TWIN RESEARCH 3
Part B
Intelligence, Personality, and Development

PROGRESS IN CLINICAL AND BIOLOGICAL RESEARCH

RECENT TITLES

See pages 289 – 290 for previous titles in this series.

TWIN RESEARCH 3

Proceedings of the Third International
Congress on Twin Studies
June 16 – 20, 1980
Jerusalem

Part B
Intelligence, Personality, and Development

Editors

Luigi Gedda
The Gregor Mendel Institute of
Medical Genetics and Twin Studies
Rome

Paolo Parisi
The Gregor Mendel Institute of
Medical Genetics and Twin Studies
Rome

Walter E. Nance
Department of Human Genetics
Medical College of Virginia
Richmond, Virginia

Alan R. Liss, Inc., New York

Address all Inquiries to the Publisher
Alan R. Liss, Inc., 150 Fifth Avenue, New York, NY 10011

Copyright © 1981 Alan R. Liss, Inc.

Printed in the United States of America.

Library of Congress Cataloging in Publication Data

International Congress on Twin Studies (3rd : 1980 :
   Jerusalem)
   Twin research 3.

   (Progress in clinical and biological research ;
v. 69)
   Includes indexes.
   Contents: pt. A. Twin biology and multiple pregnancy — pt. B. Intelligence, personality, and development — pt. C. Epidemiological and clinical studies.
   1. Pregnancy, Multiple — Congresses. 2. Twins — Congresses. 3. Twins — Psychology — Congresses. 4. Diseases in twins — Congresses.   I. Gedda, Luigi. II. Parisi, Paolo. III. Nance, Walter E. IV. Title. V. Series. [DNLM: 1. Research — Congresses. 2. Twins — Congresses. W1 PR668E v. 69 / WQ 235 I59 1980a]
RG567.I57 1980   610'.88045   81-12376
                                    AACR2

3 Volume Set ISBN 0-8451-0069-6
Part B Intelligence, Personality, and Development ISBN 0-8451-0159-5

Contents

Contributors to Part B

Frank Barron [127]
Department of Psychology, University of California, Santa Cruz, CA 95060

C. Bastin [137]
Department of Medical Psychology, University of Liège, Liège, Belgium

Silvia Borella [131, 149]
The Gregor Mendel Institute of Medical Genetics and Twin Studies, Piazza Galeno 5, 00161, Rome, Italy

Thomas J. Bouchard, Jr. [21, 179, 227]
Department of Psychology, University of Minnesota, Minneapolis, MN 55455

Gilbert F. Cardwell [169]
Department of Psychology, DePaul University, Chicago, IL 60614

J.C. Christian [35]
Department of Medical Genetics, Indiana University, Indianapolis, IN 46223

C.A. Clifford [163]
Department of Psychology, Institute of Psychiatry, DeCrespigny Park, London, SE5 8AF, England

L.A. Corey [61]
Department of Human Genetics, Medical College of Virginia, Richmond, VA 23298

J.C. DeFries [25]
Institute for Behavioral Genetics, University of Colorado, Boulder, CO 80309

L.J. Eaves [61, 73, 87]
Department of Experimental Psychology, University of Oxford, Oxford, OX1 3UD, England

Elke D. Eckert [179, 227]
Department of Psychiatry, University of Minnesota, Minneapolis, MN 55455

Siv Fischbein [43, 211]
Department of Educational Research, Stockholm Institute of Education, Box 34103, S-100 26 Stockholm, Sweden

The boldface number in brackets following each contributor's name indicates the opening page number of that author's paper.

D.W. Fulker [163]
Department of Psychology, Institute of Psychiatry, De Crespigny Park, London, SE5 8AF, England

Arleen Garfinkle [51]
Institute for Behavioral Genetics, University of Colorado, Boulder, CO 80309

Luigi Gedda [1, 149]
The Gregor Mendel Institute of Medical Genetics and Twin Studies, Piazza Galeno 5, 00161 Rome, Italy

Hugh M.D. Gurling [175]
Department of Psychiatry, Institute of Psychiatry, De Crespigny Park, London, SE5 8AF, England

David A. Hay [235]
Department of Genetics and Human Variation, La Trobe University, Bundoora, Victoria, 3083, Australia

A.C. Heath [73]
Department of Experimental Psychology, University of Oxford, Oxford, OX1 3UD, England

Leonard L. Heston [179, 227]
Department of Psychiatry, University of Minnesota, Minneapolis, MN 55455

Joseph M. Horn [17, 121]
Department of Psychology, University of Texas, Austin, TX 78712

Jaako Kaprio [189]
Department of Public Health Science, University of Helsinki, 00290 Helsinki 29, Finland

Margaret Keyes [227]
Department of Psychology, University of Minnesota, Minneapolis, MN 55455

Reuven Kohen-Raz [251]
Division of Special Education, School of Education, Hebrew University, Jerusalem, Israel

Markku Koskenvuo [189]
Department of Public Health Science, University of Helsinki, 00290 Helsinki 29, Finland

A.R. Kuse [9]
Institute for Behavioral Genetics, University of Colorado, Boulder, CO 80309

Heimo Langinvainio [189]
Department of Public Health Science, University of Helsinki, 00290 Helsinki 29, Finland

John C. Loehlin [17]
Department of Psychology, University of Texas at Austin, Austin, TX 78712

Jouko Lönnqvist [189]
Department of Psychiatry, University of Helsinki, 00290 Helsinki 29, Finland

Hugh Lytton [255, 283]
Department of Educational Psychology, University of Calgary, Calgary, Alberta, T2N 1N4, Canada

Adam P. Matheny, Jr. [279]
Department of Pediatrics, School of Medicine, University of Louisville, Louisville, KY 40292

Karen Matthews [121]
Department of Psychiatry, University of Pittsburgh, Pittsburgh, PA 15261

Judy Z. Miller [169]
Department of Psychology, Indiana University, Bloomington, IN 47405

Robin M. Murray [163, 175]
Department of Psychiatry, Institute of Psychiatry, De Crespigny Park, London, SE5 8AF, England

W.E. Nance [61]
Department of Human Genetics, Medical College of Virginia, Richmond, VA 23298

Pauline J. O'Brien [235]
Department of Genetics and Human Variation, La Trobe University, Bundoora, Victoria, 3083, Australia

Robert Plomin [25, 269]
Institute for Behavioral Genetics, University of Colorado, Boulder, CO 80309

Michael F. Pogue-Geile [169]
Department of Psychology, Indiana University, Bloomington, IN 47405

Susan Resnick [227]
Department of Psychology, University of Minnesota, Minneapolis, MN 55455

Adrianne M. Reveley [175]
Department of Psychiatry, Institute of Psychiatry, De Crespigny Park, London, SE5 8AF, England

Richard J. Rose [35, 61, 169]
Department of Psychology, Indiana University, Bloomington, IN 47405

Ray Rosenman [121]
Stanford Research Institute (SRI International), Menlo Park, CA 94025

Sandra Scarr [99]
Department of Psychology, Box 11 A Yale Station, Yale University, New Haven, CT 06520

Lauri Tarkkonen [189]
Department of Public Health Science, University of Helsinki, 00290 Helsinki, 29, Finland

M. Timsit [137]
Department of Clinical Neurophysiology, University of Liège, Liège, Belgium

M. Timsit-Berthier [137]
Department of Clinical Neurophysiology, University of Liège, Liège, Belgium

Anne Mari Torgersen [261]
Department of Child Psychiatry, Ullevål Hospital, Oslo, Norway
Svenn Torgersen [155]
NAVF's Center for Research in Clinical Psychology, University of Oslo, P.O. Box 1039, Blindern, Oslo 3, Norway
I.A. Uchida [35]
Department of Pediatrics, McMaster University Medical Center, Hamilton, Ontario, L85 4J9, Canada
Steven G. Vandenberg [9, 51]
Institute for Behavioral Genetics, University of Colorado, Boulder, CO 80309
Denise Watts [255, 283]
Department of Psychology, Board of Education, Calgary, Alberta, T2G 2L9, Canada
Patricia L. Webber [99]
Counseling Bureau, University of Minnesota, Minneapolis, MN 55455
Richard A. Weinberg [99]
Department of Psychoeducational Studies, University of Minnesota, Minneapolis, MN 55455
Lee Willerman [17]
Department of Psychology, University of Texas, Austin, TX 78712
Ronald S. Wilson [199]
Department of Pediatrics, University of Louisville School of Medicine, Louisville, KY 40292
Michele A. Wittig [99]
Department of Psychology, California State University, Northridge, CA 91330
P.A. Young [87]
Department of Genetics, University of Birmingham, BI5 2TT, England

Twin Research 3

Contents of Part A: Twin Biology and Multiple Pregnancy

Contents of Part C: Epidemiological and Clinical Studies

Preface

The Third International Congress on Twin Studies, held in Jerusalem in June 1980, was a successful event because of its site and because of the number and quality of contributors, as reflected in these proceedings. But its relevance and success were perhaps also partly due to its taking place at a particular stage in the evolution of human biological sciences. The latter, and medicine among them, can no longer do without the lead offered them by genetics, since the study of the individual needs to be approached within the context of the generational tissue. Without genetics, it is impossible to understand what takes place in the phenotype, or to forecast what will occur in the offspring.

The boom in genetics can be compared to that of nuclear physics. In fact, the study of nonliving matter requires the understanding of nuclear forces, just as the study of living matter requires that of gene forces. The energy of the gene is the force behind any gene information, and the interweaving of the primary gene products is the loom on which the generational tissue is produced, from which life and its variability depend. Our understanding of these processes, as deep as it may be, is still comparable to what one gathers looking through a keyhole. The study of twins, with its many modern refinements, can frequently offer a broader understanding of the genetic times and processes involved in the human design, both at the physical and the psychological level.

Any research into human biology can draw water from this well, as is made clear by the variety of the contributions to these proceedings, and of those already published in the 30 years of life of the journal I established in 1952, *Acta Geneticae Medicae et Gemellologiae* (the proceedings of the First International Congress on Twin Studies, held in Rome in 1974, were published in Volume 25 of this journal in 1976), as well as by the increasing membership and impact of the International Society for Twin Studies. This has been largely the result of a truly collaborative effort, to which many have contributed, from many countries and various areas of interest. They cannot all be mentioned but I should like to at least acknowledge the efforts of Gordon Allen, organizer of the Second International Congress on Twin Studies held in Washington in 1977 (the proceedings of which were published by Alan R. Liss, Inc. in 1978 in three volumes entitled *Twin Research,* edited by Walter Nance with coeditors Gordon Allen and Paolo Parisi), and Ian MacGillivray, organizer of the Aberdeen Workshop in 1979, respectively Past President and President of our International Society, as well as those of Walter Nance and Paolo Parisi, the coeditors of these proceedings.

Luigi Gedda

Twin Research 3: Intelligence, Personality,
and Development, pages 1 – 7
© 1981 Alan R. Liss, Inc., 150 Fifth Avenue, New York, NY 10011

The Human Twin

Luigi Gedda

The Gregor Mendel Institute of Medical Genetics and Twin Studies, Rome, Italy

For the geneticist, or for anyone else, to make a speech in Jerusalem means a cultural effort that is extraordinary. Like every other researcher, the geneticist must locate his scientific investigations in the context of a truth that embraces nature and the history of man. Those of us who are concerned with twin studies, however, cannot simply leave our concrete and specific field to deal with theoretical themes; rather we must extract from our research those concepts that bridge the gap between the particular truths we seek and that total truth man desires in order to resolve the mystery that surrounds his existence.

I would like to submit to the distinguished personalities who are honoring our Congress with their presence, as well as to my very dear colleagues, the idea that the best project for creating a link between our field of interest and the other interests of modern culture would be to survey the state of our knowledge about the personality of the human twin.

Therefore, I will not talk about the application of the method of twin studies, but about the identical twin, the MZ twin individual. That is, I will not talk about those dizygotic twins like Esau and Jacob, who were different. These dizygotic twins are, of course, real twins, and about twice as frequent as the monozygotic twins. But I will refer only to the twin who has another twin identical to himself, and who represents the classical model of the phenomenon of twins.

The person who derives from the same egg as another person, an egg that has been fertilized by the same spermatozoon, is first of all a very singular being from the phylogenetic point of view. This is because, in the classification of living things, the son of man is almost always unique.

From the statistical point of view, this exception occurs in about 3.5 births out of every thousand and is of clear genetical origin. That is to say, we are dealing here with a hereditary phenomenon that often is repeated in the families where it is present.

The human twin is thus a rarity of the human species in the sense that its conception is not immediate in the same way that the conception of a nontwin is. The twin is not conceived at once, when the spermatozoon fertilizes the egg, but after a brief intervening time, when the product of fertilization divides into two embryonic, totipotential groups of cells. Thus, the conception of the monozygotic twin takes place in two stages, whereas the conception of other persons occurs in a single stage.

The biological singularity of the human twin in its prenatal life is also marked by its shorter period of development within the mother's womb. The average length of a twin pregnancy is 8½ instead of 9 months, and the average weight of the single twin at birth is 2,600 instead of 3,350 grams.

The fact that the individual twin is underweight at birth does not have the same negative impact as does the underweight of single births, because the twin reaches the standard levels of the human species in the first years of life.

However, the most important biological singularity does not regard the individual human twin, but rather the MZ pair. This means the existence of two identical individuals to whom there applies a paradox like the following: One plus one equals one.

Every human being is in fact a masterwork of genetic architecture so complex and sophisticated that, from the point of view of the laws of probability, it is practically unrepeatable. But MZ twinning replicates the unrepeatable and produces a human body in duplicate.

It is as if the ancient city of Jerusalem possessed a double, with the same walls, the same streets, the same terraces, the same rooms, the same stones and much, much more, because we are not dealing with identical, fixed structures, but rather with cells, tissues, and organs that are alive, and therefore make up part of an identical process of transformation.

The existence of an identical energy formula capable of reproducing in each twin the three dimensions of sensory consciousness demonstrates how extraordinary this phenomenon is in itself, and how precious it is for the development of the anthropological sciences.

The static and dynamic identity of MZ twins is so much at the outer limits of the imagination that it sometimes happens that I ask myself: Does there really exist an authentic and original personality in the human twin?

I note in passing that I, who ask this question, am not a twin, and that I often hear this same question from others who are also not twins. But I have never heard this question from an identical twin. They never ask this question because they experience their own individual personality as something authentic and special.

This special quality that comes out when we study the human twin derives first of all from the fact that the twin is aware of the existence of an exact copy of himself. He is aware of, and generally highly appreciates and likes, the existence of his double. The pleasure of having a double is a trait that differentiates the psychology of the human twin from that of other men. For the person who is not a twin, the very thought that there could exist an individual similar to him, so similar as to violate his intimacy and to be confused with him, brings on a feeling of irritation, of frustration, of revulsion. But the human twin, on the contrary, not only appreciates his double but desires his presence, to the point of feeling acute loss if the other twin is no longer there. This is an acquired feeling, rooted in the experience of a life lived together starting in the very first days of existence. But it is, nevertheless, a trait that distinguishes the personality of the human twin.

A second aspect that characterizes the twin is the mutual relationship between the twins, which is different from the relationship each twin has with other persons of his family or, more broadly, with friends and acquaintances. There exists between the two twins a very singular relationship, based on the intuition of a psychological similarity that the twins experience and carry with them at the same time.

The thought processes of identical twins, when they develop on the basis of the same stimuli, take place with the same speed, provoke the same mental associations, and reach the same conclusions. The incident described by Galton of the two identical twins who one day are in different British cities and buy the same glassware service is not a phenomenon of telepathy but of the correct functioning of the same biological components of human thought in the face of the same stimulus, through parallel timing.

If it is true that the phenomenon of telepathy exists, it is certain that MZ twins are in the best position to demonstrate it and to use it. Up to now, telepathy between twins has been hypothesized, but not proved. On the basis of our experience, in order to explain the observed phenomena it is enough to think in terms of a mechanism for the coordination of structures and of their chronogenetic functioning. Simultaneity and agreement of thought are thus a characteristic of the psychology of twins.

The success in aerial acrobatics that made two identical twin pilots famous during the 1950s as members of the American air exhibition team, "the Skyblazers," was probably due to this simultaneity and agreement of thought, movements, and reflexes. These twins were Captains Bill and Buck Pattillo, who in their air maneuvers carried out formation flying with a distance of only 1½ meters between the wings at a speed of 800 kilometers per hour.

A third aspect has to do with the relationship of twin brothers or sisters to the environment in which they live: the family, the school, the society.

The somatic identity of the MZ twins provokes in the environment around them reactions of surprise, novelty, curiosity, and discovery. The pair of twins stands out as such, even if each of its members taken in isolation does not possess any especially attractive aesthetic, psychological, attitudinal, or pathological qualities. It is the existence of the twins "in duplicate" that strikes people and which, in a certain way, isolates the pair. We are dealing here with an isolation that can be very cordial and positive, but which is something that marks the twin in the eyes of public opinion. It is sufficient to recall the passage of the Gospel in which the apostle Thomas is mentioned: Saint John the evangelist writes of him as "the one who is called the twin." We do not know who his twin brother was, but we note the reaction of the social environment that identifies Thomas with his exceptional biological quality: He is "the twin."

This reaction of the social environment "turns back" on the psychology of the twins in the sense that it reinforces the links between them. On the one hand, they know that they attract more attention and acquire advantages if public opinion perceives them together. On the other hand, the twins have long experience of the confusion they can create and exploit using the ease with which one twin is taken for the other when they act separately in order to obtain practical advantages. For example, a twin can show up twice for the same examination, once in his own name and once for his brother. Or, one well-rested twin can take the place of his exhausted brother during half-time of a football game. It is only just to point out that phenomena of this type do not derive from the desire to deceive people, but rather from a subtle spirit of humor, with which the twins play games with their social environment.

This paired reaction to the environment is one of the marks of the personality of the human twin.

The characteristics of the human twin that I have briefly described involve primarily the subconscious. That is, they are forms of behavior that are originally instinctive and then become conscious and deliberate. Since the subconscious is linked to nervous structures, as is well known, and since these structures are spatially and chronogenetically identical, it is easy to explain the agreement of the individual and mutual psychic reactions that characterize identical twins. Now that I have said this, the question posed earlier increases in its importance: Does the human twin have his or her own personality?

By the term personality, I mean the psychological individuality of the twin which, at the unconscious level, because of the reasons I have given and because of many other reasons which I have not mentioned, is not easy to distinguish from that of the other twin. The personality of the twin emerges gradually during the course of life in the sense that the higher faculties of the mind learn to exercise judgment over the subconscious and to use self-control in regard to the instinctive reactions that appear under stress: The higher faculties come to dominate anxiety, defense, phobias, and the rest.

The personality of the twin is manifested on the level of the conscious psyche, which possesses the capacity for abstract judgment and independent choice, despite the great similarity of the unconscious, which makes it hard for an observer to recognize the individuality of identical twins.

This special situation of the human, of the difficulty of discriminating between twins on the unconscious level, and of the precise subjective and objective identification of the ego on the conscious level is shown in the context of married life.

It sometimes happens that two identical twin brothers marry two identical twin sisters, but it is more usual for the identical twins to marry partners born singly in different families. In the majority of all cases, the choice involved is absolutely individual and does not raise any problems. Cases of marital competition—that is, two twin brothers who court the same woman—are exceptional and attract attention precisely because they are so rare. I know of no cases of the wife of a twin leaving him for his twin brother. This shows the psychological uniqueness of the identical twin with respect to his cotwin both in the active sense—that is, in making an individual choice—and in a passive sense, in being chosen instead of the cotwin. Each twin is himself, feels that he is, and in the intimacy of his ego demonstrates it, despite the identity of the body and the notable equivalence of the subconscious.

The marital relationship is therefore a test of the real personality of the human twin, and the twin couple is a very specific test for studies in experimental psychology applied to the differentiation of conscious and unconscious psychic functions and of afferent and efferent psychosomatic relations.

The special psychological situation that emerges from the study of twins yields results that are worth analyzing so that the picture we have of the human twin may be clearer for scientists.

The first result concerns the simultaneous starting point of what we call, by analogy, the assemblyline of the organism. Because of the fact that they start at the same time, the phases that follow are concurrent, in terms of physiological or normal phases, as well as of pathological phases of sickness. Obviously this is true, all other things being equal—that is to say, in similar environments.

Einstein and Langevin had the idea of comparing twins to two watches that are synchronized. In order to explain the theory of relativity, they used the famous "twin paradox." If one twin stays on earth and the other twin is launched into space and returns after a certain time, this second twin will be younger than the twin who stays on earth. In reality, the twins who pass their lives in a similar environment exhibit a very special phenomenon, which we call "twin synchronism." That is, they mark the same parallel times in the life cycle.

This synchronism produces, in turn, a special cognitive effect located in the "objective" or "external" or "depersonalized" knowledge of his own physical and psychic qualities, which the twin acquires every time he observes himself in his cotwin. In fact, all of his own hereditary qualities are present and objectifiable in the other twin. This knowledge enriches the human twin.

The ancient maxim of the Oracle at Delphi, "Know thyself," is easier to fulfill for the human twin who has the ability of perceiving himself from the outside by studying his twin partner. The single-born person does not have this possibility.

A second effect consists in the possibility of knowing the inner life of one's own twin partner with an accessibility which no single-born person can have in regard to another individual. This possibility corresponds to the task of an actor, who must "impersonate" a character. The actor divests himself of his own personality and behaves according to the personality of the character he is playing. This task is not easy, and is therefore a profession. But the twin can play the role of his cotwin with an instinctive naturalness and with a depth of insight that is all his own and which allows him to know what his cotwin is thinking and doing, because the thought and behavior of the cotwin correspond to his own. Here again we have a psychological mechanism that looks like telepathy but is not.

The higher level of knowledge that the twin has about his cotwin gives him concrete opportunities, like his ability to evaluate and treat his cotwin in an exemplary way. The twin can exercise this potential either in praise, correction, or emulation, but always in a positive and useful way.

The classic case here is that of the Belgian MZ twin brothers, Auguste and Jean-Felix Piccard. Auguste began to explore the stratosphere by inventing a special balloon, which carries him to an altitude of 16,770 meters. Then he explored the sea bottom, building a bathyscaphe with which he reached a depth of 3,150 meters in the Gulf of Naples. Jean-Felix, in turn, built another stratospheric balloon with which he broke his brother's record by reaching 17,500 meters of altitude. Auguste died in Lausanne in 1962 and Jean-Felix in Minneapolis in 1963.

The exceptions to this mutuality of thought are frequently mythological, like the murder of Remus by Romulus, or attributable to sickness, alcohol, or drugs.

The totality of normal cases shows that there exists in a pair of twins a type of heightened sociality which, as a human phenomenon, offers both positive and negative aspects which we must study, in order to accentuate the positive and eliminate the negative.

The microsociety of the twins is negative when it isolates its members from the rest of the community. Here we sometimes find phenomena like cryptophasia, or a secret language between the two twins, who make up phonemes, words, and grammatical constructions that are incomprehensible to outsiders, and which are extremely harmful for the twins who use this primitive means of communication. In the files of more than 15,000 pairs of twins that exist at the Mendel Institute in Rome we have, tape-recorded, the secret language used by several pairs of identical twins. I think that cases of this type can be useful for the specialists doing research on the formation of human language, but I feel strongly that this secret language is harmful and must be avoided, because it delays the psychological maturation of the twin, just like everything else that isolates him from the social context, whether it be identical dress, identical beds, or the same toys. With these considerations, I now come to touch on the problem of the education of twins, which is a delicate problem especially for their parents. In the human species the birth of a single child in each pregnancy has profound significance in that an intelligent and free man must be the object of special attention on the part of parents who give him not only life, but the experience of their own lives, and a civilization.

When we are dealing with identical twins, we find that their parents are not capable of correctly posing the problem of the twins' education, which is not just a double problem, given the fact that there are two children, but in reality a triple problem, because the educational process must overcome the special link between the twins. This is another reason for the delay in the psychological maturation of the human twin—the need to free the twin from his twin conditioning as well as from all forms of psychic contagion connected with this. We need to educate the parents of twins to carry out their task with wisdom.

The microsociety of the twins also presents interesting and useful lessons for the broader society to which all men belong. It was once believed, as a result of the work of Schulte and von Bracken, that within each pair of twins there was a leading twin who made the most important decisions, or a twin foreign minister whose job it was to negotiate, orally and in writing, in the name of the other twin in external relations in the family, at school, in sports, shopping, and so on. But today we think that these and other individual tasks of judgment and behavior are done in rotation, according to the psychic characteristics of each single twin in the light of his original or acquired abilities.

In each pair of twins there is a division of labor, not according to the psychoanalytic model of a dominant subject and a dominated subject, but rather in the mutual respect governed by greater competence or efficiency. This would come as no surprise in the dizygotic pairs, because there the twins are different. But it does come as a surprise in the case of identical twins, and demonstrates the existence of a distinct personality of each human twin, on the level of the higher faculties of mind, of intelligence, and of freedom.

Finally, here in the city of Jerusalem, at the crossroads of the world, here where spoke the prophets and Jesus Christ, I am happy to point out that twins give us a meaningful and exemplary image of that commandment which says: "Love thy neighbor as thyself." What other man knows his neighbor as himself, what other man loves his neighbor as the human twin loves his twin?

"Love thy neighbor as thyself" is thus the message of peace that twins, throughout their lives, bring to the world.

Twin Research 3: Intelligence, Personality,
and Development, pages 9 – 16
© 1981 Alan R. Liss, Inc., 150 Fifth Avenue, New York, NY 10011

In Search of the Missing Environmental Variance in Cognitive Ability

S.G. Vandenberg and A.R. Kuse
Institute for Behavioral Genetics, University of Colorado, Boulder

After reviewing causes of inequality, Jencks et al [4,5] have called attention to our current inability to account for large proportions of the total variance in socioeconomic status, salary, and cognitive ability. They attribute this variation to "luck" and random factors, an attitude about the possibilities of scientific explanation that we feel is unnecessarily pessimistic.

Some of the "missing" variance is probably systematic, but of a more subtle nature than is captured by the gross indices of socioeconomic status and other demographic characteristics used by Jencks and his colleagues in their analyses. For instance, childrearing attitudes and other parental personality variables have been found to influence children's cognitive performance, even though they have generally not been included in behavior genetic studies.

A search for the missing variance seems especially necessary now, because recent estimates of the genetic variance in cognitive ability are considerably lower than the 50–80% previously reported. This is particularly true for studies of infants, although it is also true for studies of older persons. For infants, it may be that the course of development in infancy is uneven and so rapid that measures at one particular time cannot meaningfully characterize the infant's status. For older persons, recent results have generally been corrected for the effects of age, which inflated resemblance in the older studies. In their recent review, Plomin and DeFries [8] conclude that the additive genetic variance in a number of recent studies is at most 0.50.

Let us now look at some recent efforts to measure environmental influences on cognitive ability.

In the Hawaii Family Study of Cognition (HFSC), a special effort was made to assess a number of environmental factors that may affect a child's cognitive performance [see 15]. Data were obtained on a variety of environmental variables for 1,120 children of European ancestry and 379 children of Japanese ancestry whose families took part in the study. These variables were reduced to 44, which were then entered into stepwise multiple regressions in order to establish the influence of each on four cognitive factor scores (verbal ability, spatial ability, perceptual speed and accuracy, and visual memory) and on the first principal component (a measure of general intelligence) derived from a battery of 15 cognitive tests. The relative influence of the environmental variables was very consistent across differing cognitive abilities within ethnic groups, and was relatively consistent across ethnic groups (except in the case of visual memory). Environmental variables usually accounted for less than 20% of the variance in cognitive scores, and socioeconomic status alone accounted for only a small proportion of the environmental variance.

Only a brief summary of the HFSC data can be presented here. The cognitive tests are listed in Table 1, together with the loadings of the 15 tests on the four specific ability factors and the first principal component. Table 2 shows the 44 "environmental" variables. It can be seen that some of these — such as family income [11], Duncan socioeconomic status of father's occupation [13], father's education [16], and mother's education [27] — may reflect genetic attributes of the parents. They were included, however, because their influence is at least as much nongenetic, or cultural, as it is hereditary. Table 2 also shows the variables that contributed to the multiple regression equation predicting each of the four specific ability factors and general intelligence for children of European ancestry (AEA) and of Japanese ancestry (AJA), respectively. Table 3 shows that the multiple R ranges from 0.191 (AEA) and 0.187 (AJA) for verbal ability to 0.046 (AEA) and 0.125 (AJA) for perceptual speed. That is to say, the total effect of the 44 "environmental" variables accounted for only less than 20% of the variance in verbal ability and an even smaller percentage for the other ability factors. Of course, individual variables contributed even less; many of them added only 1% to the variance accounted for when the contributions of the other variables were removed. In fact, the intercorrelations that went into producing the multiple correlations show that the environmental variables constitute a veritable spider web of interconnecting relations.

In a similar study conducted in Boulder, Colorado, we used the questionnaire developed by Schludermann and Schludermann [10, 11], based on Schaefer's [9] Parental Attitude Research Instrument (PARI), to assess the parental childrearing attitudes of 110 families. Using a questionnaire called "Growing Up," we also asked the children how they viewed their parents. The results of this study are summarized in Table 4. For the daughters, we see that some attributes of the fathers accounted for 21% of the variance in verbal ability; for the sons, some attributes of the mothers accounted for 25% of the variance in perceptual speed scores. The multiple correlations for the other abilities and the same familial relationships were not significant.

Finally, we shall look at another study being conducted in Boulder — the Colorado Adoption Project. It should be kept in mind that the results to be discussed here are preliminary and are based only on data for 1-year-old infants. This is probably too early an age to see any major consequences of parental practices; however, one can probably feel quite confident about the importance of any influence detected so early in development. Data have been analyzed for 119 adopted children and for 79 "control" children being reared by their biological parents.

The Mental Index of the Bayley Scales of Infant Development [1] and four scales from the Uzgiris-Hunt Ordinal Scales of Psychological Development [13] were administered as measures of infant intelligence. Several approaches were used to assess environmental influences (including videotaping of mother-child interac-

TABLE 1. Cognitive Tests, Test Times, Reliabilities[a] and Factor Loadings

Test[b]	Test time	Reliability[c]	Verbal	Spatial	Perceptual speed	Visual memory	First principal component
PMA Vocabulary	3 min	0.96 (PUBL)	0.80	0.10	0.25	0.09	0.71
Visual memory (immediate)	1-min exposure/ 1-min recall	0.58 (KR-20)	0.13	0.08	0.06	0.85	0.34
Things (a fluency test)	2 parts/ 3 min each	0.74 (CRα)	0.68	0.22	-0.09	0.01	0.55
Shepard-Metzler mental rotations (modified for group testing by Vandenberg)	10 min	0.88 (KR-20)	0.16	0.80	-0.09	0.05	0.56
Subtraction and multiplication	2 parts/ 2 min each	0.96 (CRα)	0.20	0.15	0.81	-0.02	0.53
Elithorn mazes ("lines and dots"), shortened form	5 min	0.89 (PUBL)	0.04	0.62	0.13	-0.01	0.45
ETS word beginnings and endings	2 parts/ 3 min each	0.71 (CRα)	0.67	0.11	0.27	0.04	0.62
ETS card rotations	2 parts/ 3 min each	0.88 (CRα)	0.13	0.76	0.18	0.05	0.63
Visual memory (delayed recall)	1 min	0.62 (KR-20)	0.08	0.05	0.06	0.85	0.29
PMA pedigrees (a reasoning test)	4 min	0.72 (PUBL)	0.58	0.28	0.41	0.17	0.75
ETS hidden patterns	2 parts/ 2 min each	0.92 (CRα)	0.32	0.58	0.26	0.11	0.69
Paper form board	3 min	0.84 (KR-20)	0.36	0.64	0.09	0.07	0.67
ETS number comparisons	2 parts/ 1.5 min each	0.81 (CRα)	0.14	0.13	0.84	0.14	0.52
Whiteman test of social perception	10 min	0.69 (KR-20)	0.71	0.21	0.08	0.13	0.66
Raven's progressive matrices, modified form	20 min	0.86 (KR-20)	0.51	0.54	0.15	0.10	0.74

[a]From Wilson et al [14].
[b]PMA = Primary mental abilities; ETS = Educational Testing Service.
[c]PUBL = from test manual; KR-20 = Kuder-Richardson Formula 20; CRα = Composite Reliability Coefficient [3, 6].

TABLE 2. Cognitive Factors Predicted by Environmental Variables[a]

Environmental variable		Cognitive factor predicted[b]	
		AEA	AJA
1. AGE	Age of subject at time of testing	S,M	
2. AMTTV	Amount of television subject reports watching		P
3. ANXIETY	Anxiety rating from Multiple Affect Check List		P
4. BIRTHORD	Birth order of subject	M	
5. BOOKREAD	Number of books read per month	V,G	
6. BOOKSOWN	Number of books in home	V,S,G	V,G,M
7. DEPRESS	Depression rating from Multiple Affect Check List	S	
8. DEVPROB	Mother's report of whether she had development problems with offspring.	V,S,G,P	P
9. ELEMINTR	Number of elementary and intermediate schools attended		
10. FAGEBIR	Father's age at birth of offspring	S	
11. FAMINCOM	Parents' estimates of family income	G	
12. FATHAWAY	Was father absent for a year or more?		V,S,G,P,M
13. FATHSES	Duncan SEI rating of father's occupation		V
14. FJOBMOB	Father's SEI rating of first job subtracted from rating of present job		V,M
15. FRNLANG	Amount of foreign language known.		
16. FYREDC	Father's years of education	V,G	
17. GRDSFRD	Grades of subjects vs grades of friends	V	
18. HANDWRIT	With which hand does subject write?		S,G
19. HOMEWORK	Average hours of homework done per week		P
20. HOMVISTS	Number of friends who visit the home per month	V,S,G,P,M	V,S
21. HOUSE	Size of home		
22. JOB	Does subject have a job?		
23. MAGEBIR	Mother's age at birth of subject		P

No.	Variable	Description		
24.	MAGREAD	Number of magazines read per month	P,M	V,S,G
25.	MATH	A rank ordering of mathematical ability with 3 other abilities	S,P	V,S,G,P,M
26.	MYREDC	Mother's years of education		S,G
27.	NOFETALD	Number of fetal deaths reported by mother		V,M
28.	NOPREG	Number of pregnancies of mother	P	V,G,P,M
29.	NURSERY	Whether subject attended nursery school	S,G,P,M	G
30.	PIDGIN	Amount of pidgin spoken in home and with friends	M	V,M
31.	PREPROB	Mother's report of whether she had pregnancy problems		
32.	PSCHOLAR	Factor score for "scholar" from parents' average rating of subject on 12 personal adjectives	V,S,G,M	V,S,G,P,M
33.	PTEMPERM	Factor score for temperament from parents' average rating of subject on 12 personal adjectives		V,S,G,P,M
34.	READING	A rank ordering of reading ability with 3 other abilities	V,S,M	
35.	ROOMMATE	Number of roommates the subject has		V,M
36.	SCHOLAR	Factor score for "scholar" from the offsprings' self-ratings on 12 personal adjectives		V,S,G,M
37.	SEX	Sex of subject	P	S,G
38.	SIZECITY	Size of city in which subject was born	M	P
39.	SIZESIB	Number of brothers and sisters		
40.	SOCIALPR	Chapin's (1942) index of social participation	V,S,G,P,M	V,S,G,P,M
41.	SPELLING	A rank ordering of spelling ability with 3 other abilities	S,G	M
42.	TEMPERMT	Factor score for temperament from the offsprings' self-ratings on 12 personal adjectives		S
43.	YRSEDC	Years of education subject had	S	V,S,G,P,M

[a]From Wilson et al [15].
[b]V = Verbal ability; S = spatial ability; G = general intelligence; P = perceptual speed; M = memory for drawings.

TABLE 3. Stepwise Multiple Regressions for the AEA Ethnic Group[a]

Verbal ability		Spatial ability		1st Principal component		Perceptual speed		Memory	
Variable	Multiple R	Variable	Multiple R	Variable	Multiple R	Variable	Multiple R	Variable	Multiple R
BOOKREAD	0.257	PSCHOLAR	0.158	PSCHOLAR	0.275	PSCHOLAR	0.233	PSCHOLAR	0.099
SOCIALPR	0.313	SPELLING	0.211	BOOKSOWN	0.336	DEVPROB(-)	0.277	MAGREAD	0.125
PSCHOLAR	0.347	BOOKSOWN	0.247	SOCIALPR	0.372	SOCIALPR	0.301	HOSTILTY(-)	0.144
BOOKSOWN	0.373	DEVPROB(-)	0.266	DEVPROB(-)	0.397	HOMVISTS	0.316	HOMVISTS(-)	0.160
ROOMMATE(-)	0.388	SOCIALPR	0.280	BOOKREAD	0.413	NURSERY	0.328	SIZECITY	0.172
HOMVISTS	0.412	MATH	0.295	NURSERY	0.427	MATH	0.337	BIRTHORD	0.183
FYREDC	0.422	FAGEBIR	0.307	HOMVISTS	0.437	MAGREAD	0.347	NURSERY	0.191
DEVPROB(-)	0.430	HOMVISTS	0.316	FAMINCOM	0.447	SEX	0.355	AGE	0.198
FRNLANG	0.437	NURSERY	0.324	FRNLANG	0.453	NOPREG	0.360	SOCIALPR(-)	0.204
		AGE	0.331	SPELLING	0.458			ROOMMATE(-)	0.209
		YRSEDC	0.338					PIDGIN(-)	0.215
		ROOMMATE(-)	0.343						
		DEPRESS	0.348						
R^2	0.191		0.121		0.130		0.046		0.210

Stepwise Multiple Regressions for the AJA Ethnic Group

Verbal ability		Spatial ability		1st Principal component		Perceptual speed		Memory	
Variable	Multiple R	Variable	Multiple R	Variable	Multiple R	Variable	Multiple R	Variable	Multiple R
FATHAWAY	0.195	MATH	0.182	FATHAWAY	0.171	TEMPERMT	0.159	FATHAWAY	0.137
BOOKSOWN	0.264	FATHAWAY	0.234	BOOKSOWN	0.228	MATH	0.214	TEMPERMT	0.189
MAGREAD	0.303	SEX	0.254	MATH	0.264	PTEMPERM	0.243	PTEMPERM	0.242
PSCHOLAR	0.318	MAGREAD	0.274	TEMPERMT	0.293	BOOKSOWN	0.302	BOOKSOWN	0.256
PTEMPERM	0.349	TEMPERMT	0.286	MAGREAD	0.312	PSCHOLAR	0.319	MATH	0.268
FATHNORC	0.361	PTEMPERM	0.302	SEX	0.331	FATHAWAY	0.336	NOFETALD(-)	0.280
ROOMMATE(-)	0.368	HANDWRIT	0.314	NURSERY	0.341	NOPREG	0.351	SOCIALPR	0.289
NOPREG(-)	0.376	MYREDC	0.324	PSCHOLAR	0.348	SIZESIB	0.363	FJOBMOB	0.300
SIZESIB	0.385	PSCHOLAR	0.332	PTEMPERM	0.381	DEVPROB(-)	0.370	SCHOLAR	0.307
TEMPERMT	0.393	SCHOLAR	0.341	MYREDC	0.387	MAGEBIR(-)	0.378	SIZESIB	0.314
FJOBMOB	0.401	HOMVISTS	0.347	SIZESIB	0.395	AMTTV(-)	0.388	ROOMMATE(-)	0.320
HOMVISTS(-)	0.410	SIZESIB	0.353	HANDWRIT	0.402	SIZECITY(-)	0.394	NOPREG(-)	0.326
NOFETALD	0.417	SPELLING	0.359	SCHOLAR	0.407	ANXIETY	0.400	PSCHOLAR	0.332
SCHOLAR(-)	0.422			NOPREG	0.412	HOMEWORK		PIDGIN(-)	0.337
MATH(-)	0.427								
PIDGIN(-)	0.432								
R^2	0.187		0.129		0.160		0.125		0.170

[a]Directionality of relationships that are not obvious include the following: the more frequent the home visits and social participation, the higher the scores on the verbal factor and the first principal component. Greater knowledge of foreign language is positively associated with performance on the first principal component. Females are superior on the perceptual speed variable. The larger the city in which the subject was born, the higher the score on the memory factor. The later the offspring in birth order, the lower the score on the memory factor.

TABLE 4. Effect of Parents' Environmental Measures on Cognitive Ability of Sons (N = 83) and Daughters (N = 82)[a]

	Cognitive ability	R^2	P	Environmental variable	Beta	P
Father's attributes						
Sons	All 4 ability factors	<0.16	NS			
Daughters	Verbal ability	0.21	<0.05	Growing Up 3[b]	0.25 ± 0.11	<0.05
				Number of books read	0.32 ± 0.13	<0.05
				Growing Up 2[b]	0.33 ± 0.13	<0.05
				Interest in reading	−0.30 ± 0.12	<0.05
				"Highbrow" interests	−0.31 ± 0.14	<0.05
	Other 3 ability factors	<0.03	NS			
Mother's attributes						
Daughters	All 4 ability factors		NS			
Sons	Perceptual speed	0.25	<0.01	SES	0.37 ± 0.12	<0.01
				Personality 1	0.28 ± 0.11	<0.05
				Protestant	−0.60 ± 0.23	<0.05
				PARI 3[b]	0.30 ± 0.13	<0.05
				Roman Catholic	−0.81 ± 0.24	<0.01
	Other 3 ability factors	<0.04	NS			

[a]From Spuhler [12].
[b]Growing Up 3 measures "perceived autonomy"; Growing Up 2 measures "perceived consistency"; PARI 3 measures "autonomy".

tions, which will not be discussed here). During each home visit, the tester filled out the Home Observation for the Measurement of the Environment (HOME) form [2], while the parents completed the Moos [7] Family Environment Scales (FES). We were not surprised to find that there are few significant correlations between our measures of environment and infant intelligence at 1 year of age. HOME responsivity is correlated with the Bayley Mental Index and the Uzgiris-Hunt total score in both adoptive and control families. This is not a new observation, but it is comforting to find it replicated in our study. A few other significant correlations need not be taken too seriously because they are not found in both adoptive and control families.

In summary, we have reviewed three studies in which an effort was made to search for environmental contributions to cognitive ability factors. Some variables related to parental childrearing attitudes have been found to be important, but further work is needed to clarify their effects, and genotype-environment interaction and correlation may be responsible for some of the unexplained varience. Future efforts will have to be directed at revealing the extent to which these factors account for the missing environmental variance in cognitive ability.

REFERENCES

1. Bayley N: "Manual for the Bayley Scales of Infant Development." New York: Psychological Corporation, 1969.
2. Caldwell BM, Bradley RH: "Home Observation for the Measurement of the Environment." Little Rock, University of Arkansas, 1978.
3. Guttman L: A basis for analyzing test-retest reliability. Psychometrika 10:255–282, 1945.
4. Jencks C, Smith M, Acland H, Bane MJ, Cohen D, Gintis H, Heyns B, Michelson S: "Inequality: A Reassessment of the Effect of Family and Schooling in America." New York: Basic Books, 1972.
5. Jencks C, Barlett S, Corcoran M, Crouse J, Eaglesfield D, Jackson G, McClelland K, Mueser P, Olneck M, Schwartz J, Ward S, Williams J: "Who Gets Ahead? The Determinants of Economic Success in America." New York: Basic Books, 1979.
6. Lord FM, Novick MR: "Statistical Theories of Mental Test Scores." Reading, Massachusetts: Addison-Wesley, 1968.
7. Moos RH: "Preliminary Manual for Family Environment Scale, Work Environment Scale, and Group Environment Scale." Palo Alto: Consulting Psychologists Press, 1974.
8. Plomin R, DeFries JC: Genetics and intelligence: Recent data. Intelligence 4:15–24, 1980.
9. Schaefer EA: Development of a parental attitude reseach instrument. Child Dev 29:339–361, 1958.
10. Schludermann S, Schludermann E: Conceptualization of maternal behavior. J Psychol 75:205–215, 1970.
11. Schludermann S, Schludermann E: Conceptual factors of parental attitudes of fathers. J Psychol 75:193–204, 1970.
12. Spuhler KP: "Family Resemblance for Cognitive Performance: An Assessment of Genetic and Environmental Contributions to Variation." Unpublished doctoral dissertation, University of Colorado, Boulder, 1976.
13. Uzgiris IC, Hunt JMcV: "Assessment in Infancy." Urbana, Illinois, University of Illinois, 1975.
14. Wilson, JR, DeFries JC, McClearn GE, Vanderberg SG, Johnson RC, Rashad MN: Cognitive abilities: Use of family data as a control to assess sex and age differences in two ethnic groups. Int J Aging Hum Dev 6:261–276, 1975.
15. Wilson KW, Johnson RC, Vanderberg SG, McClearn GE, Wilson JR: Intelligence (in press), 1981.

Twin Research 3: Intelligence, Personality,
and Development, pages 17 — 19
© 1981 Alan R. Liss, Inc., 150 Fifth Avenue, New York, NY 10011

Generalizability of Heritability Estimates for Intelligence From the Texas Adoption Project

Joseph M. Horn, John C. Loehlin, and Lee Willerman
Department of Psychology, University of Texas at Austin

Small sample sizes have generally precluded attempts by adoption researchers to examine the influence of varying environmental circumstances upon estimates of heritability for intelligence. However, in the Texas Adoption Project [1], intellectual assessments are available for 300 pairs of adoptive parents, their natural as well as adoptive children, and the biological mothers of the adopted children. The purpose of the present report is to communicate the results of our effort to subdivide our sample according to the intellectual and socioeconomic status of the adoptive family and test for significant effects on estimates of the importance of additive genes and common environment in intellectual development. Readers are referred to our earlier report for details concerning the sample, methods of intellectual assessment, and data analysis.

The socioeconomic index used here is the Duncan occupational index [3]. This scale has a mean of 44.6 and standard deviation of 25.5 for U.S. white males aged 35–44 in 1973. The Texas Adoption Project families have a mean of 59.7 and standard deviation of 24.0 on this index. The average midparent IQ (Wechsler Adult Intelligence Scale) for our sample is 113.8 with a standard deviation of 8.7.

Table 1 gives the correlations for performance IQ between all the pairs of biological relatives and pairs of unrelated individuals used to estimate genetic and environmental parameters according to the method of Loehlin [2]. Loehlin's method also requires correlations between SES and intelligence. These are also given in Table 1. The correlations for the full sample can be compared to those obtained when the families are divided first at the mean on the Duncan index and second at the average midparent WAIS IQ. The estimates for the influence of additive genes (h^2) and common environment (c^2) derived from these correlations are given at the bottom of Table 1.

The results indicate that estimates of h^2 and c^2 are quite stable across the

Table 1. Correlations of Revised Beta IQs (Adults), Wechsler Performance IQs (Children), and Socioeconomic Status of Adoptive Family, for Families Below and Above the Mean on the SES Index and Midparent WAIS IQ

Pairing	Full sample		Lower SES families		Higher SES families		Lower IQ families		Higher IQ families	
	r	N	r	N	r	N	r	N	r	N
Father—Natural child	0.29	144	0.26	67	0.27	76	0.26	59	0.29	83
Mother—Natural child	0.21	143	0.25	67	0.12	75	0.25	59	0.12	83
Father—Adopted child	0.12	405	0.11	170	0.07	231	0.10	167	0.04	225
Mother—Adopted child	0.15	401	0.20	173	0.04	224	0.17	167	0.03	225
Unwed mother—Her child	0.28	297	0.32	129	0.18	167	0.27	122	0.26	163
Adopted—Adopted child	0.05	132	0.03	51	0.03	79	0.07	47	0.04	78
Natural—Natural child	0.33	40	0.29	18	0.31	22	0.09	16	0.41	24
Adopted—Natural child	0.24	159	0.29	69	0.18	88	0.29	56	0.20	99
Unwed mother—Other adopted	0.15	202	0.22	82	-0.03	119	0.27	67	0.02	124
Unwed mother—Other natural	0.06	143	0.09	69	-0.11	73	0.17	56	-0.06	84
Father—Mother	0.24	292	0.21	131	0.14	159	0.05	131	0.03	157
Unwed mother—Father	0.11	339	0.09	149	-0.03	189	0.05	141	-0.02	187
Unwed mother—Mother	0.14	337	0.14	150	-0.05	186	0.18	141	-0.07	187
Unwed mothers	0.07	132	0.09	27	-0.11	40	0.23	22	-0.06	41
Father—SES	0.36	295	0.46	132	-0.01	163	0.18	130	0.03	156
Mother—SES	0.32	293	0.24	133	0.00	160	0.22	130	-0.07	156
Unwed mother—SES	0.32	342	0.13	151	0.13	191	0.26	140	0.24	187
Adopted child—SES	0.16	406	0.17	174	0.02	232	0.13	165	0.08	223
Natural child—SES	0.21	144	0.35	68	0.05	76	0.34	58	0.06	83
h^2	0.38		0.45		0.35		0.45		0.52	
c^2	0.18		0.23		0.10		0.23		0.12	

half-samples generated by splits at the mean on SES and parental IQ. Since all estimates of c^2 fall outside the range of values for h^2, conclusions regarding the relative roles of heredity and environment from full-sample data would not be affected by considerations of within-sample variation in SES or parental intelligence. This means, of course, that we do not know if our results generalize to samples with SES scores and parental IQs outside the range for the families in the Texas Adoption Project.

REFERENCES

1. Horn JM, Loehlin JC, Willerman L: Intellectual resemblance among adoptive and biological relatives: The Texas Adoption Project. Behav Genet 9:177, 1979.
2. Loehlin JC: Combining data from different groups in human genetics. In Royce JR, Mo LP (eds): "Theoretical Advances in Behavior Genetics" Netherlands: Sijthoff and Noorhoff, Alphen aan den Rijn, 1979.
3. Reiss AJ, Duncan OD, Hatt PK, North CC: "Occupations and Social Status." Glencoe, Illinois: Free Press, 1961.

Twin Research 3: Intelligence, Personality,
and Development, pages 21 – 23
© 1981 Alan R. Liss, Inc., 150 Fifth Avenue, New York, NY 10011

The Study of Mental Ability Using Twin and Adoption Designs

Thomas J. Bouchard, Jr.
Department of Psychology, University of Minnesota, Minneapolis

Behavior genetic studies of intelligence with twins and adopted individuals are experiments of nature. Unfortunately, nature does not conduct clean experiments. These studies all have biases of one sort or another. As a result, the problem of demonstrating hereditary influence on intelligence is a problem in construct validation and the only workable approach is methodological and measurement triangulation.

In spite of some criticism of the method, I believe the only way to arrive at a heritability statistic that usefully summarizes the environmental and genetic factors at work in a population is to fit a reasonably complex model that uses many different familial relationships. Whereas biases in the data are not magically done away with, they are balanced out to some extent.

This same idea should be extended to research within degrees of familial relationships. The bulk of twin and adoption studies are conducted with children. There is nothing wrong with this, but most of us would be more confident in the findings if they were confirmed in adult twins and adult adoptees. Most twin studies, for example, recruit via mothers-of-twins clubs. The possible bias in favor of DZ twins of greater than average similarity is great. Epidemiologists learned the importance of comprehensive enumeration and unbiased sampling long ago. The traditional twin design assumes the DZ twins have half their genes in common. The validity of this assumption should be tested in some manner in every study. I understand that methods are being worked out to do this using blood groups. We can, however, report the correlations for finger ridge count, finger pattern intensity, height, weight, and head length and width. Although these data will not solve the representativeness of sampling problem, they will shed some light on it. They will do one other thing: They will provide a within-study frame of reference.

The physical data will also provide a good between-study frame of reference. One of my graduate students and I have just finished updating the Erlenmeyer-Kimling survey of familial resemblance in IQ. We find the weighted average correlation for single parent-offspring to be 0.41. The weighted average for total finger ridge count (3 studies, 2,108 pairs) is 0.42. This suggests that the cross-generational similarity is as great for IQ as for finger ridge count, a trait determined in the first trimester of life.

Another useful way of providing a frame of reference in a twin study is to include other family members, parents or siblings or both.

Selection bias also occurs in adoption studies. Parents with serious child-rearing problems and those whose SES has dropped a great deal are much less likely to participate. It seems to me that we need more studies that recruit via the twins and adoptees themselves. Such studies will introduce their own biases, but, and this is important, they will be different. In our study we have found adopted twins with extremely poor childrearing backgrounds. One example is a DZ twin who went through 14 foster homes in 15 years. Such twins and adopted children are very interested in participating in research studies if only to help prevent such abuses.

The other side of the triangulation issue is triangulation of constructs. It seems to us that we could do a far better job of chosing traits and instruments. This is a difficult problem because the array of instruments from which we can choose is nothing to brag about. Nevertheless, it is my impression that behavior geneticists will analyze any dependent variable no matter how poorly measured or conceptualized. This indiscriminate behavior can do nothing but erode our credibility as serious scientists. Constructs and measures should be justified on grounds other than that they exist.

I would like to make the distinction between intelligence and mental abilities. Some psychologists do not believe intelligence is a useful construct and prefer to speak only of mental abilities. Others, like myself, think of intelligence as *the* major mental ability, but willingly recognize a large number of additional special mental abilities. I think of intelligence as the general factor "g" underlying a broad sample of mental ability tests of appropriate difficulty for the sample being studied. I would therefore choose the WAIS over the Raven as a measure of IQ. A good behavior genetic study of mental abilities should measure both intelligence and a reasonable array of special mental abilities. Special mental abilities should not be measured with a single, brief test. We have found in our twin work that very minor misinterpretations of instructions can lead to large score differences. My own opinion is that, at a minimum, each special ability should be measured with at least two tests using different item content. The tests should also be intermixed rather than sequential (eg, not all spatial, all vocabulary, etc).

Lastly it seems to me that we need a more systematic assessment of the environment. Benjamin Bloom pointed out long ago that we have numerous multiple aptitude batteries for measuring individual differences in organisms but no tools for measuring the characteristics of environments.

My laboratory is working on two projects designed to yield multiple environmental batteries. It is widely believed that parental interests and childrearing patterns determine children's interest patterns. John Holland [1] has in fact presented "speculative statements" regarding the specific environmental influences that shape each of his six vocational types: realistic, investigative, artistic, social, enterprising, conventional. One of my students and I have scaled these environmental influences and administered our instrument, as well as the Strong Campbell interest inventory, to 122 families. The average correlation between appropriate environmental scales and interests were 0.17 for fathers and 0.10 for mothers. Not very impressive correlations.

In a second study, which is not yet complete, we have developed measures of specific environmental influences that should theoretically be related to the following traits: verbal comprehension, verbal fluency, spatial visualization, perceptual speed and accuracy, artistic interests. Our instruments have been administered to over 200 families of high school students. We are eagerly awaiting the results.

We are developing these instruments on typical families with full knowledge that genetic and environmental effects are confounded. Our rationale is that, if reasonable relationships cannot be found within natural families, it does not make sense to administer the instruments to adoptive families or twin families.

Earlier in this paper I argued that it was important to justify the inclusion of a measure in a twin or adoption study. Let me illustrate such a justification. In the study discussed above, all the traits show sex differences. Our environmental measures are also sensitive to this question. A behavior genetic study that focused on these traits and included environmental measures would be far superior to and more informative than one that simply selected an array of mental ability tests for no specific reason.

Twin Research 3: Intelligence, Personality,
and Development, pages 25 – 33
© 1981 Alan R. Liss, Inc., 150 Fifth Avenue, New York, NY 10011

Multivariate Behavioral Genetics and Development: Twin Studies

Robert Plomin and J. C. DeFries
Institute for Behavioral Genetics, University of Colorado, Boulder

INTRODUCTION

The earliest studies of human behavioral genetics were developmental. For example, Galton's [5] original twin study in 1875 addressed the question whether the initial similarity or dissimilarity of twin pairs changed during development. Subsequent studies by Thorndike [15] in 1905 and Merriman [10] in 1924 concerned the same issue. In all three studies, no evidence was found for different twin correlations in younger and older groups, suggesting that twin similarity remains relatively constant from childhood through adolescence.

Although this early developmental focus of twin studies was thereafter lost for several decades, the longitudinal Louisville Twin Study [18], initiated in the 1960's, marked a return to important questions of development. Moreover, the recent interest in development appears to be accelerating—at the first two International Congresses on Twin Studies, few developmental papers were presented; however, at the Third International Congress, two symposia and numerous papers addressed issues of developmental concern.

One issue of concern to developmental human behavioral genetics is differential heritability as a function of age. Genes that influence mental ability may turn on and off at various stages of development, thereby changing the heritable nature of individual differences. Environmental influences, of course, may also change as children experience more varied environments outside the home. Thus the relative importance of genetic and environmental influences is expected to vary as a function of age. Several recent twin studies [3, 4, 7] have specifically addressed this issue of differential heritability during development.

Although the issue of differential heritability is informative, it does not address the question of genetic continuity throughout development. At least in

Supported in part by grants from the National Institute of Child Health and Human Development (HD-10333) and the National Science Foundation (BNS-7826204). The report was written while the first author was supported by a Research Scientist Development Award (AA-00041) from the National Institute on Alcohol Abuse and Alcoholism.

theory, the heritability of a character could be relatively constant from one stage of development to another, even though entirely different gene systems were operating. The methods of multivariate behavioral genetics, previously applied to different characters measured at the same age rather than the same character at different ages [see 11], may be employed to assess genetic and environmental continuity. These methods yield estimates of longitudinal genetic and environmental correlations, measures of the extent to which a character at different ages is influenced by the same genes and by the same environmental influences.

The primary objective of this paper is to discuss possible applications of multivariate behavioral twin studies to developmental issues. We begin with a consideration of the relationship between heritability and stability (the correlation between an adult measurement and a measure of the same character at an earlier age) and then suggest a method for testing hypotheses of stage development from the structure of longitudinal genetic and environmental correlation matrices.

DIFFERENTIAL HERITABILITY AND STABILITY

Although the early studies of Galton, Thorndike, and Merriman found no change in twin similarity between childhood and adolescence, twin correlations do change at earlier ages. For example, it is not until about 7 years of age that twin correlations for IQ reach levels comparable to those of adolescent and adult twins. Changes in twin correlations during early childhood, of course, result in changes in heritability. In Figure 1, the heritability of IQ measurements (estimated by doubling the difference between the MZ and DZ twin correlations) during the preschool and early school years is plotted from data reported by the Louisville Twin Study [17, 18]. Heritabilities are low through 4 years of age, but then rise rapidly to levels characteristic of adolescent [9] and adult [12] populations.

For the sake of comparison, the heritability of height (also estimated from data reported by the Louisville Twin Study) is plotted in Figure 2. Whereas the heritability of IQ changes dramatically during the preschool years, it may be seen that the pattern for height is considerably different. The heritability of height is moderately high by 1 year of age (about 0.4). It then increases to about 0.7 by 2 years of age, remains relatively constant through 4 years, and then increases to adult levels.

Stabilities (the correlation between measures of a character at a given age and adult measurements) of IQ and height are also plotted in Figures 1 and 2 from data collected by Honzik et al [8] and by Tanner et al [14]. As may be seen, stability tends to parallel heritability. Several factors could account for this relationship. One possible explanation is that a third variable, such as reliability, may be responsible for the correlation between heritability and stability. Obviously, neither heritability nor stability will be found in the absence of reliable measurement. Thus, if the reliability of IQ measurements increased during early development, this could result in both greater heritability and stability. However, although infant measures are poor predictors of later IQ, they are

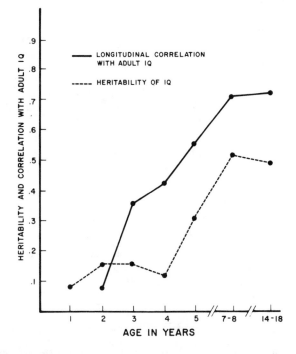

Fig. 1. Stability and heritability of IQ. Correlations between child and adult status (at 18 years) were reported by Honzik et al [8]; the results are similar to those of other longitudinal studies. Heritabilities were estimated from twin data reported by Wilson [18] for 1–5 years, Wilson [17] for 7–8 years, and Loehlin and Nichols [9] for adolescents. Although Loehlin and Nichols's study focused on general scholastic ability, the results of their study are the same as the weighted average results of other large twin studies of IQ [see 12].

nonetheless reliable (eg, [1]). Moreover, the low heritability of infant IQ measurements is not due to low twin correlations. On the contrary, both MZ and DZ twin correlations are relatively high, suggesting substantial reliability.

Another possible explanation for the relationship between heritability and stability is differential validity. If the validity of a measure increases during development, both stability and heritability would increase concomitantly. Although measures need not be valid in order to be stable or heritable, developmental differences in validity (eg, different item content at different ages) could lead to apparent developmental changes in both stability and heritability.

Genetic Correlations and Environmental Correlations

A more interesting possibility is that the relationship between heritability and stability is causal. A path diagram in Figure 3 depicts the relationship between

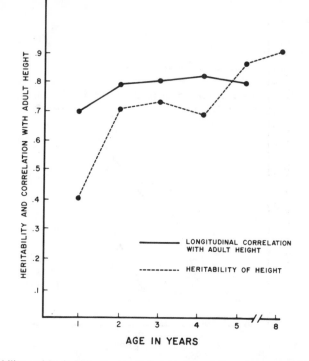

Fig. 2. Stability and heritability for length/height. Correlations between child and adult status (at 25–30 years) were reported by Tanner et al [14]; the results are similar to those of other longitudinal studies that did not extend into adulthood. Heritabilities were estimated from twin data reported by Wilson [16, 19], the only longitudinal twin study reporting data for height.

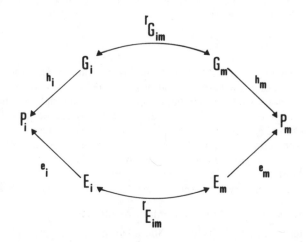

Fig. 3. Path diagram of longitudinal stability. See text for explanation.

the measured phenotype of an individual at a given age (P_i) and a measurement of the same character at maturity (P_m). G and E symbolize genetic values and environmental deviations, respectively, at the different ages and the path coefficients (h and e) are square roots of heritability and environmentality [13]. The genetic correlation (r_{Gim}) and environmental correlation (r_{Eim}) between the measurements of ages i and m are due to genetic and environmental influences that are salient at both ages.

We have defined stability as the correlation between P_i and P_m. From path analytic theory, this phenotypic correlation may be partitioned into its genetic and environmental parts as follows:

$$r_{Pim} = h_i h_m r_{Gim} + e_i e_m r_{Eim} \qquad (1)$$

Thus, stability (r_{Pim}) is obviously a function of heritability (h_i^2). If all other variables were held constant, an increase in h_i^2 would result in a corresponding increase in r_{Pim}. However, as h_i^2 increases, e_i^2 decreases. Therefore the relationship between heritability and stability is not as simple as it first appears.

Stability is also a function of genetic and environmental correlations during development. Changes in heritability during development will affect stability only if the genetic correlations between the ages are nonzero. Although genetic correlations have previously been estimated for different characters measured at the same age, the methodology could also be applied to measurements of the same character at different ages. Thus, instead of estimating the genetic correlation between characters X and Y at time i, we estimate the genetic correlation between character X at times i and m.

Genetic correlations and environmental correlations can be estimated from twin data by methods that are perfectly analogous to those used to estimate heritability and environmentality [11]. The heritability of a character at time i is estimated by doubling the difference between the MZ and DZ correlations:

$$h_i^2 = 2(r_{MZi} - r_{DZi}) \qquad (2)$$

where r_{MZi} and r_{DZi} are the phenotypic (intraclass) identical and fraternal twin correlations at time i. Environmentality, the proportion of variance due to environmental influences is estimated by subtraction:

$$e_i^2 = 1 - h_i^2$$

In exactly the same manner, $h_i h_m r_{Gim}$ may be estimated by doubling the difference between the MZ and DZ cross-correlations:

$$h_i h_m r_{Gim} = 2(r_{MZim} - r_{DZim}) \qquad (4)$$

where r_{MZim} and r_{DZim} are the MZ and DZ cross correlations of a character in twin one at time i with the same character in twin two at time m. (For computer analysis of large data sets, a double-entry procedure may be used to approximate the intraclass cross-correlation.) Also, $e_i e_m r_{E_{im}}$ may be estimated by subtraction:

$$e_i e_m r_{E_{im}} = r_{P_{im}} - h_i h_m r_{G_{im}} \tag{5}$$

It should be noted that $h_i h_m r_{G_{im}}$ and $e_i e_m r_{E_{im}}$ reduce to h_i^2 and e_i^2 when $i = m$.
These genetic and environmental contributions to $r_{P_{im}}$ are equivalent to phenotypically standardized covariances [11]:

$$h_i h_m r_{G_{im}} = CovG_i G_m / \sigma_{P_i} \sigma_{P_m} \tag{6}$$

and

$$e_i e_m r_{E_{im}} = CovE_i E_m / \sigma_{P_i} \sigma_{P_m} \tag{7}$$

Thus these phenotypically standardized genetic and environmental covariances sum to yield stability, a phenotypically standardized phenotypic covariance.

Given estimates of $h_i h_m r_{G_{im}}$, $e_i e_m r_{E_{im}}$, h_i^2, and h_m^2, we can solve for $r_{G_{im}}$ and $r_{E_{im}}$. Estimates of these genetic and environmental correlations would be useful for addressing questions about the causal nature of longitudinal stability. For example, do the same genes influence a character at ages i and m or are different sets of genes involved? However, a genetic correlation between measurements at times i and m could be high, but the genetic contribution to observed phenotypic resemblance (ie, $h_i h_m r_{G_{im}}$) would be low if either h_i^2 or h_m^2 is low. Similarly, heritabilities at both ages could be high, but the genetic contribution to stability would be low if $r_{G_{im}}$ is low. Therefore, although genetic and environmental correlations are important for understanding the causal nature of genetic and environmental continuity, phenotypically standardized genetic and environmental covariance matrices are more relevant indices of the genetic and environmental contributions to phenotypic stability.

Bivariate Heritability and Environmentality

The *relative* importance of genetic and environmental causes of phenotypic covariance for measurements of a character over time may be assessed by two recently defined quantitative genetic parameters, bivariate heritability and environmentality [11]:

$$h_{im} = CovG_i G_m / CovP_i P_m = h_i h_m r_{G_{im}} / r_{P_{im}} \tag{8}$$

and

$$e_{im} = CovE_i E_m / CovP_i P_m = e_i e_m r_{E_{im}} / r_{P_{im}} \tag{9}$$

where h_{im} and e_{im} are bivariate heritability and environmentality. As is the case for univariate h_i^2 and e_i^2, bivariate heritability and environmentality sum to one.

However, unlike the univariate case, h_{im} and e_{im} may be greater than one or less than zero if r_{Gim} and r_{Eim} differ in sign. Nevertheless, bivariate heritability and environmentality provide indices of the relative contributions of genetic and environmental influences to longitudinal stability.

Speculations in the Absence of Data

To date, the methods of multivariate behavioral genetics have not been applied to developmental data. Thus, in the absence of empirical results, we can only speculate about the causes of longitudinal stability. However, we can make some educated guesses about the findings plotted in Figures 1 and 2.

In the case of nondevelopmental analyses, it has often been found that genetic and environmental correlations are similar in direction, if not in magnitude [see 2]. Although not predicted a priori, this observation that genetic correlations and environmental correlations are correlated seems reasonable in retrospect [6]. Thus, in the absence of information to the contrary, we may assume that r_{Gim} and r_{Eim} are roughly equal. If this assumption is approximately correct, we can then obtain "ballpark" estimates of bivariate heritability and environmentality. For example, the heritability of IQ is about 0.5 by 7 years of age. Therefore we predict that genetic and environmental factors contribute about equally to longitudinal stability from age 7 to maturity, ie, bivariate heritability and environmentality are approximately equal in this case (see Eq 1). The heritability of height, however, is about 0.9 by 7 years of age. As a consequence, we predict that bivariate heritability for height is much greater than bivariate environmentality.

Given estimates of stability and heritability, we can also predict the size of the genetic and environmental correlations. For example, stability for IQ at 2 years of age is about 0.1, whereas heritabilities at this age and at adulthood are approximately 0.15 and 0.50, respectively. Upon substitution of these values into equation 1,

$$0.1 = [(0.15)\,(0.50)]^{1/2} r_{G2m} + [(0.85)\,(0.50)]^{1/2} r_{E2m} = 0.27 r_{G2m} + 0.65 r_{E2m} \quad (10)$$

Thus r_{G2m} and r_{E2m} must both be relatively small. If both correlations are positive, which certainly seems reasonable for longitudinal data, then the maximum value that r_{G2m} could attain is 0.37 (if r_{E2m} were zero), whereas r_{E2m} could not exceed 0.15. If r_{G2m} and r_{E2m} were equal, they would be less than 0.11.

However, the size of the genetic and environmental IQ correlations apparently increases dramatically by 7 years of age. At this age, stability is about 0.7 and heritability is approximately 0.5. Substituting into Eq 1,

$$0.7 = 0.5 r_{G7m} + 0.5 r_{E7m} \quad (11)$$

suggesting that the genetic and environmental correlations are both bounded by 0.4 and 1.0 at 7 years of age. In other words, many of the same genes and environmental factors appear to affect IQ at age 7 and at maturity. Also, these arguments suggest that the relationship between heritability and stability can be seen as causal, involving increases in both heritability and genetic correlations from the preschool years to the early school years.

MULTI-AGE BEHAVIORAL GENETIC ANALYSIS

Previous behavioral genetic analyses of development have focused on differential heritability and environmentality as a function of age, and we discussed how genetic and environmental correlations may be employed to partition longitudinal stability into genetic and environmental parts. However, the methods of multivariate behavioral genetics may have other important developmental applications.

Consider, for example, a large longitudinal twin study where members of MZ and DZ twin pairs have been measured for one character at each of N different ages. Using the methods outlined in the preceding section, one could estimate matrices of genetic and environmental correlations among the measures at the different ages (see Table 1). As previously discussed, the finding of a large genetic correlation between measures at two different ages would indicate that individual differences in the two measures are due to many of the same genes. Likewise, a large environmental correlation would suggest that similar environmental influences are being manifested. Therefore, if there are biologically organized stages of development, it would seem reasonable to expect that measurements taken during the same stage would be more highly correlated genetically or environmentally than measurements taken during different stages. If this is correct, then factor analysis of such genetic and environmental correlation matrices would provide useful information about the organization and timing of developmental stages.

It is important to distinguish the methods proposed in this paper from those employed by Wilson [17, 18] in his analysis of age-to-age change (spurts and lags) and overall level for data from the Louisville Twin Study. MZ correlations generally exceed DZ correlations for both age-to-age change and overall level, which suggests some heritable bases for these developmental phenomena. However, both age-to-age change and overall level are complex functions of heritabilities at each age and genetic and phenotypic correlations among the ages. In contrast, our methods assess the extent to which observed phenotypic correlations among measures of a character at different ages are due to shared genetic and environmental influences. Both approaches provide important information for understanding development and should not be viewed as being competing methodologies.

In summary, multivariate behavioral genetic analyses of development can go well beyond the question raised by Galton about changes in twin similarity as a function of age. In addition to providing information about differential heritability and environmentality, longitudinal analyses of twin data can provide estimates of the relative contributions of genetic and environmental influences to longitudinal stability. The significance of this approach lies in its power to assess the correlational structure of the genetic and environmental causes of continuity, thereby providing insight into the biological organization and timing of stages of development.

TABLE 1. Genetic and Environmental Correlations Among Measures of a Character Taken at Different Ages

	Ages				
	1	2	3	. . .	N
1	1	r_{G12}	r_{G13}	. . .	r_{G1N}
2	r_{E12}	1	r_{G23}	. . .	r_{G2N}
3	r_{E13}	r_{E23}	1	. . .	r_{G3N}
.	.	.	.	. . .	.
.	.	.	.	. . .	.
.	.	.	.	. . .	.
N	r_{E1N}	r_{E2N}	r_{E3N}	. . .	1

REFERENCES

1. Bayley N: "Bayley Scales of Infant Development." New York: Psychological Corporation, 1969.
2. DeFries JC, Kuse AR, Vandenberg, SG: Genetic correlations, environmental correlations, and behavior. In Royce JR, Mos LP (eds): "Theoretical Advances in Behavior Genetics." Alphen aan den Rijn The Netherlands: Sijthoff & Noordhoff International, 1979.
3. Fischbein S: "Heredity-Environment Influences on Growth and Development During Adolescence." Stockholm: Institute of Education, 1979.
4. Foch TT, Plomin R: Specific cognitive abilities in 5- to 12-year-old twins. Behav Genet 10:507–520, 1980.
5. Galton F: The history of twins as a criterion of the relative powers of nature and nurture. J Anthropol Inst 5:391–406, 1875.
6. Hegmann JP, DeFries JC: Are genetic correlations and environmental correlations correlated? Nature 226:284–286, 1970.
7. Ho HZ, Foch TT, Plomin R: Developmental stability of the relative influence of genes and environment on specific cognitive abilities during childhood. Dev Psychol 16:340–346, 1980.
8. Honzik M, Macfarlane J, Allen L: The stability of mental test performance between two and eighteen years. J Exp Ed 17:309–334, 1948.
9. Loehlin JC, Nichols RC: "Heredity, Environment and Personality: A Study of 850 Sets of Twins." Austin, Texas: University of Texas Press, 1976.
10. Merriman C: The intellectual resemblance of twins. Psychol Monogr 33:whole no. 152, 1924.
11. Plomin R, DeFries JC: Multivariate behavioral genetic analysis of twin data on scholastic abilities. Behav Genet 9:505–517, 1979.
12. Plomin R, DeFries JC: Genetics and intelligence: Recent data. Intelligence 4:14–24, 1980.
13. Plomin R, DeFries, JC, McClearn GE: "Behavioral Genetics: A Primer." San Francisco: Freeman, 1980.
14. Tanner JM, Healy MJR, Lockhart RD, Mackenzie JD, Whitehouse RH: Aberdeen growth study, I. The prediction of adult body measurements from measurements taken each year from birth to 5 years. Arch Dis Child 31:372–381, 1956.
15. Thorndike EL: Measurement of twins. Arch Philos Psychol Sci Meth 1:1–64, 1905.
16. Wilson RS: Concordance in physical growth for monozygotic and dizygotic twins. Ann Hum Biol 3:1–10, 1976.
17. Wilson RS: Twins and siblings: Concordance for school-age mental development. Child Dev 48:211–223, 1977.
18. Wilson RS: Synchronies in mental development: An epigenic perspective. Science 202:939–948, 1978.
19. Wilson RS: Twin growth: Initial deficit, recovery, and trends in concordance from birth to nine years. Ann Hum Biol 6:205–220, 1979.

Twin Research 3: Intelligence, Personality,
and Development, pages 35 – 41
© 1981 Alan R. Liss, Inc., 150 Fifth Avenue, New York, NY 10011

Placentation Effects on Cognitive Resemblance of Adult Monozygotes

Richard J. Rose, I. A. Uchida, and J. C. Christian
*Department of Psychology, Indiana University, Bloomington (R.J.R.),
Department of Pediatrics, McMaster University Medical Centre, Hamilton,
Ontario (I.A.U.), and Department of Medical Genetics, Indiana University
School of Medicine, Indianapolis (J.C.C.)*

INTRODUCTION

The classic twin study evaluates genetic variance by contrasting intrapair differences of mono- and dizygotes. The contrast assumes no systematic differences are associated with twin type other than the proportion of genes identical-by-descent. Yet it long has been known [16] that twins differ not only in zygosity, but in placentation as well. And placental differences in monozygotic (MZ) twins afford a research tool of promise in the search for nongenetic sources of behavioral variation [11].

The type of placentation in MZ twins is determined by the stage of early embryonic development at which separation of the cell mass occurs. Dichorionic MZ twins are assumed to result from separation of early blastomeres within 72 hours after ovulation [1, 9, 20]; their placentation is similar to that of dizygotic (DZ) twins in which each developing fetus has its own amnion and chorion. Although the two placentas may fuse if implantation occurs in close proximity, they remain structurally separate. The more common process of MZ twinning arises through duplication of the inner cell mass beyond the fourth day; the two embryos develop within a single chorionic membrane and share a common placenta in which some vessels join via anastomosis. Separation after the tenth day duplicates the embryonic rudiment of the germ disc and results in twins delivered within a single amnion as well as a single chorion. The causal factors that create differences in timing of MZ twinning are unknown and cannot be assumed to be uniform.

Population surveys of newborn Caucasian twins reveal that about 77% are dichorionic, the remaining 23% monochorionic [10]. Zygosity determinations suggest that 10% of the dichorionic twins are monozygotes, permitting the inference that about one-third of MZ twins arise from dichorionic placentation [3]. That inference was confirmed in replicated results of three recent surveys; examination of twins delivered in the 14 participating centers of the Collaborative Perinatal Project [15], in a series of consecutive twin deliveries in Indiana and Virginia [8] and Florida [13], yield estimates of dichorionic placentation in MZ twins of 32.4, 31.4, and 35.1% respectively.

Recent comparisons of MZ twins differentiated by placental type suggest that mono- (MC) and dichorionic (DC) monozygotes differ in birthweight [8, 11], dermatoglyphics [17], and cord blood cholesterol [7]. For 19 of 84 dermatoglyphic variables, within-pair mean squares significantly differed in 108 MZ twin pairs distinguished by chorion type [17]. Since the dermal ridges are established early in fetal life and are, thereafter, immune to environmental effects, dermatoglyphic variables may provide an index trait for systematic appraisal of difference among monochorionic and dichorionic MZ twin pairs. For cord blood cholesterol [7], variation within 22 pairs of dichorionic MZs was five times that of 30 MC-MZ pairs. For birthweight, studies in Indiana and Virginia [8] and in Oxford and Aberdeen [11, 12] suggest that within MZ pairs, placental proximity results in greater within-pair differences and smaller intraclass correlations. Fused dichorionic placentas apparently lower birthweight correlation in both MZs and DZs, permitting the hypothesis [12] that adjacent implantation in DC-MZs may lead to nutrient competition.

Family histories of early- and late-forming monozygotes may also differ. There are only limited data on the epidemiology of the several types of MZ twinning, but promising leads can be found in a report [4] of the family histories of mirror-image twins identified on the basis of the timing and structure of dental asymmetries, direction of hair whorl, patterns of clothing wear, etc. Families of these twins differed from other twin families in 1) increased frequency of familial MZ twinning, 2) elevated prevalence of lefthandedness, and 3) distortions of sex ratio in sibships of the parental generation. These results were interpreted [4] as evidence of a genetically transmitted tendency to produce zygotes that split late in embryogenesis.

Placental effects on tested IQ have been reported for 7-year-old Caucasian twins evaluated with the WISC as part of the Collaborative Perinatal Project [14]. Significant effects were found only in white twins, and the sample, while representative, was small (9 DC-MZs, 23 MC-MZs). However, the within-pair variation of DC-MZs was significantly greater (P<0.01) than that of monochorionic white pairs. In another report from the Collaborative Perinatal Project, the IQs of 4-year-olds measured with the Stanford-Binet, were not associated with chorion type [2], and at 18 months, an evaluation of 24 white MZ twin pairs (14 MC-MZ, 10 DC-MZ) from the Indiana Newborn Panel [22] failed to find a placentation effect on Bayley scores. These results may reflect the fact that until about age 6, birthweight and headsize differences account for a significant part of intrapair variance in mental and motor development [23]; by age 7, however, the effect of those variables is diluted and systematic genetic and environmental influences become evident.

METHOD

Study Population

Since 1978, we have been studying a unique sample of adult twins whose chorion type is known. The twins are part of a large cohort born in Toronto hospitals during the period 1936–1959. At birth, the placental membranes were separated under cold running water, and in the case of fused placentas, latex was injected into the umbilical cord of one placenta to evaluate transfer. Determination of zygosity of twins who volunteered for this study was based on extensive analyses of red cell antigens and enzymes, HLA typing, dermatoglyphic comparison, and evaluation of similarity of facial photographs. In all, some 25 polymorphic blood markers including HLA were employed, and the likelihood of zygosity error is near zero. The 60 twin pairs included in this preliminary report comprise 28 DZ, 17 MC-MZ, and 15 DC-MZ pairs.

Test Procedure

Behavioral testing was accomplished during the twins' participation in a program of research directed by the second author [21]. The behavioral test battery includes two subtests from the Wechsler Adult Intelligence Scale (WAIS), Vocabulary and Block Designs. The two subtests were chosen because they form the best dyad predictor of total IQ, because both exhibit significant heritability, but importantly differ in that vocabulary is significantly associated with socioeconomic status and educational achievement and, accordingly, exhibits assortative mating, while blocks does not [18]. In other research, we have shown that the vocabulary tests exhibit significant maternal effects [19] not found for block designs. Both tests were administered by a trained examiner and results were coded and scored blindly. Vocabulary test data were taped and subsequently scored from verbatim transcripts.

Analyses

TWNAN analyses [6] incorporating tests of assumptions, evaluations of homogeneity of means and variance across twin type, and distributional properties of the behavioral measures were employed. The analyses and the form in which they are here reported parallels the report from the Collaborative Perinatal Project [14].

RESULTS AND DISCUSSION

Means for the two WAIS subtests are compared in Table 1 and homogeneity of means evaluated with the t' test [5]. Neither zygosity nor chorion type is associated with mean performance on either vocabulary or block designs.

The representativeness of this small and selected sample is evaluated in Table 2, which estimates genetic variance from the conventional comparison of MZ and DZ twin pairs. Both tests permit inferences of significant genetic variance, and there is no association of total variance with twin type.

TABLE 1. Means of Vocabulary and Block Design Scores for Three Twin Types

	MC-MZ pairs	DC-MZ pairs	DZ pairs
Vocabulary			
No.	17	15	28
Mean	56.8	58.6	53.4
SD	15.5	11.3	15.0
	$t' = -0.36$	$t' = 1.23$	
	$P > 0.7$	$P > 0.2$	
Block design			
No.	17	15	28
Mean	39.6	37.5	41.2
SD	7.5	7.1	6.4
	$t' = 0.88$	$t' = -1.67$	
	$P > 0.3$	$P > 0.1$	

Differences between means were evaluated with the t' test proposed by Christian and Norton [5]; means for the 28 DZ pairs were compared to the means for the 32 MZ pairs.

TABLE 2. Estimates of Genetic Variance From Comparison of MZ and DZ Twin Pairs

	Vocabulary		Block design	
	MZ	DZ	MZ	DZ
Analysis of variance				
Among mean square	367.31	353.67	94.06	59.35
Within mean square	9.86	101.38	14.96	22.82
Sum of mean squares	377.17	455.04	109.03	82.17
Tests of twin model				
Equality of total variance	$F' = 1.21, P > 0.5$		$F' = 1.32, P > 0.3$	
Equality of covariance	$F = 3.48, P < 0.001$		$F = 2.60, P < 0.007$	
Estimates of genetic variance				
Comparison of within mean squares	$F = 10.28, P < 0.001$		$F = 1.52, P = 0.12$	
Intraclass correlations	0.947	0.554	0.725	0.444
	$P < 0.001$		$P < 0.05$	

An analysis of variance of the MZ twin pairs differentiated by twin type is reported in Table 3. Vocabulary exhibits no association with chorion type, with the intraclass correlations of MC-MZ and DC-MZ pairs replicating one another. By contrast, however, the block design test shows a significant effect of chorion type. Total variance for the block design subtest is equivalent in the two chorion types, but intraclass correlations are 0.92 for the MC-MZ group but only 0.48 for the DC-MZ group.

Finally, an evaluation of genetic variance of the two MZ groups compared to the DZ pairs is presented in Table 4. For both vocabulary and block design tests the MC-MZ twins exhibit significantly greater resemblance than do the

TABLE 3. Analysis of Variance of MZ Twin Pairs Differentiated by Chorion Type

	MC-MZ		DC-MZ	
	Mean square	DF	Mean square	DF
Vocabulary				
Among	483.92	16	256.00	14
Within	12.56	17	6.80	15
Sum	496.48	16.8	263.60	14.7
Equality of total variance		$F' = 1.88, P > 0.2$		
Intraclass correlation	0.949		0.948	
Block design				
Among	112.47	16	74.64	14
Within	4.74	17	26.56	15
Sum	117.21	17.3	101.20	23.0
Equality of total variance		$F' = 1.15, P > 0.7$		
Intraclass correlation	0.919		0.475	

TABLE 4. Evaluation of Genetic Variance by Chorion Type

	MC-MZ	DZ	DC-MZ
Vocabulary			
Within mean square (MS_W)	12.56	101.38	6.80
Comparison of MS_W	$F = 8.07, P < 0.001$		$F = 14.90, P < 0.001$
Intraclass correlations	0.949	0.554	0.948
	$P < 0.001$		$P < 0.001$
Block design			
Within mean square (MS_W)	4.74	22.82	26.56
Comparison of MS_W	$F = 4.81, P < 0.001$		$F = 0.86, P > 0.8$
Intraclass correlations	0.919	0.444	0.475
	$P < 0.003$		$P > 0.9$

DZ pairs. The DC-MZ twins also reliably differ from the DZs for vocabulary, but for the block design test, the DC-MZ twins are no more alike than are the DZs.

These results suggest an effect of placentation on the abilities measured by the Block Design Subtest of the WAIS. As such, they comprise the first evidence of a lasting influence of placental variation on adult intellectual performance. It is, of course, necessary to underscore the preliminary nature of these data, the small samples on which they are based, and the obvious need for replication with larger samples and more diverse tests.

Interpretation of our evidence of greater dissimilarity of DC-MZ pairs remains uncertain. The effect may represent variation in vascular communication in utero, competitive effects of placental proximity, or differential timing of the initial embryological division underlying early and late MZ twinning. In any case, these results are consistent with a report from the Collaborative Perinatal

Project and warrant further investigation. Our studies of the unique McMaster twin panel are continuing.

In summary, significant population variance in tested IQ is attributable to prenatal and maternal factors, and specific effects are evident in the correlations of childhood IQ scores with birthweight, placental weight, head circumference, and presence of anemia during pregnancy. Data from adult MZ cotwins, carefully classified by chorion type, may provide important new evidence of prenatal effects on cognitive ability.

ACKNOWLEDGMENTS

We thank Patricia M. Cino, Marilyn Parsons, and A. Dea Clark for their assistance. Ascertainment and genotyping of twins was made possible by a contract from the National Heart, Lung & Blood Institute (I. A. Uchida, principal investigator). Behavioral testing was supported by BRS grant S07 RR 7031 to R. J. Rose and by the Indiana University Human Genetics Center, GM 21054.

REFERENCES

1. Benirschke K: Origin and clinical significance of twinning. Clin Obstet Gynecol 15:220–235, 1972.
2. Brown B: Placentation effects on birth weight and IQ in MZ twins. Presented at meetings of Society for Research in Child Development, New Orleans, 1977.
3. Bulmer MG: "The Biology of Twinning in Man." Oxford: Clarendon Press, 1970.
4. Carter-Saltzmann L: Mirror twinning: Reflection of a genetically mediated embryological event? Behav Genet 9:442–443 (abstr), 1979.
5. Christian JC, Norton JA, Jr: A proposed test of the difference between the means of monozygotic and dizygotic twins. Acta Genet Med Gemellol 26:49–54, 1977.
6. Christian JC: Testing twin means and estimating genetic variance: Basic methodology for the analysis of quantitative twin data. Acta Genet Med Gemellol 28:35–40, 1979.
7. Corey LA, Kang KW, Christian JC, Norton JA Jr, Harris RC, Nance WE: Effects of chorion type on variation in cord blood cholesterol of monozygotic twins. Am J Hum Genet 28:433–441, 1976.
8. Corey LA, Nance WE, Kang KW, Christian JC: Effects of type of placentation on birthweight and its variability in monozygotic and dizygotic twins. Acta Genet Med Gemellol 28:41–50, 1979.
9. Corney, GW: The observed embryology of human single ovum twins and other multiple births. Am J Obstet Gynecol 70:933–951, 1955.
10. Corney G: Placentation. In MacGillivray I, Nylander PPS, Corney G (eds): "Human Multiple Reproduction." London: WB Saunders, 1975, pp 40–76.
11. Corney G: Twin placentation and some effects on twins of known zygosity. In Nance WE, Allen G, Parisi P (eds): "Twin Research: Biology and Epidemiology." New York: Alan R Liss, 1978, pp 9–16.
12. Corney G: Multiple and singleton pregnancy: Differences between mothers as well as offspring. Presented at 3rd International Congress on Twin Studies, Jerusalem, June 1980.
13. Levine RS, Hennekens CH: Blood pressure in infant twins: Birth to 6 months of age. Hypertension 2 (Suppl 1) I:29–33, 1980.
14. Melnick M, Myrianthopoulos NC, Christian JC: The effects of chorion type on variation in IQ in the NCPP twin population. Am J Hum Genet 30:425–433, 1978.
15. Myrianthopoulos NC, Melnick M: Malformations in monozygotic twins: A possible example of environmental influence on the developmental genetic clock. In Inouye E, Nishimura H (eds): "Gene-Environment Interaction in Common Diseases." Baltimore: University Park Press, 1977, pp 206–220.

16. Price B: Primary biases in twin studies: A review of prenatal and natal difference — producing factors in monozygotic pairs. Am J Hum Genet 2:293–352, 1950.
17. Reed T, Uchida IA, Norton JA Jr, Christian JC: Comparisons of dermatoglyphic patterns in monochorionic and dichorionic twins Am J Hum Genet 30:383–391, 1978.
18. Rose RJ, Harris EL, Christian JC, Nance WE: Genetic variance in nonverbal intelligence: Data from the kinships of identical twins. Science 205:1153–1155, 1979.
19. Rose RJ, Boughman JA, Corey LA, Nance WE, Christian JC, Kang KW: Data from kinships of monozygotic twins indicate maternal effects on verbal intelligence. Nature 283:375–377, 1980.
20. Strong SJ, Corney G: "The Placenta in Twin Pregnancy." Oxford: Pregamon Press, 1967.
21. Uchida I, Feinleib M, Christian JC: Comparisons of coronary heart disease risk factors in monozygotic and dizygotic twins by chorion type. Presented at 3rd International Congress on Twin Studies. Jerusalem, June 1980.
22. Welch P, Black KN, Christian JC: Placental type and Bayley mental development scores in 18-month-old twins. In Nance WE (ed): "Twin Research: Psychology and Methodology." New York: Alan R Liss, 1978, pp 145–149.
23. Wilson RS: Synchronies in mental development: An epigenetic perspective. Science 202:939–948, 1978.

Twin Research 3: Intelligence, Personality,
and Development, pages 43 – 50
© 1981 Alan R. Liss, Inc., 150 Fifth Avenue, New York, NY 10011

Intelligence-Test Results in Opposite-Sex Twins

Siv Fischbein
Department of Educational Research, Stockholm Institute of Education

INTRODUCTION

Many intelligence tests are designed to eliminate or at least minimize sex differences. This implies that a choice of test items is made not to discriminate against either sex. This is true, for example, for the Stanford-Binet. Tests of specific abilities, however, often show differences between sexes in either direction, depending on the items included in the test. Sex differences thus tend to be more or less pronounced, depending on both the type of test and the age at which the test is given.

It is well known that tests heavily loaded on *verbal ability* tend to favour girls. Both language development and overall linguistic ability seem to be more advanced in girls before the age of 3 [15]. After that age, sex differences in verbal ability are fairly small up to age 11, when girls again, on average, perform better than boys on these types of tests. This seems to be mainly due to an excess of boys at the lower level of performance. At the upper level of test scores, however, there does not seem to be much difference in the numbers of boys and girls [10].

On measures of *quantitative ability,* however, there seem to be only minor differences between boys and girls. At least this is true for children growing up under normal circumstances and up to puberty. In disadvantaged populations the girls tend to be slightly ahead of the boys. From puberty upwards, most studies find consistent differences in favour of boys on these types of tests.

In a Swedish study, Ljung [13] has discussed sex differences during puberty, using results from achievement tests constructed to equalize marks in the compulsory school system. He also found that girls, on the average, perform better than boys in the verbal comprehension factor and that boys perform better than girls in the mathematics factor. The difference was more pronounced for the latter, however, and the picture was complicated by apparent differences in the onset of the growth spurt for the two sexes.

Supported by the Swedish Council for Social Science Research.

From about age 6–8, boys show an advantage on tests measuring *spatial ability*. The differences between the sexes also seem to increase with advancing age.

Studies of *analytic ability* often show some superiority of boys over girls. This is especially true for tests of field independence from the beginning of puberty. Maccoby and Jacklin define field independence as skill "in a large range of tasks that require ignoring a task-irrelevant context or focusing upon only selected elements of stimulus display" [15, p 104]. For problem-solving ability involving set-breaking the results are equivocal.

Reasoning ability has been measured by different types of inductive and deductive reasoning tests. Up to adolescence, studies are consistent in showing an absence of sex differences. At higher ages, research evidence is somewhat more inconsistent, sometimes presenting advantages for girls and sometimes for boys depending on the type of test.

Tests of *perceptual speed* seem to favour girls. Jarvik [11] reports, for instance, that eight out of ten studies find such differences. Broverman et al [2] also report female superiority on clerical aptitude tests. This superiority was found to be present from the fifth grade through the senior year of high school.

From this brief overview of comparisons between boys and girls on different types of tests, it can be seen that a verbal content often tends to favour girls, whereas a quantitative, spatial, or analytical content would give boys an advantage. This tendency is more evident from adolescence upwards. The average differences, however, are rather small and the variation for both boys and girls is large, so the distributions overlap to a great extent.

A pertinent question related to sex differences in intellectual abilities is therefore comparisons of variability for boys and girls on these types of tests. For verbal ability there seems to be a trend for boys to show greater variability from about 12 years of age. There are, however, some studies reporting greater variability for girls. For quantitative ability, there is a fairly consistent trend in the direction of greater male variability. This also seems to be true for spatial ability. The greater variability in verbal ability for boys found in some studies often implies more low scores among the boys than among the girls. For quantitative ability, however, there is an opposite trend, so that boys outnumber girls at the upper end of the distributions.

Several explanations have been offered to account for the greater variability more often found for males than for females on different types of tests. One of these is that greater male variability in intelligence is caused by a genetic sex linkage. Some evidence has been presented to support this theory at least concerning sex differences in spatial ability [1, 12]. For verbal ability there seems to be no evidence of a sex linkage.

Another explanation for sex differences found in intellectual abilities has been activation by sex hormones [17] of different mental functions. This hypothesis has been tested by experimentally injecting sex hormones in an experimental group and comparing it to a control group [2]. The results suggest that "estrogens are more potent activating agents than are androgens."

Brain lateralization differing for boys and girls is another theory presented to explain differential variation in the sexes. Buffery and Gray [3] claim, for instance, that an earlier and stronger development of lateralization in females facilitates their verbal development, but that spatial skills call for a more bilateral cerebral representation and hence are facilitated in men, in whom laterality is not so strong or developed so early.

In spite of all these more or less hypothetical explanations to differences found between boys and girls, Petersen [17] asserts that "while these sex-related differences in cognitive functioning may turn out to have some biological component, such influences would not limit any cognitive ability to one sex or the other and, indeed, would produce small differences at most."

Differential socialization or upbringing of boys and girls is therefore also always a factor contributing to the sex differences found in intellectual abilities. Training of intellectual capacities has sometimes led to diminished sex differences on later trials [9]. If this tendency is corroborated for many intellectual abilities, it would confirm the importance of environmental factors in the appearance of sex differences. Biological and social determinants of sex differences are also not operating independently of each other. Instead, biological factors interact during development with environmental components of sex-role socialization [6, 18].

In summary, studies on sex differences in intellectual abilities tend to show increasing differences from puberty upwards. This is often found for verbal and perceptual speed abilities where girls excel and for quantitative and spatial abilities where boys show an advantage over girls. There is, however, a large variation for both sexes, but especially for boys, and the distributions overlap to a considerable degree.

It must also be taken into account that there is a considerable difference in the onset of puberty for the two sexes. During this period it has also been shown that a successive differentiation between, and integration within, abilities is taking place [13].

The influence of biological and environmental factors on sex differences has often been studied by comparing parent-child similarity or identical and fraternal male and female twins [15]. Opposite-sex twins have often been compared with like-sex dizygotic pairs. Contrary to predictions, it has often been found that the like-sex pairs are not more similar than opposite-sex pairs [16, 19].

A more unusual approach has been to compare opposite-sex twin pairs with nonrelated boy-girl pairs matched for age and attending the same classes as the twins. This could, however, contribute to the understanding of biological and environmental factors influencing sex differences, since the twin pairs have both half of their genes in common, on average, and are brought up in the same home environment. The controls, however, could be hypothesized to show some kind of "pure" sex difference, not contaminated by specific heredity-environment influences. This hypothesis is tenable under the assumption that school influences, such as belonging to the same class, are supposed to be of minor importance for the outcome studied.

MATERIALS AND METHODS

In 1964 a longitudinal study of physical and mental growth in twins and controls of matched age (the SLU project) started at the Department of Educational Research at the Stockholm Institute of Education. The data presented in this paper have been collected in the SLU study. The twins were taken from the 40 largest cities and towns in Sweden and their controls were attending the same classes as the twins. Originally the sample consisted of 94 pairs of MZ twins, 133 DZ pairs of the same sex, 96 DZ pairs of different sex, and 1,194 controls. There were no separated twin pairs included in the study, so the twins in a pair were brought up in the same home.

For every twin pair, control pupils in the same classes as the twins were included in the study. The controls were of the same sex as the twins and approximately of the same age. The data collection has been more complete for the twins, however, who were followed through school irrespective of change of classes or schools, whereas this was not the case for the controls. This means that data could be missing for one or both of the control pupils, which sometimes makes comparisons difficult.

The twins and their controls were followed through school from grades 3 to 9, and different kinds of measurements were collected: physical growth data (eg, height and weight measurements), school achievement and test results, self ratings, ratings by others, and socioeconomic data.

The test battery included a group-administered intelligence test in grade 5, when the twins and controls were approximately 12 years old. It is a differential ability test (DBA) including three subtests: a verbal test, an inductive test, and a clerical speed test. The verbal test consists of opposites where one is supposed to name the opposite of a given word. The inductive test consists of four letter groups, one of which is different in its logical construction than the other three. The clerical speed test is made up of two-digit numbers and one is supposed to mark the numbers appearing more than once. Raw scores for the three tests have been transformed into a stanine scale.

Of the 96 opposite-sex twin pairs included in the SLU study, 58 pairs had taken the above-mentioned intelligence tests in grade 5; 74 control pupils of different sex born within a two-month interval from the twins had also taken the tests. Unfortunately, data for only 27 complete control pairs were collected, since for many pairs one control had not taken the tests and then the other one also had to be excluded.

Intraclass correlation coefficients were used to make within-pair comparisons for opposite-sex twins (DZ-OS) and controls (CO). The coefficients show the magnitude of within-pair variance relative to between-pair variance. The formula used is

$$R = \frac{V_{bp} - V_{wp}}{V_{bp} + V_{wp}}$$

where R = intraclass coefficient, V_{bp} = variance between pairs, and V_{wp} = variance within pairs. (For a more detailed discussion of this method and for a description of the data program used for computing, see Ljung [14].

RESULTS

Of the tests used in the SLU study, the verbal and perceptual speed tests could be expected to favour girls, whereas the inductive reasoning test results are more difficult to predict. A comparison of test results by sex for the total control group has been made by Fischbein [4]. Girls have a higher average score than boys on all three tests, but the difference is slight and insignificant for the verbal test score. For the inductive test the sex difference is somewhat larger and indicative at the 10% level (P < 0.10). The clerical speed test, however, shows a significant sex difference in favour of the girls (P < 0.01). The standard deviations seem to be of the same magnitude for both boys and girls on the three tests.

A comparison of average test results for the total group of opposite-sex twins and for their controls has been made for the verbal, inductive, and clerical speed test and is presented in Table 1.

TABLE 1. Intelligence Test Results for Opposite-Sex Twins and Controls

	DZ (opposite-sex)			Controls			
Test	M	SD	N*	M	SD	N	Z
Verbal test	4.65	1.51	58	5.45	1.81	75	2.78**
Inductive test	4.79	1.69	58	5.15	1.81	75	1.18
Clerical speed test	4.62	1.81	56	4.99	1.90	73	1.13

*The mean for each twin pair is used as an observation.
**P < 0.01.

For all three tests, the twin group tends to have somewhat lower average scores than their controls. The smaller standard deviations for the twin group can be expected since the twin pairs are treated as observations. The average difference in test scores is significant, however, only for the verbal test. Lower average test scores for twins in comparison to controls is a result often found in different twin studies. Possible explanations to this difference has been discussed by, among others, Fischbein [4] and Mittler [16].

The items included in the DBA tests are not specifically trained at school and the control pairs can therefore not be expected to show more than random similarity on these types of tests [17]. The twins, however, share both a common inheritance and home environment that could be expected to result in a within-pair correlation of around 0.50 [16, p 78].

Within- and between-pair variances have been estimated for the opposite-sex twins and their controls. They are presented in Table 2 as well as intraclass correlations (within-pair correlations) for the two groups. As can be seen from Table 2, only 27 control pairs with test results for both individuals in the pair are left of the original 37 pairs. A comparison of the results for the remaining and missing pairs has therefore been made for all three tests. The test results were very similar for the two groups and none of the differences were significant (P > 0.05).

TABLE 2. Intraclass Correlations Based on Analysis of Variance. Verbal, Inductive, and Clerical Speed Test Results for DZ-OS Twins and Control Pairs (CO)

	Verbal test		Inductive test		Clerical speed test	
	DZ-OS	CO	DZ-OS	CO	DZ-OS	CO
No. of pairs	58	27	58	27	56	27
V_{bp}	4.58	3.70	5.74	4.48	6.53	3.40
V_{wp}	2.37	2.50	2.97	2.35	3.31	3.35
$F (V_{bp}/V_{wp})$	1.93	1.48	1.94	1.91	1.97	1.01
R	0.32	0.19	0.32	0.31	0.33	0.01

From the results in Table 2 it is evident that the relationship of within- to between-pair variance and also the intraclass correlations (R) are practically identical on the three tests for the opposite-sex twin pairs. The correlations are just above 0.30 irrespective of type of test. The F ratios are also significant at the 5% level for the verbal test and at the 1% level for the other two tests. The correlations are lower, however, than would be expected from the results presented by Mittler [16]. This is probably an effect of the differences in onset of puberty for the two sexes [16].

The results for the control pairs are very similar to results for the twins on the inductive test (R_{CO} = 0.31 and R_{DZ-OS} = 0.32). None of the F ratios for the controls are significant at the 1% level, however, and the comparatively high intraclass correlation for the inductive test could be a random effect, considering the small number of control pairs. For the verbal and clerical speed test results DZ-OS twins have higher within-pair correlations than the controls. This is particularly evident for the last-mentioned test, where the within- and between-pair variances are practically the same for the controls resulting in an intraclass correlation coefficient of around 0.00.

DISCUSSION

Of the three intelligence tests used in the SLU study, only the clerical speed test shows a significant sex difference in favour of the girls. As has been pointed out, female superiority on this type of test is very often found. This is also the test where the largest difference for the twin groups and the controls in within-pair similarity can be noticed. The twins tend to be more similar than the controls on this type of test, an effect of both common inheritance and a more similar environment. Hormonal causes or differential brain lateralization for the sexes do not seem to be plausible explanations to this sex difference, since the control pairs as well as the twin pairs can be assumed to be similar in these respects.

For the other two tests, the intrapair difference between the twins and their controls is surprisingly small, considering that the twins have the same parents and are living in the same homes. For the inductive test, for instance, there is practically no difference between the two groups.

The intraclass correlations of around 0.30 for the opposite-sex twins could also be compared with the corresponding correlations for monozygotic (MZ) and dizygotic (DZ) like-sex twins. Fischbein [5] has reported intraclass correlations for these groups of twins on the three types of ability tests used in the SLU study. There is a tendency for male DZ pairs to be more similar on these tests than female DZ pairs. This is also true for the MZ pairs but not to the same extent. Many studies, comparing intraclass correlations for like-sex and opposite-sex DZ twins, have reported coefficients for the opposite-sex pairs of approximately the same magnitude or even higher than for the like-sex twins [16, 19]. This could probably, however, be due to both male and female pairs being included in the like-sex twin group. We have seen that for DZ-OS pairs the correlations are around 0.32 on the three tests. For the DZ like-sex pairs in the SLU study, the average correlation for the three tests is 0.44 for male pairs and 0.28 for female pairs [5]. As can be seen, the DZ-OS correlation tends to be somewhere in between these two figures.

In summary, a comparison has been made of intelligence test results for opposite-sex twin pairs and control pairs of boys and girls matched for age and attending the same classes as the twins. Within-pair correlations were of approximately the same magnitude for the twins and their controls on the inductive test. The verbal test showed the twins to be a little more similar than their controls ($R_{DZ-OS} = 0.32$ and $R_{CO} = 0.19$). The largest difference between the two groups, however, was on the clerical speed test ($R_{DZ-OS} = 0.33$ and $R_{CO} = 0.01$). This was also the only test showing a significant sex difference in favour of the girls for the total control group included in the SLU material (N = 569). One explanation of this difference seems therefore to be a combination of specific heredity-environment influences existing for the twins but not for the controls.

REFERENCES

1. Bock DR, Kolakowski D: Further evidence of sex-linked major-gene influence on human spatial visualizing ability. Am J Hum Genet 25:1–14, 1973.
2. Broverman DM, Klaiben EL, Kobayaski Y, Vogel W: Roles of activation and inhibition in sex differences in cognitive abilities. Psychol Rev 75:23–50, 1968.
3. Buffery AWH, Gray JA: Sex Differences in the development of spatial and linguistic skills. In Ounsted C, Taylor DC (eds): "Gender Differences: Their Ontogeny and Significance. Baltimore: Williams & Wilkins, 1972.
4. Fischbein S: Att vara tvilling. (Being a twin). Report No. 2 from the Department of Educational Research at the Stockholm School of Education, 1976.
5. Fischbein S: Lika och olika tvillingar. (Like and unlike twins). Report No. 4 from the Department of Educational Research, Stockholm Institute of Education, 1977.
6. Fischbein S: Heredity-environment interaction in the development of twins. Int J Behav Dev 1:313–322, 1978.
7. Fischbein S: Intra-pair similarity in IQ of monozygotic and dizygotic male twins at 12 and 18 years of age. Ann Hum Biol 6:495–504, 1979.
8. Fischbein S: "Heredity-Environment Influences on Growth and Development During Adolescence." Lund: Liber, 1979.
9. Goldstein AG, Chance JE: Effects of practice on sex-related differences in performance on embedded figures. Psychonom Sci 3:361–62, 1965.
10. Jacklin CN: Epilogue. In Wittig, Petersen (eds): "Sex-Related Differences in Cognitive Functioning." New York: Academic Press, 1979.

11. Jarvik LF: Human intelligence: Sex differences. Acta Genet Med Gemellol 24:189–211, 1975.
12. Lehrke RG: Sex linkage: A biological basis for greater male variability in intelligence. In Osborne, Noble, Weyl (eds): "Human Variation." New York: Academic Press, 1978.
13. Ljung, B-O: The adolescent spurt in mental growth. Stockholm: Almqvist & Wiksell, 1965.
14. Ljung B-O: Intraklasskorrelation (Intraclass correlation). Report No. 16. Stockholm: Department of Educational Research, School of Education, 1966.
15. Maccoby EE, Jacklin CN: "The Psychology of Sex Differences." Palo Alto, California: Stanford University Press, 1974.
16. Mittler P: The study of twins. London: Penguin Books Ltd, 1971.
17. Petersen AC: Hormones and cognitive functioning in normal development. In Wittig, Petersen (eds): "Sex-Related Differences in Cognitive Functioning." New York: Academic Press, 1979.
18. Seaver JW: "The Sex Differentiated Interaction of Environmental and Hereditary Determinants of Intelligence." Eric Documents No. 131946, 1972.
19. Wilson RS: Twin growth: Initial deficit, recovery, and trends in concordance from birth to nine years. Ann Hum Biol 6:205–220, 1979.

Twin Research 3: Intelligence, Personality,
and Development, pages 51 – 60
© 1981 Alan R. Liss, Inc., 150 Fifth Avenue, New York, NY 10011

Development of Piagetian Logicomathematical Concepts and Other Specific Cognitive Abilities

Arleen Garfinkle and Steven G. Vandenberg

Institute for Behavioral Genetics, University of Colorado, Boulder

INTRODUCTION

A number of twin studies have investigated various cognitive abilities. However, only two studies reported by Wilson [25,26,27] and by Foch and Plomin [8] have considered the development of cognitive abilities in young children. All of this research has been based on a standard psychometric approach to cognition, which recently has been criticized on the ground that studies of cognition should have a theoretical framework, such as Piaget's, addressing the origins of intellectual functioning [4,15,16].

Many researchers have investigated the effects of various general environmental factors (eg, socioeconomic status) on cognitive abilities. However, very little research has been done on the relationships between cognitive abilities and more specific environmental factors [14,21,23]. In addition, very few studies have investigated environmental influences on the early development of logiocomathematical concepts, or the possible relationships of verbal, reasoning, and memory functions to such development.

The present research, based on Piaget's theory of cognitive development, examined genetic and environmental influences on Piagetian logicomathematical concepts and other specific cognitive abilities in young children. We also investigated the interrelationships among these cognitive abilities.

METHODS AND MATERIALS

Twin pairs were solicited through school districts and mothers-of-twins clubs in the greater Denver-Boulder area. Following the precedent of Cohen et al [2], zygosity was determined by a mother's questionnaire about twin similarities

Supported in part by The Spencer Foundation, the University of Colorado Committee on Research and Creative Work, and NIMH training grant MH-11167.

and differences, phenylthiocarbamide (PTC) tasting, and fingerprinting. Blood-typing for 16 genetic markers was performed for 32 twin pairs of questionable zygosity. The zygosity determination in this sample was considered to be 98% accurate [9]. The sample of 209 Caucasian twin pairs consisted of 137 MZ pairs (58 male and 79 female) and 72 DZ pairs (38 male and 34 female). The twin pairs were relatively equally distributed among 4-, 5-, 6-, and 7-year-old groupings, with a mean age of 71 months (SD = 13 months).

This volunteer sample was upwardly biased in parental socioeconomic status. Provider's occupation was coded according to the Duncan modification of the National Opinion Research Center occupational prestige scale [19]. This sample covered the entire possible range (20–93), with a mean of 73.0 (SD = 10.5) representing a technical worker. Level of parental education ranged from completing 6th grade to obtaining a professional degree (PhD, MD, etc). On the average, fathers completed 4 years, and mothers completed 3 years of college, although the distribution of parental educational levels exhibited one mode at completing high school and a second mode at obtaining a BA degree. Each twin pair averaged 1.4 additional siblings, with a range of 0–7 additional siblings per twin pair.

Twins were individually administered four cognitive tests: 1) The Piagetian Mathematical Concepts Battery (PMCB) consists of 15 tasks representing the three Piagetian concepts of Conservation, Classification, and Seriation. The PMCB has an α reliability of 0.89 and a test-retest reliability of 0.85 [12]. 2) The Raven Coloured Progressive Matrices (PM) is the child's form (4–11 years) of the well-known adult Progressive Matrices, a nonverbal test of reasoning ability. Among 422 twins, 48–107 months old, it has a reliability of 0.82 [10]. 3) The Peabody Picture Vocabulary Test (PPVT) is also a well-known standardized test, with a Form A–Form B reliability of 0.77 [5]. 4) Visual Memory, immediate and delayed (VM), described by Wilson et al [24], has a test-retest reliability of 0.62 among 4- to 8-year-olds [9].

Parents of the twins completed the following two questionnaries as independent measures of the environment: 1) The Attitudes Toward Education (ATE) Scale consists of three factors: Attitude Toward Basic Academic Education (ATE I), Attitude Toward Parental Participation in Education (ATE II), and Attitude Toward General Utility of Education (ATE III). For the parents of this twin sample (N = 384), the ATE α reliability is 0.61 [9]. 2) The Moos Family Environment Scale (FES) consists of 10 subscales: Cohesion, Expressiveness, Conflict, Independence, Achievement Orientation, Intellectual-Cultural Orientation, Active-Recreational Orientation, Moral-Religious Orientation, Organization, and Control. Moos [17] reported KR-20 reliabilities of these ten subscales ranging from 0.65 to 0.79, and test-retest reliabilities between 0.68 and 0.86.

RESULTS AND DISCUSSION

Because there were no significant (P < 0.01) mean or variance differences between sexes in cognitive performance, all data were pooled across sex for the subsequent analyses. There were also no significant mean or variance differences in test performance, age, or any of the environmental variables between the MZ and DZ groups. Therefore, except for the MZ and DZ intraclass correlational analyses, results were determined for the entire sample. Out of 105 possible, the PMCB mean was 74.9 (SD = 19.1). Out of 150 possible, the PPVT mean was 59.7 (SD = 9.2). Since this test is meant for subjects up to 18 years old, this mean is not unreasonable. For VM, out of 40 possible, the mean was 12.2 (SD = 9.6). This mean is low because the youngest children did not do very well on this visual memory task. However, performance by the older children was comparable to previous findings [9]. Out of 36 possible, the PM mean was 19.0 (SD = 5.2). Although the PM was actually administered to 229 pairs of twins, 48–107 months old, the data presented here are based on a sample of 211 twin pairs, which included 19 pairs of 8-year-olds and excluded 17 pairs of 4- and 5-year-olds in which one twin did not finish the PM [10].

As expected, the PMCB had the highest correlation with age (r = 0.75). Correlations for the PPVT, the PM, and the VM were 0.70, 0.64, and 0.43, respectively. Because of such high correlations with age, the effects of age were partialed out of performance in most subsequent analyses (except where indicated).

For the sample of 418 children, correlations among the age-corrected test scores were calculated. A correlation of only 0.23 between the PPVT and the PM indicated that these tests do indeed measure separate abilities which are differentially related to performance on the Piagetian battery. As expected, since they both measure nonverbal reasoning, the PMCB and PM correlated most highly (r = 0.41). The verbal element to PMCB performance is indicated by its correlation of 0.36 with the PPVT. Visual Memory is only slightly (although significantly, $P < 0.01$) related to performance on the other three tests, as indicated by the smaller correlations with the PMCB (0.22) and with the PM and the PPVT (0.19).

Intraclass Correlations

With the effects of age removed, the residual scores were used to calculate intraclass correlations presented in Table 1. As a check on these results, the same calculations were performed for height and weight. All the MZ-DZ intraclass correlation comparisons are in the expected direction. The intraclass correlations for height and weight are within the range of previously reported values from the Louisville Twin Study [25].

The DZ intraclass correlation for VM was not significantly different from zero, even when corrected for test-retest reliability. The MZ intraclass correlation was significantly different from zero ($P < 0.05$), and therefore from the DZ intraclass correlation. These correlations indicate only a small amount of genetic variance in VM performance, which increased somewhat when the intraclass correlations were corrected for test-retest reliability (see Table 1). For the PM, there was no significant difference between the MZ and DZ intraclass correlations, even after correction for α internal consistency reliability. These PM and VM results are consistent with those found by Foch and Plomin [8] for their 5- to 12-year-old sample of 84 twin pairs.

There was a significant ($P < 0.05$) difference between the MZ and DZ intraclass correlations for both PMCB and PPVT performance. The heritability estimate of 0.34 for both of these tests is comparable to estimates obtained by

TABLE 1. Intraclass Correlations (t) and Estimates of "Broad" Heritability (h^2) for the Cognitive Tests, and for Height and Weight for 137 MZ and 72 DZ Twin Pairs[a]

Measure	Intraclass correlation (t)		$h^{2\,b}$
	MZ	DZ	
PMCB	0.73 ± 0.04 (0.86)	0.56 ± 0.08 (0.66)	0.34[d] ± 0.18 (0.40)[e]
PM[c]	0.47 ± 0.07 (0.57)	0.39 ± 0.10 (0.48)	0.16 ± 0.24 (0.18)
PPVT	0.69 ± 0.04 (0.90)	0.52 ± 0.09 (0.68)	0.34[d] ± 0.19 (0.44)[e]
VM	0.17 ± 0.08 (0.27)	−0.08 ± 0.12 (−0.13)	
Height	0.94 ± 0.01	0.54 ± 0.09	0.80[e] ± 0.17
Weight	0.91 ± 0.01	0.67 ± 0.06	0.48[e] ± 0.13

[a]Numbers in parentheses are the appropriate values corrected for test reliability. The reliability estimates used in these corrections are: PMCB, 0.85 test-retest; PM, 0.82 α internal consistency; PPVT, 0.77 Form A-Form B; VM, 0.62 test-retest. All calculations, except the PM α reliability, are based on age-corrected scores.
[b]"Broad" heritability, $h^2 = 2(t_{MZ} - t_{DZ})$, from Falconer [6]. The approximate standard error of the heritability estimate for 137 MZ and 72 DZ twin pairs was calculated from a formula given by Loehlin and Nichols [13], originally from Jensen [11].
[c]All calculations are based on 74 DZ and 137 MZ twin pairs, 48–107 months old, who finished the PM.
[d]P < 0.05 for h^2.
[e]P < 0.01 for h^2.

TABLE 2. Correlations Among the Cognitive Tests and the Independent Environmental Variables (N = 358)[a]

Variable	PMCB	PM	PPVT	VM
Number of sibs	0.01	−0.06	−0.10	−0.04
Provider's occupation	0.18	0.10	0.13	−0.05
Father's education	0.22	0.10	0.24	0.04
Mother's education	0.26	0.12	0.19	0.09
Moos Family Environment Scale				
Cohesion	0.10	−0.03	0.19	0.08
Expressiveness	0.02	−0.03	0.13	−0.01
Conflict	0.05	0.04	0.02	−0.01
Independence	0.08	−0.06	0.04	0.01
Achievement	−0.14	−0.16	−0.07	−0.03
Intellectual-Cultural	0.16	0.06	0.20	0.13
Active-Recreational	0.11	0.01	0.05	0.03
Moral-Religious	−0.01	0.02	−0.07	−0.05
Organization	−0.02	−0.06	−0.04	0.00
Control	−0.07	0.01	−0.09	−0.05
Attitudes Toward Education				
Factor I	0.10	−0.02	0.13	−0.06
Factor II	−0.13	0.02	−0.09	−0.02
Factor III	−0.10	−0.07	−0.08	−0.07

[a]For N = 358, the critical value (P < 0.01) of the correlation coefficient is 0.14. All correlations are corrected for the effect of age.

Wilson [27] for 5- and 6-year-old WPPSI IQ, and for 7- and 8-year-old Verbal and Performance IQ [26]. However, this is the first study to find genetic variance in Piagetian mathematical conceptualization tasks in young children.

Age Trends In Intraclass Correlations

Although this was not a longitudinal study, the age span did allow for an investigation of possible age trends in the MZ and DZ concordances for the cognitive tests. For each cognitive test, the within-pair difference in test scores was plotted against age for the MZ and DZ samples separately. For all four tests, there was no MZ or DZ relationship between within-pair score difference and age. These results indicate no changes with age in the MZ and DZ intraclass correlations. This was verified by a stepwise multiple regression technique, which found no significant interaction between age and the intraclass correlation in analyses performed separately on the MZ and DZ samples for each cognitive test.

Environmental Analyses

The magnitude of the age-corrected PMCB, PPVT, and PM intraclass correlations (see Table 1) led to the examination of specific between-family environmental influences on test performances. Since none of the mean or variance differences between MZs and DZs for any of the environmental comparisons was significant ($P > 0.05$), the environmental analyses were performed on the entire sample. The environmental variables considered were number of siblings, provider's occupation, father's and mother's educational levels, average family scores on the ten subscales of the FES, and average family scores on the three ATE factors. We recognize that parental educational levels are to some extent influenced by parental ability and therefore partly due to genetic factors. At the same time, parental educational levels are indicators of the total socioeconomic condition of the family, which is predominantly an environmental factor [14]. Therefore, although parental educational levels could be considered as a source of either genetic or environmental variance [12], they were interpreted as environmental variables for the first series of stepwise multiple regression analyses (see below). Parental educational levels were not included in the second series, and provider's occupation was also excluded in the final environmental analyses.

Table 2 presents the age-corrected correlations of the four cognitive tests with the environmental variables. Because some parents did not return all questionnaires, the sample size for these analyses was 358. The significant correlations in Table 2 indicate that mother's and father's educational levels, provider's occupation, and intellectual-cultural and achievement orientation are related to PMCB performance. Similarly, achievement orientation appears to be negatively related to PM performance. Also, mother's and father's educational levels, cohesion in the family, and intellectual-cultural orientation seem to predict PPVT performance in this sample of 358 twins. None of the environmental variables were correlated significantly with memory (VM).

Table 3. Significant Variables in Three Series of Stepwise Multiple Regressions of Cognitive Test Performance on Environmental Variables (N = 358)

Test	Variable entered	Percent of variance accounted for[a]		
		With parental education and occupation	Without parental education	Without parental education and occupation
PMCB	Age	57[b]	57[b]	57[b]
	Parental education	3[b]	—	—
	ATE III—general education	1		
	Provider's occupation		1[b]	—
	Intellectual-cultural orientation			1[c]
	Other minor variables			
	Total R^2	62	61	61[b]
PPVT	Age	48[b]	48[b]	48[b]
	Parental education	3[b]	—	—
	Cohesion in the family	1[c]		
	Intellectual-cultural orientation		2[b]	2[b]
	Provider's occupation			—
	Other minor variables			
	Total R^2	56	55	55
PM	Age	35[b]	35[b]	35[b]
	Achievement orientation	2[c]	2[c]	2[c]
	Parental education	—		—
	Provider's occupation			—
	Other minor variables			
	Total R^2	41	41	40
VM	Age	18[b]	18[b]	18[b]
	Intellectual-cultural orientation	2[d]	1[d]	1[d]
	Provider's occupation			—
	Other minor variables			
	Total R^2	23	23	22

[a]Percentage of the total variance in the dependent variable accounted for by the independent variable in the regression equation. The sum of these percentages is the total squared multiple correlation, R^2.
[b]$P \leq 0.001$.
[c]$P \leq 0.01$.
[d]$P = 0.013$.

Three series of stepwise multiple regressions were used to determine the significant amounts of unique variance in cognitive performance for each test accounted for by the independent between-family environmental variables listed. The significant ($P < 0.01$) influences on the four cognitive tests for the three series of stepwise multiple regressions are presented in Table 3. Rather than starting with age-adjusted scores, age was included as an independent variable so that its effects could be partialed out of all the other variables during the stepwise multiple regression procedure. For all four tests, age was the single most important independent variable. Age accounted for 57% of the total variance (R^2) in PMCB, 35% in PM, 48% in PPVT, and 18% in VM performance. These results confirm the high correlations between age and the cognitive test scores.

For the Piagetian battery, the only other significant effect in the first stepwise multiple regression was education (mother's), accounting for 3% of the total variance in PMCB performance (see Table 3). This result agrees with previous finding of SES differences in Piagetian task performance [1,7,22]. Thus age and parental education accounted for 60% of the total variance in PMCB performance. When parental education was excluded from the stepwise multiple regression, provider's occupation was the only additional significant effect, accounting for 1% of the total variance in PMCB performance (see Table 3). When both parental education and occupation were excluded from the regression, intellectual-cultural orientation in the family became the only additional significant influence, accounting for 1% of the total variance (see Table 3).

In the first stepwise multiple regression analysis for the PPVT, parental education (father's) yielded an R^2 of 0.03. As with the PMCB, this result is also in keeping with previous findings relating SES to cognitive performance, particularly to verbal ability [12,14,20,27]. Cohesion in the family, the only other variable to predict PPVT performance significantly, accounted for 1% of the total variance. These results are easily interpreted, since family cohesion probably facilitates verbal communication (cohesion and expressiveness correlated 0.38), and more educated parents have more extensive vocabularies to which their children are exposed. Age, parental education, and family cohesion accounted for 52% of the total variance in PPVT performance. When parental education and then provider's occupation were excluded from the stepwise multiple regression, intellectual-cultural orientation in the family became the only other significant variable, accounting for 2% of the total variance in PPVT performance (see Table 3).

The results of these two analyses indicate that intellectual-cultural orientation in the family is one aspect of socioeconomic status which can be isolated. However, intellectual-cultural orientation partially represented parental educational level, since these two variables correlated 0.47 (after controlling for twins' age).

In the first stepwise multiple regression analysis, achievement orientation was inversely related ($P < 0.01$) to PM performance, accounting for 2% of the total variance (see Table 3). This result supports Piaget's [18] contention that pressure for competitive achievement inhibits abstract reasoning and possibly other aspects of cognitive development in young children. Taken together, age and achievement orientation accounted for 37% of the total variance in PM performance (see Table 3). These results were not altered in the two subsequent regression analyses, which excluded parental education and then also provider's occupation. Apparently, socioeconomic status does not affect the reasoning ability involved in PM performance.

Finally, Table 3 indicates that age was the only significant predictor of VM performance in the first stepwise multiple regression. Intellectual-cultural orientation bordered on significance (P = 0.013) and accounted for 2% of the total variance in VM performance. A family intellectual-cultural orientation apparently is conducive to visual memory. A possible explanation is that these families provide their children with stimulating experiences to retain in the mind's eye, such as visits to museums and art exhibits. Thus age and intellectual-cultural orientation accounted for 20% of the total variance in VM performance (see Table 3). It must be kept in mind, however, that at least 75% of the variance in VM performance was within-family variance, which could not be identified in this between-family environmental analysis. In fact, about 38% of VM variance was due to test-retest unreliability (1.00 — 0.62 = 0.38), which is included in the estimate of the within-family variance. As with the PM, these results were not affected by excluding parental education and occupation from the regression equation (see Table 3).

CONCLUSIONS

The present study is the first large-scale twin study to use Piagetian tasks and to report significant genetic variance in Piagetian logicomathematical conceptualization. As previously reported for adolescents and adults, we have also found a heritable influence on vocabulary among young children. However, our results indicate no significant genetic variance for Raven Coloured Progressive Matrices performance among children 4 through 8 years old, although family resemblance has been reported for Raven Standard Progressive Matrices scores (and Visual Memory) among adolescents and adults [3,20]. Similarly, our results are only suggestive of significant genetic variance for visual memory.

The environmental analyses suggest the need for measures of parental intellectual functioning in conjunction with measures of twins' abilities. This is necessary in order to separate genetic and environmental components of the effect of parental education. A striking result of the environmental analysis is our finding of a relatively small amount of total variance accounted for by the environmental variables. This finding underscores how much is yet to be learned about the influence of the environment on the development of specific cognitive abilities.

ACKNOWLEDGMENTS

We sincerely thank all of the cooperating school districts and mothers-of-twins clubs, and all of the twins and their families who made this research possible. We also thank the many staff members who collected, scored, and coded the data.

REFERENCES

1. Almy M et al: "Logical Thinking in Second Grade." New York: Teachers College Press, 1970.
2. Cohen DJ, Dibble E, Grawe JM, Pollin W: Reliably separating identical from fraternal twins. Arch Gen Psychiatry 32:1371–1375, 1975.

3. DeFries JC, Johnson RC, Kuse AR, McClearn GE, Polovina J, Vandenberg SG, Wilson JR: Familial resemblance for specific cognitive abilities. Behav Genet 9:23–43, 1979.
4. DeVries R: Relationships among Piagetian achievement and intelligence assessments. Child Dev 45:746–756, 1974.
5. Dunn LM: "Peabody Picture Vocabulary Test Manual." Circle Pines, Minnesota: American Guidance Service, 1965.
6. Falconer DS: "Introduction to Quantitative Genetics." Edinburgh: Oliver and Boyd, 1960.
7. Figurelli JK, Keller HR: The effects of training and socioeconomic class upon the acquisition of conservation concepts. Child Dev 43:293–298, 1972.
8. Foch TT, Plomin R: Specific cognitive abilities in 5- to 12-year-old twins. Behav Genet 10:507–520, 1980.
9. Garfinkle-Claussner A: "Genetic and Environmental Influences on the Development of Piagetian Logico-Mathematical Concepts and Other Specific Cognitive Abilities: A Twin Study." Unpublished doctoral dissertation, University of Colorado, Boulder, 1979.
10. Garfinkle-Claussner A, Vandenberg SG: Internal-consistency reliability and genetic variance for the Raven Coloured Progressive Matrices. Behav Genet 10:477 (Abstr), 1980.
11. Jensen AR: Estimation of the limits of heritability of traits by comparison of monozygotic and dizygotic twins. Proc Natl Acad Sci USA 58:149–156, 1967.
12. Loehlin J, Lindzey G, Spuhler J: "Race Differences in Intelligence." San Francisco: Freeman, 1975.
13. Loehlin J, Nichols P: "Heredity, Environment, and Personality." Austin: University of Texas Press, 1976.
14. Majoribanks K: Socioeconomic status and its relation to cognitive performance as mediated through the family environment. In Oliverio A (ed): "Genetic, Environment and Intelligence." Amsterdam: Elsevier/North Holland Biomedical Press, 1977, pp 385–403.
15. Meyers CE: Can Piaget's theory provide a bettery psychometry? In Magary JF, Poulsen M, Lubin GI, Coplin G (eds): "Proceedings of the Second Annual UAP Conference on Piagetian Theory and the Helping Professions." Los Angeles: University Publishers, 1972.
16. Mittler P: "The Study of Twins." Baltimore: Penguin Books, 1971.
17. Moos R: "Family Environment Scale and Preliminary Manual." Palo Alto, California: Consulting Psychologists Press, 1974.
18. Piaget J: Foreword. In Inhelder B, Sinclair H, Bovet M (eds): "Learning and the Development of Cognition." Boston: Harvard College, 1970.
19. Reiss J: "Occupations and Social Status." New York: The Free Press of Glencoe, 1961.
20. Scarr S, Barker W: "The Effects of Family Background: A Study of Cognitive Differences Among Black and White Twins." Unpublished manuscript, 1977.
21. Spuhler KP, Vandenberg SG: Relationship between family environment and children's and parents' cognitive performance. Behav Genet 8:114–115 (Abstr), 1978.
22. Tuddenham R: A "Piagetian" test of cognitive development. In Dockrell WB (ed): "On Intelligence." London: Methuen, 1970, pp 49–70.
23. Vandenberg SG: Twin studies. In Kaplan AR (ed): "Human Behavior Genetics." Springfield, Illinois: Charles C Thomas, 1976, pp 90–150.
24. Wilson JR, DeFries JC, McClearn GE, Vandenberg SG, Johnson RC, Rashad, MN: Cognitive abilities: Use of family data as a control to assess sex and age differences in two ethnic groups. Int J Aging Hum Dev 6:261–276, 1975.
25. Wilson RS: Concordance for physical growth for monozygotic and dizygotic twins. Ann Hum Biol 3:1–10, 1976.

26. Wilson RS: Twins and siblings: Concordance for school-age mental development. Child Dev 48:211–216, 1977.
27. Wilson RS: Synchronies for mental development: An epigenetic perspective. Science 202:939–948, 1978.

Twin Research 3: Intelligence, Personality,
and Development, pages 61 — 71
© 1981 Alan R. Liss, Inc., 150 Fifth Avenue, New York, NY 10011

Relevance of the Marriages of Twins to the Causal Analysis of Nonrandom Mating

W.E. Nance, L.A. Corey, R.J. Rose, and L.J. Eaves

*Department of Human Genetics, Medical College of Virginia, Richmond
(W.E.N., L.A.C., L.J.E.), and the Department of Psychology, Indiana
University, Bloomington (R.J.R.)*

INTRODUCTION

Nonrandom mating can dramatically alter the distribution of phenotypes in both natural and experimental populations. In human populations, departures from random mating have traditionally been detected through an analysis of the marital correlation between husband and wife. Marital choices may be either assortative or disassortative, mate selection with respect to sex being a trivial example of the latter type. In theory, positive or negative marital correlations could arise either from the nonrandom pairing of phenotypes at the time of marriage or from the common home environment that couples share after marriage. Depending on whether a trait is determined largely by genetic or cultural factors and how it is transmitted, these two alternatives could have quite different implications for the offspring phenotypes.

The foregoing examples, however, do not exhaust the inherent possibilities for nonrandom mating in a population. For example, it has long been recognized from studies in lower organisms that intensive mate selection may exist even when the resulting matings are not uniformly assortative or disassortative in nature. In polygynous species, nonassortative mating preferences constitute a potent mechanism for evolutionary change and play an important role in the origin of sexual dimorphisms according to Darwin's [3] and Fisher's [6] theories of sexual selection. When one or a few individuals are preferred by all, a few matings will be assortative whereas the others will be sufficiently disassortative that there may actually be no net marital correlation in the population despite the presence of intense marital selection. In monogamous species, mating preferences generally do not carry the same potential for rapid evolutionary change unless different mating combinations are associated with variable fitness. However, Darwin suggested an ingenious mechanism by which mating preference could lead to selective change even in monogamous species: If matings that involve preference tend to occur earlier in

This is paper 111 from the Department of Human Genetics of the Medical College of Virginia and was supported in part by USPHS grants HD 10291 and GM 21054.

the mating season, Darwin speculated that they might be associated with greater fecundity. Subsequent observations in several species of birds have confirmed this insight [14]. When mating preferences are uniformly assortative (or disassortative), their effects may readily be detected by a departure of the proportions of various mating types from those expected with random mating. However, no method has previously been proposed for the detection of nonassortative mating preferences in a monogamous species when the sequence of matings in a population is not known [15]. In this paper we suggest that if marital preferences are conditioned by either genetic or cultural factors, a comparison of the choices of related individuals would provide a method of detecting nonrandom mate selection regardless of whether it is largely assortative or disassortative, or whether preferential matings of both types occur. It seems intuitively reasonable to suppose that, for some traits, certain individuals in a population may mate assortatively while others mate at random or even disassortatively. However, this type of heterogeneity in mating behavior cannot be detected from an analysis of nuclear families, since the marital correlation will reflect only the mean or net effect of all mating preferences in the population.

If heterogeneity in mating preferences does exist within a population, we must also consider the possibility that males and females may not contribute equally to nonrandom mate selection for every trait. As is true of other types of heterogeneity, sexual asymmetry in mate selection cannot be detected in nuclear families but could readily be inferred from a comparison of the phenotypic correlation between the spouses of related male family members in comparison with those of related females. Further progress in the resolution of the genetic and environmental causes for marital correlation and the detection of heterogeneity and sexual asymmetry in mating preferences will clearly require an extension of the analysis of mate selection beyond the confines of the nuclear family unit. Data on the marriages of twins provide one approach by which these goals can be achieved.

A CAUSAL MODEL

The marriages of male and female twins give rise to four distinct correlations for twins of each sex. These are the twin correlation r_{TT}, the marital correlation r_{HW}, between husband and wife, the twin-spouse correlation, r_{TS}, between one twin and the spouse of the cotwin, and the spousal correlation, r_{SS}, between the two spouses of the twins. Nance et al [13] have suggested that the expected value of these correlations may be expressed in terms of the eight variables shown in Table 1. These variables are: h^2 and c^2, the genetic and environmental variances respectively; a, the genetic component of the marital correlation; u, the component of the marital correlation that is attributable to the common home environment of marital partners; t, the component of the twin environmental correlation that is attributable to the residual effect of their shared childhood environment; k, a pervasive kinship environmental effect that influences all members of the kinship; and s, a component of the phenotypic correlation between the spouses that arises from the tendency of twins to assort concordantly in their mate selection. One would expect the genetic correlation between the spouses of two phenotypically identical but unrelated individuals to be a^2. Consider, for example, a sample of marriages

TABLE 1. Expected Values or Correlations Among MZ Twins and Spouses

Correlation	Expected values	
	Male twin marriages	Female twin marriages
r_{TT}	$h^2 + c^2 (k_M + t)$	$h^2 + c^2 (k_F + t)$
r_{HW}	$h^2 a + c^2 (k_M + u)$	$h^2 a + c^2 (k_F + u)$
r_{TS}	$h^2 a + c^2 k_M$	$h^2 a + c^2 k_F$
r_{SS}	$h^2 (a^2 + s_M) + c^2 (k_M + s_M)$	$h^2 (a^2 + s_M) + c^2 (k_F + s_F)$

Equation of determination $1 = h^2 + c^2$

involving unrelated individuals that is stratified by the stature (height) of the husband. If the couples contained within a narrow stratum are randomly paired (the stratum containing husbands taller than 6'3" but less than 6'4", for example) the result would be the creation of "pseudo-twins," who were phenotypically similar but genetically unrelated. The expected genetic correlation for the spouses of these pseudo-twins would be the product of the genetic component of the marital correlation or a^2. However, if genetically identical individuals tend to assort concordantly in their mate selection, then the genetic and environmental correlations appropriate for phenotypically identical but unrelated pseudo-twins will be augmented by an amount measured by s. Both concordant assortative and concordant disassortative matings contribute to the spousal correlation, whereas the marital correlation reflects only the average or net effect of these two processes. In a random mating population, both the marital and spousal correlations will be zero. However, if the mating behavior of related individuals is correlated, nonrandom mating of the latter type may be detected by analysis of the correlations between the spouses of relatives, such as the spouses of twins.

It can be seen from the expected values of the correlations shown in Table 1 that any observed difference between the marital correlation, r_{HW}, and the twin spouse correlation, r_{TS}, can provide a measure of the contribution of a common home environment to the observed marital correlation. Similarly, a comparison of the spousal and marital correlations can indicate the relative importance of concordant assortation for the trait in question. The variables s and k are subscripted to allow for sex differences in the kinship environment provided by male and female twins and the degree to which males and females may differ in their mating preferences for a given trait. For example, in view of the dominant role of the male in determining the socioeconomic status of nuclear families, one might expect a higher correlation among individuals in the families of male twins for traits that are influenced by socioeconomic factors. Similarly it seems plausible to assume that males and females may vary in their contributions to preferential mating for different traits. For example, if we assume that females have no concern about the stature of their spouses while males are highly selective, one would expect a low correlation between the multiple spouses of polyandrous females and a high correlation between the multiple spouses of polygynous males. The marriages of MZ twins provide an equivalent set of relationships that permit the detection of such asymmetries but are, at the same time, not biased by the behavioral and social

TABLE 2. Stature: Observed Correlations Among MZ Twins and Spouses

Correlation	Male twins		Female twins	
	df	r	df	r
Twin-twin, r_{TT}	50	0.93**	76	0.92**
Spouse-spouse, r_{SS}	50	0.24	51	0.01
Husband-wife, r_{HW}	98	0.23*	121	0.21*
Cotwin-spouse, r_{TS}	98	0.22*	121	0.21*

*P<0.05; **P<0.01.

complexities that frequently surround the contemporary causes of sequential polygamy [2]. When the eight expectations shown in Table 1 are combined with an equation of determination, they provide a total of nine relationships from which estimates of the various parameters may be obtained by a weighted least-squares procedure [7]. Alternative solutions may be compared by a χ^2 goodness of fit.

RESULTS

The model can be illustrated by data on the stature of MZ twins and their spouses as well as by observations on the Blocks, Information, and Verbal Subtests of the Wechsler Intelligence Scale. These data were collected from white, predominantly middle-class twins seen at the University of Indiana while the senior author was Principal Investigator of the Indiana University Human Genetics Center as well as from twins identified through the Medical College of Virginia Twin Registry.

Stature

Measurements of height were obtained from the total of 129 MZ twin pairs and their spouses including 52 male and 77 female pairs, and the eight correlations derived from the data are shown in Table 2. The twin correlations are high, as one might expect for a trait that is strongly influenced by genetic factors. The husband-wife and twin-spouse correlations are all significantly different from zero, and virtually identical in magnitude, suggesting the existence of a substantial degree of assortative mating preference with no evidence for an effect of postmarital environment. This is not too surprising since stature is a trait that is usually fully manifested before marriage. Although neither of the spousal correlations was significant in this small body of data, the estimate for female twins was substantially smaller than that for male twins, raising the possibility that there may be a fundamental asymmetry in the process of mate selection for stature in this sample. In Table 3 the results of fitting several genetic models to the data are given. A simple genetic model (I) could not adequately explain the data as indicated by the large χ^2 goodness of fit. The inclusion of a^2, the assortative mating parameter (II), dramatically improved the fit, giving a solution that provided an entirely adequate explanation for the data, as indicated by the P value of 0.90. The inclusion of a third parameter, s_M, to account for the apparent tendency of male twins to assort concordantly in their mate selection, led to a further improvement in the goodness of fit. However, additional observations will be required to determine with certainty

TABLE 3. Stature: Comparison of Causal Models

Parameters	Causal models			
	I	II	III	IV
h	0.96	0.97 ± 0.005	0.96 ± 0.005	0.85
a		0.24 ± 0.03	0.23 ± 0.03	
s_M			0.19 ± 0.09	
k				0.71
h^2	0.92	0.94	0.92	0.72
c^2	0.08	0.07	0.08	0.28
χ^2	23.0	2.1	0.47	2.43
df	7	6	5	6
P	0.002	0.90	0.99	0.88

TABLE 4. Information: Observed Correlations Among MZ Twins and Spouses

Correlation	Male twins		Female twins	
	df	r	df	r
Twin-twin, r_{TT}	41	0.80**	40	0.75**
Spouse-spouse, r_{SS}	33	0.46**	23	0.43**
Husband-wife, r_{HW}	75	0.56**	60	0.51**
Cotwin-spouse, r_{TS}	76	0.50**	60	0.44**

**$P < 0.01$.

whether an asymmetric pattern of marital preference is in fact characteristic of some populations. Confirmation of this trend would indicate that marital selection for stature is largely a concern of the male rather than the female marriage partner.

Information

Scores for the Information Subtest of the Wechsler Intelligence Scale were obtained by individual testing of 41 male and 40 female MZ twins and their spouses. The observed correlations in the marriages of male and female twins are shown in Table 4. As was true of stature, the twin-twin correlations are substantial. The marital, spousal, and twin-spouse correlations are even larger for information than they were for stature, are all highly significant, and show no clear evidence for sexual asymmetry in mate selection, although all four of the correlations derived from the marriages of female twins are somewhat smaller than the corresponding correlations for male twins. This is a pattern that one might expect if there were differences in the environmental kinship correlations for male and female twins (ie, $k_M \neq k_F$). As shown in Table 5, a simple genetic, random environmental model could be excluded as an explanation for the data. The inclusion of the assortative mating and concordant assortation parameters (II, III) markedly improved the fit and yielded parameter estimates that were considerably larger than their standard errors. If accepted, model III would imply that twins do not behave independently

TABLE 5. Information Subtest: Comparison of Causal Models

Parameter	I	II	III	IV	V
			Causal models		
h	0.88	0.88 ± 0.02	0.88 ± 0.02	0.53 ± 0.04	0.58 ± 0.10
a		0.68 ± 0.04	0.65 ± 0.05		0.21 ± 0.31
s			0.12 ± 0.08		
k				0.68 ± 0.03	0.66 ± 0.07
h^2	0.77	0.77	0.77	0.28	0.34
c^2	0.23	0.23	0.23	0.72	0.66
χ^2	82.1	2.0	1.2	1.5	1.2
df	7	6	5	6	5
P	~0	0.92	0.94	0.96	0.94

TABLE 6. Vocabulary: Observed Correlations Among MZ Twins and Spouses

Correlation	Male twins		Female twins	
	df	r	df	r
Twin-twin, r_{TT}	46	0.82**	54	0.72**
Spouse-spouse, r_{SS}	39	0.45**	35	0.34*
Husband-wife, r_{HW}	86	0.45**	87	0.46**
Cotwin-spouse, r_{TS}	86	0.40**	87	0.39**

*P < 0.05; **P < 0.01.

in their mate selection for this variable. If one twin selects a marriage partner with a similar score, the other twin is more likely to do the same. However, if one twin selects a partner with a dissimilar score, the cotwin again is likely to behave in the same manner. In this way, we can explain why the spousal correlations are nearly as large as the marital and twin-spouse correlations. However, as shown by model IV, the correlations can also be readily explained by the assumption that environmental factors common to all members of the kinship contribute to the trait, along with additive genetic factors. Finally, model V, in which additive genetic, kinship environmental and assortative mating effects are assumed, gives a χ^2 identical to that observed from model III. For these two models the design is indeterminant. However, the inclusion of offspring data in the analysis, or data from the marriages of DZ twins, should permit a distinction to be made between solutions which lead to heritability estimates as divergent as 0.77 and 0.34.

Vocabulary

Vocabulary Subtest scores were obtained for 46 male and 54 female MZ twins and their spouses, and the observed correlations are shown in Table 6. The pattern of correlations is quite similar to that observed for the Information Subtest (Table

TABLE 7. Vocabulary Test Scores: Comparison of Causal Models

Parameter	Causal models				
	I	II	III	IV	V
h	0.87	0.87	0.87 ± 0.02	0.58 ± 0.04	0.60 ± 0.06
a		0.60	0.56 ± 0.05		0.08 ± 0.19
s			0.16 ± 0.08		
k				0.65 ± 0.03	0.62 ± 0.05
h^2	0.76	0.76	0.76	0.33	0.36
c^2	0.24	0.24	0.24	0.66	0.64
χ^2	7.78	3.76	2.0	2.1	2.0
df	7	6	5	6	5
P	~0	0.71	0.85	0.91	0.85

TABLE 8. Blocks: Observed Correlations Among MZ Twins and Spouses

Correlation	Male twins		Female twins	
	df	r	df	r
Twin-twin, r_{TT}	41	0.68**	39	0.69**
Spouse-spouse, r_{SS}	35	−0.15	23	0.04
Husband-wife, r_{HW}	76	0.16	59	0.08
Cotwin-spouse, r_{TS}	75	0.27*	59	0.05

*$P<0.05$; **$P<0.01$.

7). As was true of the Information Subtest, two three-parameter models could not be distinguished, although they led to quite different estimates of genetic determination.

Blocks

Data on the Blocks subtest were collected on 41 male and 39 female MZ twins and their spouses, and the observed correlations are shown in Table 8. The pattern of correlations for Blocks was quite different from that observed for the other two subtests. The twin correlations were again found to be substantial in their magnitude but the remaining correlations were small and either not significant or only marginally significant. The parsimonious additive genetic random environmental solution (Table 9, I) could not be excluded as an explanation for the data, in contrast to the data from all of the other variables.

DISCUSSION

In 1976, Nance and Corey described a new research design involving the analysis of data from the families of MZ twins and showed how the relationships contained within the families could permit an improved resolution of genetic, environmental, and maternal effects and possibly even the detection of epistasis [7]. They also suggested that the marriages of twins might be of value for a more detailed analysis of

TABLE 9. Blocks Subtest: Comparison of Causal Models

Parameter	Causal models		
	I	II	III
h	0.82 ± 0.03	0.82	0.76
a		0.20	
k			0.25
h^2	0.69	0.68	0.57
c^2	0.31	0.32	0.43
χ^2	8.81	3.24	5.01
df	7	6	6
P	0.27	0.81	0.54

mating behavior. The design has subsequently been used for the causal analysis of many variables including blood pressure [5,17], birthweight [10], total ridge count [11], immunoglobulin levels [4], serum cholesterol [1,9] and several psychological traits [8,16,18]. The present examples show how the relationships contained within the marriages of twins can allow a resolution of the genetic and environmental causes for marital correlation, as well as the detection of concordant assortation by related individuals and sexual asymmetry in mating preference for height. Analysis of the Information and Vocabulary Subtest scores revealed a substantial degree of genetic determination and assortative mating, and the high spousal correlations also adumbrate the presence of concordant assortation for these traits. All possible causal models cannot be resolved when data are available only on MZ twins and their spouses and two plausible models postulating largely genetic and environmental determination could not be distinguished for those two traits. However, it seems likely that if data on other relationships, such as the MZ twins' offspring, the marriages of DZ twins, or the marriages of adoptive siblings were included in the analysis, a choice could be made among the alternatives. Finally, the data on Blocks showed a quite different pattern of correlations with little evidence for nonrandom mating.

Assortative mating acts to increase the variation in the population and, as previous authors have emphasized, the magnitude of its effects can be substantial. In the case of global IQ, marital correlations in the range of 0.3–0.4 have frequently been reported, and are known to account for a substantial proportion of the total variation in the natural population. Indeed, if matings occurred at random with respect to IQ, the frequency of individuals with IQs greater than 130 would be reduced to approximately 1/3 of their present number, whereas only about 1/6 as many individuals with IQs above 140 would be expected. Clearly, the world would be a very different place if all matings occurred at random. In addition to reducing the total variance, as noted previously, panmixia would rapidly submerge racial and ethnic differences. These facts serve to emphasize the great social importance of the mating structure of the population. Although assortative mating alone can-

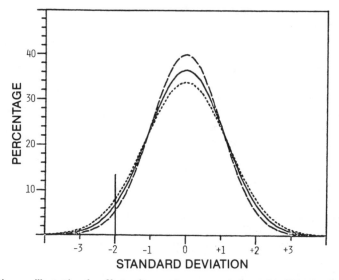

Fig. 1. Diagram illustrating the effects of truncation on populations with different variances. Dashed and dotted lines show populations with 20% smaller or 20% greater variance than that of base population, indicated by solid line. Truncation removes a larger proportion of the subpopulation with the greatest variance.

not alter the mean value of an additive genetic trait in a population, it can change the frequency of individuals who show extreme deviation from the population mean and, when combined with selective factors or threshold effects, could lead to differences in the population mean as well as its variance. This is illustrated in Figure 1 where two subpopulations are shown whose variances are 20% less and 20% greater than that of a pooled population (solid line). If the distributions were truncated at the −2 SD point, and the mean values of the residual populations were compared, the subpopulation with the greater variance would appear to have a higher mean since more low values would have been excluded. For IQ measurements, this process would correspond to comparing the IQs of school children under the assumption that children with IQs lower than 70 do not enter the system. It is of interest that, if there is a true difference in the population mean (but not the variance), truncation would have the opposite effect and the observed difference in the means of the truncated samples would underestimate the true difference in the population means. In view of all that has been written about racial differences in IQ, it is surprising that full consideration has not been given to the possible contribution that racial differences in the pattern of mating preferences might have in accounting for observed variation in the distribution of phenotypes among populations or ethnic groups. This hypothesis could readily be tested by a detailed cross-cultural comparison of the dynamics of mating preference in different populations.

In his treatise on *Genetic Models of Sexual Selection*, O'Donald distinguishes between "assortative preferential mating," which leads to a nonrandom distribution of mating types in the population, and what he characterizes as "random preferential mating," and argues that the latter should be a more common phenomenon than the former [15]. The present analysis suggests that "nonassortative mating preference" might be a more suitable term for matings that occur by preference between individuals with either similar or dissimilar phenotypes. If related individuals display a correlated mating behavior, preferences of this type can hardly be regarded as being "random." Finally, a more incisive analysis of nonrandom mating will be of critical importance to any serious attempt to extend genetic analysis from nuclear sibships to larger kindreds, since sexual asymmetry in marital selection can mask or mimic a true maternal effect, whereas concordant assortation by genetically related individuals could falsely inflate the evidence for genetic effects derived from an analysis of the correlations of distant relatives. The marriages of twins would seem to provide a useful paradigm for the recognition and estimation of these effects.

REFERENCES

1. Christian JC, Kang KW: Maternal influences on plasma cholesterol variation. Am J Hum Genet 20:462, 1977.
2. Cloninger CR, Rice J, Reich T: Multifactorial inheritance with cultural transmission and assortative mating. Am J Hum Genet 31:176, 1979.
3. Darwin CR: "The Descent of Man, and Selection in Relation to Sex." London: John Murray, 1871.
4. Escobar V, Nance WE, Bixler D, Biegel A, Corey LA: The inheritance of immunoglobin levels. In Nance WE (ed): "Twin Research: Clinical Studies." New York: Alan R Liss, 1978, pp 171–176.
5. Ewell LW, Corey LA, Winter PM, Boughman JA, Nance WE: Blood pressure studies on monozygotic twins and their families. In Nance WE, Allen G, Parisi P (eds): "Twin Research: Part C. Clinical Studies." New York: Alan R Liss, 1978, pp 29–38.
6. Fisher RA: The genetical theory of natural selection. Oxford: Clarendon Press, 1930.
7. Nance WE, Corey LA: Genetic models for the analysis of data from the families of identical twins. Genetics 88: 811–826, 1976.
8. Nance WE: The use of twins in clinical research. Birth Defects: Orig Art Ser 13(6): 19–44, 1977.
9. Nance WE, Corey LA, Boughman JA: Monozygotic twin kinships: A new design for genetic and epidemiologic research. In Morton NE, Chung CS (eds): "Genetic Epidemiology." New York, Academic Press, 1978, pp 87–132.
10. Nance WE: Genetic studies of the offspring of identical twins. Acta Genet Med Gemell 25:96–104, 1979.
11. Nance WE: The role of twin studies in human quantitative genetics. Prog Med Genet 3 (New Ser):73–107, 1979.
12. Nance WE: A note on assortative mating and maternal effects. In Sing CF, Skolnick M (eds): "The Genetic Analysis of Common Diseases: Applications to Predictive Factors in Coronary Heart Disease." New York: Alan R Liss, 1979, pp 453–464.
13. Nance WE, Corey LA, Eaves LJ: Marital selection for stature by monozygotic twins: Evidence for a sex difference. Acta Genet Med Gemell (in press).

14. O'Donald P, Davis JWF: A demographic analysis of the components of selection in a population of Arctic Skuas. Heredity 36:343–350, 1976.
15. O'Donald P: "Genetic Models of Sexual Selection." Cambridge: Cambridge University Press, 1980.
16. Rose R, Harris EL, Christian JC, Nance WE: Genetic variance in non-verbal intelligence: Data from the kinships of identical twins. Science 205:1153, 1979.
17. Rose RJ, Miller JZ, Grim CE, Christian, JC: Aggregation of blood pressure in the families of identical twins. Am J Epidemiol 109:503, 1979.
18. Rose RJ, Boughman JA, Corey LA, Nance WE, Christian JC, Kang KW: Maternal effects on verbal intelligence: Data from the kinships of MZ twins. Nature 283:375–377, 1980.

Twin Research 3: Intelligence, Personality,
and Development, pages 73—86
© 1981 Alan R. Liss, Inc., 150 Fifth Avenue, New York, NY 10011

Sex-Limitation and "Asymmetric" Assortative Mating

L.J. Eaves and A.C. Heath
Department of Experimental Psychology, University of Oxford

INTRODUCTION

A detailed understanding of the human mating system is fundamental to any study of human biology or genetic epidemiology. Although there have been various treatments of the human mating system and its consequences for the similarity between relatives, virtually all have assumed that the measured phenotype reflects the effects of genes which contribute equally to the sexual attractiveness of both sexes. Although suggestions have been made to the contrary [eg, 6, 7], serious consideration of this possibility has been hampered by the failure to present a consistent theory and parsimonious mathematical model.

This paper develops such a model from a few very simple and plausible propositions and illustrates some of the consequences of so-called "asymmetric assortation" for the similarity between relatives. Although the model is developed in very elementary terms, the treatment is powerful enough to show many of the intrinsically exciting possibilities for the study of twins and their close relatives and provides a valuable starting point for the more detailed analysis of the causal basis of assortative mating.

The logic of the approach is very simple. The conventional twin study concentrates on the phenotypes of the twins themselves. By examining the variances and covariances of these phenotypes, we attempt to deduce something of the genetic and cultural basis of the measured differences. Eaves [4] has discussed in some detail the conditions under which the twin study can be used to detect the effects of the family environment, the interaction between twins, and the sex-limitation of gene effects. Table 1 summarises the crude "rules of thumb" that may be used in a preliminary examination of twin data to decide between alternative explanations. The model-fitting approaches described by

This work is part of a program supported by the British Medical Research Council for the extension and application of biometrical genetics to the analysis of human variation.

TABLE 1. Elementary Deductions From Twin Data*

Case	Correlations	Total variances	Deduction
I	$r_{MZ} = 2r_{DZ}$	$V_{MZ} = V_{DZ}$	? Random mating, additive gene action, no family environment
II	$r_{DZ} > \frac{1}{2}r_{MZ}$	$V_{MZ} = V_{DZ}$	? Family environment, assortative mating
III	$r_{DZ} < \frac{1}{2}r_{MZ}$	$V_{MZ} = V_{DZ}$	? Nonadditive gene action
IV	$r_{DZ} < \frac{1}{2}r_{MZ}$	$V_{DZ} > V_{MZ}$	? G-E covariance due to twin competition
	r_{DZ} ? $-ve$		
V	$r_{DZ} > \frac{1}{2}r_{MZ}$	$V_{MZ} > V_{DZ}$	? G-E covariance due to twin cooperation
VI	r_{DZ} unlike sex $< r_{DZ}$ like sex	Sex differences	? Different genes expressed in each sex (sex limitation)

*The formal models underlying these deductions and methods for estimation and significance testing are discussed in Eaves [4].

Eaves [4, 5] are simply methods that judge the significance of inferences more rigorously and estimate the parameters of the best-fitting model more efficiently.

The use of twins for the study of the mating system depends on the simple recognition of the fact that the spouses of twins may be regarded as an extension, or expression, of the phenotypes of the twins themselves. Therefore any of the inferences that could apply to the phenotypes of twins (see Table 1) could equally be extended to the correlations between the phenotypes of twins' spouses, to a first approximation. Thus, by examining the spouses of male and female MZ and DZ twins, it should be possible to detect the contribution of genetic and cultural effects, and the effects of sibling interaction and sex-limitation, on the process of mate selection.

Unfortunately, the intuitive simplicity of this idea does not engender a very simple model even for the case in which transmission is purely genetic, because several parameters are likely to be necessary to describe the correlations between relatives. The reasons for this will become clear as the model is developed.

BASIC ASSUMPTIONS

The general model depends on three main propositions, which are outlined in turn. 1) The genes segregating in a population can be divided into those that affect mate selection and those that do not. We shall use the term "fitness" to describe the aspect of the phenotype on which mate selection is based, although we recognise that this might have unnecessarily precise connotations. "Sex appeal" might be more appropriate, but may be thought to have pejorative connotations! 2) A particular measured aspect of the phenotype, for example height or blood pressure, may be influenced both by genes contributing to mate selection and by genes that do not. 3) Genes that affect mate selection, and those that do not, may show sex differences in the magnitudes of their effects.

The crucial concept in the model is the separation between the phenotype that is measured and that on which mate selection is primarily based. This formal separation permits a more general model to be written from which various instructive special cases may be derived. The distinction is important biologically and psychologically since it cannot be supposed, necessarily, that the phenotypes we measured are the sole or primary components of the principal dimensions of the mating system. The second critical concept is that of sex-limitation. That is, the expression of genes may differ between the sexes. It turns out that most of the inconsistencies of earlier approaches [eg, 7] can be resolved by treating so-called "asymmetric" assortment as a particular example of sex-limitation for the genes affecting mate selection.

In order to make the problem tractable, we make a number of subsidiary assumptions common to most path-analytic approaches to genetics. The first assumption is that of genetic additivity. This is likely to be the most critical assumption from the biological point of view since it is expected that the effects of genes on fitness are likely to have a substantial nonadditive component. The second main approximation is that, within any of the sets of genes defined in the above propositions, the effects of individual loci are equal and consistent in direction.

In this elementary treatment it is assumed that transmission between generations is due entirely to genetic inheritance and that any additional environmental contribution to variation is independent of genotype, additive, and uncorrelated with respect to members of the same family. It is more tedious, though not impossible, to develop the model for cases of nongenetic transmission along the now familiar lines suggested by such authors as Cavalli-Sforza and Feldman [1], Eaves [3], Rao et al [8], and Cloninger et al [2]. Notwithstanding these approximations, we feel that the model we present may have heuristic value.

DEVELOPING THE MODEL

The starting point for considering the phenotypic correlations between relatives is the correlation between their genotypes. We begin with the general form of the correlation between the genotypes (G) of twins and their relatives for a set of genes that is presumed to affect some measured aspect of the phenotype (P). We consider a pair of twins, T1 and T2, with their spouses, S1 and S2, respectively, two offspring of T1 and S1, (O1, 1 and O1, 2), and a single offspring of T2 and S2 (O2, 1). Figure 1 expresses the causal relationships between the genotypes of these individuals in the form of a path diagram. The coefficients of ½ between parent and offspring represent the implicit assumption of genetic additivity. The correlation between twins (w) will depend on whether the twins are monozygotic (MZ) or dizygotic (DZ). Clearly, w will be unity for MZ twins, but will not necessarily be ½ for DZs unless mating is random. The other correlations in the system, a, b, and c, will be zero if mating is random. Otherwise their values will depend on several factors: the genet-

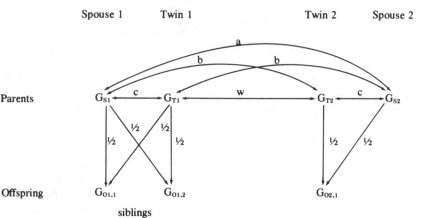

Fig. 1. The correlations between genotypes in the pedigrees of twins: the basic additive model.

ic correlation between spouses (c in Fig. 1) will be the same whatever the sex and zygosity of the twins as long as we are assuming that the matings of twins represent those in the population as a whole. The correlations a and b in the diagram, however, will depend on both the sex and the zygosity of the twins whenever mate selection is partly genetically determined and there is sex-limitation in gene expression.

For twins of a given zygosity and sex, for which w, a, b, and c were known, the principles of path analysis yield the genetic correlations of Table 2 for twins and their relatives. As it stands, however, this is not a proper "model" because it does not make explicit any of the relationships that might exist between a, b, c, and w within one type of pedigree, and it does not suggest anything about the relationships between the same parameters from different types of pedigree. In order to have a model that is theoretically powerful and practically useful, we need to discover which substitutions can be made for the empirical parameters (a, b, c, and w) in the correlations between different kinds of twins and their relatives. It is hoped that such a model will offer both insight and parsimony.

THE GENETIC CONTRIBUTION TO MATE SELECTION

The first step in obtaining the expectations for the genetic correlations between twins and their spouses is to consider the relationship between the genes, G, the measured phenotype, P, and "fitness" or "sex appeal" (F). Figure 2 presents the model for these relationships which embodies the propositions already formulated above. P and F are used to denote the phenotypes and fitnesses of males. P' and F' denote the corresponding traits in females. It is assumed that the genes in question (G) contribute both to fitness (F) and phenotype (P), but that the contribution to fitness in females (f'_1) may not be the same as the contribution to fitness in males (f_1). Similarly, the contribution of these genes to the phenotype measured may not be the same in the two sexes (ie, $h_1 \neq h'_1$). Thus the model permits specification of sex-limitation at two levels: the level of the contribution of the loci to fitness and at the level of their contribution to the phenotype measured. Both may contribute to sex-limitation at the phenotypic level but with somewhat different consequences for the correlations between relatives. For our purposes it is the differences between f_1 and f'_1 that are theoretically important since they permit some types of sex limitation for mating preference to be specified.

The diagram also represents other features of the system that are significant for understanding all the implications of the model. The genes represented by G contribute both to P and F. It must be recognised in principle that not all the genes affecting F will affect P and vice versa. An ideal treatment, of course, would assign individual effects to each locus. Here an approximation is made by assuming that some of the loci affecting P make no contribution to F. These loci are designated by G'' in the diagram, with the associated paths to measured phenotype h_2 and h'_2 in males and females, respectively. Similarly, some of the genes that affect F are assumed not to affect P. These are denoted by G', with

TABLE 2. Correlations Between Genotypes in Twin Pedigrees: The Basic Expectations*

Individual	S1	T1	T2	S2	01,1	01,2	02,1
S1	1	c	b	a	½(1+c)	½(1+c)	½(a+b)
T1		1	w	b	½(1+c)	½(1+c)	½(w+b)
T2			1	c	½(w+b)	½(w+b)	½(1+c)
S2				1	½(a+b)	½(a+b)	½(1+c)
01,1					1	½(1+c)	¼(a+2b+w)
01,2						1	¼(a+2b+w)
02,1							1

*w, a, b, c, depend on the mating system, sex, and zygosity of the twins. See text and subsequent tables.

Male

Female

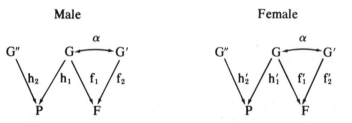

Fig. 2. The contribution of a set of genes to the measured phenotype (P) and to "fitness" (F) in males and females. Note: Uncorrelated residual components of P and F are not shown. Assumptions and parameters described in the text.

the associated paths f_2 and f_2'. The model assumes that the partition of the loci is the same for males and females. That is, it is assumed that sex-limitation is a matter of sex differences in the *scale* of gene expression rather than one of sex differences in which genes are actually expressed. Such additional complications can be incorporated but are beyond the scope of this initial treatment, since they add much by way of tedium but little by way of insight.

It will be noted that a correlation, α, is included between G and G' since these loci will be correlated as a consequence of the mating system. It is assumed, however, that the loci in the set G" will be independent as they do not contribute to the selection of a mate. Hence no correlation is presumed between G" and G or G'.

The model thus recognises that the expected phenotypic correlations between relatives can be decomposed into two components. The first, because of genes that do not contribute to mate selection, will follow the expectations for randomly mating populations. The second, because of genes that do contribute to mate selection, will follow the contributions derived on the basis of an appropriate model for assortative mating. A few examples of how this works are given in Table 3.

TABLE 3. Example Correlations Between Relatives for Measured Phenotypes*

Relationship	Assortative + random component		
	Male-male pair	Male-female pair	Female-female pair
Parent-offspring	$\frac{1}{2}(1 + c)h_1^2 + \frac{1}{2}h_2^2$	$\frac{1}{2}(1 + c)h_1h_1' + \frac{1}{2}h_2h_2'$	$\frac{1}{2}(1 + c)h_1'^2 + \frac{1}{2}h_2'^2$
Sibling/DZ twin	$\frac{1}{2}(1 + c)h_1^2 + \frac{1}{2}h_2^2$	$\frac{1}{2}(1 + c)h_1h_1' + \frac{1}{2}h_2h_2'$	$\frac{1}{2}(1 + c)h_1'^2 + \frac{1}{2}h_2'^2$
Avuncular	$\frac{1}{2}(w + b)h_1^2 + \frac{1}{4}h_2^2$	$\frac{1}{2}(w + b)h_1h_1' + \frac{1}{4}h_2h_2'$	$\frac{1}{2}(w + b)h_1'^2 + \frac{1}{4}h_2'^2$

*All nongenetic effects are assumed to be specific to individuals.

For ordinary nuclear families, consisting of parents and offspring, the significant unknown in the expectations (Table 2) is the genetic correlation between spouses, c. Writing μ for the correlation between "fitness" for spouses, Figure 3 can be exploited to derive the expectation of c in terms of the marital correlation and other parameters of the model. Since c is a secondary consequence of a primary correlation between spouses, the path from F' to G has been reversed and, following the rules of path analysis, $\emptyset'$ is given the value of the correlation between G and F', ie: $\emptyset' = f'_1 + \alpha f'_2$. If we also write $\emptyset = f_1 + \alpha f_2$, then the expression for c is simply $c = \emptyset \emptyset' \mu$. Obviously, if $f_1 = f'_1$ and $f_2 = f'_2 = O$ (the classic case of assortative mating) this reduces to the familiar $c = f_1^2 \mu$. At this stage it should be noted that the presence of environmental factors that are correlated with genotype serve only to redefine f_1 and f'_1. They do not seriously alter the form of the model.

Given this result, it is possible to work out the expectation of w for DZ twins, which is the same as that for siblings derived from the path diagram for nuclear families in Figure 4, ie: $w = \frac{1}{2}(1 + \emptyset \emptyset' \mu)$. This result is required subsequently.

THE GENETIC CORRELATIONS BETWEEN THE SPOUSES OF TWINS

We have now defined most of the elements required for a derivation of the genetic correlations between twins and their spouses. The diagram required for this stage is given in Figure 5, for male twins. The form of the figure would be the same for female twins and for unlike-sex pairs. In the case of female twins, however, $\emptyset'$ is substituted for $\emptyset$, f'_1 and f'_2 for f_1 and f_2. For pairs of unlike sex, the substitution is made for one twin and spouse only.

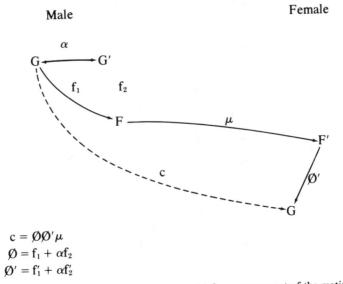

$$c = \emptyset \emptyset' \mu$$
$$\emptyset = f_1 + \alpha f_2$$
$$\emptyset' = f'_1 + \alpha f'_2$$

Fig. 3. The genetic correlation between spouses (c) for a component of the mating system.

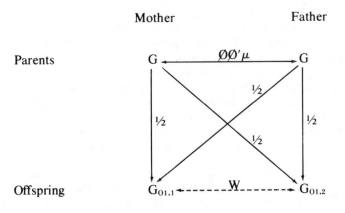

$$w = 2.\tfrac{1}{2}.\tfrac{1}{2}(1 + \emptyset\emptyset'\mu) = \tfrac{1}{2}(1 + \emptyset\emptyset'\mu)$$

Fig. 4. The genetic correlation between siblings (w) for a component of the mating system.

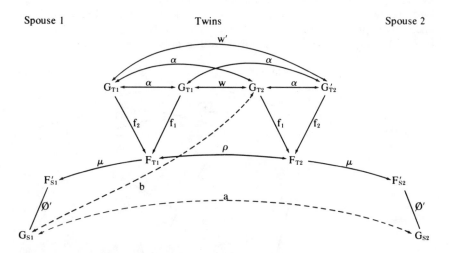

Fig. 5. The correlations between male twins and their spouses for a genetic component of the mating system: the additive model. Note: The diagram for female twin pairs is the same except $\emptyset$ is substituted for $\emptyset'$, f_1' and f_2' for f_1 and f_2. For unlike sex-pairs the substitution is made for one twin and spouse only.

The genetic correlations are summarised in Table 4, but some explanation is required and certain salient features must be indicated. By analogy with the derivation of w', the correlation between G'_{T1} and G'_{T2} for DZ twins is $\frac{1}{2}(1 + \Psi\Psi'\mu)$, where $\Psi = f_2 + \alpha f_1$ and $\Psi' = f'_2 + \alpha f'_1$. Since it is assumed that the correlation between G and G' arises as a result of assortative mating and is therefore due to parental effects, it may be assumed that the correlation between G'_{T1} and G_{T2} is the same as that between G'_{T1} and G_{T1}, ie, α.

The important point is that the genetic correlation between spouses of twins (a) and that between a twin and the spouse of his or her twin (b) involves the effects of genes which, while not contributing directly to the measured phenotype, do create variation in the dimension of "fitness" upon which mate selection is based. This result can be seen most strikingly in the correlation between twins' spouses which involves a term of the form $k\rho$, where ρ is the twin correlation for "fitness" and involves all the genes contributing to F and F', not just those that also contribute to P and P' (cf Table 4).

Although the expectations of Table 4 seem complicated in their form, they are all derived from Figure 5 (and comparable diagrams for other kinds of twin pairs), and achieve a considerable degree of parsimony by permitting substitution for the various parameters from different sex and zygosity groups of components expressed in terms of relatively few path coefficients and correlations, namely: f_1, f'_1, f_2, f'_2, α, and μ. Furthermore, if the population is in equilibrium under assortative mating, the correlation, α, can be expressed as a root of a quadratic in α of which the coefficients are functions of the four f's and the marital correlation for fitness μ. From Figure 6 it can be seen that the correlation between G and G' among children of assortatively mating parents is $\alpha = \frac{1}{2}\alpha + \frac{1}{4}\mu(\emptyset'\Psi + \emptyset\Psi')$. At equilibrium this yields: $\frac{1}{2}\alpha - \frac{1}{4}\mu(\emptyset'\Psi + \emptyset\Psi') = O$, but $\emptyset$, $\emptyset'$, Ψ, Ψ' must be expressed in terms of f's and α giving the quadratic in α: $\frac{1}{2}\alpha - \frac{1}{4}\mu[(f'_1 + \alpha f'_2)(f_2 + \alpha f_1) + (f_1 + \alpha f_2)(f'_2 + \alpha f'_1)] = O$. Although this looks awkward, it presents no practical barrier to

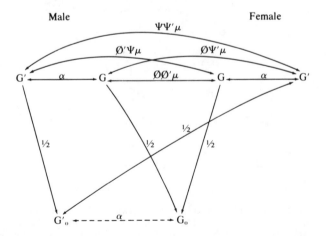

Fig. 6. The correlation between components of the mating system.

TABLE 4. The Genetic Correlations Between Twins and Their Spouses (cf, Fig. 5)

Correlation	MZ male	MZ female	DZ male	DZ female	DZ male-female
			Twin type		
w	1	1	$\frac{1}{2}(1+\emptyset\emptyset'\mu)$	$\frac{1}{2}(1+\emptyset\emptyset'\mu)$	$\frac{1}{2}(1+\emptyset\emptyset'\mu)$
w'	1	1	$\frac{1}{2}(1+\Psi\Psi'\mu)$	$\frac{1}{2}(1+\Psi\Psi'\mu)$	$\frac{1}{2}(1+\Psi\Psi'\mu)$
ρ	$f_1\emptyset + f_2\Psi$	$f_1\emptyset' + f_2\Psi'$	$f_1[\emptyset-(1-w)f_1]+$ $f_2[\Psi-(1-w')f_2]$	$f_1[\emptyset'-(1-w)f_1]+$ $f_2[\Psi'-(1-w')f_2]$	$f_1[\emptyset'-(1-w)f_1]+$ $f_2[\Psi'-(1-w')f_2]$
c	$\emptyset\emptyset'\mu$	$\emptyset\emptyset'\mu$	$\emptyset\emptyset'\mu$	$\emptyset\emptyset'\mu$	$\emptyset\emptyset'\mu$
a	$\emptyset'^2\mu^2\rho_{MZm}$	$\emptyset^2\mu^2\rho_{MZf}$	$\emptyset'^2\mu^2\rho_{DZm}$	$\emptyset^2\mu^2\rho_{DZf}$	$\emptyset\emptyset'\mu^2\rho_{DZmf}$
b	c	c	$c-f_1\emptyset'\mu(1-w)$	$c-f_1\emptyset\mu(1-w)$	either ρ_{DZm} or ρ_{DZf}

Note: $\emptyset = f_1 + \alpha f_2$; $\emptyset' = f_1' + \alpha f_2'$; $\Psi = f_2 + \alpha f_1$; $\Psi' = f_2' + \alpha f_1'$.

analysis because the value of α can be obtained numerically by any of the current approaches to numerical optimisation.

The expression for a, b, and c, from Table 4, can now be substituted in the appropriate expectations of Table 2 to give expected correlations between those components of the genotypes which contribute to both F and P. On the assumption of pure genetic transmission between generations and random environmental components uncorrelated between families, these can then be employed as in Table 3 to give the expected phenotypic correlations between relatives.

THE CONSEQUENCES OF ASYMMETRY ILLUSTRATED BY AN EXTREME CASE

It is difficult to grasp all the implications of the model simultaneously, so it may be helpful to consider a particular extreme case of interest in which entirely different genes are responsible for fitness in males and females. This amounts to saying that f_2 (say) is zero in males and f_1' is zero in females. This has the effect of making the measured phenotypes a component of fitness in males but not in females. The complementary situation, in which the phenotype is a component of fitness in females but not in males, would be given by setting f_1 and f_2' to zero. Substitution of these values (for the case of assortation based on a component of the male phenotype) in the above formulae shows that $\emptyset = f_1$, $\emptyset' = \alpha f_2'$, $\Psi = \alpha f_1$, $\Psi' = f_2'$.

Now, for illustration, let us assume $\mu = 0.5$ and that "fitness" is completely heritable (ie, $f_1 = f_2' = 1$). The parameters required for substitution in Table 2 are given in Table 5. Solving the quadratic above yields $\alpha = 0.382$. The principal points to note are that the correlations between DZ twins for G, (ie, w) exceed the values predicted under random mating, but the effect is less than would be the case under classical assortation if $\mu = \frac{1}{2}$, and selection is symmetric.

The correlation does not depend on the sex composition of the pair. However, the correlation for "fitness" for unlike-sex pairs (which is not measured

TABLE 5. Equilibrium Values of Parameters When $\mu = \frac{1}{2}$; $f_1 = f_2' = 1$; $f_1' = f_2 = 0$

	MZ		DZ		
Parameter	Male	Female	Male	Female	Unlike-sex
w	1	1	0.596	0.596	0.596
w'	1	1	0.596	0.596	0.596
p	1	1	0.596	0.596	0.382
c	0.191	0.191	0.191	0.191	0.191
a	0.036	0.25	0.022	0.149	0.036
b	0.191	0.191	0.114	0.114	0.114

Note: $\alpha = 0.382$; $\emptyset = \Psi' = 1$; $\emptyset' = \Psi = 0.382$.

directly) would be less than that for like-sex pairs because of sex limitation. The surprising fact is that the correlation of DZ twins for "fitness" is so high, and reflects the substantial effect of assortative mating on α. Under random mating ρ_{dz} would be zero.

As far as phenotypic correlations are concerned, the most important difference is that between the spouses of twins (a), which is greater in the spouses of female than male twins in this case, because the genes being assayed in the phenotype (G) contribute to fitness in males but not in females. Notice that under this model the correlation between twins' spouses (a) for MZ females actually *exceeds* phenotypic correlation of spouses (c).

The parental correlations may be employed to predict those between offspring, and the intergenerational correlations. Of particular interest is the correlation between the "half-sibling" offspring of MZ twins mated to different males. This is given by substitution in the expression $\frac{1}{4}(a + 2b + w)$ from Table 2, using the numerical values in Table 5. For the offspring of *male* MZ twins, we have: $\rho_{MZhs} = 0.3545$ and for *female* MZ twins, the half-sibling offspring correlation is 0.4080.

Thus, as Nance [7] pointed out on grounds that were intuitively appealing but mathematically inconsistent, asymmetric assortment can give the appearance of maternal effects in studies of half-siblings, because the correlation between maternal half-siblings may exceed that for paternal half-siblings as a result of the mating system rather than maternal effects in the strict sense. We believe our model provides the theoretical rationale for the basis of this claim and offers a foundation for a more fruitful general development. Notice that the mechanism we propose, while simulating maternal effects in cousins and half-siblings, should not be mistaken for maternal inheritance in data from complete MZ and DZ families for two reasons. The first reason is that the effects of asymmetric assortment should be detected in the correlations of twins' spouses. Additional information should be gained from the correlations between offspring and the spouses of their twin "aunt" or "uncle." The second reason why asymmetric assortment should not be confused with maternal effects is that the former gives identical expectations to the mother-offspring and father-offspring covariances, whereas any but the most bizarre model for genotypic maternal effects predicts that the covariance of mother and offspring should exceed that for father and offspring.

CONCLUSION

We have proposed a theory of "asymmetric" assortative mating that avoids the inconsistencies of earlier models and provides a much stronger theoretical framework for the discussion of such effects. It is recognised that "asymmetry" does not reside in the marital correlation as Nance [7] proposed, since such a model is simply inconsistent; rather, it lies in the sex-limitation of the expression of genes that contribute to "sex appeal" or "fitness." The relatively simple model developed here, and illustrated still more simply for the case of complete asymmetry; shows how data from twins and their relatives may produce a rich source of empirical correlations to permit many of the model's implications to be explored. The treatment we have offered in this paper does not exhaust all the subtleties of sex limitation for mate selection, nor does it consider all the implications of asymmetry in the presence of cultural transmission and genotype-environmental covariance. As we have suggested already, the algebra of such intricacies is not so much difficult as tedious. Our main hope is that the possible subtleties of the mating system, which have generally been ignored in correlational studies to date, might now become the serious object of theoretical and empirical investigation.

REFERENCES

1. Cavalli-Sforza LL, Feldman MW: Cultural versus biological inheritance. Am J Hum Genet 25:618–637, 1973.
2. Cloninger CR, Rice T, Reich T: Multifactorial inheritance with cultural transmission and assortative mating. Am J Hum Genet 31:178–188, 1979.
3. Eaves LJ: The effect of cultural transmission on continuous variation. Heredity 37:41–57, 1976.
4. Eaves LJ: Inferring the causes of human variation. J R Stat Soc (A) 140:324–355, 1977.
5. Eaves LJ: Young PA, Last KA, Martin NG: Model-fitting approaches to the analysis of human behaviour. Heredity 41:294–320, 1978.
6. Eaves, LJ: The use of twins in the analysis of assortative mating. Heredity 43:399–409, 1980.
7. Nance WE: A note on assortative mating and maternal effects. In Sing CF, Skolnick M: "Genetic Analysis of Common Diseases." New York: Alan R Liss, 1978, pp 453–464.
8. Rao DC, Morton NE, Yee S: Analysis of family resemblance. Am J Hum Genet 26:331–359, 1974.

Twin Research 3: Intelligence, Personality,
and Development, pages 87—97
© 1981 Alan R. Liss, Inc., 150 Fifth Avenue, New York, NY 10011

How Stable Are Personality Traits?

L.J. Eaves and P.A. Young
*Department of Experimental Psychology, University of Oxford and
Department of Genetics, University of Birmingham*

Almost without exception, twin studies of personality have revealed a significant genetic contribution to personality differences and have suggested that the
shared environment of twins has very little effect on the development of adult
personality. That is, whatever physiological systems underlie observed personality differences, they are established at a time when the organism is largely
immune from the influences of environment or they reside in parts of the nervous system that remain immune from such influences during postnatal development.

The twin study, allied to the model-fitting approaches of modern quantitative
genetics, has played a key role in establishing the compatibility of data with
such a strong theory of personality [see, eg, 2, 4, 5]. Other authors [eg, 10],
while not using the same statistical methodology, have confirmed that the twin
correlations of the National Merit Twin Study are consistent with such models
of personality. The recent adoption studies [eg, 13] also present data generally
consistent with this view.

The basis for this very strong position may be summarised briefly. The twin
data on the major dimensions of personality *are consistent with* a model which
assumes there are *no family environmental effects*. The twin data on the major
dimensions of personality, however, are *not consistent with* an equally simple
model which assumes *no genetic effects*. Allowing for the possible effects of
the family environment in addition to those of the genotype leads neither to
significantly better ability to predict the results of twin studies nor to estimates
of the effects of the family environment which differ significantly from zero.

These findings have been replicated repeatedly on a very large scale [see 6].
The argument and method may be illustrated clearly by the data from the National Merit Twin Study [10] kindly made available by Dr. Nichols. They
record scores on the major dimensions of extraversion (E) and neuroticism (N)
derived by applying to their questionnaire data a scoring key suggested by

This work is part of a research programme supported by the British Medical Research Council. P.A.
Young was the recipient of an S.R.C. C.A.S.E. studentship.

TABLE 1. Mean Squares for Transformed Neuroticism and Extraversion Data From the NMSQT Twin Study*

Twin type	Item	df	Extraversion			Neuroticism		
			MS	F	r	MS	F	r
MZ female	Between pairs	266	13.2	4.55	0.64	41.9	2.89	0.49
	Within pairs	267	2.9			14.5		
MZ male	Between pairs	178	11.7	3.66	0.57	53.8	3.84	0.59
	Within pairs	179	3.2			14.0		
DZ female	Between pairs	176	10.6	1.89	0.31	34.2	1.58	0.22
	Within pairs	176	5.6			21.7		
DZ male	Between pairs	110	9.5	1.46	0.09	37.8	1.54	0.21
	Within pairs	111	6.5			24.6		

*Computed from data kindly made available by Dr. Nichols.

Eysenck. The raw scores, in common with those of most other personality dimensions measured by questionnaire, have scalar properties that reflect the relative lack of information about the extremes of personality. For this reason, Young derived an empirical transformation that ensured that the error variance of the scores was homogeneous over the range of measurement. The National Merit Scholarship Qualifying Test (NMSQT) data on the twins, after transformation, were then subjected to a nested (one-way) analysis of variance. The results of this analysis are given for both extraversion and neuroticism (Table 1). For comparison with traditional approaches, the intraclass correlations (r) are also tabulated for each group.

The key observation is that, on average, the DZ correlation for both traits is approximately half (numerically rather less than half) that for MZ twins. The recurrent problem of the traditional approach to twin data analysis is providing tests of such comparisons. While it is easy enough to decide whether two correlations differ, the usual approach does not provide tests of more specific hypotheses like "Is the MZ correlation significantly different from twice the DZ correlation?". Yet it is upon testing such precise and explicit hypotheses that a detailed understanding of the mechanisms of transmission, whether social or genetic, depends. Such tests are no problem for the model-fitting approach, based either on maximum likelihood or some close relative such as weighted least-squares. Indeed, the primary thrust of these approaches is toward providing tests of competing hypotheses and yielding the most cost-effective estimates as can conveniently be achieved.

Table 2 gives three competing models for the mean squares for MZ and DZ twins. The first model allows for random within-family environmental effects (E_1) and additive genetic effects (G). The second model allows for E_1 and between-family ("shared") environmental effects (E_2). The third model specifies the joint effect of all three. Gene action is assumed to be additive. The coefficients of G reflect an underlying assumption of random mating. These models

TABLE 2. Three Models for Twin Data

Mean square	Expected mean squares		
	Model I	Model II	Model III
Between MZ pairs	$E_1 + 2G$	$E_1 + 2E_2$	$E_1 + 2G + 2E_2$
Within MZ pairs	E_1	E_1	E_1
Between DZ pairs	$E_1 + 1\frac{1}{2}G$	$E_1 + 2E_2$	$E_1 + 1\frac{1}{2}G + 2E_2$
Within DZ pairs	$E_1 + \frac{1}{2}G$	E_1	$E_1 + \frac{1}{2}G$

TABLE 3. Model-Fitting Results for NMSQT Neuroticism Data

Data set	Model	Parameter estimate			"Fit"	
		$\hat{E}_1$	$\hat{G}$	$\hat{E}_2$	χ^2	df
Both sexes	I	14.4***	15.6***	—	5.34	6
	II	17.6***	—	12.4***	31.48***	6
	III	14.2***	17.9***	-2.2	4.88	5
Females only	I	14.6***	13.5***	—	0.06	2
	II	17.4***	—	10.7***	11.02***	2
	III	14.5***	14.5***	-0.9	0.01	1
Males only	I	14.1***	18.7***	—	0.88	2
	II	18.1***	—	14.8***	15.49***	2
	III	13.9***	23.3***	-4.29	0.41	1

are very simple. We should not delude ourselves into thinking that any further degree of subtelty is possible with twin data. Traditional approaches based on the visual comparison of correlations do not avoid these problems. They simply fail to take account of them.

The results of fitting the three possible models to the mean squares from the NMSQT data are given in Table 3 for neuroticism and Table 4 for extraversion. Each model was fitted separately to males and females, and then jointly to the mean squares for both sexes. This permits a test of significance to be conducted for sex differences in genetic and environmental components. Each model is tested using the chi-square statistic (the column labeled "Fit" in the results tables). If the chi-square is significant, it means that the model cannot predict the observed relationships between the values of the several mean squares. That is, the model must be rejected. If the chi-square is not significant, it means that the model can, to a degree of imprecision which only reflects sampling error, predict the observed relative magnitudes of the mean squares. The significance of individual parameter estimates is assessed from a knowledge of the standard errors which can also be derived from the model-fitting analysis.

TABLE 4. Model-Fitting Results for NMSQT Extraversion Data

Data set	Model	Parameter estimate			"Fit"	
		$\hat{E}_1$	$\hat{G}$	$\hat{E}_2$	χ^2	df
Both sexes	I	3.1***	4.9***	—	3.41	6
	II	4.2***	—	3.7***	49.01***	6
	III	3.0***	5.6***	−0.8	2.51	5
Females only	I	2.9***	5.2***	—	0.05	2
	II	4.0***	—	4.9***	26.87***	2
	III	2.9***	5.4***	−0.2	0.1	1
Males only	I	3.4***	4.4***	—	1.84	2
	II	4.5***	—	3.21***	19.51***	2
	III	3.2***	6.0***	−1.59	0.28	1

The results of the analysis are quite striking. In each case, the pure environmental model (model II) fails significantly to predict the twin data. This is true for both sexes, individually and jointly, and for both the main dimensions of personality. The model that assumes no family environmental effects (model I), however, fits the entire data set uniformly. Furthermore, it is as capable of fitting both sexes simultaneously (with identical parameter estimates) as it is of fitting the results for the sexes separately. The power and value of the first model is strengthened by the finding that allowing for *both* genetic factors (G) *and* the family environment (E_2) does not lead to a significant reduction in the value of chi-square (ie, the "fit" of the model is not significantly improved); neither is there any suggestion that the estimated contribution of the family environment differs significantly from zero.

The analysis thus converges on a remarkably simple interpretation of the twin data relating to personality. Genetic variation seems to be additive. The shared environment of family members seems to make a comparatively trivial contribution. There is no suggestion whatever that the distribution of genetic and environmental factors is affected by the mating system, as far as personality differences are concerned.

It has sometimes been argued informally, though rarely in print, that the striking simplicity of the analysis of personality is an artefact of the method rather than anything to do with the nature of personality. The argument goes that the method is somehow "biased" to detect genetic effects and to accept a genetic explanation. This is nonsense. Examples of analyses have been published repeatedly that show that the model-fitting approach is as capable of identifying social factors in twins as it is of detecting genetic factors. Examples are given, eg, by Eaves et al [5]. Furthermore, simulation studies reveal [12] that the twin study allied to the model-fitting approach has as much inherent power, if not more, to reject the simple genetic model as the simple environmental one. The family environment has been clearly indicated in studies of social attitudes, and the social interaction between twins has also been suggested for aspects of parent-child interaction [5]. The method is therefore intrinsically far more powerful than the traditional methods: it simply requires greater flexibility to specify a range of competing hypotheses and the assumptions that underlie any analysis.

Thus personality measurements, at least as far as the major dimensions are concerned, stand by themselves in suggesting a remarkably simple mechanism of variation that is not shared by cognitive measures, by the major dimensions of socially significant variables [1] or by many components of social attitudes. What does this mean? One possibility has already been suggested, namely that personality measures reflect the inherent variation in primitive physiological systems which are largely insulated from the effects of the social environment, both developmentally and phylogenetically. Such suggestions as have been advanced for the physiological bases of neuroticism and extraversion [see, eg, 9] would lend some credibility to this position. If this model for personality turns out to be valid indeed in the long run, then it would appear that personality measurements are part of the "background noise" of human differences: immune from the social environment, quite uninvolved in the basic processes of mate selection, and probably not directly related to man's recent evolutionary past. This seems to be in stark contrast to other measures, in which the family environment and the mating system appear to play a more significant role. From the clinical point of view the model has its attractions, because it suggests that the computation of risk for neurotic disorders would be a fairly simple matter, and that simple social manipulations may not be the most effective strategy for ameliorating neurotic symptoms.

We have chosen Nichols's data merely to illustrate the point. The basic components of the model, however, have been vindicated by a far broader data set on twins. The results of other large twin studies are subjected to detailed analysis by Eaves and Young [6]. Although it is clear that the assumption of genetic additivity may need to be revised for extraversion in the light of the recent large Swedish study [8], the broad features of the model remain unchallenged. The data do nothing to suggest that the family environment or the mating system is seriously involved in personality determination.

The attraction of the twin design is the degree of control it apparently provides over the expression of genetic factors. Almost without fail, twins are studied at the identical stage of development since members of a twin pair are always studied at the same chronological age. While this approach makes the detection of genetic effects more powerful, since both age-specific and age-dependent genetic effects are assayed simultaneously, it also introduces a major potential source of bias in any attempts to generalise from twin studies to the population as a whole. In effect, the twin study is in danger of overestimating the risk to relatives (or the correlation between relatives) because it does not provide for the estimation of age-specific gene effects. It also may overestimate the contribution of genetic factors to prospective risk because the genes assayed at one stage of development are not those that will be expressed later in development.

Thus, although the "once-off" twin studies suggest that genetic factors play a significant role in personality development, they do not allow us to separate the stable effects of genes on personality from those that reflect particular idiosyncratic, but nevertheless genetic, features of the developmental process. A design is clearly needed that can resolve the long-term effects of genes on personality from the relatively short-term fluctuations occasioned by the synchronous switching on and off of specific genetic effects in response to individual profiles of development in genetically related individuals.

One or two studies have concerned the generalisability of personality findings over repeated measures. Only one [3] has involved sufficiently large samples to permit reliable inference and has combined the analysis of variance approach to psychometric investigation [7] with the model-fitting approach to the testing of models for genetic and environmental causation. Their design involved the repeated study of some 400 twin pairs at a 2-year interval. Neuroticism responses were secured from MZ and DZ twins on a short (eleven-item) scale. The preliminary analysis of variance of the data identified and estimated, for each zygosity and sex group in the sample, the main effects of subjects, occasions, and items with all the possible interactions between them. In addition, however, the main effects of subjects and all interactions involving subjects were partitioned into the components within and between twin pairs. The analysis of the data, however, was pursued further than the conventional psychometric investigation by estimating the contribution of various genetic and environmental factors to the main effects and their interactions. The resulting analysis sheds important light on the interactions between persons and situations, which has become such a key issue in contemporary personality research [11].

In common with many earlier analyses of questionnaire data, the results showed that components of interaction were equally as important as the main effects of neuroticism but further identified their genetic and environmental components. The results are summarised in Table 5. Particularly marked is the finding that the individual profile of response over items is as much influenced by genetic factors as by the specific environmental experiences of individuals. That is, genetic effects on personality responses are as specific and idiosyncratic as environmental effects. However, changes in neuroticism scores over the 2-year period were not influenced either in their direction or magnitude by genetic factors. Although they are greater than those associated with the sampling, such differences do not reflect the switching on and off of genetic factors over this period, but are a result of intervening short-term idiosyncratic environmental factors. Neither for the main effect of subjects, nor for their interaction with items and occasions, was there any suggestion at all that the family environment was a significant component of variation. This study therefore suggests that genes are highly specific as well as general in their effects on personality, but does not implicate genetic factors in relatively short-term changes in adult personality.

The problem of extending this approach to the relatively long-term fluctuations is the difficulty of securing a sufficiently large sample of cooperative and traceable subjects spanning the far greater age range necessary for long-term

TABLE 5. The Contribution of Genetic and Environmental Factors to Differences in Neuroticism, the Interaction of Subjects and Occasions, and the Profile of Item Responses to an 11-Item Neuroticism Scale*

Source	Trait Neuroticism	Interaction		Error	Total
		Profile	Occasions		
Genetic (G)	11.4	14.0	—	—	25.4
Environmental (E₁)	8.6	15.5	3.4	46.9	74.5
Total	20.0	29.5	3.4	46.9	
"Heritability"	0.57	0.47	0	0	

*Assuming "fixed" choice of items. The assumption that items are chosen at random makes little difference to the analysis of variance. Contributions are expressed as percentages of variance of individual responses.

risk calculations. We conclude with an account of a study that exploits our current knowledge of the genetics of adult personality derived from twin studies, in the attempt to examine how far the model we have described really can explain the long-term consistency of personality measurements from preadolescence into adulthood.

Young et al [14] describe in detail a study that has critical bearing on the issue, as well as revealing the inherent power of the model-fitting approach, to show when assumptions of the classical models fail and to suggest viable alternatives. The design was a much-extended twin study that provided a direct test of many of the assumptions implicit in the strong model described above for the MNSQT data. The design consisted of adult twins, as before, together with juvenile twins and singletons. The parents of the juveniles also participated in the investigation.

The study now embodied a number of critical controls. The comparison of adult MZ and DZ twins provides a test of genetic effects in the adults. The same comparison for juvenile twins permits estimation of genetic and environmental effects in juveniles. In addition, however, the availability of parents has several important implications. First, they provide a sample of nontwin adults that can be used to check on the consistency of the adult twin data with that of the rest of the population. Second, the husband-wife correlation provides a direct test of the assumption of random mating. Third and most significantly, the design allows us to check whether the parent-offspring covariance is consistent with the predictions made from the twin data, on the assumption that genetic effects are stable over the relatively long term. Thus we can ask, "On the assumption of genetic additivity, and long-term consistency of gene expression, is the parent-offspring covariance what we would expect?". If the answer to the question is "Yes," then the theory of stable personality differences is strengthened still further. If the answer is "No," then we must seriously begin to doubt whether long-term predictions based on the stability hypothesis can be justified. An additional check on the assumptions of the model was provided by the data on singleton juveniles. As well as providing check on the sampling consistency of juvenile twins and nontwins, they also provide a baseline for the detection of the effects on personality of social interactions between twins.

Since the family structure no longer justifies analysis of variance, the data are summarised instead by the covariance matrices between family members for each of the five different groups of twins and the two groups of singletons. The full analysis was conducted for the three main dimensions of Eysenck's personality theory, extraversion, neuroticism, and psychoticism, and for the "lie scale." Only one set of covariance matrices is reproduced here (Table 6) to illustrate the structure of the data summary. Those for other variables are tabulated by Young et al [14]. The precise details of the numerical analysis are not important here. The method of maximum likelihood was used to analyse the total structure of the covariances to obtain parameter estimates and compare alternative hypotheses. The model that is especially important for our purpose is that of Table 7, which assumes no familial environment, random mating, and additive gene action. In other words, this is the basic model that we already know can account for adult variation in personality according to many large studies. Two critical adjustments have been made to the model. The first is to identify separate genetic and environmental components for adults and juveniles (G_A, G_J and E_{1A}, E_{1J}). These permit any scalar difference between adult and juvenile measures to be incorporated. Then we identify the genetic covariance between adults (parents) and juveniles (twins and singletons), G_{AJ}. If G_{AJ} is small or zero, we would argue that there can be very little long-term consistency in genetic effects on personality, no matter how large the genetic components in adults and juveniles are separately (G_A and G_J). In general, the correlation between adult and juvenile gene expression, r_{GAJ}, cannot exceed unity, ie, $r_{GAJ} = G_{AJ} \cdot (G_A \cdot G_J)^{-1/2} \leq 1$. If r_{AJ} does not differ significantly from unity, it may be safely assumed that the expression of genetic differences in personality is stable over time. Otherwise, we may suspect that a substantial contribution to measured personality differences arises from gene effects which are highly age-specific.

In Table 8, the results are given for each of the three main dimensions of personality and for the "lie scale," which are represented in the adult (EPQ) and junior (JEPQ) versions of the Eysenck Personality Questionnaire. The main point is that the model fits all three personality measures. That is, both adult and juvenile data are consistent with the assumption of additive gene action and environmental influences within, rather than between, families. Other possible models for these dimensions are discussed by Young et al [14].

There are two important features of the results, however, which go beyond those of the previous studies. The first is that the genetic consistency of the personality measures is variable. That for neuroticism is high ($r_{AJ} = 0.81$), suggesting a good degree of long-term stability in gene expression. Those for extraversion and psychoticism suggest either that there is an inordinate amount of genetic nonadditivity or that the same genes are not contributing both to adult and juvenile personality. In every case, it should be noticed that the parent-off-

TABLE 6. The Structure of the Family Data Illustrated by Covariances (Upper Triangles), Variances (Diagonals), and Correlations (Lower Triangles) Between Relatives for Neuroticism

Group	df	Juvenile twin/singleton families				df	Adult twins	
		Mother	Father	Child 1	Child 2		Twin 1	Twin 2
MZ_m	58	0.078	0.009	0.010	0.011	69	0.070	0.037
		0.144	0.054	0.017	0.013		0.511	0.076
		0.153	0.291	0.059	0.030			
		0.149	0.211	0.456	0.072			
MZ_f	49	0.070	−0.011	0.032	0.023	232	0.065	0.028
		−0.155	0.070	0.018	0.012		0.425	0.065
		0.460	0.257	0.069	0.029			
		0.342	0.178	0.436	0.065			
DZ_m	39	0.079	−0.009	0.028	0.004	46	0.054	0.001
		−0.153	0.042	−0.005	−0.003		0.021	0.059
		0.381	−0.085	0.069	0.000			
		0.059	−0.057	0.007	0.058			
DZ_f	36	0.059	0.000	−0.004	0.022	124	0.063	0.004
		−0.005	0.068	−0.007	−0.005		0.066	0.065
		−0.082	−0.138	0.037	0.016			
		0.427	−0.081	0.403	0.045			
DZ_{mf}	75	0.041	0.001	0.009	0.008	67	0.069	0.011
		0.027	0.057	0.022	0.001		0.167	0.060
		0.156	0.329	0.077	0.023			
		0.146	0.010	0.293	0.077			
Singleton m	84	0.086	0.001	0.019				
		0.015	0.071	0.006				
		0.263	0.089	0.058				
Singleton f	96	0.058	−0.005	0.022				
		−0.089	0.060	0.002				
		0.359	0.040	0.063				

TABLE 7. A Simple Model for the Variances and Covariances of Twins, Singletons, and Their Relatives

Relationship	Statistic	Expectation
Adults	Variance	$G_A + E_{1A}$
Juveniles	Variance	$G_J + E_{1J}$
Adult MZ twins	Covariance	G_A
Adult DZ twins	Covariance	$\frac{1}{2}G_A$
Juvenile MZ twins	Covariance	G_J
Juvenile DZ twins	Covariance	$\frac{1}{2}G_J$
Spouses	Covariance	O
Parent-offspring	Covariance	$\frac{1}{2}G_{AJ}$

TABLE 8. Estimates of Parameters and Chi-Square Tests of the Model for the Simple Genotype-Environment Model Fitted to the Four Scales of the EPQ and JEPQ

Parameter	Extraversion	Neuroticism	Psychoticism	Lie scale
E_{1A}	0.035 ± 0.003	0.038 ± 0.003	0.24 ± 0.02	0.021 ± 0.001
G_A	0.073 ± 0.007	0.053 ± 0.006	0.46 ± 0.04	0.040 ± 0.004
E_{1J}	0.017 ± 0.002	0.036 ± 0.004	0.25 ± 0.03	0.016 ± 0.002
G_J	0.041 ± 0.006	0.056 ± 0.010	0.36 ± 0.06	0.044 ± 0.005
G_{AJ}	0.024 ± 0.006	0.046 ± 0.007	0.13 ± 0.05	0.025 ± 0.004
χ^2	73.80	87.20	70.11	145.47*
Consistency				
(r_{GAJ})	0.44	0.84	0.32	0.60

*$P < 0.001$.

spring covariance is nonetheless significantly different from zero, which argues for some degree of long-term stability even though it may not be substantial. The second major finding is that the "personality model" comes nowhere near predicting the findings for the "lie scale." That is, although there is significant similarity between all kinds of relatives in the study, their pattern bears no significant resemblance to that which might be predicted from the simple model, which ignores social interactions and the effects of the mating system.

Once again, therefore, the model-fitting approach, rather than confirming our predictions about genetic factors, has actually revealed that these are grossly lacking. The analysis of the "lie scale," however, does not end here. It is not enough to reveal the inadequacies of the simple genotype-environmental model. It is equally important to identify these inadequacies and to suggest a possible alternative that is consistent with the facts. Young et al therefore report a much more extensive analysis of the same data, in which they suggest finally that the determination of juvenile lie scores is social rather than genetic. Furthermore, the similarity of juvenile twins is created by two mechanisms, the influence of parent on child, and the mutual reinforcement of one twin by the other. A model that assumes either mechanism by itself cannot account for the observations. By the time adulthood is reached, however, many of the social interaction effects have dissipated, and there is detectable genetic variation. The lie scale therefore represents an important example of the principle that the mechanism underlying individual differences in behaviour can change qualitatively with time, and that findings based on one age group may be quite different from those based on another. They also suggest that the analytical approach we adopt is capable of doing far more than simply estimate "heritabilities," but can reveal greater subtleties and inconsistencies in the data than traditional, weaker approaches.

As far as the main dimensions of personality are concerned, we are left with a theory that is very strong in some aspects but relatively weak in others. The strongest claim, for which the data still provide much support, is that personality reflects genetic differences rather than the effects of the social environment created by the family. Insofar as environmental effects are important (including sampling variation, they account for about half the variation), they seem to be of a highly specific and individual nature, depending upon the "slings and hazards of outrageous fortune" for their origin. The strength of this claim lies in its replication over many sets of twin data for the same measures and the fact that other measurements, apart from personality, do not show the same mechanism when analysed by the identical methods. The weak aspects of the theory concern the fact that at least half the genetic variation in personality responses is highly idiosyncratic. It reflects either specific genetic effects on individual items of a scale, or the relatively short-term effects of genes on behaviour. These, while creating a rich diversity of gene expression, do not add greatly to our capacity to predict behaviour across occasions or scales of measurement. On the biological and physiological side, the results of the analysis of these personality dimensions leave a crucial question still with us: What is it about the ontogeny, phylogeny, or, indeed, the measurement of personality, that has ensured that its principal dimensions are immune from the effects of the social environment?

REFERENCES

1. Behrman J, Taubman P, Wales, T: Controlling for and measuring the effects of genetic and family environment in equations for schooling and labor market success. In Taubman P (ed): "Kinometrics." Amsterdam: North Holland, 1977.
2. Eaves LJ, Eysenck HJ: The nature of extraversion: A genetical analysis. J Pers Soc Psychol 32:102–112, 1975.
3. Eaves LJ, Eysenck HJ: Genetic and environmental components of inconsistency and unrepeatability in twins' responses to a neuroticism questionnaire. Behav Genet 6:145–160, 1976.
4. Eaves LJ, Eysenck HJ: A genotype-environmental model for psychoticism. Adv Behav Res Ther 1:5–26, 1977.
5. Eaves LJ, Last KA, Young PA, Martin NG: Model-fitting approaches to the analysis of human behaviour. Heredity 41:249–320, 1978.
6. Eaves LJ, Young PA: Genetical theory and personality differences. In Lynn R (ed): "Dimensions of Personality." London: Pergamon Pren, 1981.
7. Endler NS, Hunt J McV: Sources of behavioral variance as measured by the S-R inventory of anxiousness. Psychol Bull 65:336–346, 1966.
8. Floderus-Myrhead B, Pedersen N, Rasmuson I: Assessment of heritability for personality based on a short form of the Eysenck Personality Inventory. Behav Genet (in press), 1980.
9. Gray JA: The psychophysiological basis of introversion-extraversion. Behav Res Ther 8:249–266, 1970.
10. Loehlin JC, Nichols RC: "Heredity, Environment and Personality: A Study of 850 Sets of Twins." Austin, Texas: University of Texas Press, 1976.
11. Magnusson D, Endler NS: "Personality at the Crossroads—Current Issues in Interactional Psychology." New Jersey: Lawrence Erlbaum, 1977.
12. Martin NG, Eaves LJ, Kearsey MJ, Davies P: The power of the classical twin study. Heredity 40:97–116, 1978.
13. Scarr S, Webber PL, Weinberg RA, Wittig MA: Personality resemblance among adolescents and their parents in biologically-related and adoptive families. In Gedda L, Parisi P, Nance W (eds): "Advances in Twin Research. 2. Intelligence, Personality, and Development." New York: Alan R. Liss, 1981.
14. Young PA, Eaves LJ, Eysenck HJ: Intergenerational stability and change in the causes of variation in personality. Pers Indiv Diff 1:35–55, 1980.

Twin Research 3: Intelligence, Personality,
and Development, pages 99 – 120
© 1981 Alan R. Liss, Inc., 150 Fifth Avenue, New York, NY 10011

Personality Resemblance Among Adolescents and Their Parents in Biologically Related and Adoptive Families

Sandra Scarr, Patricia L. Webber, Richard A. Weinberg, and Michele A. Wittig
*Department of Psychology, Yale University, New Haven, Connecticut, (S.S.),
Counseling Bureau (P.L.W.) and Department of Psychoeducational Studies,
University of Minnesota, Minneapolis (R.A.W.); and Department of
Psychology, California State University, Northridge M.A.W.)*

INTRODUCTION

The essence of personality is behavioral consistency across time and place. People are said to "have" certain personality characteristics when they are observed by others or themselves to behave in predictably similar ways over variable events and situations. The very notion of personality was challenged by Mischel [22], who proposed that 1) consistencies are so low as to be trivial, and 2) whatever consistency exists is primarily in the eye of the beholder. He emphasized the situational inconsistency in people's behaviors. Throughout the history of personality study there have been arguments over the relative importance of situational determinants of behavior versus individual consistency in behavior. Advocates of the importance of situationalism necessarily favor environmental explanations of behavior; advocates of personal consistency have often proposed some genetic basis for individual differences in personality.

Despite the popularity of situationalism over the past 15 years, there is growing awareness that personal consistency does exist, at least for "some of the people some of the time" [1]. And there is growing awareness that the claims of extreme situationalism are based in (large) part on unreliable measurements of behaviors, which necessarily result in low correlations across times and places [23]. At the other extreme, ideas of fixed traits have given way to more moderate views of person-situation interactions that shape personality development.

If personal consistency develops from combinations of genetic background and individual experiences, then biologically related persons should be more similar in personality than unrelated persons. People who live together should share more common experiences and therefore be more similar in their behaviors than others who do not live together. Thus, parents and their genetic offpsring and biologically related siblings should score more similarly on personality measures than unrelated adoptive parents and their children or unrelated children reared as siblings. Unrelated persons who live together should be more similar than unrelated persons reared apart. Monozygotic (MZ) twins should be more similar than first-degree relatives, including dizygotic (DZ) twins.

TWIN STUDIES

Studies of personality resemblance between adolescent and young adult co-twins are numerous and fairly consistent in finding moderate similarity among MZ twins and greater MZ than DZ twin resemblance. Nichols [24] reviewed the published studies of personality resemblance of twins and reported a weighted mean correlation of 0.52 for MZ and 0.25 for DZ twins. There were no consistent differences among personality measures in the magnitude of their broad heritabilities, which in twin studies are calculated from the differences between MZ and DZ coefficients [$h^2 = 2(r_{iMZ} - r_{iDZ})$], that in turn can be adjusted for parental assortative mating. Dozens of personality scales administered to thousands of twin pairs in more than 30 studies yielded the result that all measured aspects of personality seem to be equally heritable.

Twin correlations for personality measures were found to be consistently lower than those for measures of ability. Nichols's [24] review of twin studies of abilities yielded a weighted mean correlation of 0.82 for MZ pairs and 0.59 for DZ pairs. For measures of general ability, identical twins are about as similar as the same person tested twice, which Plomin and DeFries [25] estimated as 0.82, whereas MZ twin correlations for personality measures do not approach the reliability of contemporary personality measures, which range in the high 0.70s and 0.80s.

Curiously, however, the *differences* between the MZ and DZ correlations are about the same for measures of ability and personality. The implication of this result is that the heritabilities of ability and personality measures are the same! In their book *Heredity, Environment, and Personality*, Loehlin and Nichols [19] concluded:

> Identical twins correlate about 0.20 higher than fraternal twins, give or take some sampling fluctuation, and it doesn't matter much what you measure — whether the difference is between 0.75 and 0.55 on an ability measure, between 0.50 and 0.30 on a personality scale, or between 0.35 and 0.15 on a self-concept composite (p 35).

Both Loehlin [18] and Nichols [24] attribute the higher correlations of ability than personality measures, for both MZ and DZ twins, primarily to the effects of common home environment (or differences among homes) on the development of abilities, but not personality. The reasoning behind their conclusion is as follows:

1) There is no consistent difference in the broad heritability estimates for abilities or personality; that is, the difference between MZ and DZ coefficients is similar for both kinds of measures (for ability, $0.82 - 0.59 = 0.23$; for personality, $0.52 - 0.25 = 0.26$, which when the ability formula is adjusted for parental assortative mating of about 0.40, yields almost identical heritabilities for ability and personality, of about 0.50).

2) The larger correlations for ability than personality measures for both MZ and DZ twins must reflect primarily the effects of being reared in the same home environment on the development of abilities but not personality.

3) In fact, there is no evidence from twin studies of *any* effect of common home environment on the development of personality resemblance; given the usual finding of no parental assortative mating for personality, twice the MZ-DZ difference yields an average broad heritability of 0.52 for personality measures, which is exactly the correlation for persons who have all of their genes in common (MZs), and twice the correlation of persons who have half of their genes in common (DZs). In other words, the estimated degree of genetically determined resemblance accounts for *all* of the personality resemblance among twins. There is no additional resemblance to be accounted for by *common rearing environment*. Experiences that are unique to the individual, unique genotype-environment correlations, interactions, and errors of measurement must account for the remaining half of personality variance. Errors of measurement may account for one-quarter of the total variance [18].

By contrast, the estimated broad heritability for measures of mental abilities — about 0.50 — does not account for an MZ twin correlation of 0.82 or a DZ correlation of 0.59. Both kinds of twins seem to show substantial effects on ability measures of being reared in the same families, neighborhoods, schools, etc. If half of the ability differences in the population from which the twins are drawn result from genetic differences, then MZ twins should correlate about 0.5 and DZ's about 0.275, given a parental assortative mating coefficient of 0.4 for general ability. The resemblance of twins over and above these levels must result from their common rearing environment, genotype-environment correlations, and other nonadditive genetic effects that are shared by MZs and, to a much lesser extent, by DZs.

Predictions From Twin Studies

If we accept the twin results, the predictions for personality resemblance among other relatives are clear. Ordinary biological siblings should have the same level of correlation as DZ twins; parents and their biological offspring should have coefficients similar in magnitude to those of siblings and DZ twins, unless nonadditive genetic effects are important sources of variation; and adopted, unrelated siblings and parents and children should not resemble each other in personality at all.

If, however, the results of family studies do not support conclusions about heritability or lack of environmental differences between families, we will need to rethink conclusions based on the study of twins. It may be, for example, that twins have special experiences that create greater personality resemblance between DZ cotwins than between ordinary sibs. Or it may be that adopted children reared together develop some degree of personality resemblance that cannot be attributed to selective placement.

Family Studies of Personality

Many studies of parental childrearing practices suggest that the characteristic ways in which parents behave toward their children are correlated with the children's personality [eg, 16]. Many studies show also that the personality characteristics of parents are modestly related to those of their offspring. Crook, in 1937, reported an average biological parent-child correlation of 0.16 for personality measures, and an average sibling correlation of 0.18 [5]. Given that both parent-child and sibling pairs share about half of their genes, the coefficients are modest indeed. In addition, siblings share more similar rearing environments than parents and children, but sibling resemblance hardly exceeds that of parents and children. Given that siblings were more likely to have been given the same personality measures, because they are more nearly the same ages, whereas parents were often given an adult test, the slightly greater similarity of sibling than parent-child pairs may be nothing more than measurement similarity.

What happened to the effects of similar rearing environments? Although some argue that no two siblings share remotely similar rearing environments, the extremity of that position is evident when it is equated with the statement that siblings' rearing environments (with the same parents!) are no more similar than those of randomly paired individuals in the population. Few would subscribe to that statement or leave it unchallenged.

Perhaps, the measurement of personality has improved greatly over the past 40 years, so that the old studies of parent-child and sibling resemblance underestimate the degree of both genetic and environmental variance shared by first-degree relatives who live together. The best test of the hypothesis that personality resemblance in families has been underestimated in the old studies is to administer current, very reliable measures to biological relatives all of whom are old enough to take the same tests. To separate the effects of shared genes from shared environments, adoptive families can be compared to biological ones.

The major study to be reported in this paper included both adoptive and biologically related families with adolescent and young adult children who were old enough to complete the same personality measures as the parents. This is the first study of its kind. For comparison, the results of two studies of young adopted and biologically related children and their parents will be reported first.

Studies of Young Adopted and Biologically Related Children

Two recent adoption studies have included children whose average ages were between 7 and 10 years. The Texas Adoption Project [15] reported personality correlations for about 200 families in which the children were old enough to complete a paper and pencil personality inventory. Although all of the families had adopted children, many also had biological offspring. Similarly, Scarr and Weinberg [30, 31] reported on 101 adoptive families who had each adopted at least one black or interracial child, but who also had many biological offspring and some adopted children of other races. In the Texas Adoption Project, the average age of the children was about 8 years; in the Minnesota Transracial Study, the adopted children averaged age 7 and the biological offspring averaged about age 10.

The striking finding in the Texas study is the lack of personality resemblance for people who live together regardless of their genetic resemblance. Loehlin [18] reported a median correlation of 0.05 for 24 pairs of biological siblings and 0.04 for 109 pairs of adopted siblings for 13 personality scales (from Cattell 16 PF). There is certainly no striking support for genetic differences on personality scales or for common environment. Children who have lived together all of their lives and those who are genetically related by half might as well be strangers on personality inventories.

Parent-child correlations were equally discouraging. The Texas parents' personality scores correlated 0.09 with their biological offspring (N = 178) and 0.08 with their adopted children (N = 409). Loehlin's careful analysis of the patterns of resemblance for the various personality scales revealed no consistent pattern of results.

In the Minnesota study, the three scales of the Junior Eysenck Personality Inventory yielded a mean sib correlation of 0.19 for 40 biologically related pairs, −0.12 for 34 adopted-biological pairs, and 0.14 for 32 pairs of adopted children. The weighted average correlation for unrelated children was 0.01. Thus in the Minnesota study of young children there is *evidence* for genetic differences in the personality scales of the Junior EPI, but no support for the effects of environmental differences among families.

The Minnesota parents' Eysenck Personality Inventory scores correlated with their biological children's scores on the Junior version of the test 0.01 (N = 162) and with their adopted children 0.05 (N = 92). The parent-child data provide no evidence for the powerful effects of genetic differences or the effects of common family environment. The necessity of different tests for parents and children, however, renders the results ambiguous.

One might argue that the problem with assessing personality in children so young is that their personalities have not developed or differentiated to the extent of their adult parents and thus cannot be assessed as similar. Or one might argue that the measurements of children's personalities are simply unreliable, although the evidence for the reliability of the Junior version of the Eysenck test is impressive [9].

Compared to several thousand DZ twins (young adults), whose weighted mean correlation for personality measures was found to be 0.25, the weighted mean correlation for 64 biological pairs of siblings in the two adoption studies is only 0.14. Clearly, the personality resemblance of ordinary siblings is not so high as that of DZ twins, which implies that there is something special about the twin environment that increases the similarity of siblings who happen to be the same age and sex. Furthermore, the newer studies even modify downward the modest conclusions of older studies of personality resemblance. Crook [5] reported a personality correlation of 0.16 for biological parent-child pairs and 0.18 for biological siblings. The new studies report 0.05 for parent-young-child pairs and 0.14 for siblings. Alas, whatever happened to genetic or environmental differences among families?

Lest the reader slip over these results, let us make explicit the implications of these findings: Upper-middle-class brothers who attend the same school and whose parents take them to the same plays, sporting events, music lessons, and therapists, and use similar childrearing practices on them, are little more similar in personality measures than they are to working-class or farm boys, whose lives are totally different. Now perhaps this is an exaggeration of the known facts, but not by much. The degree of resemblance of biological sibs on personality measures is appallingly low. Parent-child resemblance is even lower.

The major question of this study is what is the degree of parent-child and sibling resemblance on personality measures for first-degree relatives and unrelated relatives reared in the same environment who were tested in late adolescence and early adulthood, at the same ages as the twins reported by Nichols [24] and Loehlin and Nichols [19].

METHOD

Subjects

This project was part of a larger family adoption study [28, 32]. Families with adolescents adopted in infancy and families with biologically related adolescents were given a large battery of cognitive, personality, and attitude measures. The present report includes analysis of both typological and trait measures of introversion-extraversion (I-E) and measures of neuroticism and trait anxiety.

Biological families. A total of 120 biological families contributed data to this study. Not all family members completed each of the seven personality measures reported here. The number of subjects taking each test is: I-E, 495; closeness, 469; potency, 469; impulsivity, 469; neuroticism, 495; social anxiety, 479; and physical anxiety, 479. There were a total of 234 children who were between the ages of 16 and 22 years at the time of testing. Their mean age was 18.5 years. Biological families were largely recruited by means of newspaper stories and ads. (See [32] for details.)

Adoptive families. A total of 115 adoptive families contributed data to this study. As was true of the biological families, not all family members completed each of the seven personality measures. The number of adoptive family members taking each test is: I-E, 409; closeness, 394; potency, 394; impulsivity, 394; neuroticism, 409; social anxiety, 400; and physical anxiety, 400. At the time of testing, the adopted children were between the ages of 16 and 22 years with a mean age of 18.5. The adoptive families were recruited with the assistance of the Minnesota Department of Public Welfare, Adoption Unit, and newspaper stories and ads. As with the biological families, the adoptive families were paid a small fee for their participation in the study.

Of the 194 adopted children, 91% were placed in their adoptive homes by 6 months of age. All were placed before 12 months. The demographic characteristics of the biological and adoptive families were very similar [32]. There were no differences that affected personality results in the slightest.

Measuring Instruments

The Eysenck Personality Inventory, Form A (EPI). The EPI consists of true/false items which form three scales: extraversion, E, with 24 items; neuroticism, N, with 24 items; and a validity scale, Lie, with 9 items. The EPI is one instrument of a series resulting from extensive experimental and factor analytic research by H. J. Eysenck and his co-workers. Results from twin studies using instruments theoretically and structurally related to the EPI (the PEN, Maudsley Personality Inventory, and Junior Eysenck Personality Inventory) indicate the E scale is a measure of a heritable dimension of personality [6, 7, 8]. However, family studies using these instruments have failed to find significant similarity among family members [4, 16].

Although the E and N scales represent orthogonal factors, there are data that suggest that impulsive items on the E scale are associated with higher scores on the N scale and that the sociability items are associated with lower scores on the N scale [11, 13].

The Differential Personality Questionnaire, Form 9 (DPQ). The DPQ [34] is the product of iterative factor analytic studies of temperament. The three scales from the DPQ administered in this study are social closeness, social potency, and impulsiveness. These scales probably represent the major components of broad concepts and measures of introversion-extraversion.

Like the EPI, the DPQ has a true/false format and the three scales administered are approximately the same length as the EPI E and N scales: social closeness, 22 items; social potency, 27 items; and impulsiveness, 25 items. For a combined sample of 218 females and 218 males, the social closeness and social potency scales are essentially independent of impulsiveness with correlations of -0.09 and 0.05, respectively. Social closeness and social potency are correlated 0.31 for the same sample (A. Tellegen, personal communication).

The Activities Preference Questionnaire, 1973 revision (APQ). The APQ was developed to measure trait anxiety: a disposition to be fearful, shy, or apprehensive [20]. Separate scores for social and physical anxiety are provided as well as a total anxiety and validity scale. The social and physical anxiety scales are each 30 items long, and the validity scale consists of 14 items. Social and physical anxiety items are combined for the total anxiety scale.

The APQ requires the subject to indicate which two situations he/she would least prefer. Each pair of alternatives includes a potentially anxiety-provoking situation and an onerous situation. Factor analysis provides evidence that individual differences in anxiety, and not differences in avoidance of onerous situations, are being measured. Although the social anxiety and physical anxiety scales correlate only at approximately 0.40 in a normal population, twin data provide evidence that the two scales measure aspects of a single trait.

Reliability Data

Eysenck and Eysenck [12] have published test-retest reliability coefficients for the I-E scale, based on two adult samples: 92 subjects retested after one year (r = 0.82) and 27 subjects retested after 9 months (r = 0.97). The test-retest reliability coefficients for the N scale [12], based on the same subjects and over the same time periods as those for the I-E scale are: 1 year, 0.84, and 9 months, 0.88. Dr. Auke Tellegen (personal communication, 1975) has provided test-retest reliabilities for each of the three trait scales included in the DPQ separately by sex, each over a 2-week interval, for 92 males and 147 females. The reliability coefficients are: social closeness: males, 0.89; females, 0.91. *The Manual for the Activities Preference Questionnaire* [20] provides test-retest reliabilities for each of the two trait anxiety scales separately by sex, each over a 2-week period, for 101 males and 161 females. The reliability coefficients are: social anxiety: males, 0.87; females, 0.85; physical anxiety: males, 0.90; females, 0.89.

Biases in Twin and Family Studies?

Identical twins, it is said by critics of twin studies, are treated more similarly by their parents and others than fraternal twins; therefore, the usually greater behavioral similarity of MZ twins is due not to their greater genetic relatedness but to the more similar environmental response to their identical appearance [17].

Three approaches have been taken to testing the effects of greater environmental similarity of MZ than DZ twins. First, Scarr [27] and Scarr and Carter-Saltzman [29] compared the actual intellectual, personality, and physical similarities of twins who are correctly and incorrectly classified as MZ and DZ by themselves, their parents, and others. There appeared to be little bias from the belief in zygosity, and the incorrectly classified MZs and DZs were as similar on most measurements as the correctly classified pairs. On intellectual measures, belief in zygosity had no significant effect on actual similarity. On personality and physical measures, both actual zygosity and belief in zygosity were related to measured similarities. It is hard to imagine that twins grow taller or shorter or have greater or lesser skeletal maturity because someone believes them to be identical or fraternal twins. Thus we concluded that for personality and physical measures, actual similarity is a basis for the judgment of zygosity, not likely the reverse.

Lytton [21] has taken a second approach to the issue of environmental similarity between MZ versus DZ twins. With extensive observations of the parental response and initiation of interactions with very young twins, Lytton showed that the parents of MZs treat their children more similarly than do the parents of DZs, because the MZs give the parents more similar stimuli to which to respond. He observed no difference in parental treatment of MZs and DZs that would create additional similarities or differences to bias comparisons between the types of twins.

A third approach to the study of the role of more similar environment for MZ than DZ twins was developed by Plomin et al [26]. Their reasoning was as follows: If identical twins are more similar *because* they are treated more similarly, then those MZs who experience more similar environments will behave more similarly than those MZs who experience less similar environments. Sharing the same room, friends, classrooms, and receiving similar parental treatment, for example, should increase the behavioral similarity of some MZs over that of others. In short, those ought to affect the degree of similarity *among* identical twins as well. (Fraternal twins were not used, because some pairs are genetically more similar than others, a confounding factor in any analysis of greater and lesser environmental similarity. To some extent, greater genetic similarity may lead some DZ pairs to select and receive more similar environments than others.) The result of Plomin's analysis of the effect of greater similarities on the environmental factors that differentiate between MZ and DZ twins was clear: Greater environmental similarity does not inflate actual similarities among identical twins on intellectual or personality dimensions. Rather, it seems likely that more similar genotypes develop greater behavioral similarity and select more similar environments more often than less similar (eg, DZ) genotypes. The greater environmental similarity of MZ than DZ twins is, therefore, primarily a result and not a cause of behavioral similarity.

Comparisons of adopted and biologically related relatives assume that the greater behavioral similarity usually found among biological relatives is due to their greater genetic similarity. Critics of behavior genetic methods assert, to the contrary, that important biases creep into comparisons of genetically related and unrelated families or members of families through parental and child expectations of greater similarity among biological than adoptive relatives. If biological parents see themselves in their offspring and expect them to develop greater similarity to the parents, then the children may develop more similarly in many ways. Adoptive parents, knowing that there is no genetic link between them and their children, may expect less similarity and thus not pressure their children to become like the parents. The greater expectation of similarity among biological than adoptive relatives could well bias the comparisons of genetically related and unrelated families, confounding genetic relatedness with environmental pressures toward similarity that run in the same direction. The greater behavioral similarity of biological relatives might be due as much as or more to parental and child expectations than to differences in genetic relatedness.

To test the hypothesis that knowledge of biological or adoptive status influences actual similarity, we [33] correlated absolute differences in objective test scores with ratings of similarity by adolescents and their parents in adoptive and biological families. Although biological family members see themselves as more similar than adoptive family members, there are also important generational and gender differences in perceived similarity that cut across family type. There is moderate agreement among family members on the degree of perceived similarity, but there is no correlation between perceived and actual similarity in intelligence or temperament. However, family members are more accurate about shared social attitudes.

Knowledge of adoptive or biological relatedness is associated with the degree of perceived similarity, but perceptions of similarity are not related to objective similarities and thus do not consititue a bias in comparisons of measured differences in intelligence or temperament in adoptive and biological families.

RESULTS

Mean Scores of Biological and Adoptive Relatives

Tables 1 and 2 give the mean scores of the biological and adoptive family members on the measures of introversion-extraversion and neuroticism, and their components. According to the norms given for the traits by Eysenck [8], these are essentially normal samples. Differences among the groups by sex, generation, and family type are given in Tables 1a and 2a for MANOVA and univariate tests. In the I-E domain, females have higher extraversion scores than males, particularly on the measure of social closeness. Children are more extraverted than their parents, particularly on the component of impulsivity. It should be noted, however, that parents have slightly higher scores on the social closeness measure. There were no differences between the biologically related and adoptive families on measures of extraversion. On scales of anxiety and neuroticism females' scores exceed those of males, childrens' exceed those of parents, and adoptive families' exceed those of biological families. Only for physical anxiety is the parent score higher than the offspring score. These results are given in Table 2a.

Predictably, there were large differences between the sexes on physical anxiety, those sex differences being even larger for parents than for children (perhaps women are becoming less afraid of physical dangers). The mean differences between biological and adoptive families on neuroticism and social anxiety were small (0.11 and 0.10 of SD, respectively) and of no consequence practically or statistically, because we standardize all of the personality scores by gender, generation, and family type before proceeding with correlations among measures or the analyses of family resemblance.

Correlations Among Measures of Introversion and Neuroticism

Measures of introversion-extraversion and neuroticism were chosen because they seemed to represent two of the more stable traits of human personality. Since the study was conducted, Loehlin and Nichols [19] have ridiculed efforts to demonstrate that one aspect of personality is more heritable than another. Nonetheless, the data from longitudinal studies suggest that introversion and anxiety may be two of the more stable individual differences in personality. Buss and Plomin [2] argue that emotionality, activity, sociability, and impulsivity are the most reliably stable personality characteristics. Our measures of introversion include sociability and impulsivity, and the measures of neuroticism include emotionality and anxiety.

Correlations among the so-called type measures (EPI introversion and EPI neuroticism) and the trait measures from the DPQ and the APQ show adequate discriminant and convergent validity for the I-E measures but not for the measures of anxiety, as shown in Figure 1. The EPI measure of introversion-extraversion is correlated 0.44 to 0.46 with the three DPQ measures of social closeness, social potency, and impulsivity, none of which is correlated with each other more than 0.26. The measures of anxiety, which are supposed to be related to neuroticism and not I-E, are indeed not related to I-E. Thus the measures in the domain of I-E have appropriate convergent and discriminant validity. The type measure of neuroticism is supposed to be related to trait measures of anxiety, here measured by the APQ scales physical anxiety and social anxiety. Although the social anxiety scale is related to neuroticism 0.27, the next highest correlation with neuroticism is impulsivity, from the I-E cluster. Physical anxiety is not related to neuroticism, but it is positively correlated with introversion to a significant extent. Thus physical anxiety belongs more to the I-E cluster than to the neuroticism cluster, because people who are physically anxious are more introverted than they are generally anxious. People who are anxious about social material are more neurotic by Eysenck's standards, and those who are neurotic are also more impulsive. Given that these correlations are based on 879 adults, they are quite reliable (95% confidence interval = ±0.065).

Parent-Child Resemblance

The resemblance of parents and their biological and adopted children is given in Appendix Tables A1–A9. A summary of these results is given in Table 3, which reports the midparent-child correlations for the ten personality measures of the study. The median midparent-child correlation for the personality measures was 0.20 for biologically related pairs and 0.08 for adoptive pairs. Single parent-child resemblance was 0.15 for biological pairs and 0.04 for adoptive pairs. These results are in accord with the older studies of parent-child resemblance and not congruent with the studies of DZ twins. The heritability that could be estimated from parent-child resemblance is 0.22, substantially less than the 0.52 estimated from studies of MZ and DZ twins.

Sibling Resemblances

Biologically related sibling resemblance in personality traits is more like that of DZ twins, with a median of 0.20 for the ten measures in this study. The median correlation for unrelated siblings is 0.07, significantly lower than the coefficient for biologically related sibs. Table 4 shows the correlations of biological and adopted sibs, compared with the correlations of MZ and DZ twins. The most notable feature of the table is the far higher heritability estimate from twin than sibling studies. Whereas MZ twin correlations exceed those of DZs by 0.27 for the traits measured, the biological sib correlation exceeds the adopted sib coefficient by only 0.13, or half as much. Note that the degree of resemblance is 1.00 versus 0.50 and 0.50 versus 0.00 in the two

TABLE 1. Eysenck Personality Inventory, Introversion-Extraversion, and Three Subcomponents, Closeness, Potency, and Impulsiveness, from the Differential Personality Questionnaire (Means and Standard Deviations for Family Members)

		Biological				Adoptive				All Ss
		Fa	Mo	So	Da	Fa	Mo	So	Da	
Eysenck introversion-extraversion	N	120	120	113	142	107	112	87	103	904
	$\overline{X}$	10.66	11.36	11.75	12.86	10.99	10.71	13.87	14.38	12.05
	SD	4.07	3.70	3.73	3.80	4.24	4.02	4.00	3.25	4.06
DPQ closeness	N	114	113	106	136	103	108	85	98	863
	$\overline{X}$	13.13	16.39	13.75	16.21	14.35	15.59	14.93	15.99	15.07
	SD	5.01	4.23	4.92	4.70	4.78	4.35	4.65	4.76	4.80
DPQ potency	N	114	113	106	136	103	108	85	98	863
	$\overline{X}$	12.02	10.56	11.44	11.76	10.96	9.59	11.71	12.83	11.36
	SD	6.61	6.30	5.85	6.05	6.71	6.50	5.88	6.22	6.30
DPQ impulsiveness	N	114	113	106	136	103	108	85	98	863
	$\overline{X}$	7.32	8.23	10.77	11.17	7.94	7.89	12.74	12.89	9.81
	SD	4.87	5.11	5.99	5.96	5.08	5.37	5.47	5.37	5.79
IE/C/P/I	N	462	459	431	550	416	436	342	397	
	M	10.78	11.63	11.93	13.00	11.06	11.20	13.32	14.03	

TABLE 1a. Multivariate and Univariate Analyses of Eysenck I-E and DPQ Scores (Summary of Significant Effects and Their Directions)

Source	Significant effects via MANOVA I: (IE, C, P, I scales)	Post-hoc comparisons via univariate F-test			
		Introversion	Closeness	Potency	Impulsivity
Sex (male, female)	11.68<12.46**	11.69<12.31*	13.97<16.06***		7.84<11.78****
Generation (parent, offspring)	11.17<13.03****	10.93<13.13****	14.86>12.30*		
Family type (biological, adoptive)	n.s.				
Sex × generation	n.s.				
Sex × family type	n.s.				
Generation × family type	see Table 1** for means				
Sex × generation × family type					

* = P < 0.05.
** = P < 0.01.
*** = P < 0.001.
**** = P < 0.0001.

TABLE 2. Eysenck Personality Inventory, Neuroticism, and Three Subcomponents, Social Anxiety, Physical Anxiety, Total Anxiety, from the Activity Preference Questionnaire (Means and Standard Deviations for Family Members)

		Biological				Adoptive				All Ss
		Fa	Mo	So	Da	Fa	Mo	So	Da	
Eysenck neuroticism	N	120	120	113	142	107	112	87	103	904
	$\bar{X}$	7.48	8.58	10.23	11.72	7.78	9.60	11.41	12.04	9.86
	SD	4.46	5.00	4.23	4.56	4.20	5.10	4.21	4.56	4.85
APQ social anxiety	N	115	114	110	140	103	108	88	101	879
	$\bar{X}$	10.50	11.76	12.66	14.26	11.61	12.88	13.90	14.89	12.84
	SD	4.85	5.74	4.47	4.80	5.61	5.14	5.52	4.59	5.26
APQ physical anxiety	N	115	114	110	140	103	108	88	101	879
	$\bar{X}$	17.40	22.83	12.86	17.56	18.47	23.92	13.65	16.10	17.86
	SD	5.94	4.75	5.71	4.41	5.77	3.70	5.37	5.52	6.33
APQ total anxiety	N	115	114	110	140	103	108	88	101	879
	$\bar{X}$	27.90	34.60	25.53	31.82	30.08	36.80	27.55	30.99	30.69
	SD	8.46	8.24	8.17	7.31	9.25	7.63	9.20	8.30	8.98
SA, PA	N	350	348	333	422	313	328	263	305	
	$\bar{X}$	11.73	14.29	11.90	14.50	12.56	15.40	12.99	14.33	

TABLE 2a. Multivariate and Univariate Analyses of Eysenck N and APQ Scores Summary of Significant Effects and Their Direction

Source	Significant effects via MANOVA II: (N, SA, PA Scales)	Post-hoc comparisons via univariate F-test		
		Neuroticism	Social anxiety	Physical anxiety
Sex (male, female)	12.24<14.62****	9.08<10.50****	12.07<13.46****	15.67<20.02****
Generation (parent, offspring)	13.49<13.51****	8.35<11.36****	11.67<13.93****	20.66>15.26****
Family type (biological, adoptive)	13.19<13.87**	9.59<10.12**	12.39<13.28**	
Sex × generation	see Table 2 for means*			see Table 2 for means*
Sex × family type	n.s.			
Generation × family type	n.s.			
Sex × generation × family type	n.s.			

* = P < 0.05.
** = P < 0.01.
*** = P < 0.001.
**** = P < 0.0001.

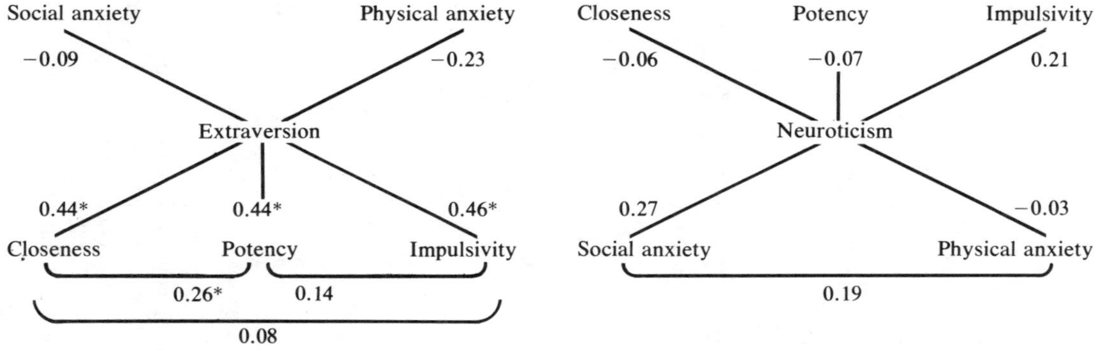

Figure 1. Schematic Diagram of Intercorrelations of Seven Personality Measures (N = 879)

TABLE 3. Summary of Midparent-Child Resemblance on Personality Measures of Introversion-Extraversion and Neuroticism-Anxiety

	Biological	Adoptive	t
Introversion-extraversion	0.19	−0.00	1.78*
Social closeness	0.28	−0.00	2.93**
Social potency	0.21	0.10	1.10
Impulsivity	0.14	−0.02	1.53
Neuroticism	0.25	0.05	2.09*
Social anxiety	0.03	0.17	−1.43*
Physical anxiety	0.21	0.06	1.56
Total anxiety	0.14	0.11	0.29
Defensiveness (Lie)	0.20	0.06	1.53
Midparent median r	0.20	0.06	$h^2 = 2(r_{iB} - r_{iA}) = 0.22$
Single parent-child median r	0.15	0.04	$h^2 = (r_{iB} - r_{iA}) = 0.14$

TABLE A1. Introversion-Extraversion: Family Correlations Based on Scores Standardized by Sex, Generation, and Family Type (Eysenck Personality Inventory)

	r_{bio}	r_{adopt}	r_{bio}-r_{adopt}	t_{corr}
Fa-Mo	−0.13	0.01	(0.14)	1.03
Fa-child	0.21	0.05	0.16	1.72*
Fa-da	0.29	−0.01	0.30	2.37**
Fa-son	0.10	0.10	0.00	−0.03
Mo-child	0.04	−0.03	0.07	0.66
Mo-da	0.03	−0.08	0.11	0.84
Mo-son	0.06	0.03	0.03	0.24
MP-child	0.19	−0.00	0.19	1.78*
MP-da	0.24	−0.05	0.29	2.22*
MP-son	0.12	0.08	0.04	0.30
Child-child	0.06	0.07	(0.01)	−0.04
Son-son	0.28	—	—	—
Da-da	0.02	—	—	—
Son-da	0.04	0.04	0.00	0.00

TABLE A2. Closeness: Family Correlations Based on Scores Standardized by Sex, Generation, and Family Type (Differential Personality Questionnaire)

	r_{bio}	r_{adopt}	r_{bio}-r_{adopt}	t_{corr}
Fa-Mo	0.14	0.10	0.04	0.30
Fa-child	0.16	0.00	0.16	1.57
Fa-da	0.22	0.04	0.18	1.33
Fa-son	0.08	−0.03	0.11	0.74
Mo-child	0.28	0.08	0.20	2.14*
Mo-da	0.28	0.12	0.16	1.22
Mo-son	0.35	0.03	0.32	2.28*
MP-child	0.28	−0.00	0.28	2.93**
MP-da	0.31	0.04	0.27	1.76*
MP-son	0.29	−0.04	0.33	2.29*
Child-child	0.10	0.13	(0.03)	−0.22
Son-son	0.11	—	—	—
Da-da	0.23	—	—	—
Son-da	0.03	0.11	(0.08)	−0.45

*P < 0.05, one-tailed; **P < 0.01, one-tailed.

cases, an equally disparate comparison. Thus one must conclude that the evidence from family studies is not congruent with the findings of twin studies. The correlations of siblings and parents and children support the conclusion that only about 25% of the personality variance is due to genetic differences among individuals.

DISCUSSION

Unlike the several family and many twin studies of abilities, which yield congruent results about the heritability of intelligence, family studies of personality do not agree with studies of MZ and DZ twins, even when the ages of the par-

TABLE A3. Potency: Family Correlations Based on Scores Standardized by Sex, Generation, and Family Type (Differential Personality Questionnaire)

	$r$bio	$r$adopt	$r$bio-$r$adopt	$t$corr
Fa-mo	0.02	0.06	(0.04)	0.29
Fa-child	0.16	0.14	0.02	0.22
Fa-da	0.25	0.06	0.19	1.48
Fa-son	0.06	0.26	(0.20)	−1.35
Mo-child	0.15	0.02	0.13	1.36
Mo-da	0.16	0.00	0.16	1.16
Mo-son	0.14	0.04	0.10	0.71
MP-child	0.21	0.10	0.11	1.10
MP-da	0.27	0.04	0.23	1.76*
MP-son	0.14	0.19	(0.05)	−0.35
Child-child	0.20	0.07	0.13	0.95
Son-son	0.11	—	—	—
Da-da	0.03	—	—	—
Son-da	0.17	0.02	0.15	0.86

TABLE A5. Neuroticism: Family Correlations Based on Scores Standardized by Sex, Generation, and Family Type (Eysenck Personality Inventory)

	$r$bio	$r$adopt	$r$bio-$r$adopt	$t$corr
Fa-mo	0.07	0.14	(0.07)	−0.53
Fa-child	0.14	−0.09	0.23	2.37**
Fa-da	0.15	−0.04	0.19	1.45
Fa-son	0.12	−0.12	0.24	1.65*
Mo-child	0.21	0.12	0.09	1.03
Mo-da	0.31	0.12	0.19	1.55
Mo-son	0.10	0.13	(0.03)	−0.24
MP-child	0.25	0.05	0.20	2.09*
MP-da	0.31	0.08	0.23	1.74*
MP-son	0.15	0.01	0.14	0.92
Child-child	0.28	0.05	0.23	1.74*
Son-son	0.23	—		
Da-da	0.40	—		
Son-da	0.21	−0.02	0.23	1.12

TABLE A4. Impulsiveness: Family Correlations Based on Scores Standardized by Sex, Generation, and Family Type (Differential Personality Questionnaire)

	$r$bio	$r$adopt	$r$bio-$r$adopt	$t$corr
Fa-mo	−0.04	−0.08	(0.12)	0.29
Fa-child	0.09	−0.04	0.13	1.26
Fa-da	0.02	−0.12	0.14	1.04
Fa-son	0.17	0.06	0.11	0.80
Mo-child	0.10	−0.03	0.13	1.30
Mo-da	0.06	0.05	0.01	0.06
Mo-son	0.15	−0.11	0.26	1.82*
MP-child	0.14	−0.02	0.16	1.53
MP-da	0.06	0.01	0.05	0.38
MP-son	0.23	−0.04	0.27	1.83*
Child-child	0.20	0.05	0.15	1.10
Son-son	−0.12	—	—	—
Da-da	0.35	—	—	—
Son-da	0.26	0.58	(0.32)	−2.25**

TABLE A6. Physical Anxiety: Family Correlations Based on Scores Standardized by Sex, Generation, and Family Type (Activity Preference Questionnaire)

	$r$bio	$r$adopt	$r$bio-$r$adopt	$t$corr
Fa-mo	0.05	0.30	(0.25)	−1.88*
Fa-child	0.13	0.07	0.06	0.63
Fa-da	0.15	−0.03	0.18	1.40
Fa-son	0.16	0.18	(0.02)	−0.17
Mo-child	0.18	0.01	0.17	1.82*
Mo-da	0.15	−0.03	0.18	1.39
Mo-son	0.25	0.04	0.21	1.45
MP-child	0.21	0.06	0.15	1.56
MP-da	0.20	−0.06	0.26	1.94*
MP-son	0.28	0.18	0.10	0.71
Child-child	0.24	0.04	0.20	1.50
Son-son	0.51	—	—	—
Da-da	0.37	—	—	—
Son-da	0.16	0.02	0.14	0.82

ticipants are limited to those who can answer the same personality instruments. If we believe the twin studies, about half of the variance in personality traits is due to genetic differences among people. If we believe the studies of ordinary siblings and parent-child pairs, the explanatory power of genetic differences shrinks to about 0.25. What are we to make of this contradiction?

First, one should note that the degree of resemblance among biological siblings cannot be fully explained by the estimates of heritability from family studies, even those of late adolescents. If the magnitude of genetic effects on individual differences is 0.25, then siblings (and DZ twins) should correlate about 0.125 on genetic bases; the obtained correlations are higher than pre-

TABLE A7. Social Anxiety: Family Correlations Based on Scores Standardized by Sex, Generation, and Family Type (Activity Preference Questionnaire)

	r_{bio}	r_{adopt}	r_{bio}-r_{adopt}	t_{corr}
Fa-mo	0.23	0.31	(0.08)	−0.63
Fa-child	0.12	−0.01	0.13	1.36
Fa-da	0.05	−0.01	0.06	0.40
Fa-son	0.18	−0.01	0.19	1.33
Mo-child	−0.06	0.27	0.21	−3.39**
Mo-da	−0.06	0.38	(0.44)	−3.41**
Mo-son	−0.09	0.17	(0.26)	−1.78*
MP-child	0.03	0.17	(0.14)	−1.43
MP-da	−0.01	0.24	(0.25)	−1.87*
MP-son	0.06	0.12	(0.06)	−0.44
Child-child	0.17	0.36	(0.19)	−1.50
Son-son	0.30	—	—	—
Da-da	−0.01	—	—	—
Son-da	0.22	0.34	(0.12)	−0.76

TABLE A8. Total Anxiety: Family Correlations Based on Scores Standardized by Sex, Generation, and Family Type (Activity Preference Questionnaire)

	r_{bio}	r_{adopt}	r_{bio}-r_{adopt}	t_{corr}
Fa-mo	0.09	0.35	(0.26)	−1.99*
Fa-child	0.17	0.02	0.15	1.55
Fa-da	0.16	−0.06	0.22	1.61
Fa-son	0.12	0.02	0.10	0.66
Mo-child	0.03	0.14	(0.11)	−1.14
Mo-da	0.02	0.16	(0.14)	−1.08
Mo-son	−0.02	0.09	(0.11)	−0.76
MP-child	0.14	0.11	0.03	0.29
MP-da	0.11	0.05	0.06	0.48
MP-son	0.12	0.15	(0.03)	−0.24
Child-child	0.32	0.29	0.03	0.24
Son-son	0.45	—	—	—
Da-da	0.31	—	—	—
Son-da	0.29	0.20	0.09	0.56

TABLE A9. Defensiveness (Lie): Family Correlations Based on Scores Standardized by Sex, Generation, and Family Type (Eysenck Personality Inventory)

	r_{bio}	r_{adopt}	r_{bio}-r_{adopt}	t_{corr}
Fa-mo	0.11	0.06	0.05	0.37
Fa-child	0.22	0.07	0.15	1.61
Fa-da	0.28	0.12	0.16	1.28
Fa-son	0.17	0.02	0.15	1.08
Mo-child	0.09	−0.01	0.10	0.97
Mo-da	0.18	0.03	0.15	1.16
Mo-son	0.01	−0.06	0.07	0.44
MP-child	0.20	0.06	0.14	1.53
MP-da	0.31	0.13	0.18	1.42
MP-son	0.11	−0.01	0.12	0.86
Child-child	0.18	0.26	(0.08)	−0.62
Son-son	0.36	—	—	—
Da-da	0.22	—	—	—
Son-da	0.10	0.32	(0.22)	−1.35

dicted. Genetically unrelated siblings should not, of course, have correlated personality measures at all; yet their degree of resemblance is generally positive and sometimes significantly so (see Table A7). Family studies suggest either that the adoption agencies exercise selective placement of infants with adoptive families according to the natural mother's personality (of which they had no measures except in the Texas Adoption Project, whose results do not differ from the other studies) or that living in the same family from infancy to adolescence has a slight effect on the development of personality resemblance to those with whom one lives. The latter hypothesis seems more reasonable.

TABLE 4. Correlations of Twins and Siblings for Personality Test Scores in Late Adolescence

Personality measure	Twins (and genetic correlation)		Siblings (and genetic correlation)	
	MZ (1.00)	DZ (0.50)	Biological (0.50)	Adopted (0.00)
Introversion-extraversion	0.52*	0.25	0.06	0.07
Social closeness			0.10	0.13
Social potency			0.20	0.07
Impulsivity	0.48*	0.29	0.20	0.05
Neuroticism	0.52*	0.22	0.28*	0.05
Social anxiety			0.17	0.36
Physical anxiety			0.24	0.04
Total anxiety			0.32	0.29
Defensiveness			0.18	0.26
Median:	0.52[a]	0.25[a]	0.20[b]	0.07[b]
	$h^2 = 2(r_{IMZ} - r_{IDZ}) = 0.54$		$h^2 = 2(r_{IB} - r_{IA}) = 0.26$	

*MZ > DZ; biological > adopted.
[a]27 CPI scales [4].
[b]10 listed measures.

Second, the larger average correlation between DZ cotwins than ordinary sibs must be explained by the greater prenatal or postnatal environmental similarity of twin pairs. We favor the latter type of environment, because no one, to our knowledge, has shown any prenatal effects on personality that last into the early 20s.

Third, the sibling correlations are consistently larger than those of parents and their children. The smaller parent-child than sibling correlation could be due to the greater similarity of rearing environments for sibs. Another possible explanation for the lower parent-child correlations could be nonadditive genetic effects that are partially shared by sibs but not by parents and offspring. Again, in the absence of evidence for nonadditive genetic effects and in the presence of the DZ-sib discrepancy, an environmental explanation seems most plausible.

Before one jumps to the conclusion that family environments are very important for the development of individual differences in personality, it would be wise to look at the magnitude of family environmental effects suggested by the adoption studies. About 4–7% of the variance in personality may be accounted for by common rearing. The difference between parent-child and sibling resemblance suggests that perhaps 3% of the variance is common to sib environments and not to parents and children. The difference between DZ twin and sib correlations suggests that another 5% of the variance may be due to "twinness" or unusually similar environments. All in all, there is not too much explained variance for environmentalists to be excited about. We are left, of course, with the largest part of the variance unexplained.

Studies of twins exaggerate the degree to which personality differences in the population are explained by genetic differences and underestimate slightly the importance of environmental differences among families. Unlike studies of mental abilities, personality studies of twins and families give quite different pictures of the sources of variance. In addition, measures of family demographic characteristics (income, education, occupation) are not correlated with personality measures, whereas they are correlated with measures of ability. It is not feasible to explain any of the effects of family environment on personality by the ordinarily indexed differences among families.

Most of the variance in personality measures is not accounted for by either genetic differences or by environmental differences *between* families. Most of the variance (not explained by errors of measurement) in personality must lie with individuals within families. That is, the experiences of siblings must be sufficiently different that personality development proceeds quite differently for even biologically related members of the same family. It is clear that we need much more complex models of how individual environments work to shape personality. Individuals within families are vastly different in the personality characteristics we measured, and psychology has no theory to explain that individuality.

If, as the twin studies suggest, the heritability of personality traits is 0.5, then the resemblance of genetic relatives should be far greater than we found it to be. It may be, however, that individual genotypes evoke and select different responses from their environments, thereby creating genotype-environment correlations of great importance. Lytton's study [21] of parental responses to the behaviors of MZ and DZ twins supports the notion that parents react to the individual differences of their offspring in ways that correlate with the genotypes of the children. Thus it may be for individual children; their unique genotypes may determine much of the enviornment they experience and explain much of the variance we are unable to measure in studies of personality.

ACKNOWLEDGMENTS

The present study was supported by the William T. Grant Foundation and National Institute of Child Health and Human Development (HD-08016). The manuscript was prepared while the first author was a Fellow at the Center for Advanced Study in the Behavioral Sciences, with support from the Spencer Foundation and NIMH.

This study was conducted with the full collaboration of the Minnesota State Department of Public Welfare, Adoption Unit, directed by Ruth Weidell and assisted by Marjorie Flowers. Their help was invaluable. The additional support of the Open Door Society, Lutheran Social Service, and The Children's Home Society, all of Minnesota, facilitated the study.

We are very grateful for the assistance of Louise Carter-Saltzman, Harold Grotevant, Margaret Getman, Marsha Sargrad, Joanne Bergman, William Thompson, and Carol Peterman in the collection of the data and the preparation of this report.

REFERENCES

1. Bem DJ, Allen A: On predicting some of the people some of the time: The search for cross-situational consistencies in behavior. Psychol Rev 81 (6):506–520, 1974.
2. Buss, AH, Plomin R: "A Temperament Theory of Personality Development." New York: John Wiley & Sons, 1975.
3. Cattell RB, Eber HW: "Handbook for the Sixteen Personality Factor Questionnaire." Champaign, Illinois: Institute for Personality and Ability Testing, 1970.
4. Coppen A, Cowie A, Slater D: Familial aspects of neuroticism and extraversion. Br J Psychiatry 111 (470):70–83, 1965.
5. Crook: Intra-family relationships in personality test performance. Psychol Rec 1:479–502, 1937.
6. Eaves LJ: The structure of genotypic and environmental covariation for personality measurements: An analysis of the PEN. Br J Soc Clin Psychol 12:275–282, 1973.
7. Eaves LJ, Eysenck HJ: The nature of extraversion: A genetical analysis. J Pers Soc Psychol 32:102–112, 1975.
8. Eysenck HJ: The inheritance of introversion-extraversion. Acta Psychol 12:95–110, 1956.
9. Eysenck SBG: "Junior E.P.I." San Diego: Educational and Industrial Testing Service, 1965.
10. Eysenck H, Eysenck SBG: "Manual for the Eysenck Personality Inventory." San Diego: Educational and Industrial Testing Service, 1963.
11. Eysenck SB, Eysenck HJ: On the dual nature of extraversion. Br J Soc Clin Psychol 2:46–55, 1963.
12. Eysenck HJ, Eysenck SB: "Manual for the Eysenck Personality Inventory." San Diego: Educational and Industrial Testing Service, 1968.
13. Farley FH: Further investigation of the two personae of extraversion. Br J Soc Clin Psychol 9:377–379, 1970.
14. Harrington DM, Block JH, Block J: Intolerance of ambiguity in preschool children: Psychometric considerations, behavioral manifestations, and parental correlates. Dev Psychol 14(3):242–256, 1978.
15. Horn JM, Loehlin JC, Willerman L: Intellectual resemblance among adoptive and biological relatives: The Texas adoption project. Behav Genet 117–207, 1979.
16. Insel PM: Maternal effects in personality. Behav Genet 4:133–143, 1974.
17. Kamin LJ: "The Science and Politics of IQ." Potomic, Maryland: Lawrence Erlbaum Associates, 1974.
18. Loehlin, JC: "Adoption Studies of Personality." Paper presented at the BGA Meetings, Middletown, Connecticut, June 1979.
19. Loehlin JC, Nichols RC: "Heredity, Environment, and Personality: A Study of 850 Sets of Twins." Austin, Texas: University of Texas Press, 1976.
20. Lykken DT, Tellegen A, Katzenmeyer CG: "Manual for the Activity Preference Questionnaire (APQ)." Reports from the Research Laboratories. Department of Psychiatry, University of Minnesota, Report No. PR-73-4. Minneapolis, 1973.
21. Lytton H: Do parents create, or respond to, differences in twins? Dev Psychol 13(5):456–459, 1977.
22. Mischel W: "Personality and Assessment." New York: Wiley, 1968.
23. Moskovitz DS, Schwarz JC: "In Search of Better Personality Measures: The Validity of Informants Ratings and Behavioral Count Scores." Unpublished manuscript, University of Connecticut, Storrs, Connecticut: 1980.
24. Nichols RC: Heredity and environment: Major findings from twin studies of ability, personality, and interests. Invited address presented at the American Psychological Association meeting. Washington, DC, September 4, 1976.
25. Plomin R, DeFries JC: Genetics and intelligence: Recent data. Intelligence 4:15–24, 1980.

26. Plomin R, Willerman L, Loehlin JC: Resemblance in appearance and the equal environments assumption in twin studies of personality. Behav Genet 6:43–52, 1976.
27. Scarr S: Environmental bias in twin studies. Eugen Quart 15(1):34–40, 1968.
28. Scarr S: "IQ: Race, Social Class and Individual Differences, New Studies of Old Problems. Hillsdale, New Jersey: Lawrence Erlbaum Associates (in press) 1980.
29. Scarr S, Carter-Saltzman L: Twin method: Defense of a critical assumption. Behav Genet (in press) 1980.
30. Scarr S, Weinberg RA: IQ test performance of black children adopted by white families. Am Psychol 31:726–739, 1976.
31. Scarr S, Weinberg RA: Intellectual similarities within families of both adopted and biological children. Intelligence 32(8):170–191, 1977.
32. Scarr S, Weinberg RA: The influence of "family background" on intellectual attainment. Am Sociol Rev 43:674–692, 1978.
33. Scarr S, Scarf E, Weinberg RA: Perceived and actual similarities in biological and adoptive families: Does perceived similarity bias genetic inferences? Behav Genet (in press).
34. Tellegan A: "Differential Personality Questionnaire," mimeo, University of Minnesota, 1973.

Twin Research 3: Intelligence, Personality,
and Development, pages 121 — 125

Blood Groups, Physical Appearance, and Personality Similarity in Adult Dizygotic Twins

Joseph M. Horn, Karen Matthews, and Ray Rosenman
*Department of Psychology, University of Texas, Austin (J.M.H.), Department
of Psychiatry, University of Pittsburgh (K.M.), and Stanford Research
Institute (SRI International), Menlo Park, California (R.R.)*

INTRODUCTION

Since pairs of dizygotic twins vary in percentage of genes identical by descent, they afford twin researchers a good opportunity to investigate the degree of genetic control over behavioral traits in a context where assumptions about environmental differences between monozygotic (MZ) and dizygotic (DZ) twins need not be invoked. Given the frequent utilization of bloodtyping as a means of separating twins into MZ and DZ groups, it would seem feasible to present correlations between bloodgroup differences and behavioral trait differences in DZ twins as a check on the inferences drawn from inspection of differences between MZ and DZ twins. A few such reports have appeared but, in terms of confirming results obtained when the two types of twins are compared, the approach has been a disappointment. For example, Carter-Saltzman and Scarr-Salapatek [1] reported that neither cognitive nor personality measures were consistently related to bloodgroup differences in their sample of DZ twins, even though the bloodgroups did predict differences in physical traits, and previous work by numerous investigators comparing MZ and DZ twins had identified a genetic component to the personality and cognitive measures they utilized in their study.

Among twin researchers, one response to such negative findings has been to question the adequacy of bloodgroups as a good sample of the genotype. Another possible explanation for the disagreement between the two types of twin studies is that comparisons of MZ and DZ twins have overestimated the degree of genetic control for some personality traits. If some factor unique to MZ twins happens to increase their similarity, differences between MZ and DZ correlations can be inflated, producing an elevation of heritability estimates. One important source of such distortion could derive from associations between physical appearance and personality.

Since MZ twins are usually identical in appearance whereas many DZ twins are not, any relationship between morphology and personality will elevate the MZ correlation for the personality trait. Lindzey [4] surveyed the literature on morphology and behavior and concluded that "the most firmly based evidence we now possess suggests the existence of important associations" in this area. Studies designed to estimate the direct relationship between observer ratings of personality and morphological variables formed a major part of Lindzey's review.

If the mechanism behind the association of personality and physical traits involves a set of biological factors influencing behavior and morphology jointly, it may not be correct to consider MZ correlations inflated. However, if physical traits determine a person's social-stimulus value for others, and thereby exert some control over social learning experiences, it seems reasonable to question the appropriateness of basing heritability estimates on comparisons of MZ and DZ twins.

The purpose of the present report is to see if within-pair differences in physical appearance can be related to differences in personality for a sample of DZ twins and to illustrate the impact of such a relationship on measures of personality similarity for both MZ and DZ twin pairs. Bloodgroup differences within DZ twin pairs are used as a measure of genetic similarity and correlated with within-pair differences in both personality and physical appearance in order to see if gene overlap can account for any relationship between physical appearance and personality.

MATERIALS AND METHODS

Sample

A total of 110 DZ and 114 MZ twin pairs from the NHLI Twin Study of cardiovascular disease risk factors [2] formed the study population. These twins are part of the Twin Registry maintained by the Medical Follow-Up Agency of the National Research Council [3]. All twins were adult males living in California at the time of assessment.

Measures of Physical Traits

Height, eye color, hair color, hair type, baldness, site of baldness, and handedness were selected for study because each trait was thought to contribute importantly to overall physical appearance. Each twin's report[1] of his own physical makeup was used to classify each twin pair as similar or dissimular on each dimension, and the sum of all dissimilar classifications was used as a mea-

---

[1]Each twin evaluated his own characteristics according to the following schemes: 1) Eye color: blue, gray, brown, hazel, or other. 2) Hair color: blond, brown, black, or red. 3) Hair type: straight, curly, other. 4) Baldness: none, beginning, moderate, or complete. 5) Site of baldness: none, crown, temple, or forehead. 6) Handedness: right, left, or both. 7) Height: actual measurements used—if more than an inch apart in height, the twins were classified as different.

Twin pairs were classified as different for a given trait if they gave themselves different ratings for the trait.

sure of overall difference. The modal difference between twin pairs was 3 and the variance was 1.7. On the average, approximately 60% of pairs were the same on a single trait.

Bloodgroups

In the original project, 15 bloodgroups were used to classify twins as MZ or DZ. However, all twins were not assessed on all bloodgroups and the gene frequencies were such that sufficient within-pair variability was present in only eight of the 15 bloodgroups. Each twin pair was classified as same or different at each of these eight loci. The sum of all differences was then used as an overall measure of bloodgroup difference. The mode for this index was 2 and the variance was 1.2. On the average, approximately 75% of the twin pairs were the same at a single locus. Only 86 twin pairs had been typed for all eight of these bloodgroups.

Measure of Personality

The only personality test administered to all of these DZ twins was the California Personality Inventory (CPI). The two major personality dimensions represented in this test are extroversion and psychological stability. Nichols and Schnell [5] have constructed a 55-item scale called Person Orientation from the CPI items that measure extroversion, and this measure does not correlate significantly with their 110-item scale, Value Orientation, designed to measure psychological stability. Both scales are used in this investigation.

RESULTS

Table 1 gives the correlations between the numbers of within-pair physical trait or bloodgroup differences and the differences in personality for this sample of DZ twins. The sum of the scale differences across all 18 CPI scales was significantly related to the differences in physical traits but failed to show any relationship to differences in bloodgroups. However, not all of the scales of the CPI contribute equally to this result. The significant correlation between differences in Value Orientation and differences in physical traits coupled with the lack of any relationship between Person Orientation and physical differences, indicates that the CPI scales measuring the dimension of psychological stability are responsible for the overall relationship between physical traits and personality.

Table 2 reveals the effect of the correlations observed in Table 1 on the intraclass correlations for both MZ and DZ twins by displaying correlations for both types of twins according to number of physical trait differences. Since so few MZ twins showed two or more physical trait differences, no significance can be attached to the lower intraclass correlations for the relatively dissimilar MZ twins, but DZ twins with above the modal number of physical differences (four or more) correlate only 0.01 on Value Orientation, whereas DZ twins with fewer physical differences correlate 0.30 on this trait.

TABLE 1. Correlations Between Number of Physical Trait[1] or Bloodgroup[2] Differences and Differences in Personality for DZ Twins

	Differences in physical traits (N = 110 pairs)	Differences in bloodgroups (N = 86 pairs)
Differences on 18 CPI scales	0.254*	–0.045
Difference in Person Orientation (extroversion)	0.014	0.100
Difference in Value Orientation (psychological stability)	0.212*	0.010

[1]Physical traits: height, eye color, hair color, hair type, baldness, site of baldness, handedness
[2]Bloodgroups: A, Le^a, s, C+C^w, JK^a, c, P, Fy^a
*P <0.05.

TABLE 2. Personality Similarity (Intraclass Correlations) for DZ and MZ Twins Classified According to Number of Physical Trait Differences

	DZ twins			MZ twins	
	0 or 1 (N = 26)	2 or 3 (N = 42)	4-7 (N = 43)	0 or 1 (N = 101)	2 or 3 (N = 13)
Person Orientation	0.12	0.15	0.19	0.52	0.32
Value Orientation	0.30	0.31	0.01	0.43	0.31

This array of correlations also shows that if twin comparisons are limited to those groups of MZ and DZ twins with the same degree of physical similarity, the heritability estimate for Value Orientation would be lower than that obtained when all MZ are compared to all DZ twins. Degree of physical similarity does not moderate MZ-DZ differences for the trait of Person Orientation since there was no correlation between these variables in the DZ twins.

The correlation between the bloodgroup differences and the physical trait differences measured in this investigation was only 0.02.

DISCUSSION

These results point to what may be a problem in the application of the twin method to the study of personality. The absence of any correlation between personality and genetic similarity (as judged by bloodgroup data), coupled with a significant correlation between personality and physical appearance, may mean that the personalities of MZ twins are more alike than the personalities of DZ twins for nongenetic reasons. However, not all personality traits show this pattern of results and no qualification may be necessary if twins are used to study Person Orientation (extroversion).

It is interesting to note that there is a positive correlation between difference in Person Orientation and difference in bloodgroups for the DZ twins. Number of bloodgroup differences is only a crude index of genetic similarity and perhaps, if the better measure of percentage of genes identical by descent were used, the correlation would reach an acceptable level of statistical significance. This work is currently underway.

A word needs to be said about the measure of physical appearance and the method of judging differences in appearance that are utilized in this investigation. We picked traits that, in our judgment, are used frequently in everyday life to distinguish individuals from one another. Each twin rated himself on these characteristics, and our comparisons of these ratings produced the difference measures. These traits and methods vary from those used by other researchers in this area. Carter-Saltzman and Scarr-Salapatek [1] used three techniques to generate measures of difference in physical appearance: 1) Twins responded to questions such as "Do you and your twin look as alike as carbon copies?". 2) Graduate student judges rated similarity from black and white photographs. 3) Actual measures of morphological variables such as stature, sitting height, skeletal age, weight, and upper arm circumference were taken. Height is the only physical trait common to both investigations, and the methods of judging differences do not overlap at all. This variance between studies may account for the fact that we did not obtain a significant correlation between differences in physical appearance and bloodgroup differences, whereas Carter-Saltzman and Scarr-Salapatek did find a relationship between their measures of these variables. However, the fact that our measures concentrated on various aspects of the head and face may have been responsible for the emergence of the significant correlation between physical appearance and personality. The contribution of each physical trait difference, taken alone, to differences in personality will be evaluated in a later report.

REFERENCES

1. Carter-Saltzman L, Scarr-Salapatek S: Blood group, behavioral, and morphological differences among dizygotic twins. Soc Biol 22:372, 1975.
2. Feinleib M, Christian JC, Borhani NO, et al: The NHLI twin study of cardiovascular disease risk factors: Methodology and summary of results. Am J Epidemiol 106:284, 1977.
3. Jablon S, Neel JV, Gershowitz H, Atkinson GF: The NAS-NRC twin panel: Methods of construction of the panel, zygosity diagnosis, and proposed use. Am J Hum Genet 19:133, 1967.
4. Lindzey G: Behavior and morphological variation. In Spuhler JN (ed): "Genetic Diversity and Human Behavior," Chicago: Aldine, 1967.
5. Nichols RC, Schnell RR: Factor scales for the California Psychological Inventory. J Consult Psychol 27:228, 1963.

Twin Research 3: Intelligence, Personality,
and Development, pages 127 – 130
© 1981 Alan R. Liss, Inc., 150 Fifth Avenue, New York, NY 10011

Twin Resemblances in Personality

Frank Barron
Department of Psychology, University of California, Santa Cruz

The search continues for an elegant taxonomy of personality traits. The usual method in modern research is the intercorrelation and subsequent factor analysis of person-descriptive terms, whether as they occur in the natural language and are revealed by clusters of approximate synonyms and antonyms (in a thesaurus, for instance), or as applied by persons to themselves, or as used by others to describe a given individual. Notably omitted in almost all such attempts is any attention to interpersonal dimensions (Leary [5], however, is an exception). The present study presents one possible method of approach to this problem, which becomes especially important to the twin method itself because of the well-known "'couple effect" [9].

The example to be presented in this paper employs the Gough Adjective Check List (ACL), a set of 300 personally descriptive adjectives or phrases, selected to represent established factors in personality traits. The list has been used extensively in research, both in pursuit of a comprehensive taxonomy of personality and in relation to creativity. Gough [3] has reported a meta-analysis of more than a dozen samples comprising several thousand persons for whom ratings and measurements of creativity were available. The present study is a novel application of the ACL to the problem of personality description in twins, with particular attention to zygosity-related self-descriptions and expectations of how one will be described by one's cotwin.

METHOD

A total of 61 pairs of like-sex Italian twins, 36 monozygotic (MZ) and 25 dizygotic (DZ) approximately equally divided between male and female pairs, were tested at the Mendel Institute in Rome. Valid data were obtained for 57–61 pairs for the Barron-Welsh Art Scale, the Perceptual Acuity Test, the Gottschaldt Figures, and the Child Esthetic Preference Test. The sample was reduced to 32 pairs for the M-threshold Inkblots and the Gough ACL, and to 28 pairs for the Franck Drawing Completion Test.

Acknowledgment is gratefully made to Paolo Parisi of the Mendel Institute in Rome for assistance in data collection and to James L. Dwyer for research assistance in data analysis. The study was supported financially by a grant from the U.S. Office of Education, Division of the Arts.

The twins were asked to go through the 300-item ACL under three different conditions: first, describing themselves; second, describing the cotwin as the cotwin would describe self; and third, guessing at which adjectives the cotwin would check under condition 2. These latter two conditions were inserted with a view to discovering whether accurate perception of twins by one another is related to their zygosity.

In what follows, we shall consider the Adjective Check List survey alone. An earlier, partial report of this analysis has been made, and some of the results are supported by the analysis of the perceptual and aesthetic measures on the larger sample [1].

For the ACL portion of the present study, 20 MZ and 12 same-sex DZ twin pairs participated. Complete data were gathered on seven MZ female pairs, 13 MZ male pairs, four DZ female pairs, and five DZ male pairs. The zygosity of the pairs was determined both from birth records and by serological examination with a high level of confidence. The age of the twins ranged from 18 to 25.

Each twin was asked to complete an Italian translation of the ACL. The twins checked the appropriate adjectives under three instructional sets: A) Check those adjectives which describe you. B) Check those adjectives which you expect your twin to use when he/she describes him/her self. C) Check those adjectives which you expect your twin to use when guessing your responses. This procedure resulted in a set of six ACL profiles or sets of checked adjectives for each twin pair. The six will be identified as A1, B1, and C1 for the abitrary first twin, and A2, B2, and C2 for the second twin.

Item Analyses

The adjectives for which a significantly greater proportion (P <0.05) of DZ profile comparisons were in disagreement (check on one profile and not on the other) than MZ profiles are presented in Table 1. The adjectives in Table 1 are ranked according to an estimate of H' computed from dichotomous data. It is most interesting that on the A1-A2 comparison the adjective *artistic* emerges prominently, and 67% of the variance in that trait is indicated to be genetic in origin. This supports a finding by Loehlin and Nichols [6] using the same list of adjectives.

The interpretation of the ACL results is rather complex. Some of the results of the overall comparisons are puzzling. When the twins describe one another (B1-B2), the MZ twins are more similar. When their self-descriptions are compared (A1-A2), however, there is no greater similarity among MZ twins. There are at least two possible explanations for this result. First, the self-description instructional set may be dominated by social desirability response styles that are not heritable when the description of the other twin is more objective. This line of reasoning would support a genetic explanation of the greater similarity of MZ twins on the B1-B2 comparison. Alternatively, the greater MZ twin similarity on B1-B2 may have resulted from a socialization experience that encourages identical twins to describe one another more similarly than do like-sex DZ twins.

TABLE 1. Adjectives Agreed Upon by a Significantly (P <0.05) Greater Proportion of MZ Twins Than DZ Twins—Crude Estimates of H′

A1–A2		B1–B2		C1–C2	
forgetful	0.838	slipshod	0.655	inventive	0.790
artistic	0.672	deceitful	0.639	absent-minded	0.745
honest	0.624	inventive	0.578	practical	0.578
informal	0.465	mild	0.397	hasty	0.431
wary	0.465	simple	0.397	greedy	0.397
interests wide	0.073	confused	≤0.000	leisurely	≤0.000
		evasive	≤0.000		
		peculiar	≤0.000		
		silent	≤0.000		
A1–B1		**A1–C1**		**B1–C1**	
A2–B2		**A2–C2**		**B2–C2**	
dreamy	0.600	wise	0.744	forceful	0.685
forgetful	0.524	mature	0.732	unselfish	0.577
capable	0.522	imaginative	0.675	conscientious	0.479
artistic	0.515	idealistic	0.601	imaginative	0.475
conscientious	0.462	unstable	0.574	self-denying	0.469
understanding	0.416	restless	0.559	dreamy	0.450
silent	0.282	confused	0.441	complicated	0.447
dependent	0.233	hasty	0.402	mature	0.412
		defensive	0.310	reliable	0.397
		reserved	≤0.000	stingy	0.367
		submissive	≤0.000	hasty	0.293
A1–B2		**A1–C2**		**B1–C2**	
B1–A2		**C1–A2**		**C1–B2**	
slipshod	0.733	absent-minded	0.489	temperamental	0.699
forgetful	0.579	forgetful	0.466	original	0.566
original	0.376	wise	0.466	peculiar	0.545
independent	0.342	hasty	0.398	evasive	0.328
loyal	0.296	emotional	0.368	leisurely	0.243
organized	0.234	confused	0.347	stingy	≤0.000
peculiar	0.216	artistic	0.252		
reserved	0.013	stingy	≤0.000		

The overall comparisons A1-B2, B1-A2, and B1-C2 may be seen as measures of the ability of one twin to take the role of the other twin. For this sample of twins it is clear that identical twins are much better at this task than are fraternal twins. Again, this result may be explained genetically or in terms of differential socialization of identical and fraternal twins.

Relevance to Artistic Potential Creativity

The most important aspect of the ACL analysis for our present concern is revealed in the sets of specific adjectives that show greater concordance among

MZ twins. As Table 1 shows, zygosity effects, taking all conditions into account, most frequently occur for adjectives like *artistic, inventive, dreamy, imaginative,* and *original,* all of which occur in various of the ACL scales developed to identify traits of the creative personality [2, 3, 4, 7, 8]. The indicated heritability, if these are considered as a cluster, is in the range of 0.60–0.80; thus approximately two-thirds of the variance in artistic creativity, assuming accuracy of self-description as well as description of self by cotwin, may be due to genetic factors.

REFERENCES

1. Barron F, Parisi P: Twin resemblances in creativity and in esthetic and emotional expression. Acta Genet Med Gemellol 25:213–217, 1976.
2. Domino G: Identification of potentially creative persons from the Adjective Check List. J Consult Clin Psychol 35:48–51, 1970.
3. Gough HG: A creative personality scale for the Adjective Check List. J Pers Soc Psychol 37:1398–1405, 1979.
4. Harrington DM: Effects of explicit instructions to "be creative," on the psychological meaning of divergent thinking test scores. J Pers 43:434–454, 1975.
5. Leary TF: "The Interpersonal Diagnosis of Personality." Princeton, New Jersey: Van Nostrand, 1957.
6. Loehlin JC, Nichols RC: "Heredity, Environment and Personality." Austin and London: University of Texas Press, 1976.
7. Smith JM, Schaefer CE. Development of a creativity scale for the Adjective Check List. Psychol Rep 25:87–92, 1969.
8. Yarnell TD: A common item creativity scale for the Adjective Check List. Psychol Rep 9:675–678, 1971.
9. Zazzo R: Les jumeaux: Le couple et la personne. Paris: Presses Universitaires de France, 1960.

Twin Research 3: Intelligence, Personality,
and Development, pages 131 — 136
© 1981 Alan R. Liss, Inc., 150 Fifth Avenue, New York, NY 10011

Heredity and Personality in Visual Perception

Silvia Borella

*Gregor Mendel Institute of Medical Genetics and Twin Research, Rome,
Italy*

INTRODUCTION

Visual perception, is considered in this study as part of the cognitive process and
as related to personality. According to the underlying principles here adopted [eg,
5, 14], perception represents the starting point of knowledge in that it consists in
the awareness of objects as they immediately appear to the subject, ie, in their concrete and singular dimension and according to a given "entirety" (we see at the
same time *chromatic* and *figural* qualities and *essential content* of the object). In
fact perception not only represents the beginning of a process, but it also prepares,
and somehow possesses, intellectual-cognitive contents. The heterogeneous com-
plexity of the perceptive content presumes in the subject a heterogeneity of functions responsible for the receiving of a specific category of content (color or form
or meaning). On the other hand visual perception, as an act involving the subject
as a whole, is an expression of his personality, this being the underlying principle
of projective personality tests based on visual stimulus [2:pp 405–410, 16].

In the realist schools of perception [see especially 3,9,10], as well as in Piagetian
operative theory [4,17] and the cognitive theories [11, 13, 15], visual perception is
considered to result from the more or less direct participation of all cognitive functions: From the organic sensorial, imagination, memory, to intelligence and,
indirectly, emotional functions.

Considering perception as a sole but heterogeneous act brings about a distinction of *levels* in the global phenomenon according to the categories of content
and the basic functions. We will consider here three perceptive levels: 1) A *"formal
level"* primarily involving *sensuous* functions (sensorial organs, imagination,
memory), ie, those mainly responsible for the awareness of the object's formal
qualities (surface, figure-background) perceived through its chromatic qualities. 2)
An *"objective level"* primarily involving *intellectual* functions, ie, those mainly
responsible for the awareness of the object's meaning. (Although memory may
play a role, this level is to be attributed mainly to the intellect in receiving the concrete essence of the object and in orientating the entire process.) 3) A *"subjective
level,"* less specific, involving *emotional* functions, ie, those mainly responsible for

the spontaneous choice of one form or meaning, or another, when the stimulus is indefinite enough to allow consistent perceptive synthesis, so that the choice is realized on the basis of internal subjective motivations [cf 2:pp 227–237, 20].

AIM, MATERIALS, AND METHODS

The present twin study was carried out aiming to contribute to the understanding 1) of a possible role of hereditary factors, and 2) of the extent of ego uniqueness in the process of visual perception. The following techniques have been used.

For the first two perceptive levels, *formal* and *objective,* three gestaltic figures of hidden content (Fig. 1) were shown to the subjects, one after the other, with the request that they identify the object represented. The progression of the subject's perception through to complete synthesis was probed by the interviewer through

Fig. 1. Drawings no. 1 and 3 have been shown by Koffka [12: p 187] and by Fabro [5: p 292], respectively, as examples of tasks requiring a high degree of perceptive articulation or organization. The perception of the object in drawing no. 3 is attributed by Fabro to the intellect which *sees* through the senses.

Drawing no. 2 has been taken from the Thurstone Figure Recognition Test [cf 1: p 99] and has been slightly modified following a first experiment. The upper spokes of the wheel have been removed so as to make the whole more ambiguous and arouse a clearer manifestation of constructive processes.

questions. The three figures represent: 1) the face of a smoker (Hazlitt), 2) a coach driven by a man (Thurstone), and 3) a man holding an object (Street). "Total form" and "meaning" are not immediate in these figures, so that processes of construction have to be considered and the experimemtal differentiation of the above perceptive levels becomes possible. The *formal* level, which would be attained in the initial perception, was evaluated by asking the subjects a) what part of the figure they saw first, b) whether the background seemed to be immediately integrated with the figure, and c) if they proceeded immediately to correct partial images. The *objective* level would be attained a) in the complete synthesis, achieved through the discovery of the meaning of the figure; and b) in the mental processes leading to the synthesis — these two aspects having been considered separately.

For the third perceptive level, *subjective*, Zulliger's Z-test [22] — easier to administer than Rorschach test — has been used.

The twin sample consisted of 30 monozygotic (MZ) and 25 dizygotic (DZ) pairs of twins, 15–30 years of age, selected at random from the Mendel Institute's twin register and with highly homogeneous environmental characteristics. Zygosity was assessed through the usual criteria, involving both the use of genetic markers and of subjective methods.

RESULTS AND DISCUSSION

First Perceptive Level: Formal-Sensuous (Gestaltic Figures)

Concordance vs discordance values in the two zygosity groups with respect to the initial perception, related to the formal qualities of the stimulus, are shown in Table 1. Concordance in the MZ, but not in the DZ series appears to be very significantly (P << 0.001) higher than what would be expected on the hypothesis of no zygosity effect, so that hereditary factors may be strongly suspected to play a role.

Second Perceptive Level: Objective-Intellectual (Gestaltic Figures)

Concordance vs discordance values in the two zygosity groups with respect to the second level of perception, related to the discovery of the meaning or the total perceptive synthesis, are shown in Table 2. No significant difference is found when MZ vs DZ pairs are compared (Table 2A). However, when the values observed in the twin pairs of the two zygosity groups are compared to those expected in

TABLE 1. Gestaltic Figures — Initial Perception

	Concordances		Discordances		
	Observed	Expected	Observed	Expected	Total
MZ pairs	65	45.8	25	44.2	90
DZ pairs	19	38.2	56	36.8	75
Total		84		81	165

$\chi_1^2 = 36.056$, P << 0.001.

TABLE 2. Gestaltic Figures — Perceptive Synthesis

A. MZ vs DZ pairs

	Concordances		Discordances		Total
	Observed	Expected	Observed	Expected	
MZ	40	37.4	19	21.6	59
DZ	31	33.6	22	19.4	53
Total		71		41	112

B. Twin pairs vs random pairs

	Concordances + +		Concordances − −		Discordances + −		Total
	Observed	Expected	Observed	Expected	Observed	Expected	
MZ	40	27.9	31	18.0	19	44.1	90
DZ	31	23.2	22	15.0	22	36.7	75
Total	71		53		41		165

$\chi^2_2 = 40.3$, P << 0.001.

random pairs, based on the frequencies recorded for individual twins (Table 2B), the difference is highly significant (P << 0.001). Therefore, the perceptive level of the synthesis and discovery of the meaning, while apparently not zygosity-dependent, seems to be significantly influenced by the structure of the pair (environmental factors).

The concordance analysis related to the mental processes leading to the perceptive synthesis is shown in Table 3. The processes (subjectively defined), were 1) concrete intuition, 2) overall judgment of similarity, 3) constructive-inductive reasoning, and 4) constructive-verifying reasoning. The comparison of observed to expected values in the two zygosity groups clearly shows these processes to be not zygosity-dependent. In both zygosity groups, discordance values are even much larger than concordance ones.

Third Perceptive Level: Subjective-Emotional (Z-Test)

Concordance vs discordance values in the two zygosity groups with respect to the third level of perception are shown in Table 4, separately for "location" or "first area chosen" for interpretation (Table 4A) and for "content" of the answers, ie, the activity of discovery of the meaning (Table 4B) — the two separate parts respectively corresponding essentially to the first and the second levels of the gestaltic figures. In contrast to the single content of the latter, here the subjects have options, and this activity of spontaneous choice can be considered as the special realm of emotion. Both for location and content, no zygosity effect is shown by the concordance analysis, while a strong individual component is indicated by the much higher discordance values in all cases, so that this perceptive level may be interpreted as expressing the uniqueness of each personality.

TABLE 3. Gestaltic Figures – Processes of Synthesis

| | Concordances | | Discordances | | |
	Observed	Expected	Observed	Expected	Total
MZ	13	12.9	27	27.6	40
DZ	10	10.1	21	20.4	31
Total		23		48	71

TABLE 4. Z-Test

A. Location (area chosen)

| | Concordances | | Discordances | | |
	Observed	Expected	Observed	Expected	Total
MZ	20	19.6	70	70.4	90
DZ	16	16.4	59	58.6	75
Total		36		129	165

B. Content

| | Concordances | | Discordances | | |
	Observed	Expected	Observed	Expected	Total
MZ	16	14.7	74	75.3	90
DZ	11	12.3	64	62.7	75
Total		27		138	165

CONCLUSIONS

The three perceptive levels considered appear to be in fact heterogeneous in respect to each other. Hereditary factors would play a role only in the initial level of perception, the one related to the object's formal qualities. The second level of perception, that involving intellectual functions, would instead appear to be largely influenced by environmental factors, although presumably in relation to the previous experience (gathered by memory) [8]. Nevertheless, the mental-perceptive process of synthesis appears to be a more individual and autonomous activity of the subject [cf 21:pp 1–27]. Finally, it is at the third level of perception, the one involved when there is a possibility of choice, that individual originality would seem to emerge. It may be at this level that the ego comes into the perceptive phenomenon, intended as an active and autonomous center of the personality, with its own dynamism capable of overcoming other forces, whether genetic or environmental in nature.

REFERENCES

1. Ancona L: "Dinamica della Percezione," 2nd Ed. Milan: Mondadori, 1976.
2. Bohm E: "Manual del Psicodiagnostico," 4th Ed. Madrid: Morata, 1971.
3. Cesa Bianchi M, Beretta A, Luccio R: "La Percezione. Una Introduzione alla Psicologia della Visione." Milan: Franco Angelo, 1977.
4. Cote ADJ: Piaget's recent formulations on perception and intelligence. Alberta J Educ Res 13:173–179, 1967.
5. Fabro C: "La Fenomenologia della Percezione." Brescia: Marcelliana, 1961.
6. Gedda L: "Lo Studio dei Gemelli." Rome: Orizzonte Medico, 1951.
7. Gedda L: "Twins in History and Science." Springfield, Illinois: CC Thomas, 1961.
8. Gedda L: Indagine sul primo ricordo. Acta Genet Med Gemellol 22:75–89, 1973.
9. Gemelli A: Funzioni e strutture psichiche. Riv Fil Neoscol, 1–52, 1936.
10. Gemelli A: La psicologia della percezione. Boll Fil 2:1, 1936.
11. Kanisza G, Legrenzi P: "Psicologia della Gestalt e Psicologia Cognitivista." Bologna: Il Mulino, 1978.
12. Koffka K: "Principi di Psicologia della Forma." Turin: Boringhieri, 1970.
13. Legrenti P et al: "Realtà e Rappresentazione. Percezione e Linguaggio nella Teoria Cognitivista." Florence: Giunti e Barbera, 1979.
14. Lerch P: "La Estructura de la Personalidad." Barcelona: Scientia, 1966.
15. Luria AR: "Cognitive Development." Cambridge, Massachusetts: Harvard University Press.
16. Perez IMA: Normalidad y anormalidad en la fisionomia psicoetica del adolescente. Percepcion y valoracion. Antropos 2:28–38, 1978.
17. Piaget J: "Les Mecanismes Perceptifs," 2nd Ed. Paris: PUF, 1975.
18. Piaget J: L'equilibration des structures cognitives. III: Quelques aspects du développement des structures sensori-motrices perceptives et spatiales. Et Epistem Gen 33:83–114, 1975.
19. Priorini P: Autonomia dell'Io da ereditarietà e ambiente. Minotauro 3:2, 1976.
20. Rorschach H: "Psychodiagnostic," 4th Ed. Paris: PUF, 1976.
21. Smith G: Twin differences with respect to the Muller-Leyer illusion. Lunds Universitet, anskruft NF And 50:1–27, 1953.
22. Zulliger H: "Z-Diapositive Test, Italian Adaptation to the 2nd Edition." Florence: Organizzazioni Speciali, 1960.

Twin Research 3: Intelligence, Personality,
and Development, pages 137 – 148
© 1981 Alan R. Liss, Inc., 150 Fifth Avenue, New York, NY 10011

Rorschach Test and the Myokinetic Psychodiagnosis of Mira y Lopez in Twins

M. Timsit, C. Bastin, and M. Timsit-Berthier
Department of Medical Psychology, University of Liège, Belgium

The present study aims at assessing the relative importance of genetic vs environmental factors in the determination of personality components and the fluctuations of their interactions as a function of time. Some methodological problems will also be considered.

MATERIAL AND METHODS

Twin Sample

A sample of 28 monozygotic (MZ) and 27 dizygotic (DZ) twin pairs has been collected with the help of a Social Medical Institute working with twins. This means that our twins have already participated in other medical studies and certainly are cooperative subjects, although they may not be entirely representative of the general twin population.

Table 1 shows the distribution of our sample by zygosity (assessed on the basis of genetic marker analysis), sex, and age group. It can be seen that the sample splits into two age subgroups, one of adolescents and young adults, 14–22, and one of adults, 25–65.

In order to rule out possible effects of socioeconomic and intellectual level, we administered to all of our twins the Raven Progressive Matrices. A clear correlation was found with age, younger twins having better scores. However, no significant difference was found between MZ and DZ twins ($t = 0.198$). Educational methods did also not differ between MZ and DZ twins. All pairs, except one, used to be dressed alike as children and most of them had shared their bedroom until the age of 14. However, more MZ than DZ pairs had slept in the same bed (21 vs 13).

Personality Tests

The tests used in the study were the Rorschach test and the Myokinetic Psychodiagnosis of Mira y Lopez (MKP), both projective techniques and, so to say, "trap

TABLE 1. The Sample

AGE	MZ PAIRS n=28		DZ PAIRS n=27	
	MALE	FEMALE	MALE	FEMALE
14-16	3	2	3	2
17-18	2	2	3	2
18-22	3	2	3	2
Subtotal 14-22	8	6	9	6
25-35	3	2	2	2
40-50	2	4	1	4
60-65	1	2	0	3
Subtotal 25-65	6	8	3	9
TOTAL	14	14	12	15

tests" in the sense that they do not allow the subject to guess the significance of responses. However, while the Rorschach is a verbal test, based on perceptual data and symbolic processes and aiming at revealing the structure and defense mechanism of the personality, MKP is a nonverbal kinesigraphic test based on motor data and aiming at revealing what Mira y Lopez defined as the "attitudinal formula."

The Rorschach test is too well known and familiar to describe it in detail. Let us just say that it consists in presenting inkspots and asking the subject what they look like. The ambiguity of inkspots favors the emission of responses. Evaluation of responses consists of symbols belonging to a precise code for locations, determinations, and contents.

The assmption underlying MKP is that any mental set corresponds to a muscular attitude that helps the execution of the movement through which, in turn, this mental set realizes. But this muscular attitude remains latent during overt action of the subject. It is only revealed by an exploration of the postural tonus. If the subject is requested to execute oscillatory movements without eye control-- that is, without being able to correct his direction and his extension—systematic deviations occur that reveal latent components of personality. According to Mira y Lopez [12], the deviations observed on the *dominant side* (according to lateralization of the subjects) reflect the *cultural aspects of personality*—ie, the voluntary and reactional aspects. The deviations observed on the *nondominant side* (nondominant) reflect the *innate aspects of personality* —ie, the instinctive and temperamental aspects. During the test, the subject is sitting in front of a table the inclination of which can be adjusted so that two positions are obtained: horizontal and vertical. Sheets with different tracings are successively put on the table. The subject is asked to follow the tracings with a pencil—at the beginning with the hand of dominant side, and then the other hand. On the first three trials, eye control is used, but from the fourth trial on, a screen is placed before the subject so that eye control is no longer available. The subject cannot see what he or she is doing until item ends at the tenth tracing.

The lineograms—the first data obtained in this way—consist of six lines, three for the right hand and three for the left hand, drawn on three planes of space, horizontal ones in the middle, sagittal ones at the bottom, and vertical ones above (Fig. 1). Tracings other than lineograms are zigzags (Fig. 2); stairs and circles, chains, parallels, and U's. The method of measurement consists in evaluating the deviations in terms of metric distances—primary deviations, secondary deviations, and length of lines—and, in terms of degrees of angles—axial deviations; but we will not insist on the technical aspects of the procedure. From the interpretation of the results, five main components of personality can be drawn: 1) extratensivity vs intratensivity, according to the external vs internal orientation of deviations on horizontal plane; 2) environment-oriented aggressivity vs self-oriented aggressivity,

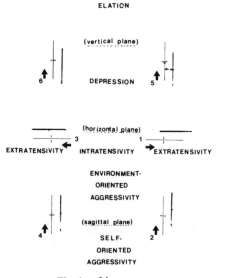

Fig. 1.   Lineograms.

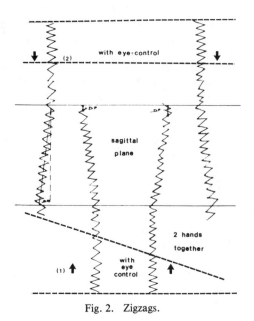

Fig. 2. Zigzags.

according to the front vs back orientation of deviation on sagittal plane; 3) psychomotor tonus with elation vs depression, according to the top vs bottom orientation of deviation on vertical plane; 4) excitation vs inhibition, according to the length of the line; and 5) emotivity, according to the amplitude of the secondary deviations.

We thought that this test could be very interesting in twin research. Our hypothesis was that tracings executed by the nondominant hand would be significantly more similar for MZ partners than for DZ partners, since they are, according to Mira y Lopez, the expression of temperamental tendencies. So we evaluated the differences between raw scores of MZ partners, and we compared them with those of DZ partners by nonparametric statistical methods (Chi-square Mann Whitney's U, Kolmogorov-Smirnov test).

RESULTS
Rorschach Test

The results obtained by means of the Rorschach test concerned essentially the location of the responses and their determination. Indeed, the score differences of "whole" and "space" responses for MZ partners were significantly less important than those of DZ partners (S, $P < 0.05$). We emphasize that this is seen only among the young population, which implies that the perception of the world is more similar in young MZ twins than in young DZ twins.

With regard to response determinant, significant results are found in MZ pairs. These concern young MZ subjects in all but one case: that of "movement" responses. Young MZ twins are characterized by a greater tendency to react similarly, when compared to DZ twins in situations where movement perception intervenes (S, $P < 0.05$). It is established that such responses, antithetic to "real" movements, reflect the capacity of internalization [16] through a fantasmatic process closely linked with the fundamental psychomotor components of personality (ie, postural tonus and attitudes [18]). Members of MZ pairs would thus share these central features.

Other response determinants for which statistics provide significant differences are "F%," the sum of "C" responses and "shadow" responses. The weaker values for intrapair differences are found, not in young MZ pairs, but in adult MZ pairs. The latter, to a greater extent than their homologous DZ, are characterized by the same tendency of the partners to use or not to use the "form" responses and, correlatively (as these response classes stand in an opposite relationship), the "color" and "shadow" responses for interpreting inkspots (S, $P < 0.05$).

It is known that "form" responses refer to a figurative activity that is little or not submitted to the imaginary life, whereas "color" and "shadow" responses indicate a psychic process that expresses the emergence of the affect and constitutes a qualitative expression of the amount of pulsional energy and its variations. It is interesting to note that while a certain number of results can be drawn from localization and determinant sources, the analysis of contents and the dynamic study of responses do not indicate any significant difference between MZ and DZ twins, among youngsters as well as adults.

MKP

For this test, it is at the level of the "extratensivity-intratensivity" dimension that heredity appears most obviously. The data collected for the nondominant hand are remarkably consistent: Among five measures, intrapair differences for young MZ twins appear smaller than in their homologous DZ. These differences are the axial deviations from egocipetal zigzags (S, $P < 0.05$), from sagittal egocifugal chains (S, $P < 0.05$), from upward vertical chains (S, $P < 0.02$), and from parallels (S, $P < 0.01$) (Fig. 3). In the adult population, on the contrary, intrapair differences for MZ twins are as important as those observed among DZ twins.

These results are obtained at the level of the nondominant or "temperamental" hand according to Mira y Lopez—that is, the hand that did not undergo the constraints of education—which strongly suggests the intervention of genetic factors in the determination of the "intratensivity-extratensivity" dimension.

Other dimensions of personality such as "aggressivity" and "excitation-inhibition" also appear significantly different between MZ and DZ twins, but these differences are found among adults and not among adolescents. So differences are obtained for primary deviations from sagittal lineograms and from zigzags on the side of the dominant hand (this allows one to evaluate the "actual" aggressive components), and intrapair differences are smaller in the adult MZ (S, $P < 0.05$ for both types of deviations).

Four measures of length of lines for zigzags and parallels for the nondominant

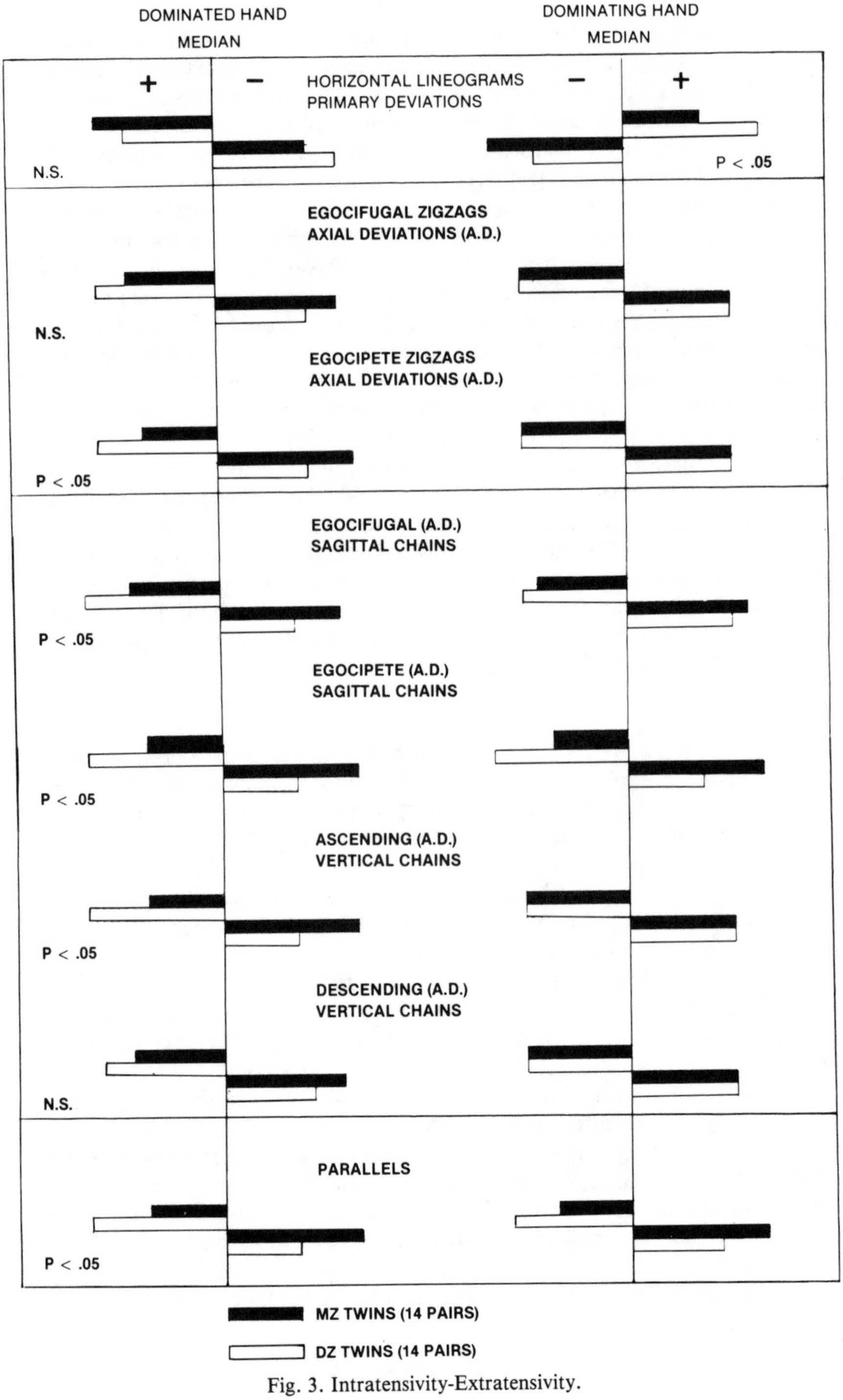

Fig. 3. Intratensivity-Extratensivity.

hand, and four measures for zigzags for the dominant hand show smaller differences in MZ adults. Such measures give information about the "excitation-inhibition" component.

A striking observation is that, on the contrary, no significant difference appears when one considers secondary deviations, which are, following Mira y Lopez, a measure of "emotivity." Such a result is made surprising by the fact that this dimension of personality is classically considered an inherited one, as far as the major form of hyperemotivity is considered (the "emotive type" of Dupre).

From all MKP data, those that support the more consistent interpretation refer to the "extratensivity-intratensivity" component of personality. This dimension clearly appears submitted to genetic determination and could thus be considered as a fundamental component. At the graphomotor level that is studied with the MKP, its meaning is to express the degree of opening to external world, which could refer, at least partly, to the notion of introversion-extraversion which is evaluated by other psychological techniques.

Progressive Matrices

Considering the data obtained with the Raven test, we see that differences between young MZ are significantly less important than those between their homologous DZ (Kd = 9 at the Kolmogorov-Smirnov test, P < 0.01). The same result, however, is not found when the scores of aged MZ partners are compared with those of their homologous DZ (Fig. 4).

Such a result calls for a double remark. First, the signification one should attribute to it will be considered. We conclude from the observed significant difference between score deviations for MZ twins that intelligence as a whole is submitted to the influence of hereditary factors.

The only thing we feel allowed to put forward is that those aspects of intellectual processes that Raven's test is measuring are likely to be dependent on genetic factors. Raven himself stressed that it would be an error to view the progressive matrices as a general intelligence test. This task appeared to him sensitive for evaluating an *observing capacity,* as well as *clarity* and *accuracy* in performing intellectual work. That such processes are under hereditary influence is consistent with the fact that, among all the adolescents of our study (MZ and DZ), only MZ partners showed very close scores, whereas both MZ and DZ twins are submitted to similar environmental influences: Most of them follow the same school life, with the same type of studies for both partners.

The second remark deals with the influence of age on this result. Before we consider, as we will later in the discussion, the hypotheses that would possibly account for the disappearance, in the adult, of an element the hereditary character of which seemed obvious in the adolescent, we shall question the fidelity of the test. According to the estimations made by the author himself, the fidelity coefficient of the progressive matrices (ie, between test and retest) diminishes with age. From 0.93 at ages under 30, it gets to 0.88 for subjects between 30 and 39, then goes down to 0.83 for people aged 50 or more [15]. Such a decrease would reflect the fact that intellectual activity tends to fluctuate the older the subjects are: In our population,

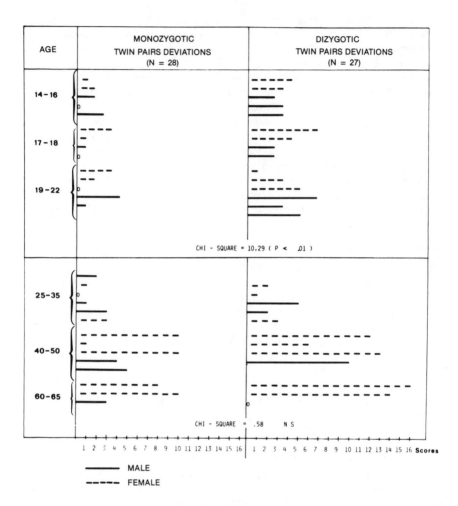

Fig. 4. Raven Progressive Matrix (Results).

such a variability of performance could mask the role of genetic factors in the determination of the capacities measured by the matrices. So, the increase as a function of age in the differentiation of scores for MZ partners, also seen in DZ partners, could be linked to some peculiarities belonging to the used test.

In summary, the two personality tests — Rorschach and MPK — and the progressive matrices enable us to draw a certain number of significant differences about monozygotic twins. The results we obtained are consistent with a hereditary

TABLE 2. Summary of Data

Procedures	Results	Population MZ twins	
		Young	Adults
Rorschach test	Location – W and S responses	+	
	Determinants – M responses	+	
	Determinants – F, color, and shadow responses		+
Myokinetic	Extratensivity-intratensivity	+	
Psychodiagnosis	Aggressivity		+
(Mira y Lopez)	Inhibition-excitation		+
Progressive matrices (Raven)	Level of intellectual processes	+	

character of the features referred to by these tests. The whole set of results is presented in a recapitulative table (Table 2).

DISCUSSION

A mere glance at Table 2 proves the fruitfulness of the method. Whichever test is used, positive results are collected. These undoubtedly favor the hereditary character of certain features, but are unequally distributed between the two groups of age that form our population. Such are the two facts we would now discuss, relating the obtained results to data from the literature, on the one hand, and evaluating the weight of the chronological variable, on the other.

As a matter of fact, the less surprising results are those obtained with the progressive matrices. They follow a long line of research about genetic influences on intellectual processes. It has been shown already that mental development was strongly submitted to genetic determinants during early life. This was based either on more concordant developmental curves in MZ than DZ twins [19] or on higher intra-pair correlation coefficient for MZ (0.92 for those reared together, 0.87 for those reared apart, against 0.53 for DZ reared together [3]). Factor analysis also revealed a variable influence of heredity according to the factor considered [11, 14].

More recently, a modified form of Raven's progressive matrices was given to 200 MZ and 260 DZ juvenile twin pairs, and to the parents of 320 of these pairs. All were tested individually. This study, in a preliminary analysis of raw total scores, reveals that a substantial progression of the variation therein (at least 50%) is attributable to additive gene action [8].

With the same perspective we can consider that data collected with the MKP for the "extratensivity-intratensivity" dimension widely agree with former conclusions about genetic determination of introversion-extraversion, though evaluated by different techniques [5]. Scarr [17] carried out a study on 28 pairs of DZ and 24 pairs of MZ twin girls aged 6–10. She was able to support the view that introversion-extraversion is the component of personality the most strongly submitted to genetic influences, as compared to other dimensions studied among the same population. This conclusion also belongs to Gottesmann [7], but was not confirmed by the recent Italian twin study carried out with an Italian translation of the Eysenck Personality Questionnaire (EPQ) on 603 pairs of twins. Extraversion differed in that a significant negative variance component for the effects of home environment was found [6].

From the data collected with the Rorschach test, only those referring to the mode of apprehension (location, W responses, and S responses) compare with results found in the literature. This type of response is indeed specific to some "perceptive mode" about which it is not uninteresting to mention that some authors report its hereditary determination. In 33 MZ pairs compared to 12 DZ pairs, 89% of the variance for this function was accounted for by hereditary factors [13]. In a large population (240 twins aged 5–11), MZ twins of different ages were found to present more similar types of exploration than did DZ twins [10].

However, we lack reference points as to the determinants that appear significantly more similar in the MZ twins we studied. We can nevertheless point out that most of our results are consistent with those Basit [1] obtained on 15 pairs of twins: This author reported that his intraclass correlation coefficient also was significant for M (movement responses), FM, FC, FC', and also for the F%.

The second point that appears to us worth discussing is the impact of the chronological variable on genetic determinism. It is puzzling to note that, using an identical technique of investigation, we found significant results in one age group and not in the other, and conversely. An "a priori" statement could consider that innate components are characterized by constancy and stability; this appears not to hold, but few studies have until now approached this highly complex question.

We shall point out that it is the adolescent group that bears the features whose hereditary character has been widely stressed in the literature: intellectual level (at the progressive matrices), apprehension type (at the Rorschach test), intratensivity-extratensivity (at the MKP), to which one should add kinesthesic ability (M responses at the Rorschach test). It is tempting to view all these features as referring to a perception phenomenon, closely linked with basal psychomotor components of personality. However, none of them gives rise to significant differences between adult MZ and their homologous DZ pairs. This leads one to think that they were modified through environmental influences, numerous and varied, among which parting of the twins seems to us a non-negligible releasing factor.

We know, indeed, through analysis of the interviews we made, that partners belonging to the adolescent group have about the same environmental influences. Most of them still live together, do the same studies, often in the same school, and spend their holidays with common friends. The adult twins, on the contrary, are separated, often because of the wedding of one of them. Their differentiation obtains through social relationships, first at the level of the family cell (spouse, children) and then with new friends and holiday mates. The differentiation is still more marked with professional relationship, as each of the twins exerts activities in a different place (even if their professions are identical).

The nature of the professional activity certainly constitutes a variable likely to modify the orientation, the intelligence type, and the mode of apprehension of external reality. It is thus probable that it results, as well as in modified social exchanges, in modified basal components of personality. Such are the mesological factors that seem to account for the disagreement between the results of young vs adult MZ twins.

In accounting for what is discovered as innate traits in MZ adults but unseen in MZ adolescents, it is helpful to consider that they are indices—bearing the label of "inneity" at the Rorschach test as well as at the MKP—referring (as a whole) to affective states: affective modulation by "color" and "shadow" responses at the Rorschach test, aggressivity at the MKP. Our opinion is that, as Zazzo [20] pointed out, at adolescence, a period of crisis, the twin bond—especially of the MZ kind—would constitute a powerful environmental force leading to differentiation from the partner. The result of that differentiation is, however, not definitely acquired, since after a transitory period inneity reappears.

What has just been discussed about the importance of the chronological variable in the evaluation of innate components of personality seems to belong for a large part to an area of research actually in progress. The present results fully confirm statements formulated by Eaves [4]: "Closer study, however, reveals that the expression of genetic factors in personality changes significantly with age. In particular, inherited differences in juvenile personality do not persist entirely into adulthood, and there are inherited differences in adult personality which are not apparent in juveniles. The higher order factors do not exhaust all the information about genetic differences which are reflected in the responses of subjects to items to different occasions."

ACKNOWLEDGMENTS

We wish to express our gratitude to Doctors P. Dodinval, Service de Génétique Humaine, and F. Pirnay, Laboratoire de Médecine et Hygiène Sociales, for their help to find the subjects of this study, and to H. Croisier-Mantanus, PhD, for her help in the English translation of this paper.

REFERENCES

1. Basit A: A Rorschach study of personality development in identical and fraternal twins. J Pers Assessm 36:23–27, 1972.
2. Bastin C: Etude des facteurs de personalité chez des jumeaux monozygotes et dizygotes, à l'aide du test de Rorschach et du psychodiagnostic myokinétique de Mira y Lopez. Mém Lic Univ Liège 1976 (ronéot).
3. Burt C: The genetic determination of differences in intelligence: A study of monozygotic twins reared together and apart. Br J Psychol 57:137–153, 1966.
4. Eaves LJ: Are personality traits stable? Third International Congress on Twin Studies, Jerusalem, 16–20 June 1980.
5. Eysenck HJ: The inheritance of extraversion-introversion. Acta Psychol 12:95–110, 1956.
6. Fulker D, Parisi P, Eysenck HJ, Gedda L: A comparative study of individual differences in personality. An Italian study. Third International Congress on Twin Studies, Jerusalem, 16–20 June 1980.

7. Gottesman II: Genetic variance in adaptative personality traits. J Child Psychol Psychiatry 7, 1966.
8. Heath AC, Eaves LJ, White PO, Last KA, et al: Preliminary findings from a study of the familial transmission of intelligence using juvenile twins and their parents. Third International Congress on Twin Studies, Jerusalem, 16–20 June 1980.
9. Johnson RC: Similarity in IQ of separated identical twins as related to length of time spent in same environment. Child Dev 34:745–749, 1963.
10. Matheny AP: Perceptual explorations in twins. J Exp Child Psychol 14:108–116, 1972.
11. Mikheev VF: The effects of heredity on the individual features of some memory processes. Voprosy Psykhologïe 4:51–67, 1972.
12. Mira y Lopez E: Le psychodiagnostic myokinétique. Ed Centre Psychol Appliquée, Paris. 1963.
13. Osborne R, Gregor AJ: The heritability of visualization, perceptual speed and spatial orientation. Percept Motor Skills 23:379–390, 1966.
14. Osborne R, Gregor AJ, Miele F: Heritability of numerical facility. Percept Motor Skills 24:659–666, 1967.
15. Raven JC: "Guide to the Standard Progressive Matrices." London: HK Lewis, 1963.
16. Rorschach H: "Psychodiagnostic." Paris: PUF, 1962.
17. Scarr S: Social introversion-extraversion as a heritable response. Child Dev 40:823–832, 1969.
18. Wallon H: "Les Origines du Caractère Chez l'Enfant." Paris: PUF, 1949.
19. Wilson RS: Twins: Early mental development. Science 175:914–917, 1972.
20. Zazzo R: "Les Jumeaux, le Couple et la Personne." Paris: PUF, 1960.

Twin Research 3: Intelligence, Personality,
and Development, pages 149–153
© 1981 Alan R. Liss, Inc., 150 Fifth Avenue, New York, NY 10011

Ego Phenomenology in the Human Twin

Luigi Gedda and Silvia Borella
Gregor Mendel Institute of Medical Genetics and Twin Studies, Rome, Italy

The study of human psychology carried out from the outside, on the basis of behavior, deserves being supplemented by a subjective approach to the *ego* [6,11,16]. We understand the latter as the central nucleus of personality and a center of freedom, also with respect to heredity and environment [12–14; see also 10]. It appears to us that ego phenomenology in twins may greatly contribute both to twin psychology and to the analysis of the ego [cf 7]. We have approached the problem through an oral survey, ie, through an interview designed to elicit and analyze the awareness of the own ego in each twin. The interviews took place at the Mendel Institute, where the twins had come for medical reasons, in a cordial and relaxed atmosphere, each twin being interviewed in the cotwin's absence.

A sample of 28 MZ and 20 DZ adult twin pairs was the object of our study. The interview involved two main points: 1) the analysis of the differences and similarities that the twin recognizes in himself with respect to the cotwin, to obtain a basic evaluation of his own ego, and 2) acceptance or rejection of the twin condition, in order to evaluate the influence of the twin condition on each twin.

RESULTS AND DISCUSSION

Basic Determination of the Ego

Overall subjective evaluation of the own ego with respect to cotwin.
Interestingly enough, most DZ as well as MZ twins consider themselves to be different from their cotwin in terms of overall personality (Table 1). This may reflect a wish to be, rather than awareness of being different, but even so may serve to elicit the nature of the ego in that it expresses a tendency of the ego toward differentiation that, although not realized, is persistent. It may be added that the few cases of twins defining themselves identical to the cotwin usually refer to individual twins, not to pairs, their cotwins usually defining themselves differently. Such a primary awareness of one's own ego would thus seem to be independent from the twin pair situation, and from zygosity.

Definition of divergent vs convergent characteristics with respect to cotwin. After considering their overall difference in respect to their cotwin, the subjects were asked to define *in which aspects* of personality they felt to be different and in which ones they felt to be similar to their cotwin. The answers were classed as 1) related to *rational* characteristics (such as intellectual or decisional attitudes or activities, largely dependent on the subject's will); 2) related to *infrarational* characteristics (such as psychosomatic reactions, states of mind, largely independent of the subject's will); and 3) related to the *twin relation* (eg, similarity can be seen in mutual affection, in mutual influence, in shared psychic times, whereas dissimilarity can be seen in a mutual relationship of dominance vs dependence.)

The results (Table 2) show the more divergent characteristics to be rational ones, both in DZ as well as in MZ twins, while infrarational characteristics are the only ones to show *inverse distributions* in MZ vs. DZ twins [cf 1]. Interestingly enough, it is the DZ twins, and not the MZ twins, who consider their mutual relationship as a factor of strong convergence — a finding that should be considered in the light of Zazzo's "couple effect" [2, 17; see also 3,5,9,].

Divergent or convergent characeristics with respect to basic ego. Table 3 shows the relation between the *basic* ego and its *particular* characteristics. It shows the reasons for the differences and similarities indicated by the twins in their self-awareness, classified as 1) reasons concerning internal factors of the ego, and 2) reasons concerning external factors of the ego. We have considered as internal factors the cases in which the characteristics of convergence or divergence are perceived as innate in the ego, ie, always present from the very beginning, or else as deriving from the autonomous action of the own ego in its specific choices and orientation. In the class of external factors we have considered cases in which the differences or similarities are attributed to the mutual influence of one twin on the other, or else to the situation of the pair or to historical or environmental circumstances like education, profession, being married or single, and so on.

The results (Table 3) are practically identical in the MZ and the DZ twins, thus clearly indicating that this self-awareness is not zygosity-dependent. The results also clearly indicate that the characteristics of divergence are perceived as the most internal to the ego, as compared to those shared with the cotwin, which are instead attributed largely to circumstances which affect the ego from the outside.

Evaluation of the Twin Condition

The results of the evaluation of the twin condition are shown in Tables 4 and 5, first in terms of acceptance vs rejection in MZ vs DZ subjects (Table 4), and then in terms of reasons for acceptance or rejection in the MZ subjects alone (Table 5), 75% of DZ subjects having been found to be indifferent, a situation that applied to none of the MZ subjects. Acceptance of the twin condition appears to be mainly determined by emotional reasons (company, mutual affection, remedy for solitude, etc), whereas rejection appears to be mainly due to pressures toward identity and lack of autonomy.

TABLE 1. Overall Subjective Evaluation of the Own Ego With Respect to Cotwin

Ego evaluation	MZ subjects N	%	DZ subjects N	%
Different	51	91	38	95
Identical	5	9	2	5
Total	56	100	40	100

TABLE 2. Definition of Divergent and Convergent Characteristics With Respect to Cotwin

Characteristics	MZ subjects (%) Divergence	Convergence	DZ subjects (%) Divergence	Convergence
Rational	66	44	66	46
Infrarational	19	40	26	15
Twin relation	15	16	8	38
Total	100	100	100	100

TABLE 3. Divergent or Convergent Characteristics With Respect to Basic Ego

Factors	MZ subjects (%) Divergence	Convergence	DZ subjects (%) Divergence	Convergence
Internal to the ego	88	45	87	45
External to the ego	12	55	13	55
Total	100	100	100	100

TABLE 4. Evaluation of the Twin Condition

Twin condition	MZ subjects (%)	DZ subjects (%)
Accepted	54	17
Rejected	46	8
Indifferent	0	75

TABLE 5. Reasons for Acceptance or Rejection of the Twin Condition in MZ Twin Individuals

Reason	Accepted (%)	Rejected (%)
Affection	87	12
Identity	7	88
Other	6	0

The following conclusions would seem to be in order: 1) MZ twins possess a basic awareness of their own ego as something unique and their own, and different from the cotwin's, similarly to what is found for DZ twins. 2) Also similarly to the DZ twins, MZ twins tend to consider the differences with respect to their cotwin as the substance which most intimately constitutes their own ego, while they tend to perceive the twin situation and the environmental circumstances as outside forces conditioning the ego toward homogeneity. In other words, both MZ and DZ twins tend to conceptualize the ego in terms of its special and unique qualities, and to locate factors of homogeneity as being outside of the ego. 3) The specialness of the ego would seem to be preponderantly located in the area of the higher faculties of personality, ie, those inherent to rationality. 4) The awareness of similarity to the cotwin with respect to the infrarational characteristics would therefore not affect, in the MZ twin, the prevalent tendency of the ego to recognize and assert its own original diversity. 5) The twin condition appears to have a markedly different value for the MZ and DZ twins. In the MZ twins, it characterizes the existential situation of the ego within the framework of emotional relations and the assertion of the self. Thus, the appreciation of the existence and the presence of the cotwin proceeds hand in hand with the authentic quest for one's own discrimination and autonomy.

REFERENCES

1. Brown AM, Stafford RE, Vandenberg SG: Twins: Behavioral differences. Child Dev 38: 1055–1064, 1967.
2. Cacciaguerra F: Studio sulle relazioni interpersonali nei gemelli. Acta Genet Med Gemellol 24:221–238, 1975.
3. Cacciaguerra F: Schema corporeo e comportamenti relazionali nei gemelli. Acta Med Auxol 89:223–234, 1976.
4. Canter S: Personality traits in twins. Unpublished paper delivered to annual conference of the British Psychological Society.
5. Cirillo S: The process of identity in twins. Acta Genet Med Gemellol 25:353–358, 1976.
6. Erikson EH: "Childhood and Society." 2nd Ed, New York: WW Norton, 1963.
7. Gedda L: Twins as object of science. What's New: 229, 1962.
8. Gedda L: Aspetti psicobiologici nei gemelli. Riv Neurobiol 10:4, 1964.
9. Koch HL: "Twins and Twin Relations." Chicago: Chicago University Press, 1966.
10. L'Ecuyer R: "Le Concept de Soi." Paris: PUF, 1978.
11. Loevinger Y: The meaning and measurement of ego development. Am Psychol 21:195–206, 1966.
12. Priorini P: Autonomia dell'io da ereditarietà e ambiente. Minotauro 3:2, 1976.
13. Russo L: Tre punti sulla questione del Sé. Minotauro 3:2, 1976.
14. Russo L: Dell'io spirituale. Minotauro 4:1, 1977.
15. Vandenberg SG: The contribution of twin research to psychology. Psychol Bull 66:327–352, 1966.
16. White LW: Competence and the psychosexual steps of development. In MR Jones (ed): "Nebraska Symposium on Motivation." Lincoln, Nebraska: University of Nebraska Press, 1960.
17. Zazzo R: The twin condition and the couple effects on personality development. Acta Genet Med Gemollol 25:343–352, 1976.

Twin Research 3: Intelligence, Personality,
and Development, pages 155—162
© 1981 Alan R. Liss, Inc., 150 Fifth Avenue, New York, NY 10011

Environmental Childhood Similarity and Similarity in Adult Personality and Neurotic Development in Twin Pairs

Svenn Torgersen
Norwegian Research Council for Science and the Humanities, Center for Research in Clinical Psychology, University of Oslo, Blindern, Norway

Originally the classical twin method assumed that the environment was not more similar for monozygotic (MZ) than for dizygotic (DZ) twin pairs. Hence, the more similar reactions in MZ than in DZ pairs had to be explained by the identical genetic makeup in MZ pairs. This assumption is of course no longer accepted. Studies have shown that MZ twin pairs are not only more similar in appearance and hence receive more similar environmental reactions; they are also more often dressed alike in childhood, are more often together, have more often the same friends, and, all in all, more often do the same things. The question is, when MZ twins not only are identical genetically, but also are exposed to a more similar childhood environment, is it then warranted to interpret the greater similarity in characteristics and reactions in MZ twin pairs as proof of the importance of genetic factors in the development of the characteristics or reactions?

One way of testing this "bias" in twin research is to investigate whether MZ twins who have been exposed to a more dissimilar environment also are more dissimilar than MZ twins who have been influenced by a more similar environment. And the same has to be done for DZ twins. It would be of special interest to compare MZ and DZ twin pairs with the same similarity in childhood environment.

Earlier studies have shown that similarity in childhood environment does not seem to make the twin partners more similar in personality, either in MZ or DZ twin pairs [1, 2, 4]. The results presented in this paper aim at confirming these results regarding personality, and also investigate whether the same is true with regard to concordance for neurotic reactions.

MATERIAL AND METHOD

This study is part of a nationwide study of all same-sexed twins born between 1910 and 1955 admitted to any of the psychiatric institutions in Norway, with a diagnosis of mild psychiatric disorder. All the twins (299 pairs) were personally interviewed, and were asked about the relationship to cotwin in childhood as well as later psychiatric symptoms.

A diagnosis formed on the basis of the information about symptoms and pathogenesis gathered during the interview and from the psychiatric records was given to the twins separately by three independent judges (one of whom is the author). A total of 229 twin probands, both female and male, were given a diagnosis of neurosis. The age ranged from 18 to 66, with a mean of 44 years. (See Torgersen [6] for more details about the procedure).

Both twins of 260 out of the 299 pairs returned a personality questionnaire that was given them during the interview. The personality questionnaire is meant to measure oral, obsessive, and hysterical personality traits [5].

Zygosity determination was based on the analysis of ten genetic markers for three-fourths of the pairs, and for all the twins on a questionnaire dealing with similarity in appearance, and how often and by whom the twins were mixed up in childhood. As there was an almost total correspondence between a zygosity determination by means of blood analysis and one by means of the questionnaire, the zygosity of the one-quarter of pairs without bloodtyping was determined by means of the questionnaire [3].

RESULTS

A childhood environmental similarity score was calculated according to the twins' answers to the questions about whether they had the same friends, whether they played a lot with each other, were strongly identified with each other, were spoken to as a unity, were dressed alike, and were in the same class at school.*

Table 1 and Figure 1 show that, as expected, the environmental similarity score is higher for MZ than for DZ twins. The distribution of the scores is different in the two twin groups. While the scores of the MZ pairs are J-curved, with a high similarity score for most of the pairs, the scores of the DZ pairs are more evenly distributed. Since the scores of the two twin groups overlap, it is possible to create parallel groups of MZ and DZ twin pairs with the same environmental similarity scores.

The mean intrapair difference of all the 17 personality traits is calculated for each twin pair, and the average of this composite personality difference score is calculated for three groups of MZ and DZ twins with the same environmental similarity scores.

Table 2 and Figure 2 show the average composite intrapair difference in personality in the three groups of MZ and DZ twin pairs with different environmental similarity scores. We see that the intrapair difference in personality is completely unrelated to similarity in childhood environment for both the MZ

*No information about childhood environmental similarity was obtained for one of the 229 probands.

Table 1. Distribution of Childhood Environmental Similarity Scores in MZ and DZ Twin Pairs

Environmental similarity	MZ pairs		DZ pairs	
	N	%	N	%
0–11	—	—	5	3.6
12–15	2	2.2	10	7.3
16–19	1	1.1	14	10.2
20–23	3	3.3	17	12.4
24–27	5	5.5	18	13.1
28–31	6	6.6	29	21.1
32–35	10	11.0	25	18.2
36–39	22	24.2	15	10.9
40–43	42	46.2	4	2.9
Total	91[1]	100.1	137[1]	99.7

[1] The twin pair is represented two times in the table if both twin partners are probands.

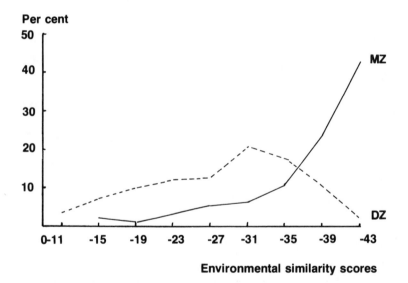

Fig. 1. Distribution of childhood environmental similarity scores in MZ and DZ.

and DZ twin groups. Furthermore, irrespective of the similarity in childhood environment, MZ twins are, as measured by our questionnaire, significantly more similar than DZ twins in personality.

The concordance for neurosis, calculated according to the proband-wise method, was also measured in the three groups of environmental similarity scores. We see from Table 3 and Figure 3 that the concordance in DZ pairs is much the same irrespective of whether the twins' childhood environment was similar or dissimilar. For MZ twins, however, the concordance is much lower

Table 2. Relationship Between Childhood Environmental Similarity Scores and Intrapair Difference of 17 Personality Traits in MZ and DZ Twin Pairs

Environmental similarity	MZ pairs			DZ pairs			
	N	Mean diff.	sd	N	Mean diff.	sd	z-score
0–31	21	3.7	1.24	108	4.5	1.32	2.62***
32–36	19	3.5	1.27	31	4.3	1.34	2.12**
37–43	65	3.8	1.29	16	4.6	1.53	1.93*

*P<0.05.
**P<0.02.
***P<0.005.

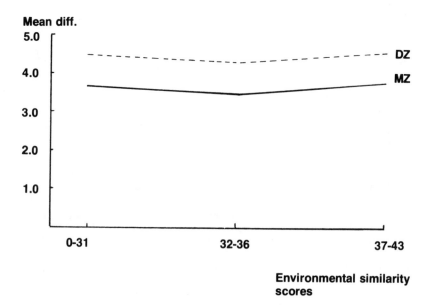

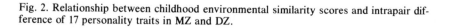

Fig. 2. Relationship between childhood environmental similarity scores and intrapair difference of 17 personality traits in MZ and DZ.

Table 3. Relationship Between Childhood Environmental Similarity Scores and Concordance for Neurosis in MZ and DZ Twin Pairs

| Environmental similarity | Concordance | | | | |
| | MZ pairs | | DZ pairs | | |
	N	%	N	%	MZ/DZ ratio
0–31	4/17	23.5	28/93	30.1	0.8
32–36	10/17	58.8	7/28	25.0	2.4
37–43	24/57	42.1	5/16	31.3	1.3
Total	38/91	41.8	40/137	29.2	1.4

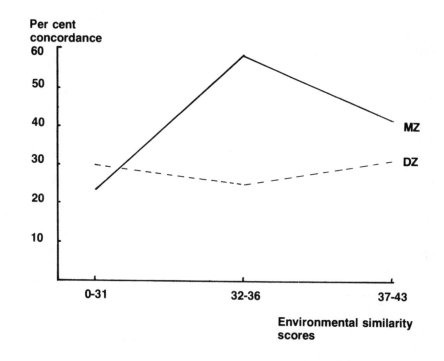

Fig. 3. Relationship between childhood environmental similarity scores and concordance for neuroses in MZ and DZ.

Table 4. Relationship Between Childhood Environmental Similarity Scores and Concordance for any Psychiatric Disorders in Cotwins of MZ and DZ Neurotic Probands

| Environmental similarity | Concordance | | | | MZ/DZ ratio |
| | MZ pairs | | DZ pairs | | |
	N	%	N	%	
0–31	7/17	41.2	35/93	37.6	1.1
32–36	10/17	58.8	10/28	35.7	1.6
37–43	30/57	52.6	5/16	31.3	1.7
Total	47/91	51.6	50/137	36.5	1.4

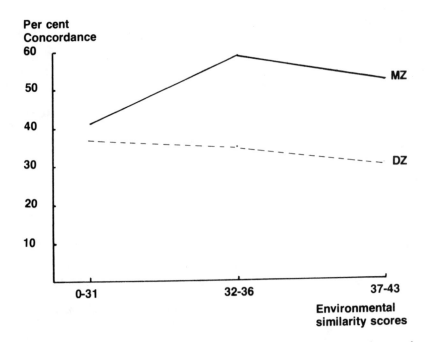

Fig. 4. Relationship between childhood environmental similarity scores and concordance for any psychiatric disorders in cotwins of MZ and DZ neurotic probands.

when the childhood environment was very different; in fact, the concordance for neurosis is lower for MZ than for DZ twins when the childhood environment was very different. When the similarity in childhood environment was moderately high or high, the concordance for neurosis in MZ twins is all the time clearly higher than for DZ twins.

In Table 4 and Figure 4 an extended concordance concept is used where concordance is defined as any psychiatric diagnosis in cotwin. We see that this analysis gives more or less the same results as when concordance is defined as neurosis in cotwin.

DISCUSSION

As measured by this study, environmental intrapair similarity is found to be unrelated to intrapair similarity in personality. This result is also supported by earlier studies. Irrespective of similarity in childhood environment, MZ twins are more similar in personality than DZ twins. [1, 2, 4].

An analysis of concordance in psychiatric disturbances in pairs where the proband had been admitted to a psychiatric institution for neurotic reactions gave, however, a more complex result. While concordance in DZ twin pairs was unrelated to similarity in childhood environment, concordance in MZ twin pairs was much lower when the childhood environment of the twin partners was dissimilar. Consequently, the difference in concordance between MZ and DZ twin pairs disappeared when the childhood environment was dissimilar for the twins.

How should these results be explained? One interpretation may be that the MZ twin pairs with very dissimilar childhood environments were wrongly diagnosed as MZ and were in reality DZ twins. This interpretation is hardly correct, because the results for personality differences showed that MZ pairs with dissimilar childhood environment were no different from MZ pairs with more similar childhood environment.

Perhaps the results may be explained by an interactionistic view upon the development of neurosis. If both environment and heredity contribute to the neurotic development, a similar childhood environment as well as an identical genetic makeup will be necessary for a high concordance rate in MZ twin pairs.

Even if the numbers in each childhood environmental group are small for statistical testing, the results of the present study point to the importance of taking into account the similarity of environment when the results of twin studies are interpreted. Twin studies will give quite different results according to how much environmental variation the study permits. A very similar environment within the twin pairs may result in quite different concordance rates between MZ and DZ pairs. Conversely, a very different childhood environment for the twin partners may give no difference in concordance between MZ and DZ pairs. Consequently, a universal estimate of the relative contribution of heredity and environment in the development of neurosis is impossible by means of the classical twin method.

REFERENCES

1. Loehlin JC, Nichols RC: "Heredity, Environment and Personality. A Study of 850 Sets of Twins." Austin and London: University of Texas Press, 1976.
2. Matheny AP Jr, Wilson RS, Brown Dolan A: Relations between twins' similarity of appearance and behavioral similarity: Testing an assumption. Behav Genet 6:343–351.
3. Torgersen S: The determination of twin zygosity by means of a mailed questionnaire. Acta Genet Med Gemellol 28:225–236, 1980d.
4. Torgersen S: The oral, the obsessive and the hysterical personality syndromes. An investigation of hereditary and environmental factors by means of the twin method. Arch Gen Psychiatry (in press), 1980a.
5. Torgersen S: Heredity - environmental differentiation of general neurotic, obsessive and impulsive hysterical personality traits. Acta Genet Med Gemellol 29:193–207, 1980.
6. Torgersen S: Genetics of neuroses. (submitted for publication), 1981.

Twin Research 3: Intelligence, Personality,
and Development, pages 163–168

A Genetic and Environmental Analysis of Obsessionality in Normal Twins

C. A. Clifford, D. W. Fulker, and R. M. Murray

Department of Psychology (C.A.C., D.W.F.) and Department of Psychiatry
(R.M.M.), Institute of Psychiatry, London

This paper reports on an investigation into genetic and environmental influences on individual differences in obsessional behaviour, as measured by the Brief Leyton Obsessional Inventory [1,11]. This inventory, which was devised to measure obsessional tendencies in both normal and patient populations, has been shown to yield four five-item subscales concerned with four type of obsessional behaviour [1]. The first of these subscales reflects a feeling of dissatisfaction and incompleteness caused by a failure to carry out everyday tasks to an internal standard of perfection. The second is concerned with excessive cleanliness and tidiness, the third relates to recurring intrusive thoughts of an unpleasant and gloomy nature, and the final subscale relates to constant repetition and checking.

The trait of obsessionality has been shown to relate to the more general trait of neuroticism [6]. In the present paper we explore this relationship further and report the results of giving the Leyton and the neuroticism scale of the Eysenck Personality Questionnaire (EPQ) [2] to 404 pairs of twins drawn from the Institute of Psychiatry's Volunteer Twin Register.

The register, which has been described in detail elsewhere [7] comprises male and female monozygotic (MZ) and dizygotic (DZ) twins as well as a number of opposite-sex pairs. It reflects the common bias in favour of MZ twins and females found in volunteer twin registers [8]. The subjects covered a wide age range from 16 to over 70 years of age, with a mean age of 31.3 years and a standard deviation 12.4.

The method of analysis we employed was a form of Jöreskog's maximum likelihood confirmatory factor analysis [5] adapted for use with genetic and environmental covariance matrices [3,9,10]. The raw data for the analysis were between- and within-pair mean cross-product matrices derived from a multivariate analysis of variance of the five measures for each of the twin types in

TABLE 1. 5 × 5 Covariance Matrices and Their Associated Degrees of Freedom

Between-pair mean cross-product matrix for MZ male twins				
1	6.9317	2.8239	2.0622	2.2562	6.0667
2	2.8239	4.6113	0.4097	1.1555	3.8539
3	2.0622	0.4097	3.8343	1.3825	4.5436
4	2.2562	1.1555	1.3825	3.5604	2.9758
N	6.0667	3.8539	4.5436	2.9758	77.8252

df = 67

Within-pair mean cross-product matrix for MZ male twins				
1	3.3623	0.7391	0.1594	0.8406	−1.0870
2	0.7391	3.1014	0.2319	0.6087	0.1159
3	0.1594	0.2319	1.8986	0.7681	1.8116
4	0.8406	0.6087	0.7681	2.5072	0.3333
N	−1.0870	0.1159	1.8116	0.3333	33.2754

df = 69

There are ten matrices in all, two for each of the twin types: MZ male and MZ female; DZ male, DZ female, and opposite-sex pairs.

TABLE 2. Expectations of Mean Cross-Products of ANOVA of MZ and DZ Twins

MZ	Between pairs	$VSE_{ij} + 2VA_{ij}$
	Within pairs	VSE_{ij}
DZ	Between pairs	$VSE_{ij} + 1\frac{1}{2} VA_{ij}$
	Within pairs	$VSE_{ij} + \frac{1}{2} VA_{ij}$

$VA_{ij} = VA_i^{1/2} RA_{ij} VA_j^{1/2}$
$VSE_{ij} = VSE_i^{1/2} RSE_{ij} VSE_j^{1/2}$

the study. One of these five pairs of covariance matrices, together with the associated degrees of freedom, is shown in Table 1 to illustrate the form of the data.

Carrying out a genetic and environmental factor analysis of the structure of these covariance matrices involves first specifying an appropriate genetic and environmental model in terms of components of covariation and then explaining the psychological structure of these two components in terms of a factor model. In general it has been found that both normal and abnormal personality traits follow the simplest of genetic and environmental models in which there is only additive genetic variance characteristic of random mating and specific environmental variance unique to the individual [11]. This simple model involves two kinds of parameters: VA_{ij}, the additive genetic covariance, and VSE_{ij}, the specific environmental covariance where the subscript i and j run from 1 to 5 according the variables involved.

On the assumption that this model is equally appropriate to male and female subjects, the expectations of the mean cross-products are shown in Table 2. These components of covariance may be reparameterized for convenience as variance components and correlations as shown at the foot of the table, where RA_{ij} is the additive genetic correlation, RSE_{ij} the environmental correlation,

TABLE 3. Components of Variance and Genetic and Environmental Correlations for Mean Cross-Product Matrices in Table 1

	Genetic correlation matrix (RA_{ij})				Variance component (VA_{ij})
1	1.00	0.57	0.43	0.80	0.50	1.45 ± 0.22
2		1.00	0.23	0.30	0.38	2.04 ± 0.24
3			1.00	0.24	0.64	1.66 ± 0.24
4				1.00	0.48	1.01 ± 0.14
N					1.00	25.13 ± 3.17

SE of correlations 0.10 or less

	Environmental correlation matrix (RSE_{ij})				Variance component (VSE_i)
1	1.00	0.26	0.28	0.18	0.09	3.20 ± 0.19
2		1.00	0.09	0.22	0.04	2.70 ± 0.20
3			1.00	0.50	0.19	2.43 ± 0.18
4				1.00	0.05	1.57 ± 0.10
N					1.00	34.38 ± 2.32

SE of correlations 0.05 or less

Model fit: $\chi^2_{120} = 43.26$, P = 0.9.

and VA_i and VSE_i are the genetic and environmental components of variance. As a preliminary step, this version of the model was fitted to the mean cross-product matrices using a maximum likelihood procedure which minimizes the log likelihood ratio statistic

$$\chi^2 = \sum_{i=1}^{10} (\log_e (\det EC_i/\det C_i) + \text{trace}C_i\ EC_i^{-1} - p)$$

where EC_i = ith expected mean cross product matrix, C_i = ith observed mean cross product matrix, and P = number of variates (5). The components of variance and the correlation matrices are shown in Table 3.

The simple genetic and environmental model fitted very well, $\chi^2_{120} = 43.26$ p = 0·9. Genetic correlations are moderate to substantial and all are highly significant. Environmental correlations are smaller but a number of them are still highly significant. The genetic correlations amongst the four scales of the Leyton are all positive but vary in size ranging from 0·23 to 0·80, suggesting the presence of a general obsessional factor as well as considerable specific variation for each of the subscales.

Of particular interest are the substantial correlations with N which are all greater than 0·37, indicating that this general factor may in large part be explained by the general factor of neuroticism. Table 4 shows the heritability estimates obtained from this analysis for each of the four subscales and for N.

In order to explore the structure of the genetic and environmental correlation matrices in more detail, a further reparameterization was carried out in terms

TABLE 4. Heritability Estimates From the Simple Genetic and Environmental Model

	$h_n^2 = VA_i/(VA_i + VSE_i)$
1 Dissatisfaction and incompleteness	0.31
2 Cleanliness and tidiness	0.43
3 Unpleasant and gloomy thoughts	0.41
4 Checking and counting	0.39
N Neuroticism as measured by EPQ	0.42

of a factor model. Uncorrelated factors were fitted to both the genetic and environmental covariances, the first being forced to loading on N but the second excluding N, the loading on N for the second factor being set to zero. In addition, specific variances were specified for each of the four subscales of the Leyton and for N, but only in the environmental structure where the presence of error variation requires it. The structure of this model is shown in Table 5. The aim of these restrictions on the factor structure was to identify the first factor in the genetic structure with N, allowing us to partial out neuroticism and assess more accurately the importance of the independent contributions of the subscales of the Leyton. This model was fitted to the mean cross-product matrices using the maximum likelihood procedure. The goodness of fit was again very good, $\chi_{123}^2 = 47.9$ p = 0.9. The majority of the loadings and specific variances were highly significant and their contributions to genetic and environmental variance are shown in Table 6. The loadings and specific standard deviations are shown in units appropriate to the genetic and environmental correlation matrices.

As far as the genetic correlation matrix is concerned, there are clearly two general factors of obsessionality. The first factor is identified with a general trait of neuroticism most strongly relating to scale 1, dissatisfaction and incompleteness, and scale 3, which represents a depressive component of gloomy, guilty, and unpleasant thoughts. The second factor, which is independent of N, represents all that is general to the four subscales once N has been partialed out. This factor relates mostly to scales 1 and 4. When we examine the loadings we can see that the first factor is truly general in that all the loadings are positive, and that the second factor contrasts subscales 1, 2, and 4 with subscale 3, the loading for this being negative. Thus this factor contrasts the obsessional personality traits of cleanliness, tidiness, and checking, and to some extent incompleteness, with a depressive component. In addition to these two general factors, a substantial amount of genetic variation is specific to the subscales, ranging from 23% to 65%, emphasizing the unique hereditary nature of the various forms of obsessional behaviour measured by the subscales. In summary, the hereditary component in obsessional traits and symptoms reflects a complex of genetic effects relating to neuroticism, a general obsessional personality independent of neuroticism, and specific factors relating to the four subscales.

TABLE 5. Factor Structure of Genetic and Environmental Covariances

	Genetic			Environmental		
	1st factor	2nd factor	Specific variance	1st factor	2nd factor	Specific variance
1	1	1	1	1	1	1
2	1	1	1	1	1	1
3	1	1	1	1	1	1
4	1	1	1	1	1	1
N	1	0	0	1	0	1

TABLE 6. The Structure of the Genetic and Environmental Correlation Matrices

	Proportions of variance (VG = 1.0)			Loadings of RG		
	1	2	Specific			
1	0.4204	0.3506	0.2290	0.6484	0.5921	0.4785
2	0.1825	0.1696	0.6479	0.4272	0.4118	0.8049
3	0.4820	0.1122	0.4058	0.6943	−0.3335	0.6370
4	0.1375	0.5492	0.3113	0.3708	0.7411	0.5597
N	1.0000	0.0000	0.0000	1.0000	0.0000	0.0000
	Proportions of variance			Loadings of RE		
	1	2	Specific			
1	0.0576	0.8805	0.0619	0.2400	0.9384	0.2488
2	0.0014	0.0949	0.9038	0.0374	0.3081	0.9507
3	0.9862	0.0138	0.0000	0.9931	0.1175	0.0000
4	0.4335	0.0102	0.5563	0.6584	0.1009	0.7459
N	0.0315	0.0000	0.9685	0.1775	0.0000	0.9841

The environmental correlation matrix is less clear and suggests a plethora of specific effects. We have not forced the first factor to be identified with N in the same way as it was in the genetic correlation matrix, and this is reflected in the loadings and the proportions of variance. As far as the genetic structure is concerned, we can assume that N is an errorless predictor of genotypic effects, and hence exclude a specific term in our factor model. This is not possible with respect to environmental variation unless we assume that the N scale is completely reliable. Since 20–30% of variance in individual differences in N is attributable to error, something in the region of 50% of the environmental variation in N would be expected to reflect this error of measurement. In short, we cannot omit the specific variance in our environmental model. In the environmental correlation matrix, factor 1 is most clearly identified with subscale 3 and to some extent with 4, but hardly at all with 1, 2, and N. Factor 2 is almost completely identified with 1; 2 and N only appear substantially as specific effects. The result of the analysis then appears to indicate an absence of general factors and emphasizes specific effects as far as environmental causes of obsessionality are concerned.

In conclusion, our analysis quite clearly shows that, although genetic effects are somewhat less important than environmental ones, those systematic features that underly obsessionality as a trait depend on genetic rather than environmental causation. This finding suggests that etiological studies of obsessionality would benefit from focusing on genetic rather than environmental causes.

REFERENCES

1. Cooper et al: Manuscript in preparation, 1980.
2. Eysenck SGB, Eysenck HJ: Manual of the E.P.Q. (Eysenck Personality Questionnaire). London: University of London Press, 1975.
3. Fulker DW: Multivariate extensions of a biometrical model of twin data. In Nance WE (ed): "Twin Research: Psychology and Methodology." New York: Alan R Liss, 1978, pp 217–236.
4. Fulker DW: Some implications of biometrical genetical analysis for psychological research. In Royce JR, Mos LP (eds): "Theoretical Advances in Behaviour Genetics." Alphen, Netherlands: Sijthoff and Noordhoff, 1979.
5. Jöreskog KG: A general approach to confirmatory maximum likelihood factor analysis. Psychometrika 34:183–202, 1969.
6. Kendell RE, Discipio WJ: Obsessional symptoms and obsessional personality traits in patients with depressive illness. Psychol Med 1:65–72, 1970.
7. Lader M, Kendell R, Kasriel J: The genetic contributions to unwanted drug effects. Clin Pharmacol Ther 16:343–347, 1974.
8. Lykken DT, Tellegen A, DeRubeis R: Volunteer bias in twin research: The rule of two-thirds. Soc Biol 25:1–9, 1978.
9. Martin NG, Eaves LJ: The genetical analysis of covariance structure. Heredity 38:79–95, 1977.
10. Martin NG, Eaves LJ, Fulker DW: The genetical relationship of impulsiveness and sensation seeking to Eysenck's personality dimensions. Acta Genet Med Gemellol, 1980 (in press).
11. Murray RM, Clifford C, Fulker DW, Smith A: Is there a genetic contribution to obsessional traits and symptoms. In Ming T (ed) "Genetics: Issue in the Psychosocial Epidemiology Monograph Series". New York: Academic Press, 1980.

Twin Research 3: Intelligence, Personality,
and Development, pages 169 – 174
© 1981 Alan R. Liss, Inc., 150 Fifth Avenue, New York, NY 10011

Twin-Family Studies of Common Fears and Phobias

Richard J. Rose, Judy Z. Miller, Michael F. Pogue-Geile, and Gilbert F. Cardwell

Department of Psychology, Indiana University, Bloomington, (R.J.R., J.Z.M., M.F.P.-G.), and Department of Psychology, DePaul University, Chicago (G.F.C.)

INTRODUCTION

A century ago, Charles Darwin accompanied his son, then 2 years and 3 months old, to the Zoological Gardens where he witnessed the child's unexpected alarm of large, caged animals. Unable to account for his son's sudden fear, Darwin asked: "May we not suspect that the . . . fears of children, which are quite independent of experience, are the inherited effects of real dangers . . . during ancient savage times?" [8] Do genetic predispositions underlie fears that were adaptive for our ancestors? Are humans, like other species [13, 14, 20], biologically prepared to exhibit fears that once promoted avoidance of real dangers? Using twin-family data, we here report an evaluation of genetic bases of fears and phobias. Our results document genetic contributions to the transmission of common fears that may have been of adaptive significance in early species survival.

Some specific fears are highly prevalent in the population; fears of snakes were expressed by over one-third of the adults interviewed in a house-to-house survey in Burlington, Vermont [2]. What process underlies the transmission of such common fears? The traditional answer has been sought in models of conditioned learning. That individuals come to fear those stimuli that are repeatedly associated with painful consequences had been an accepted fact for a half-century, and demonstrations of conditionable fear [24] are standard references in textbook accounts of human phobias. There are, however, serious limitations to conditioning models [17, 21, 25], of which the most obvious is the selectivity of common human fears. The situations frequently feared are not those most frequently associated with aversive consequences in everyday life.

Supported by a grant-in-aid from Indiana University to the first author and by the Indiana University Human Genetics Center, PHS GM 21054. We thank Meloni M. Muir and Rachel M. Loop for help with data collection.

Common fears—closed and dark spaces, deep water, snakes, thunderstorms—are limited in number and invariant in development. Their developmental histories appear unrelated to the individual environment within which development occurs. The age at which children exhibit particular fears, such as that of strangers or of the dark, reveals a normative regularity not expected if the fears are acquired in the idiosyncratic experience of each child. Nor can it be argued that such regularity reflects the development of a generalized fear response, since different fears mature at different ages. Epidemiological surveys reveal significant differences in the onset, duration, and stability of different fears. Some, eg, fear of strangers or of darkness, are common only in childhood; acquired early, they extinguish readily, and their prevalence among adults is near zero. Others, eg, fears of snakes or storms, also exhibit peak incidence in early childhood, but once acquired, they prove resistant to extinction and remain prevalent throughout adult life [1].

What accounts for marked variation in the adult prevalence of different classes of fears? Why are there apparent differences in the ease with which different fears extinguish? One hypothesis is that of biological preparedness [22]. Men and animals may be prepared by their evolutionary histories readily to exhibit some fears and unprepared to exhibit others. Prepared fears may represent unlearned reactions to specific stimulus configurations, or, alternatively, prepared learning for which minimal, nonspecific experience is requisite; in either case, they will prove resistant to change. By contrast, fears that are biologically meaningless will require extensive individual conditioning histories, will remain unstable, and will extinguish when the relevant environment changes.

Behaviors subjected to a weak stabilizing form of selection are expected to exhibit a relatively high degree of genetic variability as equilibrium is approached [3, 5]. Once highly directional, we assume that selective action on adaptive fears is now stabilized, so that variance in contemporary populations is around an intermediate level of fearfulness. Accordingly, such fears should exhibit significant familial aggregation in patterns consistent with genetic transmission. Thus we infer that biological preparedness underlies common fears for which, in the context of significant parent-offspring resemblance, conventional analyses of identical and fraternal twins yield evidence of heritable variation.

MATERIALS AND METHODS

To evaluate these ideas, we administered a fear survey schedule to twins and their parents. The survey we used [12] was empirically developed by asking college students to list their fears in an open-ended questionnaire. The 51 items included in the survey were those fears listed by two or more students in the initial sample. The instrument has high internal consistency and satisfactory test-retest reliability over short time periods; several items on the survey (snakes, spiders, rats, strange dogs) permit direct observation of fearful avoidance or physiological response to the actual stimulus, and such validation suggests that self-reported fear does correlate with other dimensions of fearful behavior [15].

We administered the fear survey to 151 like-sex twin pairs of college age, and, in 66 families, to both parents of the twin pair as well. The study sample thus includes 434 adults who comprise 91 identical (MZ) and 60 fraternal (DZ) twin pairs, and 66 pairs of parents and their twin offspring. Zygosity determination was based on multiple blood typing and dermatoglyphic comparisons.

For the present analysis we selected those fears which 1) empirically, are highly prevalent in the general population; and 2) theoretically, were of evolutionary significance to early man [10]. Factor analysis [4] of fear survey data from 1,800 undergraduates identified four orthogonal factors composed of items meeting these two criteria. The four factors, exemplified by fears of snakes, deep water, illness, and death of a loved one, account for about 30% of the total variance in the fear survey.

RESULTS AND DISCUSSION

Table 1 summarizes our twin-family data for these four factors. For each factor, the successive columns in the table report 1) the ratio of the mean square within DZ twins to that within MZ twins and the probability associated with an F-test of that ratio; 2) a test of equality of environmental covariance based on the partitioned variation among and within DZ twins; 3) the intraclass correlations of MZ and DZ twins and probability values of a test of their differences; 4) a heritability estimate based on the correlations; and, in the last column 5), the regression of midtwin on midparent.

All four factors meet conservative criteria for inferring the influence of significant genetic variance. Neither means nor total variances for factor scores or individual items were associated with twin type [6]. To protect against spurious inferences of genetic variance, we evaluated the equality of environmental covariance by a confirmatory F-test (MS_A/MS_W) of data from DZ twins [7]. The h^2 estimate $[2(^rMZ-^rDZ)]$ based on the twin correlations [11] provides an estimate of heritability assuming random mating, no dominance, and equality of environmental and genotype-environment correlations. In the absence of common (between-family) environmental variance, the regression of midtwin on midparent yields an alternate estimate of h^2 which is not affected by dominance or assortative mating [9].

Table 2 reports a similar analysis for specific fears of known contemporary prevalence and assumed historical utility. The format of the fear survey requires subjects to rate their fearfulness of each stimulus on a seven-step scale ranging from no fear at all to terror. The crudity of the rating scales led us to evaluate the distributional properties of the 14 variables reported in Tables 1 and 2. Measures of skewness and kurtosis were estimated by SPSS formulas and compared to the zero values expected for normal variates. Only one of the 28 moments estimated for the four factors and the ten individual items has a value > 1.0. The modest departures from normality found in our fear survey data will have no significant effects on our analyses or the inferences drawn from them.

Despite the relative crudity of measurement and constrained reliability of individual item analysis, consistent evidence of heritable variation is present. All items in Table 2 survive a conservative test of equality of environmental

TABLE 1. Twin-Family Analysis: Factor Scores of Fear Survey Schedule

Factor	I		II		III			IV	V
	W_{DZ}/W_{MZ}	P	A_{DZ}/W_{DZ}	P	r_{MZ}	r_{DZ}	P	h^2	Midparent midtwin
Organisms	1.80	0.005	1.70	0.02	0.62	0.26	0.01	0.72	0.45
Personal death	2.01	0.001	1.52	0.05	0.59	0.20	0.01	0.77	0.20
Water	1.84	0.004	2.20	0.01	0.55	0.37	0.09	0.36	0.20
Death of others	1.22	0.186	1.74	0.02	0.53	0.27	0.03	0.51	0.37

TABLE 2. Twin-Family Analysis. Selected Items From Fear Survey Schedule

Fear stimulus	Twin data					Midparent midtwin regressions
	Anova		Correlations			
	W_{DZ}/W_{MZ}	P	r_{MZ}	r_{DZ}	h^2	b
Snakes	1.71	<0.01	0.64	0.40	0.48	0.50
Rats and mice	1.39	<0.07	0.35	0.17	0.35	0.35
Spiders	1.23	<0.18	0.32	0.15	0.32	0.32
Stinging insects	1.35	<0.09	0.44	0.13	0.62	0.18
Thunderstorms	1.56	<0.02	0.41	0.28	0.26	0.20
Deep water	1.40	<0.07	0.52	0.40	0.24	0.37
Dark places	1.34	<0.07	0.35	0.17	0.36	0.27
Death	1.79	<0.01	0.44	0.14	0.60	0.47
Illness	1.42	<0.06	0.50	0.22	0.56	0.21
Death of loved one	1.57	<0.05	0.56	0.17	0.78	0.37

covariance. The traditional test of genetic variance, based on the ratio of within-pair mean squares, permits the inference of genetic variance, and heritability estimates derived from correlations of twin siblings and from parent-offspring regressions are satisfactorily consistent despite the age/sex differences in self-reported fears which constrain parent-offspring resemblance relative to that of age-matched, like-sex cotwins.

Fear of snakes provides an especially noteworthy example of prepared learning. While few contemporary people experience direct aversive conditioning with snakes, the prevalence of intense snake fear approximates 250/1,000 in the general population. Observations of children [16, 23] reveal a predictable, orderly development of fear of snakes quite independent of experience, and similar observations have been made for the chimpanzee [26]. In adult man, snakes possess a prepotency as conditioned stimuli for fearful avoidance, and, once acquired, conditioned fear of snakes is slow to extinguish [18, 19]. Finally, in the results here reported, estimates of genetic variance based on the correlations of twins and the regression of offspring on parent are surprisingly high and consistent with one another despite inequity in environmental covariance.

In summary, to earlier knowledge that snake fears are readily acquired and slow to extinguish, we now add evidence that such fears are highly heritable. Our results apparently confirm Darwin's suggestion that common human fears represent the inherited effects of ancient dangers.

REFERENCES

1. Abe K: Phobias and nervous symptoms in childhood and maturity: Persistance and associations. Br J Psychiatry 120:275–283, 1972.
2. Agras S, Sylvester D, Oliveau D: The epidemiology of common fears and phobia. Compr Psychiatry 10:151–156, 1967.
3. Allen G: Within group and between group variation expected in human behavioral characters. Behav Genet 1:175–194, 1970.
4. Bernstein DA, Allen GJ: Fear survey schedule (II): Normative data and factor analyses. Behav Res Ther 7:403–407, 1969.
5. Cavalli-Sforza LL, Bodmer WF: "The Genetics of Human Populations." San Francisco: WH Freeman, 1971.
6. Christian JC: A review of basic methodology for the analysis of quantitative twin data. Acta Genet Med Gemellol 28:35–40, 1979.
7. Christian JC, Feinleib M, Norton JA Jr: Statistical analysis of genetic variance in twins. Am J Hum Genet 27:807, 1975.
8. Darwin C: A biographical sketch of an infant. Mind 2:285–294, 1877.
9. DeFries JC, Ashton GC, Johnson RC, Kuse AR, McClearn GE, Mi MP, Rashad MN, Vandenberg SG, Wilson JR: The Hawaii family study of cognition: A reply. Behav Genet 8:281–288, 1978.
10. DeSilva P, Rachman S, Seligman MEP: Prepared phobias and obsessions: Therapeutic outcome. Behav Res Ther 15:65–77, 1977.
11. Falconer DS: "An Introduction to Quantitative Genetics." New York: Ronald, 1960.
12. Geer GH: The development of a scale to measure fear. Behav Res Ther 3:45–53, 1965.
13. Halliday MS: Exploration and fear in the rat. Sympos Zool Soc Lond 18:45–59, 1966.

14. Hebb DO: On the nature of fear. Psychol Rev 53:259–276, 1946.
15. Hersen M: Self-assessment of fear. Behav Ther 4:241–257, 1973.
16. Jones NE, Jones MC: Fear. Childhood Educ 5:136–143, 1928.
17. Marks IM: "Fears and Phobias." New York: Academic Press, 1969.
18. Öhman A, Eriksson A, Olafsson C: One-trial learning and superior resistance to extinction of autonomic responses conditioned to potentially phobic stimuli. J Comp Physiol Psychol 88:619–627, 1975.
19. Öhman A, Erixon G, Löfberg I: Phobias and preparedness: Phobic versus neutral pictures as conditioned stimuli for human autonomic responses. J Abnorm Psychol 84:41–45, 1975.
20. Sackett GP: Monkeys reared in isolation with pictures as visual input: Evidence for an innate releasing mechanism. Science 154:1468–1473, 1966.
21. Seligman MEP: Phobias and preparedness. Behav Ther 2:307–321, 1971.
22. Seligman MEP, Hager GE (eds): "Biological Boundaries of Learning." New York: Appleton-Century Crofts, 1972.
23. Valentine CW: The innate bases of fear. J Genet Psychol 37:394–419, 1930.
24. Watson JB, Raynor R: Conditioned emotional reactions. J Exp Psychol 3:1–14, 1920.
25. Wilson EO: "On Human Nature." Cambridge: Harvard University Press, 1977.
26. Yerkes RM, Yerkes AW: Nature and conditions of avoidance (fear) responses in chimpanzee. J Comp Psychol 21:53–66, 1936.

Twin Research 3: Intelligence, Personality,
and Development, pages 175–178

Mortality and Psychosis in Twins

Adrianne M. Reveley, Hugh M.D. Gurling, and Robin M. Murray
*Department of Psychiatry, Institute of Psychiatry, and Maudsley Hospital,
University of London*

The occurrence of twinning, particularly monozygotic twinning, is in itself an abnormal event [2]. Twinning is thus associated with an excess of in utero and obstetric complications, prematurity, birth trauma, and perinatal death [5]. Robertson [14], for instance, who studied 375 twin births in Edinburgh found that 23% of monozygotic and 10% of dizygotic twins died. Furthermore, twins show an increased frequency of congenital abnormalities including neurological deficits, particularly among the surviving members of twin pairs where one has died [4].

Davison and Bagley [3] have exhaustively reviewed the literature on the occurrence of psychosis in individuals with neurological disorders. They conclude that "in many organic CNS disorders the association of 'schizophrenia' exceeds chance expectation." Achté [1] found both affective and schizophrenic psychoses among 300 cases of head injury, and Krauthammer and Klerman [8] concluded that mania too may follow brain injury. McNeil and Kaij [9], reviewing the literature on antecedent obstetric complications in schizophrenia and other psychoses, concluded that, although retrospective ascertainment is a problem, such complications do appear to increase the risk of later psychosis. Mednick [10], who prospectively followed the "high risk" children of schizophrenics, claimed that perinatal complications were positively related to later psychiatric breakdown.

If perinatal injury does increase the risk of psychosis in later life, then we might expect that twins should be at greater risk of psychosis than singletons. Rosenthal [15] and Pollin [11] believe that the evidence does not support this conclusion, but in fact the evidence they cite is rather scanty. An alternative prediction that one might make is that the surviving members of twin pairs where one has died should have an increased risk of psychosis compared with those where both members survive past childhood. The extensive twin records of the Maudsley Hospital have enabled us to begin to address this question.

Dr. Reveley is supported by a Wellcome Foundation Fellowship. Dr. Gurling is supported by a grant from the Research Fund of the Bethlem Royal and Maudsley Hospital.

METHOD

The Maudsley Twin Register was started in 1948 as a means of obtaining an unselected sample of psychiatrically ill twins. Since then, all patients attending the hospital as either outpatients or inpatients have been routinely asked questions about twinship. If their twin survived past the age of 15, they were incorporated into the register. Patients whose cotwin had died at birth or before the age of 15 were not part of the register, but from 1967 onwards this information was stored in the computerised records of the hospital. We were therefore able to compare the frequency of psychosis in those twins, with and without a surviving cotwin, who were treated at the Maudsley and Bethlem Hospitals between 1967 and 1977.

RESULTS

A total of 540 patients were registered as twins in the 11-year period studied. Of these, 140 (26%) had cotwins deceased in childhood. In the vast majority of these (93%), the cotwin had died under the age of two years; 77% had been stillborn. There are no national data on the number of twin pairs in which one does not survive. But Robertson [14] noted that, in Edinburgh, 12.5% died in the perinatal period, whereas Record et al [12] reported on all children of twin birth born between 1950 and 1957 who later took a national examination in Birmingham. From his data it can be estimated that 17.6% of all twins were brought up alone, presumably in the majority of cases because of the death of the cotwin.

It therefore appears that twins presenting to the Maudsley Hospital between 1967 and 1977 are more likely than one might have expected to have lost a cotwin. An earlier report by Gottesman and Shields [6] showed that 30% of all persons born a twin who attended the Maudsley Hospital in the single year 1955 did not have a surviving cotwin, a figure very comparable to ours.

Table 1 shows the numbers of twin patients who were diagnosed as psychotic or nonpsychotic. It can be seen that 11% of those with a cotwin surviving had a psychotic illness compared with 24% of those with a dead cotwin. This difference is statistically significant ($\chi^2 = 14.8$; $P<0.001$).

DISCUSSION

A higher proportion of those twins with a dead rather than a living cotwin receive a diagnosis of psychosis. Our assumption is, of course, that the death of one of a pair of twins is likely to be a reflection of a more hazardous pregnancy and perinatal period which at least in part is shared by the survivor. A number of additional facts help to confirm that this is the case in our series.

We found that those with a cotwin dead, whatever their diagnosis, were more often male, whereas those with a cotwin surviving showed the usual excess of females seen in British psychiatric populations. Male twins are more often stillborn than female twins, and males are more common among those with a stillborn cotwin. Those with nonsurviving cotwins were also of lower social class, and had greater numbers of nontwin siblings—again, whatever their diagnosis (Table 2). This too corresponds with national trends which show

TABLE 1. Survival of Cotwin and Diagnosis

	Probands with cotwin survivors		Probands with cotwin nonsurvivors	
	Psychotic	Nonpsychotic	Psychotic	Nonpsychotic
No. of twins	42	358	33	107
% of twins	11	89	24	76

TABLE 2. Demographic Characteristics of the Sample

	Probands with cotwin survivors		Probands with cotwin nonsurvivors	
Diagnosis	Psychotic	Nonpsychotic	Psychotic	Nonpsychotic
Number	42	358	33	107
Sex ratio (% males)	37	45	56	53
Sibship size	4.3	4.1	5.8	5.3
Social class (%)				
I & II	14	33	14	17
III & IV	60	54	59	56
V	26	13	27	24
Totals	100	100 (from a sample of n =50)	100	100

that increased perinatal mortality is associated with greater parity and lower social class.

This sample of psychiatric patients with cotwins who died shows a number of demographic features which at the national level are associated with infant mortality. Extrinsic perinatal factors, unrelated to genetic make-up, which lead to the death of one of the twins may therefore predispose the cotwin to psychotic illness later in life. An alternative explanation for the findings could be that it is the genetic loading for psychosis that predisposes to the death of one of the twins. This is one of the explanations that Reider et al [13] proposed for their finding of an increased incidence of fetal and neonatal deaths among the offspring of schizophrenics. However, such an explanation would run counter to the physiological advantage hypothesis suggested by Huxley et al [7] and later supported by Erlenmeyer-Kimling [4], which proposes that schizophrenia is maintained in the population by selective advantage and resistance to infection.

There is no clear evidence so far, of course, that twins as a whole show an excess of psychosis compared to singletons [9, 10, 12]. Such an association would be expected if perinatal morbidity alone were contributing to psychosis. The answer may be that perinatal insults increase the risk of psychosis in genetically predisposed individuals who might not otherwise have become ill. We shall be attempting to choose between these various hypotheses in the next, more detailed phase of our study.

REFERENCES

1. Achté KA, Hillbom E, Aalberg V: Psychoses following war brain injuries. Acta Psychiatr Scand 45:1–18, 1969.
2. Boklage CE: Embryonic determination of brain programming asymmetry. Acta Genet Med Gemellol 25:244–248, 1976.
3. Davison K, Bagley CR: Schizophrenia-like psychoses associated with organic disorder of the central nervous system. In Herrington R (ed): "Current problems in Neuropsychiatry." Ashford, Kent: Headley, 1969.
4. Erlenmeyer-Kimling L: Mortality rates in the offspring of schizophrenic parents and a physiological advantage hypothesis. Nature 220:798–800, 1968.
5. Farr U: Prognosis for the Babies, Early and Late. In MacGillivray I, Nylander PPS, Corney G (eds): "Human Multiple Reproduction." London: W.B. Saunders, 1975, pp 188–211.
6. Gottesman II, Shields J: "Schizophrenia and Genetics. A Twin Study Vantage Point." New York and London: Academic Press, 1972.
7. Huxley J, Mayr E, Osmond H, Haffer A: Schizophrenia as a genetic morphism. Nature 204:220–221, 1964.
8. Krauthammer C, Klerman GL: Secondary mania. Arch Gen Psychiatry 35:1333–1339, 1978.
9. McNeil TF, Kaij L: Obstetric factors in the development of schizophrenia. Presented at the Second Rochester International Conference on Schizophrenia. May 2–5, 1976.
10. Mednick SA: Studies of high risk children. In Mednick SA, Schulsinger F, Higgins J, Bell B (eds): "Genetics, Environment and Psychopathology." North Holland: American Elsevier, 1974, pp 89–116.
11. Pollin W: The pathogenesis of schizophrenia. Arch Gen Psychiatry 27:29–37, 1972.
12. Record RG, McKeown R, Edwards JH: An investigation of the difference in measured intelligence between twins and single births. Ann Hum Genet Lond 34:11–20, 1970.
13. Reider RO, Rosenthal D, Wender P, Blumenthal H: The offspring of schizophrenics. Arch Gen Psychiatry 32:200–211, 1975.
14. Robertson JG: Twin pregnancy: Mortality and fetal mortality. Obstet Gynecol 23:330–337, 1964.
15. Rosenthal D: Confusion of identity and the frequency of schizophrenia in twins. Arch Gen Psychiatry 3:297–304, 1960.

Twin Research 3: Intelligence, Personality,
and Development, pages 179 — 188
© 1981 Alan R. Liss, Inc., 150 Fifth Avenue, New York, NY 10011

MZ Twins Reared Apart: Preliminary Findings of Psychiatric Disturbances and Traits

Elke D. Eckert, Leonard L. Heston, and Thomas J. Bouchard, Jr.

Department of Psychiatry, University of Minnesota, Minneapolis

INTRODUCTION

Monozygotic (MZ) twins reared apart since early in life present a unique opportunity to estimate directly the relative influence of genes and the environment on medical and psychological traits. In addition to a few scattered reports, there are three previous systematic investigations of identical twins reared apart. Newman et al [10] reported on 19 pairs in the United States, Shields [12] reported on 44 British pairs, and Juel-Nielsen [6] reported on 12 Danish twin pairs. In these investigations, most of the twins were separated in early childhood, but some were separated later in life. Newman et al reported on two pairs separated as late as their eighth year of life, and both Shields and Juel-Nielsen reported on twins separated in their fifth year of life. Shields and Juel-Nielsen employed a medical-psychiatric interview technique as part of their investigation, whereas Newman et al did not.

This paper will present preliminary findings of psychiatric disturbances and personality traits in MZ twins reared apart, largely as they were assessed during extensive psychiatric and medical work-up as part of a week of intensive psychological and medical investigation at the University of Minnesota.

METHODS

Fifteen MZ twin pairs, all except one pair separated within 6 weeks (SD ± 50 days) after birth and reared apart usually by parents who were not biologically related, were studied. One pair was not separated until 3 years of age. Each twin was separately interviewed in a semistructured format jointly by two psychiatrists for 1½ hours to 3 hours. Additional information from adoptive parents and previous hospital and general medical records was obtained when possible. Zygosity was determined using extensive blood grouping procedures. There were seven female and eight male MZ pairs; their age ranged from 16 to

Supported by NSF grant BNS-7926-654, a grant from the Spencer Foundation, and a grant from the Graduate School of the University of Minnesota.

57. Most of the twins live in the United States, but four female pairs came from the British Isles, and one member of one pair lives in Germany, while his twin lives in California. The twins were self-recruited, attracted by reports of re-united twins appearing in the press. No attempt was made to select twins by any psychiatric or other criteria.

RESULTS

Although differences in psychiatric traits were also found, the similarities often were striking as illustrated by the following pair.

Case History

Twenty-three-year-old male twins (pair 12 in Table 1), both unmarried, were evaluated within 6 months after they had accidentally found each other. Birth records described no abnormalities. At birth they were equal in length, but twin A, the first-born, was a little heavier (2,670 g vs 2,550 g) and taller by 5 cm at the time of our evaluation. The twins were separated and adopted in the first few weeks of life.

Separate histories obtained from each adoptive mother described remarkable similarities. Both twins had a height phobia at an early age (4–12 years), so that they refused to climb on walls and cried when placed on ledges. This phobia gradually improved over the years so that, as adults, only a mild fear of height remained.

Twin B, but not A, had enuresis until age 7.

Early speech problems were noted in both. These were described as diffi-culty pronouncing particular letters and syllables (the mothers could not recall specific letters or syllables). In kindergarten and first grade both received speech training with subsequent resolution of this problem by the third grade.

Both began to show signs of hyperactivity at about 18 months to 2 years, characterized by decreased attention span, distractibility, and inability to sit still. Both were seen by psychiatrists over several years. Twin B's parents were told that he had minimal brain damage (MBD), although a neurological examination was reported as negative. Only twin B took medication (chlor-promazine) from age 6 to 14 and again from about age 18 to age 20. Twin A was never given a formal diagnosis of MBD and medication was never recom-mended.

Probably because of the hyperactivity, both twins showed a learning disabil-ity for which they attended special classes for several years. In addition, both displayed temper outbursts as children; according to their parents both would scream and cry with little provocation. The problem was more severe in twin B, who become physically violent and threw things. Twin A was not physically violent. Medical records confirm that twin B was hospitalized twice at age 20 for temper outbursts associated with physical violence and a high anxiety state — the predominant theme was feelings of hostility towards his family, espe-cially the father, and neighbors. Twin A has never been hospitalized.

Twin B impulsively stole things on several occasions. He was placed on pro-bation for this at age 18. Twin A had no comparable history.

Both twins remained dependent on their families and had difficulties finding and holding steady employment. Both showed a marked emotional lability with a tendency to anxiety and depression, and both had recurrent suicidal feelings.

Both twins were actively homosexual. They showed a similar pattern of homosexual development, and at evaluation they were similar in many respects but they described some differences, for example, B had many more sexual partners. An interesting aspect of their homosexuality is that the incest taboo was not operative since they had an ongoing sexual relationship with each other.

Thus a surprising number of psychiatric traits were common to both, yet there were also some differences. Twin B, the shorter and the second-born, was the more severely disturbed.

Overall Results

A pattern of similarities with less striking differences in pathology, and a tendency for one twin to have more severe problems was also found in the other MZ twins studied. Similarities and differences in the 15 pairs are shown in Table 1. Several traits are listed as examples: alcohol and drug abuse, fears or phobias, speech impediments, enuresis, and a category of other traits of psychiatric interest.

The + signs indicate an abnormality in the respective trait is present, and the ++ signs indicate that the abnormality is more pronounced in one of the twins — for example, in twin pair 5: Both were enuretic, but twin B had the problem until age 10 versus age 6 for twin A. In twin pair 2, both were enuretic for roughly the same time.

Speech impediments were found in both members of two female pairs (1 and 7) and two male pairs (10 and 12), but no pairs were discordant. Both twins in pair 7 lisped as children, but they had gradually improved over the years. The other speech impediments could be classified as stuttering. Pair 1 reported a mild problem, with twin A reporting spontaneous resolution at age 13 whereas the problem of twin B, who had speech therapy, resolved earlier at age 8. Histories from the adoptive mothers confirmed that both twins of pair 10 took longer than normal to begin to speak, and they both stuttered. Their problems gradually disappeared without special training. The similar pattern of stuttering in pair 12 has already been described.

We inquired about specific fears or phobias. Both twins of female pairs 1, 2, and 5 described multiple fears and phobias which were sometimes different but sometimes strikingly similar. In pair 5, for example, both twins suffered from marked claustrophobia and fears of height and water. Both twins feared going into the ocean above knee level, and they behaved similarly in response to this situation: Both gingerly backed into the water only up to their knees. They developed this coping mechanism independently while living apart. Both members of pairs 6, 12, and 13 shared a mild height phobia. There was also discordance for fears or phobias; only twin B of pairs 4 and 7 reported mild fear of heights. Only twin A of pair 8 reported a fear of snakes, which had started when he stepped into a snake nest as a young boy and was bitten.

TABLE 1. Psychiatric Traits in MZ Twins Reared Apart

Twin pair no.	Twin	Age (yrs)	Sex	Alcohol or drug abuse	Fears or phobias	Speech impediment	Enuresis	Other psychiatric traits
1	A	54	F		+	+		"Nervous"—takes medication
	B		F		+	+		Emotionally stable
2	A	57	F	+	+		+	Emotional lability, depressive neurosis, nightmares
	B		F	+	+		+	Emotional lability, depressive neurosis, nightmares, hospitalized with psychosis
3	A	35	F					Moody, psychosomatic response to stress ++, propranalol-responsive
	B		F					Moody, psychosomatic response to stress +, propranalol-responsive
4	A	40	F					Emotionally stable
	B		F		+			Adjustment reaction with anxious mood
5	A	35	F		+		+	Adjustment reaction with anxious mood
	B		F		+		++	Adjustment reaction with anxious mood
6	A	55	F		+ +			Emotionally stable
	B		F		+ +			Depressive neurosis

Pair	Member	Age	Sex					Diagnosis
7	A	37	F			+		Adjustment reaction with depressed mood
	B		F		+	+		Adjustment reaction with depressed mood
8	A	40	M	+	+			Atypical anxiety disorder
	B		M					Atypical anxiety disorder
9	A	57	M					Grief reaction with depressive syndrome
	B		M	+				Grief reaction with depressive syndrome
10	A	16	M			++	++	Emotionally stable
	B		M			++	++	Moody, nervous sociopathic traits, hyperactive
11	A	46	M	+				Atypical depression, nervous, anger outbursts
	B		M					Narcolepsy, nervous, anger outbursts

+ = Abnormality present; ++ = abnormality more pronounced.

(Table 1 Continued on next page)

TABLE 1. Psychiatric Traits in MZ Twins Reared Apart

Twin pair no.	Twin	Age (yrs)	Sex	Alcohol or drug abuse	Fears or phobias	Speech impediment	Enuresis	Other psychiatric traits
12	A	23	M		+	+		Hyperactivity +, emotionally immature +, temper/anger outbursts +, emotionally labile with episodes of anxiety and depression, homosexual
	B		M		+	+	+	Hyperactivity ++, emotionally immature ++, temper/anger outbursts ++, emotionally labile with episodes of anxiety and depression, homosexual
13	A	24	M		+			Emotionally stable
	B		M		+			Emotionally stable
14	A	31	M					Emotionally stable
	B		M					Emotionally stable
15	A	37	M				+	Homosexual, emotionally stable
	B		M					Heterosexual, emotionally stable

+ = Abnormality present; ++ = abnormality more pronounced.

Enuresis was concordant in two female pairs and in one male pair, and was discordant in two male pairs. In pair 2, both twins reported resolution of the problem at about age 12. In pair 5, twin A reported bedwetting until age 6, and twin B until age 10. The adoptive mothers of pair 10 reported bedwetting in both: Twin A stopped at age 7, but twin B continued until age 12. Twin B also soiled his pants until about age 6. In twin pair 14, only B reported enuresis. The discordance in bedwetting in pair number 12 has already been described.

Alcohol and drug abuse problems were both concordant and discordant. In pair 2, both twins went through a prolonged period of heavy drinking between age 15 and 30, although neither would have met the Diagnostic and Statistical Manual of Mental Disorders (DSM-III) [14] criteria for alcohol abuse. However, both would have met DSM-III criteria for amphetamine abuse. Both began to use amphetamines for weight control between age 30 and 40. Twin A stated she sometimes used as many as 20 pills per day (probably 5-mg tablets); twin B was hospitalized twice with a paranoid psychosis which was most likely related to amphetamine abuse. In pair 11, twin A met DSM-III criteria for alcohol dependence during one period of his life. He showed mild withdrawal symptoms and blackouts; when drinking, he physically abused his wife. His twin avoided alcohol because it made his narcolepsy worse (see below). He never developed a drinking problem. In two other pairs, 8 and 9, only one of each pair drank heavily during a period of his life associated with major situational stress, but neither met diagnostic criteria for alcohol abuse.

In the category for "other" psychiatric traits in Table 1, an attempt was made to use DSM-III criteria whenever possible. When this was not possible, descriptions of the traits are given.

Twin pairs 1, 6, 10, 11, and 15 showed some clear discordances. Twin A in pair 1 had been treated with minor tranquilizers for feeling "nervous" during the last 5 years, whereas her twin was considered emotionally stable. Twin B of pair 6 had a depressive neurosis since menopause, but her twin had been emotionally stable. Twin B in pair 10 had been diagnosed as hyperactive in association with minimal brain damage (the diagnosis was confirmed by a neurologist during evaluation) and had been moody and nervous and had shown behavioral problems: lying, stealing, and running away from home. His twin, who also had minimal brain damage according to a neurological evaluation, had been emotionally stable.

Pairs 11 and 15 are interesting in the degree of both similarities and differences. Both members of pair 11 had recurrent anxiety and both had explosive anger. Twin A was physically violent during his anger outbursts as noted above. Twin B was never physically violent (he did not drink), but he was verbally abusive during anger outbursts to the extent that it caused him social embarrassment. Twin A of pair 11 was treated by psychotherapy during the preceding 4 years for an atypical depression with occasional suicidal thinking. His twin had no such problems. Twin B, however, suffered from narcolepsy (including sleep attacks, cataplexy, and sleep paralysis), which responded to Ritalin. Twin A did not have narcolepsy. The twins of pair 15 were stable emotionally but there was a difference in their sexual orientation, with twin A being actively homosexual while twin B had a primarily heterosexual orientation.

Members of several twin pairs experienced situational adjustment reactions (pairs 5, 7, and 9). They tended to react similarly if both members of a pair experienced similar stress. For example, both members of pair 5 were treated with minor tranquilizers for "nervousness" and "tenseness" during a period of marital turmoil when both their husbands were drinking heavily. Both twins in pair 7 reacted with similar signs and symptoms of depression for a period of months (mainly weight loss, sleep disturbance, feelings of lethargy, and crying). A's child had been hospitalized with encephalitis and B had marital trouble.

Three pairs were instructive because, while having attributes which were much the same in kind, there were also qualitative and quantitative differences within pairs with respect to these attributes (pairs 2, 3, and 12). Both twins in pair 2 showed lifelong emotional lability and an atypical depressive neurosis. They also suffered from nightmares, starting in their teens, which were described similarly: Both felt as if they were suffocating or choking and both dreamt of needles and doorknobs in their mouths. Twin B of pair 2 was twice hospitalized with a paranoid psychosis as noted above. Her twin, although she also abused amphetamines, was never psychotic.

Both twins in pair 3 tended to be moody. They described anxiety for which they were treated with a variety of medications, but they were particularly responsive to propranolol. This may be an example of the use of MZ twins for pharmacogenetic study. Both these twins tended to respond to stress with physiological symptoms, primarily gastrointestinal, respiratory, and cardiovascular. Both twins, during the week of medical and psychological evaluation, experienced anxiety with nausea and vomiting when initially confronted with test-taking situations. Twin A developed these symptoms sooner, and in her they lasted longer and were more intense than in her cotwin. Twin B of this pair experienced lightheadedness and a feeling of faintness during some of the medical procedures, in contrast to A, who responded with severe hyperventilation on two such occasions. By history, both were subject to feelings of "breathlessness" along with "tingling" in their extremities during stressful situations. Overall, it appeared that A tended to react more intensely, both physiologically and emotionally, to stress. Environmental variation may account for this difference, in that twin B was raised in an environment that required that she develop some "toughness" to survive. She also disliked the extreme responses of twin A, saying that she certainly did not want to be like her.

The variation in degree of impairment exhibited by pair 12 has already been described.

Several pairs, however, had virtually identical attributes (5, 7, 8, 9, 13, and 14). For example, both members of pair 8 described in almost the same words a fluctuating anxiety disorder (atypical by DSM-III criteria) that began in their late teens, had become worse over the past 7 years, and had been treated with partial success with diazepam.

DISCUSSION

The results in this paper are preliminary since multiple psychometric and physiological results which will amplify our understanding of these twins have not yet been analyzed. However, the many similarities and the differences in the various psychiatric traits are not without interest.

Although fears and phobias have not been thought highly heritable [4, 8, 11], the facts that three pairs of twins were concordant for multiple fears or phobias, that other pairs reported no fears, and that often the same specific fear coped with in similar ways was described, at least raise the question of an innate genetically mediated tendency to fearfulness. These data indicate that fears or phobias are largely concordant (six pairs concordant, three discordant). In Shields's data, specific fears were as often reported concordant as discordant, but Shields qualified his data by suggesting his assessments of neurotic traits could have been unreliable [12].

Speech impediments were completely concordant in our series. This makes sense because one could expect a large genetic component in speech. A higher concordance for stuttering in MZ then in DZ twins has been reported [8]. Shields, however, found "speech stammers" to be as often discordant as concordant [12].

Enuresis was sometimes concordant (3 pairs) and sometimes discordant (2 pairs) in our twins. This compares with Shields's data of seven concordant pairs and only one discordant pair, and with Juel-Nielsen's report of four discordant pairs. Hence the question of the influence of genes and environment in this condition remains unclear, although data on twins support the view that enuresis has a strong genetic component [1, 11].

Although our data are limited, drug and alcohol abuse were not strongly concordant, reflecting a pronounced environmental influence. However, we had no severe alcoholism of a type where genetic factors have been implicated [3].

Psychoneurotic and characterological traits overall appeared quite concordant, be it a tendency to react primarily with anxiety, anger outbursts, or depression. Even the specific physiological signs and symptoms associated with anxiety, or the specific symptom complex of depression, appeared to have similar features, although the degree of the expression of certain traits sometimes differed markedly. It is assumed that environmental variations were reflected in these differences. Although there is considerable variable in the literature regarding the heritability of neurotic traits [4, 9], Shields stated that if decompensation and the development of a neurosis occurs, the form that it takes probably depends on genotype [13].

Homosexuality in twins reared apart has never been reported previously, and this makes noteworthy the similar pattern of homosexual development and behavior in both members of one pair and especially their sexual attraction for each other. Similarity in homosexual pattern and behavior have been reported previously in MZ twins reared together [5, 7]. The fact that we have one concordant and one discordant pair for homosexuality matches the tendency in the literature, excepting for Kallmann [7], whose sample is acknowledged as being very biased, for concordance and discordance for homosexuality to occur about equally in MZ twins reared together.

REFERENCES

1. Bakwin H: Enuresis in twins. Am J Dis Child 121:222–225, 1971.
2. Godai U, Tatarelli R, Bonanni G: Stuttering and tics in twins. Acta Genet Med Gemollol 25:369–375, 1976.
3. Goodwin DW, Schulsinger F, Hermansen L, Guze SB, Winokur G: Alcohol problems in adoptees raised apart from alcoholic biological parents. Arch Gen Psychiatry 28:238–243, 1973.
4. Gottesman II: Differential inheritance of the psychoneuroses. Eugen Quart, 9:223–227, 1962.
5. Heston LL, Shields J: Homosexuality in twins — a family study and a registry study. Arch Gen Psychiatry 18:149–160, 1968.
6. Juel-Nielsen N: "Individual and Environment: A Psychiatric-Psychological Investigation of Monozygotic Twins Reared Apart." Acta Psychiatrica Scandinavica, Supplementum 183. Copehagen: Munksgaard, 1965.
7. Kallmann FJ: Comparative twin study on the genetic aspects of male homosexuality. J Nerv Ment Dis 115:283–298, 1952.
8. Marks IM: "Fears and Phobias." London: Academic Press, 1969.
9. Miner GD: The evidence for genetic components in the neuroses. Arch Gen Psychiatry 29:111–118, 1973.
10. Newman HH, Freeman FN, Holzinger KJ: "Twins: A Study of Heredity and Environment." Chicago: University of Chicago Press, 1937.
11. Shields J: Personality differences and neurotic traits in normal twin school children. Eugen Rev 45:213–246, 1954.
12. Shields J: "Monozygotic Twins, Brought Up Apart and Brought Up Together." London: Oxford University Press, 1962.
13. Shields J: Heredity and psychological abnormality. In Eysenck HJ (ed): "Handbook of Abnormal Psychology." London: Pitman Medical, 1973.
14. Spitzer RL et al: "Diagnostic and Statistical Manual of Mental Disorder" (Third Ed). Washington, DC: American Psychiatric Association, 1980.

Twin Research 3: Intelligence, Personality,
and Development, pages 189—198
©1981 Alan R. Liss, Inc., 150 Fifth Avenue, New York, NY 10011

Finnish Twins Reared Apart: Preliminary Characterization of Rearing Environment

Heimo Langinvainio, Markku Koskenvuo, Jaakko Kaprio, Jouko Lönnqvist, and Lauri Tarkkonen
Department of Public Health Science (H.L., M.K., J.K., L.T.), and Department of Psychiatry, University of Helsinki (J.L.)

INTRODUCTION

When the relative roles of environmental and genetic factors on the development of the individual are studied, the study of twin pairs reared apart from an early age represents a nearly ideal design. Difficulties are encountered, however, as such cases are rare and the possibly exceptional reasons for separation may cause problems in generalizing the findings. Also, the character of the rearing environment before and after separation has to be assessed.

Earlier studies of twins reared apart have consisted of fairly small series of pairs. Newman et al [7] studied 19 pairs separated under the age of 7 years (12 under the age of 1), Shields [10] studied 44 pairs separated before the age of 9, (30 under the age of 1), and Juel-Nielsen [2] studied 12 pairs separated at less than 6 years of age (9 under the age of 1). In addition, Bouchard [1] recently described a series of 15 pairs of identical twins separated at a very early age who have been extensively studied. The emphasis in these earlier studies has been on psychopathology, cognitive functions, and personality development, but biomedical aspects have not been so intensively studied.

A preliminary survey of the rearing environment of twins reared apart in Finland has been undertaken. In this paper, some characteristics of the rearing environment of adult twins raised apart from the age of 10 or less will be presented.

In addition to the characteristics of the rearing environment, the questionnaire study included three semantic differential test batteries: a 43-item battery for personality characteristics, a 20-item battery for the emotional at-

The Finnish Twin Registry has been supported in part by a grant from The Council for Tobacco Research USA, Inc.

mosphere of the childhood rearing home, and a 44-item battery for the intrapair comparison of personality. These will be presented later. After assessing the characteristics of this series, the feasibility of detailed studies will be evaluated.

MATERIALS AND METHODS

The Finnish Twin Registry consists of all Finnish adult like-sexed twin pairs (N = 17,357 pairs) born before 1958 and with both cotwins alive in 1967. All pairs of persons with the same date of birth, sex, surname at birth, and community of birth were selected from the Central Population Registry of Finland. This selection procedure yielded the data base for the Finnish Twin Registry [3]. Twinship was confirmed by a questionnaire study in 1975 and inquiries to local parish birth registers. The 1975 questionnaire covered health-related items and standardized measures of morbidity, with a total of 97 questions. The basic distributions of the questionnaire study have been documented [4–6]. The questionnaire was mailed to all pairs with both members alive in 1975. The overall response rate was 89%.

In addition to the questions on health-related items, a number of other aspects were considered: whether the twin pair lived together and, if not, at what age separation had occurred. The present frequency of intrapair contact, birth order, and handedness were also investigated and questions directed to zygosity assessment were included [8].

Definition of Present Study Groups

The sampling frame from which the study series in this investigation were drawn consisted of those adult like-sexed twin pairs of whom at least one had replied in the 1975 questionnaire study of the Registry. The sample of the twins that were considered to have been raised apart consisted of those pairs in whom at least one had replied that he had been living apart from his twin since the age of 10 or less.

This selection procedure yielded 478 Finnish-speaking pairs. All those alive in 1979 and with adequate address data were then sent, during November 1979–January 1980, a questionnaire on their childhood environment. Some 30 Swedish-speaking pairs were for the moment excluded from the study.

Three control groups were formed in order to assess which aspects of the rearing environment, personality factors, and childhood medical history of the study sample differed from those of twins of the same age and sex: 1) Age of separation 11–16, as reported by the twins in 1975; if the twins disagreed, the pair was classified by the lower age reported. 2) Age at separation >16. This group consisted of pairs not living together in 1975. 3) Twins living together. This group consisted of pairs in which both twins replied that they lived together in 1975; in case of contradictory answers, the pair was excluded.

From these three groups samples were drawn and matched for age and sex with the study group of 478 twin pairs raised apart. The questionnaire was mailed also, for pertinent parts, to the three control groups.

The questionnaire used in this study was formed from three sources. The first consisted of the questions on cause of separation and the rearing environment of the twins. This part of the study on selective placement was planned jointly with the Swedish Twin Registry, Karolinska Institute, and with Gerald McClearn, University of Colorado, to ensure comparability with a similar study ongoing in Sweden. The second source originated from the additional questions added to clarify further and to detail various aspects of the childhood environment, psychological relationships between the twins, and birth events and illnesses in childhood. The third source consisted in three personality measures that were developed to investigate the relationship of rearing conditions and adult personality. These test batteries have been validated using singletons from the general population and psychiatric outpatients.

In the whole Finnish Twin Registry, zygosity was determined by a highly accurate questionnaire method validated by blood testing [8,9]. Because this method was mainly based on similarity in appearance and confusion by other people in childhood, its reliability in the particular sample of twins reared apart has not been assessed, and therefore zygosity data are not presented here. Slightly less than a third of the pairs in the Twin Registry are monozygotic [9].

RESULTS

So far, information has been obtained on a total of 304 pairs who have been raised in separate environments from the age of 10 or less: Their distribution by age at separation (groups I–IV) and by birth year and sex is given in Tables 1 and 2. The age at separation indicated in the 1975 questionnaire and in the new questionnaire study agreed in 81% of responses. The one used here is the average of the ages given by the pair if these were not the same. If one of the twins indicated as age at separation over 10 years, the pair was excluded from the analysis pending clarification.

The most common causes of separation reported were economic conditions (29.9%), death of the mother (19.2%), single parenthood of the mother (15.5%), death of the father (12.0%), and childlessness in close relatives (8.5%) (Table 3). Other causes were indicated in 28.3%, and the reason was not known in 7.6% of cases. The distribution of causes varied by age at separation (Table 4). Compared to other groups, economic conditions (40.5%) and death of the father (19.6%) were most common in group IV. In group III maternal death was the cause of separation in 29.8% of cases, whereas in group II, single parenthood of the mother was most common (24.6%). In the pairs separated under the age of 1 year (group I), the cause of separation was unknown in 17.4% vs 3.7%–6.4% of cases in other groups. Because some causes of separation were specified by the questionnaire and others classified on the basis of the replies given to an open-ended question on "other reasons," more than one cause of separation may have been registered.

One or both of the rearing parents after separation were the biological parents in 30.4% of cases (Table 5). Women had a biological rearing parent somewhat more often (32.3%) than men (27.9%). At least one rearing parent was a relative in 30.7%, and no rearing parent was present in 11.3% of cases. The distribution of rearing parent type varied somewhat by age at separation (Table 6). The lack of a rearing parent was most common in twins in group IV, whereas among twins of group I, there was always a rearing parent present. In groups I and II, biological parents were most often the rearing parents: 31.4%

TABLE 1. Age at Separation by Sex. Number of Pairs

Age at separation	Men	Women	Total
Less than 1 year (group I)	24	27	51
1–2 years (group II)	39	34	73
3–5 years (group III)	32	34	66
6–10 years (group IV)	41	73	114

TABLE 2. Distribution of Twin Pairs Reared Apart by Birth Year and Sex

Birth year	Men	Women	Total
–1917	15	45	60
1918–1922	6	21	27
1923–1927	19	17	36
1928–1932	22	17	39
1933–1937	20	20	40
1938–1942	16	18	34
1943–1947	12	9	21
1948–1952	11	8	19
1953–1957	15	13	28
Total	136	168	304

TABLE 3. Reported Causes of Separation by Sex *

Cause of separation	Individual responses (%)		
	Men	Women	Total
Economic conditions	26.0	32.8	29.9
Maternal death	19.4	19.1	19.2
Single mother	17.9	13.7	15.5
Paternal death	13.3	11.1	12.0
Childlessness in relatives	8.2	8.8	8.5
Parental divorce	6.6	5.3	5.9
Maternal illness	5.1	5.3	5.2
Cotwin illness	5.1	4.2	4.6
War	4.6	4.6	4.6
Own illness	3.1	2.7	2.8
Parental illness	2.0	0.8	1.3
Social difficulties of parents	0.5	1.9	1.3
Going to work	0.5	1.5	1.1
Schooling, studies	1.1	1.1	1.1
Migration	0.5	0.4	0.4
Other reason	4.6	5.3	5.0
Reason unknown	8.7	6.9	7.6

*More than one reason of separation possible.

TABLE 4. Cause of Separation by Age at Separation (% Values)*

Cause of separation	0 (I)	1–2 (II)	3–5 (III)	6–10 (IV)	Total
	Age at separation				
Economic conditions	25.6	25.5	21.3	40.5	29.9
Maternal death	23.3	13.6	29.8	15.3	19.2
Single mother	14.0	24.6	18.1	9.2	15.5
Parental death	2.3	8.2	11.7	19.6	12.0
Childlessness in relatives	11.6	14.6	6.4	4.3	8.5
Parental divorce	4.7	10.0	5.3	3.7	5.9
Maternal illness	9.3	5.5	6.4	2.5	5.2
Cotwin illness	2.3	2.7	6.4	6.1	4.6
War	1.2	4.6	5.3	6.1	4.6
Own illness	0.0	4.6	0.0	4.9	2.8
Parental illness	1.2	0.9	1.1	1.8	1.3
Social difficulties of parents	1.2	0.9	0.0	2.4	1.3
Going to work	0.0	0.0	0.0	3.1	1.1
Schooling, studies	0.0	0.0	0.0	3.1	1.1
Migration	0.0	0.0	1.1	0.6	0.4
Other reason	5.8	4.6	7.5	3.7	5.0
Reason unknown	17.4	6.4	5.3	3.7	7.6

*More than one reason of separation possible.

TABLE 5. Rearing Environment (Adults) by Sex (% Values)

Adults present in rearing family after separation	Men	Women	Total
At least one biological parent	27.9	32.3	30.4
At least one foster parent, who was a relative	33.0	28.9	30.7
Other foster parents, nonrelatives	30.5	25.5	27.6
Other adults, institutions, employer only	8.6	13.3	11.3
Total	100.0	100.0	100.0

and 36.4% of cases, respectively. A rearing parent who was a relative was also most common in group I (44.2%). The combinations of rearing parent types for respondent pairs will be presented later.

Children other than the respondent were present in the rearing environment in 72.8% of families (Table 7). Biological sibs were present in 30.2%, half-sibs in 3.7%, and other related sibs in 11.3% of families. Children in the same rearing family, but who were not relatives, were present in 14.4% of cases. There were no significant differences in distribution by sex of the separated twins.

TABLE 6. Rearing Environment (Adults) by Age at Separation (% Values)

Adults present in rearing family after separation	0 (I)	1–2 (II)	3–5 (III)	6–10 (IV)	Total
At least one biological parent	31.4	36.4	28.7	26.2	30.4
At least one foster parent, who was a relative	44.2	28.2	39.4	21.3	30.7
Other foster parents, nonrelatives	24.4	29.1	28.7	26.8	27.6
Other adults, institutions, employer only	0.0	6.4	3.2	25.6	11.3
Total	100.0	100.0	100.0	100.0	100.0

TABLE 7. Rearing Environment (Children) by Sex (% Values)

Children present in rearing family after separation	Men	Women	Total
Biological siblings	27.9	31.9	30.2
Half sibs	3.6	3.8	3.7
Foster children, relatives	10.7	11.8	11.3
Foster children, nonrelatives	14.2	14.5	14.4
Other children	14.2	12.6	13.3
No children	28.9	24.0	26.1
Missing data	0.5	1.5	1.1
Total	100.0	100.0	100.0

When examined by age at separation (Table 8), the proportion of cases with biological sibs present in the rearing family was fairly constant. The proportion of foster children was highest in group III, whereas other nonfoster children were most common in group IV.

The educational level of the rearing parents (Table 9) was less than primary school in 34.6% of mothers and 33.3% of fathers, more than primary school in 10.7% of mothers and 11.1% of fathers, and unknown by 15% of respondents. Group I had relatively more mothers (45.2%) and fathers (50.7%) with less than primary school as compared to other groups (Table 10). Group III had the highest proportion of parents who had completed primary school (45.2% of mothers and 45.6% of fathers). The educational level of parents was most often unknown in group IV (mothers 19.8%, fathers 18%) and least often in group I (7.1% and 9.9%, respectively).

The occupational status of the rearing parents (Table 11) was farming in 58.7% of mothers and 52.1% of fathers, manual work in 18.3% of mothers and 32.1% of fathers, and other occupations were found in 3.9% of mothers and

TABLE 8. Rearing Environment (Children) by Age at Separation (% Values)

Children present in rearing family after separation	0 (I)	1–2 (II)	3–5 (III)	6–10 (IV)	Total
Biological siblings	31.4	28.2	25.5	33.5	30.2
Half sibs	3.5	8.2	2.1	1.2	3.7
Foster children, relatives	17.4	12.7	11.7	7.3	11.3
Foster children, nonrelatives	17.4	15.5	18.1	9.8	14.4
Other children	2.3	9.1	9.6	23.8	13.3
No children	27.9	26.4	29.8	23.2	26.1
Missing data	0.0	0.0	3.2	1.2	1.1
Total	100.0	100.0	100.0	100.0	100.0

TABLE 9. Educational Level of Rearing Parents by Sex of Twins (% Values)

Educational level	Mother or equivalent[a]			Father or equivalent[b]		
	Men	Women	Total	Men	Women	Total
Less than primary school	28.5	39.0	34.6	28.2	37.3	33.3
Primary school	47.3	33.9	39.6	44.2	37.3	40.3
More than primary school	11.3	10.4	10.7	15.4	7.7	11.1
Unknown	12.9	16.7	15.1	12.2	17.7	15.3
Total	100.0	100.0	100.0	100.0	100.0	100.0

[a]Case excluded if no rearing mother.
[b]Case excluded if no rearing father.

TABLE 10. Educational Level of Rearing Parents by Age of Twins at Separation (% Values)

Educational level	Age at separation				
	0 (I)	1–2 (II)	3–5 (III)	6–10 (IV)	Total
Mother[a]					
Less than primary school	45.2	33.7	26.7	34.4	34.6
Primary school	40.5	40.4	48.8	33.8	39.6
More than primary school	7.2	12.4	8.2	12.0	10.7
Unknown	7.1	13.5	16.3	19.8	15.1
	100.0	100.0	100.0	100.0	100.0
Father[b]					
Less than primary school	50.7	30.7	25.0	30.5	33.3
Primary school	32.4	42.1	45.6	39.8	40.3
More than primary school	7.0	11.3	13.2	11.7	11.1
Unknown	9.9	15.9	16.2	18.0	15.3
	100.0	100.0	100.0	100.0	100.0

[a]Case excluded if no rearing mother.
[b]Case excluded if no rearing father.

TABLE 11. Occupational Status of Rearing Parents by Sex of Twins (% Values)

Occupational status	Mother or equivalent[a]			Father or equivalent[b]		
	Men	Women	Total	Men	Women	Total
Farmer	63.2	55.3	58.7	52.5	51.9	52.1
Manual worker	14.9	20.9	18.3	26.0	36.6	32.1
Other	4.0	3.8	3.9	7.6	6.9	7.2
Combination of above classes	1.1	1.7	1.4	10.8	3.8	6.7
Housewife	12.6	16.2	14.7	—	—	—
Unknown	4.0	2.1	2.9	3.2	0.9	1.9
Total	100.0	100.0	100.0	100.0	100.0	100.0

[a]Case excluded if no rearing mother.
[b]Case excluded if no rearing father.

TABLE 12. Occupational Status of Rearing Parents by Age of Twins at Separation (% Values)

	Age of separation				
Occupational status	0 (I)	1–2 (II)	3–5 (III)	6–10 (IV)	Total
Mother[a]					
Farmer	70.0	53.2	55.6	57.4	58.7
Manual worker	12.5	20.2	18.5	20.3	18.3
Other	0.0	6.4	2.5	4.7	3.9
Combination of above	1.3	1.1	3.7	0.7	1.4
Housewife	12.5	17.0	17.3	13.5	14.7
Unknown	3.8	2.1	2.5	3.4	2.9
	100.0	100.0	100.0	100.0	100.0
Father[b]					
Farmer	65.3	40.9	54.3	51.5	52.1
Manual worker	25.3	37.5	27.1	35.3	32.1
Other	2.7	10.2	7.1	7.4	7.2
Combination of above	5.3	9.1	11.4	2.9	6.7
Unknown	1.3	2.8	0.0	2.9	1.9
	100.0	100.0	100.0	100.0	100.0

[a]Case excluded if no rearing mother.
[b]Case excluded if no rearing father.

7.2% of fathers. Combinations of two occupation categories were found in 1.4% of mothers and 6.7% of fathers; 14.7% of mothers were housewives.

The occupational level of the rearing parents varied somewhat by age of twins at separation (Table 12). Group I had more farmers (70% of mothers and 65.3% of fathers) and group II more manual worker fathers (37.5%). Other occupations were rarest in group I (mothers 0.0% and fathers 2.7%), but accounted for 10.2% of fathers in group II.

After separation, 65.7% of pairs did not live together again (60.7% of male and 69.5% of female pairs) and 20.6% lived together for one time period (Table

TABLE 13. Rearing Environment of Cotwins After Separation (% Values)

Characteristic	Men	Women	Total
Not lived together after separation	60.7	69.5	65.7
Lived together once after separation	20.8	20.4	20.6
Lived in different community	50.9	55.4	53.4
Attended different schools	66.7	67.2	66.9
Met cotwin half-yearly or less often	54.8	63.3	59.5
Met common friends half-yearly or less often	58.8	69.4	64.7
Met common relatives half-yearly or less often	64.8	68.8	67.0

TABLE 14. Present Contact Between Cotwins by Sex (% Values)

	Men	Women	Total
Daily or almost daily	3.6	8.4	6.3
Once a week	8.1	7.7	7.9
Once a month	20.8	17.2	18.8
Half-yearly	24.9	24.5	24.7
Rarely	35.5	34.9	35.1
Never	7.1	7.3	7.2

TABLE 15. Present Contact Between Cotwins by Age at Separation (% Values)

	0 (I)	1–2 (II)	3–5 (III)	6–10 (IV)	Total
Daily or almost daily	5.8	7.3	0.0	9.9	6.3
Once a week	9.3	8.2	2.1	10.5	7.9
Once a month	20.9	17.3	14.9	19.1	18.8
Half-yearly	27.9	24.6	26.6	21.6	24.7
Rarely	26.7	38.2	45.7	32.7	35.1
Never	9.3	4.6	10.6	6.2	7.2

13). The separated twins had lived in different communities in 53.4% of cases; 66.9% had attended different schools. Common friends or common relatives were met half-yearly or less often in 64.7% and 67%, respectively. The meeting frequency was less for female than male pairs.

The present frequency of contact, asked separately, was half-yearly in 24.7%, less often in 35.2%, and never in 7.2% of cases (Tables 14 and 15).

For older twins, birth at home, particularly in the sauna, was common. The reported frequency of complications was slightly higher among the early separated twins; further analyses for type of complication, age, sex, and year of birth, are being conducted.

DISCUSSION

Studies on twins reared apart can be very fruitful when the intrapair rearing environments are uncorrelated. In this study, the intrapair correlation of rearing environment varied greatly as it appeared from variables such as age at separation, family members, school, friends, living place, intrapair contact frequency, and education and occupation of rearing parents. However, direct interviews will be needed.

We plan to examine further the intrapair relationships of the rearing environment, both within the group of early separated twins and in the control groups. Objective data from official records, parish registers, etc, can serve to validate various aspects studied. An important source of data is the 1975 questionnaire study [3] which has the advantage of having been conducted prior to the present survey and without special identification of the twins reared apart. The 1975 postal questionnaire study data cover smoking habits, alcohol use, leisure-time physical activity, weight, height, and drug usage. Psychosocial factors such as marital status, occupational history, changes of residence and employment, extroversion and lability, and type-A behavior were also studied, as well as various symptoms and history of disease.

The cause of separation, based on a self-report, seems to be fairly often associated with some psychosocial pathology. The separation of members of a twin pair may also mean intrapair selection: It is not an ideal experimental situation, so that the generalization of results may meet with some problems. Further assessment and comparisons with singletons from the general population and with psychiatric outpatients are ongoing.

REFERENCES

1. Bouchard TJ: Developmental patterns in monozygotic twins reared apart. Third International Congress on Twins Studies, Jerusalem, 1980.
2. Juel-Nielsen N: Individual and environment: A psychiatric-psychological investigation of monozygous twins reared apart. Acta Psychtr Neurol Scand Suppl 183, 1965.
3. Kaprio J, Sarna S, Koskenvuo M, Rantasalo I: The Finnish Twin Registry: Formation and compilation, questionnaire study, zygosity determination procedures and research program. Prog Clin Biol Res 24B:179–184, 1978.
4. Kaprio J, Sarna S, Koskenvuo M, Rantasalo I: Baseline characteristics of the Finnish Twin Registry: Section II: History of symptoms and illnesses, use of drugs, physical characteristics, smoking, alcohol and physical activity. Publications of the Department of Public Health Science M37, Helsinki, 1978.
5. Kaprio J, Koskenvuo M, Artimo M, Sarna S, Rantasalo I: Baseline characteristics of the Finnish Twin Registry: Section I: Materials, methods, representativeness, and results for variables special to twin studies. Publications of the Department of Public Health Science M47, Helsinki, 1979.
6. Koskenvuo M, Langinvainio H, Kaprio J, Rantasalo I, Sarna S: The Finnish Twin Registry: Baseline characteristics, Section III: Occupational and psychosocial factors. Publications of the Department of Public Health Science M49, Helsinki, 1979.
7. Newman HH, Freeman FN, Holzinger KJ: "Twins: A Study of Heredity and Environment." Chicago: University of Chicago Press, 1937.
8. Sarna S, Kaprio J, Sistonen P, Koskenvuo M: Diagnosis of twin zygosity by mailed questionnaire. Hum Hered 28:241–254, 1978.
9. Sarna S, Kaprio J: Use of multiple logistic analysis in twin zygosity diagnosis. Hum Hered 30:71–80, 1980.
10. Shields J: "Monozygotic Twins Brought Up Apart and Brought Up Together." London: Oxford University Press, 1962.

Twin Research 3: Intelligence, Personality,
and Development, pages 199–209
© 1981 Alan R. Liss, Inc., 150 Fifth Avenue, New York, NY 10011

Synchronized Developmental Pathways for Infant Twins

Ronald S. Wilson

University of Louisville School of Medicine, Kentucky

INTRODUCTION

The study of developmental processes in twins furnishes a powerful resource for examining the role of gene-action systems in guiding the course of growth. While there is a steady and rapid progression from birth onward, the growth rate is not entirely uniform for a given child, but rather moves in episodes of acceleration and lag [2]. The timing of the growth spurts follows a distinctive pattern for each child, and consequently a child who may be smaller than average at one age may then enter a phase of rapid growth, and ultimately catch up with or surpass his peers at a later age.

The effect of such individualized patterns of growth is that many children may change in relative size from one age to the next; and in this sense it may appear that the underlying developmental processes are erratic, rather than coherent. But if there is an underlying ground plan, a chronogenetic pattern, then the distinctive developmental gradients should unfold in synchrony for twins sharing the same genetic make-up. Episodes of acceleration and lag in growth would then occur in parallel for both twins and would presumably represent the activity of timed gene-action systems, which switch on and off according to a pre-determined plan.

Physical growth data are valuable for illustrating these synchronized developmental gradients in twins, since the relationship to genetic factors is well established and the measures themselves are precise and virtually free of error. For psychological data, however, the measures are much less precise, and this has often confounded efforts to demonstrate any continuity in behavioral development during childhood.

Supported in part by grants from the Office of Child Development (OCD 90-C-922) and the National Science Foundation (BNS 76-17315).

Indeed, the age-to-age changes for each child have often been interpreted as evidence against any systematic effects of a genetic origin. But twin data recently reported for early mental development have shown a significant degree of synchrony in the profile of scores for monozygotic MZ twins [5], which might be taken as confirming a genetic influence on the spurts and lags in mental development.

The present paper examines data for both physical growth and mental development obtained from a sample of 67 MZ pairs during the first two years of life. The twins were part of a larger longitudinal study in which measures of height and mental development were routinely obtained throughout childhood [for a description of the sample and the assessment procedures, cf 5].

The data to be analyzed were obtained when the twins were 3, 6, 12, 18, and 24 months of age, and the mental development scores were obtained from the Bayley Mental Scale [1]. The twins were tested by separate examiners at each visit, who also alternated between the twins over successive visits.

The Bayley Mental Scale yields age-adjusted standardized scores (MDI scores) with a mean of 100 and standard deviation of 16; for comparison purposes the height measures were also standardized at each age, using the complete twin sample as the standardization group (n > 600). An infant of average height at every age would have scores of 100, with no variability.

But if there were episodes of acceleration or lag in growth, the standardized scores would change across ages, reflecting the relative upward (or downward) shift of the child's height in relation to his age mates. Similarly, the profile of mental development scores would reflect phases of rapid advancement or lag in the growth of mental functions, as measured by the Bayley Scale.

The basic data may be illustrated by reference to the growth curves for six pairs of MZ twins, as shown in Figure 1. Note that for some pairs the average height during the first two years was considerably different from the average mental development, as in pairs A, C, and E; in some pairs the trends moved in opposite directions, as in B, C, and E; and in some pairs the episodes of spurt and lag were very pronounced for one variable but less so for the other, as in pairs B, D, and E.

With certain exceptions, the members of each pair showed a concordant pattern of change for height and for mental development, and the strong tendency was for the twins to converge over age and match each other rather closely by 24 months. As the curves suggested, the developmental trends for height and mental functions did not seem to follow a common gradient; the two variables appeared to be independent as far as early development was concerned.

ANALYSIS OF HEIGHT

Turning to the full sample of 67 MZ pairs, the height data were analyzed first to establish a baseline estimate of individual consistency and twin concordance for a precisely measured biological variable. Initially, the height scores for each infant were intercorrelated for the five ages of measurement, and the resultant correlations are shown in Table 1.

It is apparent that the correlations for height were relatively high, especially from 12 months onward. The individual differences in height became progressively stabilized, and the changes due to spurts and lags in height gain were reduced in magnitude. Each infant's growth trajectory became more securely established in the rank-ordering of growth curves, and did not markedly deviate from one age to the next.

The consistency of each infant's height was estimated by applying a repeated-measures analysis of variance to the five height measures obtained at 3, 6, 12, 18, and 24 months [8]. The results showed that the average intercorrelation between ages was $r = 0.80$; and if a composite height measure were obtained for each infant based on all five measurements, the stability or internal consistency of this composite height measure was 0.95.

The consistency in relative height across these five ages accounted for 83.4% of the variance, whereas the spurts and lags in height gain accounted for 16.0% of the variance. From this perspective, the spurts and lags in height gain were superimposed upon a rather stable ordering of individual differences (especially from 12 months onward), and the consistency of these differences in relative height accounted for a major portion of the variance in the height curves.

Turning to the analysis of twin concordance, the within-pair correlations for the twins' height at each age are shown in Table 2. The correlations began at a strong intermediate level at 3 months, and then moved progressively upward until reaching $R = 0.89$ at 24 months. Obviously there was a substantial degree of similarity in height among these MZ twins, and some initial height differences at the early ages were progressively reduced by 24 months.

The height measures were then analyzed for twin concordance in the growth gradients during infancy by a repeated-measures twin ANOVA [6] and the results are summarized in Table 3. The results showed a high degree of twin concordance for average height (the composite of all five measures), and a significant but lesser degree of concordance for the spurts and lags in height gain ($R = 0.60$). Some of the nonconcordance for height gain was a reflection of certain pairs that were originally discordant for height at birth, and subsequently the smaller member gained more rapidly in the early months to offset the original deficit [7].

It will be noted, incidentally, that twin concordance for the composite height measure accounted for the largest proportion of variance in the data, whereas the concordance for spurts and lags accounted for a considerably smaller proportion. However, both components added together reflect the total degree of synchrony in these growth curves for MZ twins: 72.4% + 9.6% = 82.0% of the variance in height accounted for by these synchronized developmental pathways. Evidently, there is a powerful contribution of the genotype to the measured height at each age, and the pattern of height gain between ages, even during this early period of infancy.

MENTAL DEVELOPMENT

With this perspective from a physical-growth variable, we turn to the measures of mental development obtained for these twins at the same ages. The

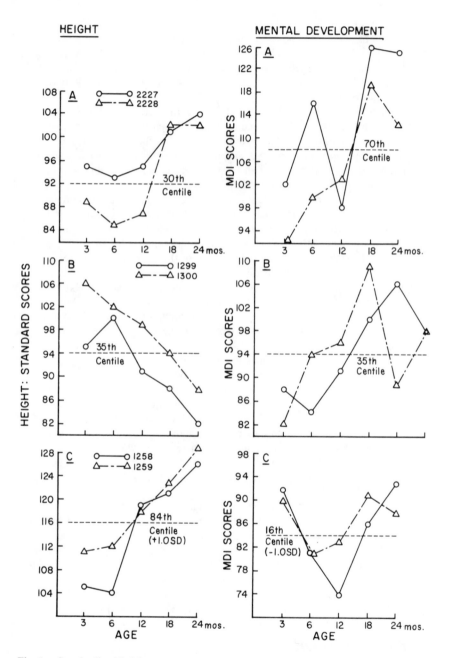

Fig. 1.   Standardized height scores and mental development scores for six pairs of MZ twins.

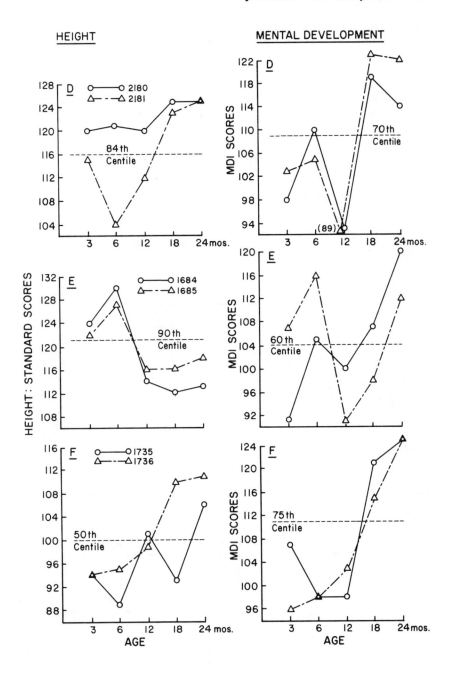

Fig. 1. (Continued).

TABLE 1. Height Measures: Intercorrelations Between Ages

Age	Age (months)			
	6	12	18	24
3	0.79	0.72	0.65	0.62
6		0.83	0.78	0.76
12			0.89	0.88
18				0.95

TABLE 2. Height Measures: Within-Pair Correlations For MZ Twins

Age (months)	3	6	12	18	24
Within pair R	0.78	0.80	0.86	0.87	0.89

TABLE 3. Summary of Twin ANOVA for Standardized Height Scores, 3–24 Months

Source of variance	df	MS	Twin correlation	Percentage of variance explained	Results signify:
Pairs (average height)	66	1868.6	0.88	72.4	Twin concordance for composite of five scores
Within pairs	67	118.1		9.8	
Ages	4	283.9		0.5	Main effects of age removed by standardization
Pairs × ages (pattern of height gain)	264	76.6	0.60	9.6	Twin concordance for spurts and lags in height gain
Within-pairs × ages	268	18.9		7.8	

TABLE 4. Mental Development Measures: Intercorrelations Between Ages

Age	Age (months)			
	6	12	18	24
3	0.42	0.33	0.41	0.37
6		0.42	0.41	0.42
12			0.48	0.51
18				0.66

correlations between mental development scores are presented in Table 4. The intercorrelations were moderate in size and did not reach the 0.60s until the final 18–24 month correlation. In contrast to height, the measures of mental development were much more affected by age-to-age changes, and the ordering of individual differences was much less consistent during infancy. The average intercorrelation was only r = 0.44, whereas for height it was r = 0.80.

These results were further confirmed by a repeated-measures ANOVA, which showed that 55.2% of the score variance was explained by each S's consistency from age to age, whereas 44.2% of the variance was attributed to changes between ages. Obviously, the fluctuations, or spurts and lags in mental development, played a much larger role than for height; and the question was whether these fluctuations represented a genuine phenomenon, or whether they were simply a by-product of unreliable measurements.

It is here particularly that twin data can provide a powerful lever for detecting some coherent pattern underlying the apparent fluctuations from age to age. If MZ twins display a synchronized pattern of change in the mental test scores, then there is a strong likelihood of a common chronogenetic influence shared by both twins.

The within-pair correlations were first calculated for the scores at each age, and the results are shown in Table 5. The correlations began in the mid-0.60s and expanded into the low 0.80s by the second year, revealing a substantial degree of concordance. In fact, the twin correlations were considerably higher than the age-to-age correlations in Table 4, so that twin A's score was a better predictor of his cotwin's score at the same age than of his own score at a later age. Thus, while there may have been substantial fluctuations in each twin's score from age to age, the changes seemed to occur in parallel for the members of MZ pairs.

This inference was tested specifically by applying the repeated-measures twin ANOVA to the mental test scores, and the results are summarized in Table 6. The results showed that twin concordance for the composite mental test score was very high (R = 0.89), equal to the concordance for height; and similarly, the concordance for spurts and lags in mental development (R = 0.56) was virtually the same as for height. From the standpoint of concordance in developmental trends, the twin correlations were comparable for height and mental development.

However, the percentage of variance explained by each component confirmed what had already been inferred from Tables 1 and 4: The age-to-age changes, or discontinuities, were much more prominent for mental development than for height. The spurts and lags in mental development contributed a much

TABLE 5. Mental Development Measures: Within-Pair Correlations

Age (months)	3	6	12	18	24
Twin correlation	0.66	0.74	0.67	0.83	0.80

larger proportion of variance, and in this sense there were considerably greater fluctuations in mental status from age to age.

But from the perspective of concordance among twins, the synchronization of mental development was as congruent or in phase as the synchronization of height gain. Therefore, the apparent discontinuities in mental development were not simply a function of measurement error or unsystematic factors inducing change, but rather reflected some systematic effects acting in age-linked fashion, and influencing both members of MZ pairs. A significant portion of these effects are chronogenetic in origin, and a detailed discussion of how timed gene-action systems might influence the development of the central nervous system and the expansion of mental functions may be found in Wilson [5].

JOINT DEVELOPMENTAL TRENDS

To what extent do the gradients for height and mental development follow a common course for each infant? Referring to the original graphs in Figure 1,

TABLE 6. Summary of Twin ANOVA for Mental Development Scores, 3–24 Months

Source of variance	df	MS	Twin correlation	Percentage of variance explained	Results signify:
Pairs (average mental status)	66	985.7	0.89	47.0	Twin concordance for composite of five scores
Within pairs	67	58.7		5.9	
Ages	4	282.4		0.4	Standardization removes age effects
Pairs × ages (pattern of mental scores)	264	162.7	0.56	23.7	Twin concordance for spurts and lags in mental development
Within pairs × ages	268	45.3		23.0	

TABLE 7. Intercorrelations Between Height and Mental Development at All Ages

Mental development at different ages	Height at different ages				
	3	6	12	18	24
3	0.33	0.15	0.12	0.03	0.04
6	0.37	0.27	0.17	0.14	0.14
12	0.21	0.08	0.08	0.00	−0.06
18	0.31	0.17	0.14	0.11	0.04
24	0.26	0.18	0.20	0.21	0.14

were the score profiles for each infant equally elevated for height and mental development, and did the episodes of acceleration or lag occur at the same time?

As a first step in answering these questions, the correlations were computed between both variables at every age, and the results are presented in Table 7. Looking first at the diagonal entries, there were significant correlations between height and mental development at 3 and 6 months, but at subsequent ages the correlations dropped to very small values that were no longer significant. As noted previously [4], prematurity had a pronounced suppressive effect on both birth size and initial developmental status, and this effect was sustained in the early months of life. However, as the premature twins recovered from the effects of prematurity, the relationship between physical size and mental development became dissociated, and the correlations regressed to an insignificant level.

There was virtually no relationship between precocity in height and precocity in mental development during the period from 12 to 24 months. Whether this would continue to be true at later ages is a matter to be explored, but it was clearly the case during one very active developmental phase of infancy.

One other relationship in the matrix is worth noting. There was a significant correlation between the 3-month height measure and each of the subsequent mental development measures, which would suggest that initial body size had some long-standing association with mental development—perhaps as a residual holdover of prematurity.

When the data were carefully examined, however, it was found that several twins had missed the 3-month visit, and therefore they did not appear in any of the correlations involving the 3-month height measures. These twins happened to be slightly larger than average for height, but somewhat below average in mental development, and so when they were included in the correlations at subsequent ages, they effectively offset the initial slight positive correlation and pulled the value toward zero. Therefore the apparent relationship between height at 3 months and later mental development was principally an artifact of these few missing cases.

Turning to the issue of correlated developmental trends for height and mental functions, this was assessed by employing a two-factor, repeated-measures ANOVA, with the principal interest being in the interaction term that represented the congruence in score profiles for the two variables. The correlation expressing this congruence was very low ($R = 0.07$), indicating that for each infant there was no linkage in the pattern of growth spurts and lags for height and mental development.

The discrepancies illustrated by the curves in Figure 1 were replicated throughout the entire sample, and it may be concluded that the developmental gradients for height and mental functions proceeded according to independent schedules during the first 2 years of life. For any given infant, the gradients might be closely related (as in pair F, case 1736); or conspicuously divergent (as in pair B, case 1299); but on a samplewide basis, the developmental gradients were orthogonal. Again, this is in reference to the individual phases of rapid growth or lag superimposed upon the basic species trajectory—the latter is a very powerful age-related process, and virtually all children grow taller and make progressive advances in mental functioning throughout the ages of childhood.

Given these results, does either variable seem to be more tightly programmed by the genotype during early development? If the percentage of variance explained by MZ twin concordance is taken as a rough index of genotypic control, then height appears to be more fully determined. Twin concordance for height accounted for 82.0% of the total variance, whereas twin concordance for mental development accounted for 70.7% of the variance. This would suggest a more complete genetic control of the manifold growth processes that culminate in linear height during the first 2 years.

It is worth noting that the MZ concordance estimates were further strengthened for both variables during the later ages of childhood. For MZ twins measured at 4, 5, and 6 years of age, the concordance for height over this period accounted for 92.4% of the variance, whereas for mental development the twin concordance accounted for 82.6% of the variance. Clearly, these MZ twins progressively converged toward a common value by school age, and early-appearing differences in many of the pairs were gradually reduced.

Height still appeared to be under tighter control of the genotype, and it is instructive to realize that the growth curves for two genetic replicates could be pulled closer together during childhood, in spite of rather large differences in birth size. Data for ten such MZ pairs were reported in detail in Wilson [7]. The growth gradients appear to be strongly canalized and capable of resuming the targeted pathway in spite of early deflections, a point that Waddington has elaborated in detail [3].

CONCLUSIONS

These results strongly suggest that developmental processes are initiated and guided by timed gene-action systems which are activated in sequential fashion, and on a schedule largely determined by the genotype. In addition to the profound species-wide programming of developmental processes, there are distinctive variations in rate and schedule superimposed upon the main trends, and these furnish the dispersion of individual differences in the population. Each zygote contains a preprogrammed set of instructions that constantly propel the developmental processes along predetermined pathways, and maintains the directional focus in the face of deflecting agents.

While the itinerary of the developmental pathways is in some ways unique for each child, there is a remarkable degree of synchrony for MZ twins, and it must represent a powerful chronogenetic influence on development. We might anticipate that if such influence is clearly demonstrable for mental development, it will also be evident in other behavioral domains as well.

REFERENCES

1. Bayley N: "Bayley Scales of Infant Development." New York: Psychological Corporation, 1969.
2. Tanner JM: Physical growth. In Mussen PH, (ed): "Carmichael's Manual of Child Psychology," vol 1. New York: Wiley, 1970.
3. Waddington CH: "The Evolution of an Evolutionist." Ithaca, New York: Cornell University Press, 1975.
4. Wilson RS: Mental development in twins. In Oliverio A (ed): "Genetics, Environment, and Intelligence." Amsterdam: Elsevier, 1977, pp 305–334.
5. Wilson RS: Synchronies in mental development: An epigenetic perspective. Science, 202:939–948, 1978.
6. Wilson RS: Analysis of longitudinal twin data: Basic model and applications to physical growth measures. Acta Genet Med Gemellol 28:93–105, 1979.
7. Wilson RS: Twin growth: Initial deficit, recovery, and trends in concordance from birth to nine years. Ann Hum Biol 6:205–220, 1979.
8. Winer BJ: "Statistical Principles in Experimental Design." New York: McGraw-Hill, 1962.

Twin Research 3: Intelligence, Personality,
and Development, pages 211 – 226

Heredity-Environment Influences on Growth and Development During Adolescence

Siv Fischbein
Department of Educational Research, Stockholm Institute of Education

INTRODUCTION

Twin studies have been used by many researchers to estimate the proportion of variance attributable to genetic factors [25, 36]. The statistical model applied to twin data has been an additive one. The assumption made is that a change in environment will contribute to a comparable change in all genotypes.

The additive model has been borrowed from agricultural genetics, where it has been found useful. It is, however, a plausible assumption that interactional effects will play a more prominent role among human beings. Such effects will lead to different reactions in genotypes exposed to the same environmental impact. If this is true, the additive model has obvious shortcomings, since it confuses genetic and interactional effects in interpreting data from monozygotic (MZ) and dizygotic (DZ) twin pairs.

The assumption made is that within-pair differences for MZ twins are due to environmental factors and for DZ twins to both genetic and environmental factors. When genotype-environment interaction or correlation is present, this assumption will not be correct [21, 26].

GENOTYPE-ENVIRONMENT INTERACTION

Genotype-environment interaction can be estimated within the frame of an additive model for assessing the proportional contribution of genetic and environmental variance to human behavioural traits. The proponents of this type of G × E interaction state that "genes can control sensitivity to the environment and that the environment can modulate the expression of genes" [5: p 17]. The interaction term is estimated for groups of individuals in an analysis of variance design and implies that individuals high in a trait will react differently from individuals low in a trait. It is thus connected to genotypic level, which presupposes a quantification of genetic contribution.

Plomin et al [38] have discussed the difference between the above-mentioned population concept and the organismic type of interaction. The latter connotes something more than the statistical type of interaction, namely that "the organism actively interacts with its environment" [38: p 310]. The authors suggest that this should be characterized as active genotype-environment correlation instead of interaction.

Buss [3] has stressed the importance of separating different kinds of interaction. He is not specifically discussing genotype-environment interaction but more generally what he calls person-environment interaction. In the person (P) are of course embedded genetic aspects, since P is a function of both genetic (G) and environmental (E) influences. $G \times E = P$ will determine the reaction toward E, which in turn will influence $G \times E = P$. In other words, there is a reciprocal relationship between environmental and person characteristics, the latter consisting of genotype combined with earlier environmental influences specific for the individual. Buss refers to Overton and Reese [37], who have developed the argument that the statistical type of interaction calculated in an analysis of variance design is linked to a mechanistic model of reasoning. The other type of interaction, however, where there is a reciprocal relationship between individual and environment, has been connected with an organismic model. Overton and Reese have argued that the two types of interaction are incompatible with each other since they are embedded in two different metaphysical systems. Buss points out that the basic difference between the mechanistic type and the organismic type of interaction is that the former predicts a nonreciprocal relationship between environmental (E) and person (P) characteristics, so that behaviour is a joint function of $E \times P$. The organismic type of interaction, however, presupposes a reciprocal relationship and focuses upon the psychological environment and the person as these affect, and are affected by, each other. This is an active process, so that individuals are affected by the environment, but also react to and change environmental conditions in which they are living. This definition of interaction could also be compared to Piaget's notion of this concept [20]. As can be seen, this way of describing interaction is also very similar to the genotype-environment correlation concept described by Plomin et al [38].

Lerner [28] is also discussing the reciprocal character of organism-environment relations. He proposes as well that the linear type of interactions so far favoured in nature-nurture research should be supplemented by a dynamic interactionism. "While this paradigm," he asserts, "leads to a theoretical view of development which necessarily takes a stance on the core nature-nurture issue, it does so in a manner which is capable of integrating not only the 'main effects' of nature and nurture variables, and the 'weak' or 'mechanistic' interactions among these variables, but in addition, is capable of integrating the entire range and types of potential interrelations among such variables" [28: pp 3–4]. Earlier twin studies have mainly concentrated on the main effects and mechanistic interactions referred to above and a consideration of dynamic interactionism will require, among other things, a developmental approach [24].

GENOTYPE-ENVIRONMENT CORRELATION

Plomin et al [38] distinguish three main kinds of G × E correlation and define this concept as "a function of the frequency with which certain genotypes and certain environments occur together." They point out that G × E correlation may be both positive and negative.

Passive G × E correlation is present when endowment and environment covary so that, for instance, bright children tend to live in a home conducive to their intellectual development. This type of correlation is called "passive" because it occurs independently of the activities of the individual in question. Of course the existence of this type of correlation does not exclude the active type of G × E correlation (see below).

Reactive G × E correlation signifies that people can react differently to persons of different genotypes, thus creating conspicuously dissimilar environmental circumstances. An example of this type of correlation is when certain personality traits are reinforced by persons in the environment. The reactive G × E correlation has often been discussed in connection with twin studies. It has been maintained that MZ twins tend to be treated more alike than DZ twins, which would make it unwarranted to assume that environments are the same.

Active G × E correlation occurs as a result of the individual's own action. People tend to create for themselves different environments related to their genetic potentials. For instance, in the same home a brighter child may choose to read more books than a less bright child, thereby creating for himself a more stimulating environment. In twin studies a few attempts have been made to separate the reactive and active type of correlation by studying wrongly classified MZ and DZ twins [4, 34, 35]. It seems as though behaviour is connected to actual genotype and not perception of zygosity. Parents also tend to perceive MZ twins as more similar than DZ twins, but knowledge of zygosity did not affect the way the parents treat their children. It consequently seems as though the active type of G × E correlation is a more powerful determinant of behaviour in these studies than reactive correlational effects.

Both Plomin et al [38] and Eaves et al [5], who have discussed the active type of G × E correlation, have stressed the difficulty to distinguish between this type of correlation and G × E interaction. This is purely a matter of definition, and it will probably be impossible to maintain a clear-cut distinction between these two concepts.

The following definition of G × E interaction has been proposed by Erlenmeyer-Kimling [8, p 187]: "What we usually mean by interaction is that genotypes can be shown to react in different ways to the same environmental treatments." This definition implies an active reaction from the individual, thus a reciprocal relationship as defined by Buss [3]. A nonreciprocal relationship would be expressed as "the same environment will affect individuals differently depending on their genotypes."

The reciprocal definition that will be used in the following will make the distinction between G × E interaction and active G × E correlation quite arbitrary. The "same" environment (eg, living in the same home or attending the same class) will tend to affect MZ twins similarly on the basis of their identical inheritance. MZ twins will also tend to react more similarly than DZ twins to the "same" environment, thus creating more similar environments, even if they objectively are experiencing the "same" environment. The extent of interactional and correlational effects will tend to vary both with environmental factors and with the characteristic studied. A further elaboration of these assumptions will be made in the following when a model for interpreting longitudinal twin data will be presented.

HEREDITY-ENVIRONMENT INTERACTION AND CORRELATION IN THE DEVELOPMENT OF TWINS

Species-specific development is obviously strongly genetically regulated in both man and animal. Even quite drastic environmental influences will probably not permanently change a normal growth curve. A severe illness, for instance, can arrest the child's growth, but after recovery, a catch-up effect will normally be evident. Human beings tend to crawl before they walk and babble before they talk, and the maturational cycle occurs in a certain temporal sequence [30]. The onset of puberty, for instance, tends to be more concordant for MZ than DZ twins [11, 18]. This is true whether the criteria are peak height velocity (PHV), menarche, or ratings of secondary sex characteristics. Intraclass correlations [31] for age at PHV, which give a measure of within-pair similarity for timing of the height spurt, are as high as 0.85 for MZ boys and 0.78 for MZ girls. For the DZ pairs the corresponding correlations are 0.42 and 0.39 [12].

Genetic and environmental influences and their interaction and correlation will tend to vary depending on *both* the characteristic studied *and* environmental circumstances. Longitudinal twin data present certain possibilities to investigate and discuss such influences [10, 13]. Before attempting to outline a model for heredity-environmental contribution, however, some theoretical arguments will be reviewed that have had great impact on the construction of the model. Evidently a common theme in these arguments is the developmental aspect on behavioural variation.

Waddington explicitly assures that "we should think not in terms of homeostasis, but rather of homeorhesis, the stabilization not of a stationary state, but of a pathway of change in time." Behavioural development is pictured as an "epigenetic landscape," where "the development of the phenotype of an individual proceeds along a valley bottom; variations of genotype, or of epigenetic environment, may push the course of development away from the valley floor, up the neighbouring hillside, but there will be a tendency for the process to find its way back, not to the point from which it was displaced — the homeostatic equilibrium — but to some later position on the canalized pathway of change, from which it was diverted" [39: p 258].

Figure 1 gives a simplified illustration of the canalization of the phenotype. The valley is the genetically regulated course of development and the ball is the phenotypic behaviour of the individual. For some characteristics, physical growth and maturity, for instance, the hillsides of the valley are steep and high and it will

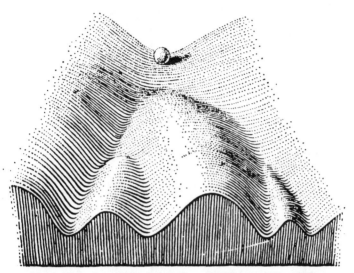

Fig. 1. The epigenetic landscape (from Waddington [39], p 259).

take very drastic environmental influences to push the ball up the hillsides. For other characteristics the hillsides will be more sloping and shallow and it will take much less environmental pressure to influence the position of the ball during the course of development. There will of course be variations in the "epigenetic landscape" depending on genotype, and the reaction to environmental influences will also differ according to individual variations, which implies both genotype-environment interaction and correlation.

Fuller and Thompson have also stressed the developmental aspects in genetic and environmental influences. "The important thing is not to stop development in order to obtain pure measures of genetic effects, but to identify the factors which produce differentiation in development" [19: p 111]. They outline possible outcomes of practice effects (in a training situation) on the relative contributions of genetic and environmental factors during a time period. The "convergence" hypothesis predicts that "when one specific response is reinforced, other responses will be extinguished, and all subjects will converge upon a common pattern" [19: pp 91–92]. This will in the long run contribute to a reduction of genetic variance. The "divergence" hypothesis, however, predicts that "subjects free to exploit their environment in a variety of fashions will by chance light upon quite different modes of adaptation." Thus there will be an increase of the relative contribution of genetic factors to behavioural variation.

The convergence and divergence hypotheses thus imply a difference in genetic contribution to a variable, depending on the amount of freedom given the phenotype to interact with environmental factors. In a restrictive environment genetic factors will contribute less to variation than in a permissive environment.

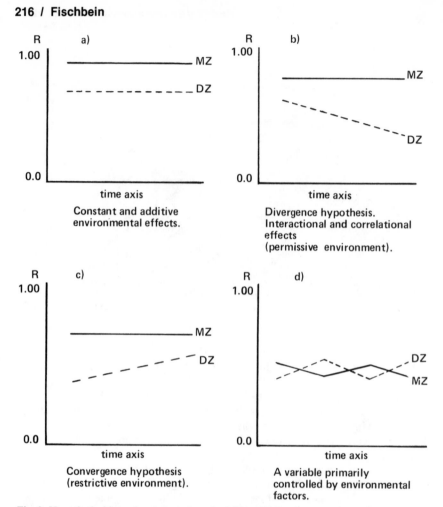

Fig. 2. Hypothetical intraclass correlations for MZ and DZ twins assuming similar environments, and varying nature-nurture contribution.

The theoretical contributions presented above have certain implications for the construction of a model of nature-nurture effects studied on longitudinal twin data. Waddington stresses variations depending on the characteristic studied, whereas Fuller and Thompson are more concerned about variations in environmental circumstances.

Model of Nature-Nurture Contribution

A model for interpreting longitudinal twin data would thus require that interactional and correlational aspects be taken into account, as well as an adaptiveness to type of characteristic studied and environmental factors relevant for its development. Figure 2 is an attempt to outline such a model. Hypothetical intrapair correlations are given for MZ and DZ pairs under the assumption that the twins in a pair are living in the "same" environment and are exposed to similar environmental impact.

Example (a) illustrates development of a characteristic primarily controlled by genetic factors, where environmental effects are assumed to be constant and additive. MZ twins, because of their identical inheritance, tend to be more similar than DZ twins and this difference tends to be of the same magnitude as long as the twins are exposed to the same environmental impact. No lowering of the intrapair correlations with increasing age is hypothesized. Example (b) illustrates the divergence hypothesis proposed by Fuller and Thompson [19]. Under permissive circumstances, MZ twins react similarly to the same environmental influences, whereas DZ twins react differently and thus get progressively less similar. A lowering of the intrapair correlations for DZ but not for MZ twins with increasing age is hypothesized. Example (c) illustrates the convergence hypothesis also suggested by Fuller and Thompson. Owing to restrictive environmental influences, negatively reinforcing genetic differences, DZ twins will get progressively more similar with increasing age. The intrapair correlations will thus increase with age for DZ twins and remain constant for MZ twins. Example (d) illustrates unsystematic environmental effects largely counteracting genetic differences. Since the identical inheritance of MZ twins does not predispose them for greater similarity, it will be rather incidental if the intrapair correlations will be higher or lower for MZ than for DZ twins.

Of course this model is not static, but the results will vary with the population studied and the cultural environment involved. What is classified in one society as a characteristic under (a) might, for instance, be susceptible to interactional and correlational effects as in example (b) under different environmental circumstances. Assuming comparable variables (similar degree of genetic regulation), constitutional factors will be of relatively minor importance in a restrictive environment and greater importance in a permissive environment.

MATERIALS AND METHODS

During the years 1964-1971, a group of twins and a control group of singletons in the same classes from grade 3 to grade 9 in the Swedish compulsory school were the object of a study concerning physical and mental growth during puberty (the SLU project).

Originally, 323 twin pairs and 1,194 controls were included in the SLU sample. The following data were collected: physical measurements (height and weight, menarche, ratings of secondary sex characteristics); ability and achievement measures (intelligence tests, standardized achievement tests); self ratings; ratings by teachers and classmates; socioeconomic background data (father's occupation and income).

The results reported so far for the twins have been mainly concentrated on the first two kinds of variables, physical and cognitive measurements, with twin ratings tending to be inflated by the greater apparent similarity for MZ than DZ pairs. Comparisons of twins and controls for physical growth and for different ability and achievement measures collected in the SLU project have been made in previous reports [9, 14, 17, 32] and the results will now be briefly reviewed.

Height and weight measurements were taken from 10 to 18 years for the male SLU twins and their controls and from 10 to 16 years for the girls [17]. Menarcheal age was also recorded for the girls [2]. There were very small differences between the twin boys and their controls, whereas twin girls were significantly shorter and weighed less than controls.

In grade 5 three subtests from a group-administered intelligence test (DBA) were given to the twins and their controls. The tests were constructed to measure verbal ability, inductive reasoning, and clerical speed. Results from a group-administered intelligence test given at enrollment to military service have also been collected for the male twins. This test consists of four subtests measuring logical reasoning, verbal, spatial, and technical ability. Twin boys tend to have somewhat lower average ability test results than their controls at both age 12 and age 18 [16]. This is in agreement with earlier twin studies [22, 36]. None of the differences are significant, however, and there is a constant trend in the SLU material toward higher similarity to controls in twin boys than girls.

In grades 3 and 6, results on standardized achievement tests, used to equalize marks in the Swedish schools [30], were collected for the SLU twins and their classmates. A comparison between the groups showed the twin girls to have lower average test scores, whereas the twin boys were very similar to singletons in school achievement.

In summary, then, twin girls, but not twin boys, in the SLU project tend to be smaller and weigh less and to have lower average test scores than controls of the same age. A twin handicap has also been found by other investigators [22, 23, 27, 36], and has often been explained by the adverse prenatal conditions that twins tend to experience. There is no obvious explanation, however, why this deficit should be greater for girls than for boys. One reason could, however, be a higher mortality for the twin boys, thus an effect of selective survival.

A final question to discuss in this chapter is whether twins are so different from singletons that this would make it impossible to generalize results found for twins to a population of singletons. For the SLU twin boys this seems not to be a serious problem, since they tend to be very similar to the control group. For the twin girls it should be kept in mind that there are certain average differences between twins and controls. The within-pair comparisons that will be presented in the following chapters, however, are only made for MZ vs DZ twins, and the group comparisons made between these two categories have shown no significant differences whatsoever [9, 17]. The estimation of the relative contribution of genetic and environmental factors to different variables is also based not on a comparison of absolute level but on within-pair similarity. It thus seems safe to conclude that generalizations from twins to singletons can be made from this kind of data.

APPLICATION OF TWIN DATA TO MODEL

Our longitudinal twin data will be discussed with reference to the previously described model of nature-nurture contribution. Each of the SLU twin pairs is living in the same home and generally the twins attend the same classes at school. It can thus be maintained that the twins are exposed to a large extent to similar environmental influences.

Physical growth

Height growth can be assumed to be a largely genetically regulated variable, at least when adequate nutritional supply is provided. Weight growth, however, is clearly much more environmentally influenced and regulated through food intake and physical activity. Different hypothetical outcomes for within-pair similarity in height and weight growth during puberty for MZ and DZ twins could therefore be predicted on the basis of the model presented earlier.

For height growth, a parallel trend in accordance with example (a) would be expected so that MZ pairs tend to be more similar than DZ pairs during puberty. No lowering of the intrapair correlations with increasing age is hypothesized.

For weight growth, a divergent trend according to example (b) is expected since, in the surplus situation prevailing in our society, the twins will be free to choose both food intake and exercise. A lowering of the intrapair correlations for DZ but not for MZ twins with increasing age is hypothesized.

As can be seen from Figure 3, MZ cotwins are very similar in height during puberty. The correlation is around 0.90 for both boys and girls as compared to 0.60–0.70 for DZ pairs.

The correlations for MZ cotwins tend to be high for weight also, around 0.80–0.90 (Fig. 4). For the DZ pairs, however, there seems to be a divergent trend so that the twins are more similar for weight at age 10 than at age 16 or 18. This is especially evident for girls, where the intraclass correlation decreases to about 0.20 at age 16.

It can thus be seen that the correlations for height largely follow the pattern illustrated in example (a) in the model, whereas the pattern for weight is much more similar to example (b). Height growth tends to be primarily controlled by

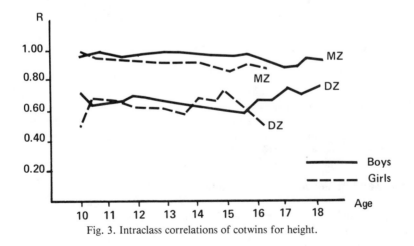

Fig. 3. Intraclass correlations of cotwins for height.

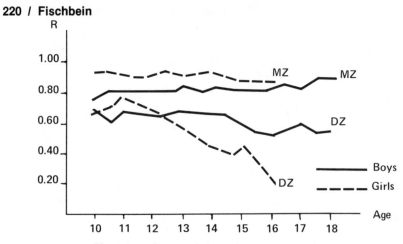

Fig. 4. Intraclass correlations of cotwins for weight.

genetic factors. Weight growth, however, is much more susceptible to interactional and correlational influences. Weight is of course a variable that is much more individually regulated than height and possibly equal consumption will produce different effects depending upon variations in metabolism. Furthermore, if an individual is beginning to get overweight, he will be able to do something about it, maybe eat less or eat another type of food, or exercise more. This regulation is also linked to hereditary factors, so that persons with different inheritances will react differently to the same environmental influences. The same offerings of food in a home will thus tend to affect the twins in a pair differently if they are DZ, but similarly if they are MZ. The within-pair similarity in MZ twins consequently includes environmental (interactional and correlational) components. From this example it can also be seen that it is very complicated to separate the two effects from each other. If identical nutrition affects the DZ twins differently, then it is an interactional effect, but if the twins react differently to the nutritional supply and choose different things, they will themselves create divergent environments and the effect would be classified as correlational.

The sex difference found for weight growth during puberty thus has a plausible explanation, since girls in this age presumably are much more concerned about their weight and regulate it more than boys. This could also be connected with the more rapid change in girls at puberty than in boys [29]. A larger amount of physical activity in boys may also contribute to a decrease in weight fluctuation during this period [6]. It is thus a plausible hypothesis that weight regulation is much more automatic and physically controlled under heavy physical training [1]. In this respect, boys could also be said to experience a more restrictive environment, limiting the expression of genetic variation.

Ability and Achievement Test Results

Verbal and inductive ability test results have been collected for the boys in grade 5 at age 12 and again at the enrollment to military service at age 18. Standardized achievement test scores in mathematics were recorded for both boys and girls in grades 3 and 6.

On the basis of the model presented earlier, hypothetical outcomes of changes over time in within-pair similarity for MZ and DZ twins can be predicted for the different types of test results. Vebal ability can, for instance, be expected to be more environmentally influenced than inductive ability and it is also conceivable that interactional and correlational effects will be more prominent for verbal than for inductive ability [16]: *For verbal ability* a divergent trend would thus be expected, so that a lowering of the intraclass correlation for DZ but not for MZ twins with increasing age is hypothesized. *For inductive reasoning ability* a parallel trend is expected, so that the difference between intraclass correlations for MZ and DZ twins is predicted to be of the same magnitude at both age 12 and age 18.

Figure 5 shows intraclass correlations for the verbal and inductive tests at ages 12 and 18 for MZ and DZ twin boys. At age 18, only pairs with equal length of schooling have been included, since this factor may influence test results. The actual correlation coefficients and the number of pairs are given by Fischbein [16].

A comparison of the intraclass correlations for verbal ability shows an increase from ~ 0.70 to 0.85 for MZ twins from 12 to 18 years of age, and a decrease from ~ 0.60 to 0.50 for DZ twins. The gap between the twin categories as regards within-pair similarity thus tends to increase from age 12 to age 18. The correlations for the inductive tests tend to increase for both MZ and DZ twins from 12 to 18 years of age (~ 0.60 to 0.80 for MZ and ~ 0.45 to 0.55 for DZ).

The divergent hypothesis thus seems to be applicable to the results for verbal ability. This would seem to imply that interactional and correlational effects are of considerable importance for explaining the variation in test scores. The verbal training received both at home and at school tends to have a differential effect for the DZ twins and a similar impact on MZ twins in a pair. On the basis of their different inheritance, the DZ pairs seem to be affected and react differently to similar environmental influences, whereas the identical twins are affected and react in a similar way to this influence.

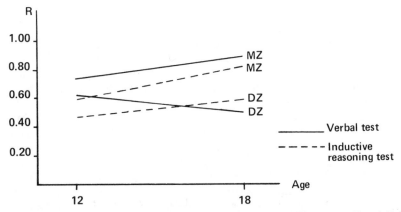

Fig. 5. Intraclass correlations for verbal and inductive reasoning ability at ages 12 and 18 for male MZ and DZ twins with the same length of schooling.

Inductive test results do not show the divergent trend described above. The correlations tend to increase for both MZ and DZ twins from age 12 to age 18. There is neither a divergent nor a convergent trend and the difference between the intraclass correlations tends to be only slightly larger at age 18. These results seem to imply that the variation in inductive ability is less susceptible to heredity-environment interaction and correlation. This explanation is of course tenable only under the circumstances given in the SLU study. The kind of ability measured by the inductive tests is probably much less influenced by parental or school activities than that measured by the verbal tests. If, however, a training of the inductive type of test items was induced, this would possibly affect the results achieved. The rise in intraclass correlations for both MZ and DZ twin pairs between age 12 and age 18 may be explained by a growth in the capacity to solve problems requiring abstract logical reasoning. At 12 years of age this kind of test is very difficult for many late maturers, and this may lead to more unexplained and unsystematic variance. The possibility must also be taken into account that the tests used on the two separate occasions are not quite comparable, and that this could contribute to the observed rise of the intraclass correlations.

Achievement test results in mathematics have been studied longitudinally in grades 3 and 6 in the SLU project. These tests, used in the Swedish school system to equalize marks, are constructed to measure advances made according to the curriculum [30, p 57ff]. They mainly check the effects of training. The hypothesis made in reference to the model would be that the more regulated and restrictive the content in school, the more concordant the trends for the two twin categories. If there is a free and permissive educational environment, however, a discordant trend would be predicted. Of course this will also depend on the type of achievement studied. For certain kinds of motor activities, eg, arm strength or vital capacity, interactional and correlational effects will have much less significance than for the types of cognitive variables discussed here [7].

The construction of the standardized achievement tests and the organization of and curriculum content in Swedish schools would lead to the assumption that, for these types of test results, interactional and correlational factors will be of great importance. Lundgren has hypothesized that "differences between children will increase cumulatively as a result of the teaching process" [33, p 227]. This could also be suspected for the reason that there has been a trend in Swedish schools toward a reduced societal pressure and use of varying control instruments. The differentiation of development with increasing age is well documented and will also lead to a formulation of the following hypothesis [30, pp 130–131]: For standardized achievement test results in mathematics, a divergent trend would be expected, so that a lowering of the intraclass correlation for DZ, but not for MZ, twins with increasing age is hypothesized.

Figure 6 gives the intraclass correlations for the mathematics test in grades 3 and 6 for MZ and DZ twin girls and boys. A thorough presentation of the results and the number of pairs on which they are based is given by Fischbein [16]. In order to make educational environment as similar as possible for the twins in a pair, only pairs attending the same classes in grades 3 and 6 have been included. In spite of this, we can see that DZ twins tend to be less concordant for achievement test results in grade 6 than in grade 3. The opposite is true for MZ pairs and this trend is the same for both boys and girls.

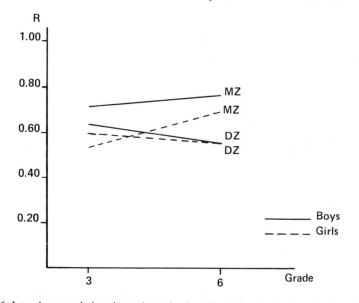

Fig. 6. Intraclass correlations in mathematics for twin boys and girls in grades 3 and 6.

Obviously a similar training does not make children more similar in the variable trained, not even if they are DZ twins living in the same homes. MZ twins, however, do tend to get more concordant, since they are affected by and react similarly to the type of environmental influences provided by the school.

In summary, then, heredity-environment interaction and correlation seem to contribute most to variation for weight growth and verbal ability as well as for mathematics achievement at school. Height growth and inductive ability tend to be primarily genetically regulated under the circumstances present in the SLU project, where the nutritional supply and environmental stimulation for most children can be considered sufficient.

DISCUSSION

It has been maintained that earlier twin studies generally have neglected effects applicable to heredity-environment interaction and correlation. True enough, such effects have been estimated in analysis of variance designs and have often been shown to be of minor importance. It can be suggested, however, that those estimates, based on comparisons of within-pair similarity of MZ and DZ twins, will tend to overestimate hereditary effects since these are inflated by interactional and correlational influences. By heredity-environment interaction is inferred a tendency for a similar environmental impact to affect individuals differentially, and by correlation, that individuals tend to react differently to environmental influences, thereby actively creating dissimilar environmental circumstances. Longitudinal twin data, such as those provided in the SLU project, give unique possibilities to study such influences during a period when the twins are experiencing the "same" environments and are exposed to similar training influences.

A model has been presented that involves determinants of individual variation for different types of characteristics and under different environmental circumstances. Varying outcomes can be predicted according to this model:

a) MZ twin pairs are uniformly more concordant than DZ pairs during a period when they are exposed to similar environmental influences. This should be applicable to characteristics where the variation is determined primarily by genetic factors and environmental influences are constant and additive.

b) There is a discordant trend so that within-pair similarity for MZ twins tends to be uniformly high, whereas DZ twins grow more discordant during similar environmental exposure. This trend can be explained by means of heredity-environment interactional and correlational effects. This assumption implies that individuals with identical inheritance will be affected by and will react similarly to environmental influences, whereas individuals with nonidentical inheritance will be affected and react differently and thus get more discordant over a time period when they are exposed to similar environmental circumstances. This trend will be especially evident for characteristics where a large amount of freedom is given to interpret environmental influences differentially.

c) A concordant trend is evident when within-pair similarity for MZ twins is uniformly high, and DZ twins also tend to grow more concordant over a time period when the twins are exposed to similar environmental influences. These will have a similar effect for both MZ and DZ and interactional and correlational effects will be negligible. The concordant trend will be especially evident for certain types of characteristics and for restrictive environmental circumstances where only certain behaviours are allowed or encouraged.

d) There is no consistent trend, either discordant or concordant, and MZ twins are not uniformly more similar than DZ. If environmental factors primarily determine variation in a characteristic, sometimes DZ and sometimes MZ twins will be more similar and this will be a random effect.

Looking at the variables available for the SLU twins, one can conclude that height growth during puberty shows a trend consistent with (a) above. MZ twins are uniformly more concordant than DZ twins for height growth from 10 to 18 years, and there is no discordant or concordant trend. This would imply that height growth during puberty is genetically regulated in our society with sufficient nutritional supply. Weight growth, however, shows a discordant trend consistent with (b) and this is especially evident for girls. Environmental factors (eg, food intake or physical exercise) tend to influence individuals differentially, depending upon their endowments, and in our society girls are probably more concerned with their weight during puberty and try to regulate it more than boys. Physical exercise should also be considered a restrictive environmental factor more prominent for boys than for girls at this age.

Cognitive growth, measured by a group-administered ability test and school achievement tests, also tends to show a discordant trend, at least for verbal ability and mathematics achievement. The trend for inductive ability is more consistent with (a) above and shows neither a discordant nor a concordant trend. It can be assumed that this is due to the verbal ability and mathematics achievement tests' being more susceptible to training than the inductive ability test. It is quite understandable that interactional and correlational effects should be of great importance for verbal ability and school achievement, since the same environmental influences will tend to be experienced differently by individuals with different endowments. In a more restrictive environment, where certain behaviours are reinforced and others extinguished, this would probably be much less evident.

It will be evident from the summary of results presented that nature-nurture influences tend to vary, depending on the characteristic studied and the existing environmental conditions. A more permissive and free environment will generally lead to greater interactional and correlational effects, whereas a more restrictive environment will lead to more variance being explained by environmental influences experienced by individuals. The heredity-environment interaction and correlation can therefore be regulated to a certain extent by environmental changes. It is thus of great importance to discuss the probable effect of such changes.

REFERENCES

1. Åstrand P-O, Rodahl K: "Textbook of Work Physiology." New York: McGraw Hill, 1970.
2. Bergsten-Brucefors A: A note on the accuracy of recalled age at menarche. Ann Hum Biol 3:71–73, 1976.
3. Buss AR: The trait-situation controversy and the concept of interaction. Pers Soc Psychol Bull 3:196–201, 1977.
4. Cohen DJ, Dibble E, Grawe JM: Parental style: Mother's and father's perception of their relation with twin children. Arch Genet Psychol 34:445–451, 1977.
5. Eaves L, Last K, Martin NG, Jinks JL: A progressive approach to non-additivity and genotype-environmental covariance in the analysis of human differences. Br J Math Statist Psychol 30:1–42, 1977.
6. Engström L-M: Physical activity in adolescence. Doctoral thesis (in Swedish) presented at the Department of Educational Research, School of Education, Stockholm, 1975.
7. Engström L-M, Fischbein S: Physical capacity in twins. Acta Genet Med Gemellol 26:159–165, 1977.
8. Erlenmeyer-Kimling L: Gene-environment interactions and the variability of behavior. In Ehrmann L, Omenn GS, Caspari E (eds): "Genetics, Environment and Behavior." New York: Academic Press, 1972.
9. Fischbein S: Being a twin. Report No. 2 (in Swedish) from the Department of Educational Research, School of Education, Stockholm, 1976.
10. Fischbein S: Like and unlike twins. A longitudinal study of within-pair differences for MZ and DZ twins. Report No 4 (in Swedish) from the Department of Educational Research, School of Education, Stockholm, 1977.
11. Fischbein S: Onset of puberty in MZ and DZ twins. Acta Genet Med Gemellol 26:151–158, 1977.
12. Fischbein S: Intra-pair similarity in physical growth of monozygotic and dizygotic twins during puberty. Ann Hum Biol 4:417–430, 1977.
13. Fischbein S: Heredity-environment interaction in the development of twins. Int J Behav Dev 1:313–322, 1978.
14. Fischbein S: School achievement and test results for twins and singletons in relation to social background. In Nance WE (ed): "Twin Research: Psychology and Methodology." New York: Alan R Liss, 1978, 101–109.
15. Fischbein S: Biosocial aspects on mathematics learning. Scand J Educ Res 1:1–14, 1978.
16. Fischbein S: Intra-pair similarity in IQ of monozygotic and dizygotic male twins at 12 and 18 years of age. Ann Hum Biol 6:495–504, 1979.

17. Fischbein S, Lindgren G: Height and weight for twins and singleton controls from 10 to 18 years. Report No. 12 (in Swedish) from the Department of Educational Research, School of Education, Stockholm, 1975.
18. Fischbein S, Nordqvist T: Profile comparisons of physical growth for monozygotic and dizygotic twin pairs. Ann Hum Biol 5:321–328, 1978.
19. Fuller JL, Thompson WR: "Behavior Genetics." New York: John Wiley, 1961.
20. Furth, HG: Piaget, IQ, and the nature-nurture controversy. Hum Dev 16:61–73, 1973.
21. Goldberger AS: "Models and Methods in the IQ Debate." Part I. Social Systems Research Institute 7801. University of Wisconsin–Madison, 1978.
22. Husén T: "Psychological Twin Research." Stockholm: Almqvist & Wiksell, 1959.
23. Husén T: Abilities of twins. Scand J Psychol 1:125–135, 1960.
24. Husén T: Policy implications of individual differences in learning ability: A comparative perspective. Scand J Educ Res 22:173–191, 1978.
25. Jensen AR: "Genetics and Education." London: Methuen & Co Ltd, 1972.
26. Kempthorne O: Logical, epistemological and statistical aspects of nature-nurture data interpretation. Biometrics 34:1–23, 1978.
27. Koch H: "Twins and Twin Relations." Chicago: The University of Chicago Press, 1966.
28. Lerner RM: Nature, nurture and dynamic interactionism. Hum Dev 21:1–20, 1978.
29. Lindgren G: "Physical and Mental Development in Swedish Urban Schoolchildren." Lund: Liber, 1979.
30. Ljung B-O: "The Adolescent Spurt in Mental Growth." Stockholm: Almqvist & Wiksell, 1965.
31. Ljung B-O: Intra-class correlation. Report No. 16 (in Swedish) from the Department of Educational Research, School of Education, Stockholm, 1966.
32. Ljung B-O, Fischbein S, Lindgren G: A comparison of growth in twins and singleton controls of matched age followed longitudinally from 10 to 18 years. Ann Hum Biol 4:405–415, 1977.
33. Lundgren UP: "Model Analysis of Pedagogical Processes." Lund: Liber, 1977.
34. Lytton H: Do parents create, or respond to, differences in twins? Dev Psychol 13:456–459, 1977.
35. Matheny AP Jr: Appraisal of parental bias in twin studies. Acta Genet Med Gemellol 28:155–160, 1979.
36. Mittler P: "The Study of Twins." Aylesbury, Bucks: Hazell Watson & Viney Ltd, 1971.
37. Overton WF, Reese HW: Models of development: Methodological implications. In Nesselroade JR, Reese HW (eds): "Life-Span Developmental Psychology: Methodological Issues." New York: Academic Press, 1973.
38. Plomin R, DeFries JC, Loehlin JC: Genotype-environmental interaction and correlation in the analysis of human biology. Psychol Bull 84:309–322, 1977.
39. Waddington CH: "The Evolution of an Evolutionist." Edinburgh: Edinburgh University Press, 1975.

Twin Research 3: Intelligence, Personality,
and Development, pages 227 – 233
© 1981 Alan R. Liss, Inc., 150 Fifth Avenue, New York, NY 10011

The Minnesota Study of Twins Reared Apart: Project Description and Sample Results in the Developmental Domain

Thomas J. Bouchard Jr., Leonard Heston, Elke Eckert,
Margaret Keyes, and Susan Resnick
Department of Psychology (T.J.B., M.K., S.R.); and Department of Psychiatry
(L.H., E.E.) University of Minnesota, Minneapolis

The Minnesota Study of Twins Reared Apart began in March of 1979 with the discovery of a pair of 39-year-old male identical twins who had recently found each other. Subsequent publicity elicited many more pairs in the United States and elsewhere. As of this writing we have conducted an exhaustive psychological and medical examination of 15 pairs of monozygotic twins reared apart and four pairs of dyzygotic twins reared apart. Wherever possible, spouses also participate in most of the psychological, but not medical, assessment. We are in touch with many additional pairs of twins whom we hope to study in the future.

THE STUDY

A sample assessment schedule is shown in Table 1. On Sunday, the study is thoroughly described and the twins (and spouses) sign informed consent forms. Since they had already been sent an exhaustive description of the project, this only takes about an hour. The schedule is self-explanatory.

The psychological inventories used are listed in Table 2. The mental ability tests are listed in Table 3. The Wechsler Adult Intelligence Scales are administered simultaneously by two professional examiners hired for that specific purpose. The Raven and Mill-Hill tests are administered separately. All other mental ability tests are administered to the twins simultaneously in the same room. They can't, however, see each other. The special mental ability tests are coded to indicate where we obtained them (CAB = Comprehensive Ability Battery, Institute of Personality and Ability Testing; H-B = Hawaii Battery, used in Hawaii and Boulder family studies; ETS = Educational Testing Service Kit of Confirmed Factor Tests; I-P = Information Processing Task). The organization of tests by factors is subjective and likely to change. The components of the medical assessment are listed in Table 4 and are self-explanatory.

Supported in part by grants from the Graduate School of the University of Minnesota, the Spencer Foundation, and the National Science Foundation (BNS 79-26654).

TABLE 1. Twins Reared Apart Assessment Schedule

Time	Sunday	Monday	Tuesday	Wednesday	Thursday	Friday	Saturday
7:30			Blood Samples				
8:00		Cardiology EKG, Chest X-ray, Echocardiogram	Breakfast		Mental Abilities	Psychomotor Tasks	Mental Abilities
9:00			Mental Abilities			Mental Abilities	
9:30					Psychomotor Tasks		Psychomotor Tasks
10:00		Mental Abilities	Stress EKG	Free Time	Voice Samples	Information Processing Tasks / Life Stress Interview	Information Processing / Scheduled Inventories
11:00			Scheduled Inventories		Scheduled Inventories	Life Stress Interview / Information Processing Tasks	Scheduled Inventories / Information Processing
		Scheduled Inventories	Heart Monitor		Wechsler Adult Intelligence Scales		
12:00		Lunch	Lunch	Dental Exam	Lunch	Lunch	Lunch
1:00		Allergy Testing			Scheduled Inventories		Scheduled Inventories
		Photo's, Fingerprints	Allergy Testing		TV Interview / Clinical Interview		
2:00	Informed Consent	Psycho-physiology	Psycho-physiology	.Eye Exam	Clinical Interview / TV Interview	Pulmonary Examination	
		Medical Life History	Medical Life History				
3:00	Scheduled Inventories	Physical Exam	Physical Exam		Joint TV Interview	Mental Abilities	Free Time
	Life History Interview						
4:00	Scheduled Inventories			Free Time	Emotional Reaction Film	Scheduled Inventories	
5:00	Life History Interview	Scheduled Inventories	Scheduled Inventories				

9:30

Sexual Life History Interview and Questionnaires

TABLE 2. Scheduled Inventories and Interviews

Personality inventories	Interests and values
Adjective check list	Jackson vocational interest survey
Activity preference questionnaire	Rokeach value survey
California psychological inventory	Strong Campbell interest inventory
Differential personality questionnaire	Study of values
Minnesota multiphasic personality inventory	Musical interest
Myers-Briggs type indicator	
	Psychomotor tests
Other personality data	Hole steadiness test (involuntary hand
Briggs life history questionnaire	movement)
Child rearing/schooling history (video inter-	Purdue pegboard test
view — 45 min)	Rotary pursuit test (2 days, 25
Clinical interview	trials/day)
Expressive style (video interview — 15 min)	Tapping test
Family environmental scale	
Fear survey	Miscellaneous tests
Life history interview	Diet questionnaire
Life stress interview	Handedness questionnaire
	Smoking questionnaire
	Television and reading questionnaire

We also ask the twins to bring with them any records they have regarding their earlier life histories. This includes birth certificates, adoption papers, letters, photographs, school report cards, graduation certificates, medical records, awards, etc.

We have not had time to collate this material. Indeed, we are still in the process of gathering medical and other life history material by mail. We maintain close contact with the twins after they participate in the study and hope to be able to gather addditional data in the future. It should be clear that the clinical data presented at this time are at best preliminary and subject to modification. We welcome any suggestions regarding changes in the design and content of the study that might improve it.

This study was not originally conceived of from a developmental or longitudinal perspective. From the very first, however, it became clear that the developmental data we gathered would be important. Our first pair of twins (case 1 below) yielded a large number of interesting developmental concordances. We believe that our data will strongly confirm the evidence being gathered in longitudinal studies indicating that genetic processes underlie spurts and lags in physical and mental development and that the onset of numerous behavioral patterns is genetically influenced. Below we present a small amount of data on four pairs of twins to illustrate our contentions.

TABLE 3. Mental Ability Tests

Factor		Tests
1. Verbal comprehension	(V)	Vocabulary CAB Vocabulary H-B Vocabulary WAIS Vocabulary Mill-Hill Sayings CAB
2. Number facility	(N)	Numerical problems CAB Multiplication-subtraction H-B Arithmetic WAIS
3. Spatial orientation − 2 dimensions	(S-O)	Card rotations CAB Card rotations H-B
4. Spatial orientation − 3 dimensions	(S-O)	Vandenberg mental rotation H-B Cube comparisons H-B Shepard-Metzler I − IP Shepard-Metzler II − IP Block design WAIS
5. Spatial visualization	(VZ)	Paper Ford board H-B Paper folding ETS
6. Speed of closure	(CS)	Incomplete word CAB
7. Flexibility of closure	(CF)	Hidden patterns H-B Hidden figures CAB
8. Perceptual speed and accuracy	(P)	Number/Letter comparisons CAB Identical pictures ETS
9. Induction (reasoning)	(I)	Letter series CAB Pedigrees H-B
10. Word fluency	(FW)	Anagrams CAB Word beginnings and endings H-B
11. Ideational fluency	(FI)	Things categories H-B
12. Flexibility of use	(XU)	Different uses H-B
13. Meaningful memory	(Mm)	Thing description memory CAB
14. Memory span	(Ms)	Memory span CAB Memory span WAIS
15. Visual memory	(Mv)	Delayed H-B Immediate H-B Sternberg paradigm − IP
16. Associate memory	(Ma)	Figure/name memory CAB
17. Spatial scanning	(SS)	Elithorn mazes H-B
18. Mechanical ability	(Mk)	Mechanical ability CAB
19. Spelling	(Sp)	Spelling CAB
20. Esthetic judgment	(E)	Barron-Welsh art scale Esthetic judgment CAB

WAIS, computer administered RAVEN, computer administered Mill-Hill.

TABLE 4. Medical Assessment

1. Medical Life History: This includes review of the complete medical history including childhood illnesses, surgery, psychiatric problems, and a review of systems. Special attention is paid to specific abnormalities and problem areas.

2. General Physical Examination: A brief general physical exam is done with emphasis on problem areas. When a special medical problem is apparent, examination by a specialist in the area may be obtained.

3. Sexual Life History Interview and Questionnaire

4. Cardiovascular examination

5. Pulmonary Examination:
   a. Pollution-exposure history
   b. Smoking history
   c. Specialized pulmonary function studies:
      1. Spirometry
      2. Flow volume loope
      3. Pletysmography
      4. Diffusing capacity
      5. Closing volume
      6. Slope of phase 3

6. Allergy Testing:
   a. Skin testing
   b. History of exposure to allergens
   c. HLA typing and IgE
   d. Serological test for allergens (RAST)

7. Basic Lab Tests:
   a. Chest x-ray
   b. Complete hematological blood count
   c. Renal chemistry battery
   d. Urinalysis

8. Special Assessments: Each pair is also treated as a unique opportunity and any special medical problems are carefully examined. Thus some twins have been examined by an orthodontist, others by an audiologist, etc.

9. Zygosity Determination Based on 20+ Genetic Markers Plus HLA

10. Anthropometric Measures:
    a. Height
    b. Weight
    c. Eye color (photographs)
    d. Photographs − front, side
    e. Ear shape (photographs)
    f. Fingerprints, palm prints
    g. Head width
    h. Head length

11. Collection of All Previous Available Medical Records When Possible

12. Eye examination

13. Dental examination

ILLUSTRATIVE CASES

Case 1

Males, 39 years of age, separated at about 37 days. Studied shortly after finding each other. Minimal contact before participation in the study.

These twins were concordant for a large number of physical and psychological characteristics. One of the most striking concordances is for headaches. Both twins developed sinus-type headaches at about age 10 years. A few years later they developed migraine-type headaches as well. The headaches are described in almost exactly the same manner and the history of headaches is very similar.

Both have a similar history of chest pain and pain traveling into the left arm. They describe the pain in the same way and both have been hospitalized for the condition. Both have reported increasing nervousness over the last 7 years and both have been treated with Valium.

Both engage in woodwork as a hobby and have done so for a considerable length of time. Both have worked on a volunteer basis for police agencies at about the same time in their lives. These are realistic occupations and both twins obtained the identical score on the Realistic Theme of the General Occupation scales of the Strong-Campbell Interest Inventory (SCII). Both work at clerical jobs and obtained identical scores on the Conventional Theme of the General Occupational scales of the SCII.

Case 2

Males, 16 years old, separated at between 8 days and 6 weeks. Minimal contact between twins before participation in the study.

Both twins had stuttering problems, which improved over the years. Clear evidence of brain damage in both but more to one than the other. Both twins had bedwetting problems. The less affected twin stopped at about 7 and the more affected twin stopped at about age 12. Both are extremely shy. They are highly discordant for behavioral problems at school and with public authorities.

Case 3

Males, 24 years old, separated at about 5 days. This pair constitutes a powerful demonstration of clocked genetic phenomena because of the sheer number of events for which they are concordant. They were both overweight until junior high school and then became extremely skinny. Both twins are overt homosexuals and were active before meeting each other. Both developed a fear of heights in childhood and showed a gradual improvement through the years (mothers' reports). Both had speech problems and training in grade school or kindergarten. Both outgrew the problem in the third grade. Both had hyperactivity which was diagnosed early (first grade or kindergarten).

Case 4

Females, 57 years old, separated at about 6 weeks. Both of these twins had nightmares, which they describe in a similar way (they imagine doorknobs and fishhooks in their mouths and feel they are smothering to death). The nightmares started in teens and gradually stopped in last 10−12 years. Both were bedwetters until age 12−13 and report remarkably similar educational and marital histories.

CONCLUSIONS

Obviously it will be necessary to attempt to relate these phenomena to various family characteristics. We do have a great deal of information about the rearing families and we will search it for clues.

We are struck, however, by the high degree of similarity between the twins in terms of relatively complex configurations of behaviors and we have no way of capturing the phenomena quantitatively and objectively. Temperamental similarities constitute a good example. Looking across the twins' educational and work histories and marriages, as well as their responsiveness in the various assessment settings, we find overwhelming patterns of similarities. Having been familiar with the literature on the heritability of temperament, we were not ready for what we found. Worse yet, we do not feel we have adequately captured the phenomenon. Many differences between the twins are variations on a theme more than anything else.

We would appreciate hearing from anyone who discovers a pair of monozygotic or dyzygotic twins reared apart from early in life.

Twin Research 3: Intelligence, Personality,
and Development, pages 235—250
© 1981 Alan R. Liss, Inc., 150 Fifth Avenue, New York, NY 10011

The Interaction of Family Attitudes and Cognitive Abilities in the La Trobe Twin Study of Behavioural and Biological Development

David A. Hay and Pauline J. O'Brien
*Department of Genetics and Human Variation, La Trobe University,
Bundoora, Victoria, Australia*

INTRODUCTION

There already exist several structured longitudinal investigations of twin children. The Louisville Twin Study [36] and the Swedish SLU project [10] demonstrate the value of such an approach compared with the more customary, cross-sectional investigations of child development [2, 25], but pose a major question for those wishing to enter this field. Given the considerable commitment of time and resources demanded by a longitudinal study, how can one go beyond simply replicating the work on physical growth, intelligence test, and school performance covered in the Louisville and SLU projects? This paper describes our solution to this problem. Although only preliminary results are presented, the test procedure is in itself a result, being the product of a 2-year pilot study followed by a 1-year questionnaire development and full-scale testing involving some 600 children. There exist several accounts of the planning behind major longitudinal studies [17, 33], but none of these studies involved twins and the specific biological, behavioural, and social problems present in the twin situation.

Our approach has been to try to devise a battery of behavioural tests, relevant both to some of the verbal [30] and nonverbal [37] skills reported to differ between twins and singletons, as well as to current issues in cognitive psychology. Apart from the question of general or specific abilities and their inheritance [5], many other issues lend themselves to the methodology of a developmental twin study, including the relation of standard psychometric tests to Piagetian stages and measures of learning, and the use of speed or power strategies in test performance

Supported by National Health and Medical Research Council (Australia).

[9]. To date the numerous studies on these topics have rarely involved either developmental or genetic analyses. For example, there has been one major longitudinal project on Piagetian skills [17] and this incorporated no genetics. Conversely, the one genetic study on this topic of adequate sample size [12] covered only a restricted age range.

Developmental and genetic analyses are not independent when one is investigating the relationship between different approaches to cognition. The correlations between the measures may change with age, but what does this imply? There could equally well be task-specific environmental factors or age-dependent changes in the genetic determinants. Even if the correlations remained the same at different ages, the relative contribution of genetics and environment may well be changing. This has been demonstrated several times in the behaviour of experimental organisms [13], where the mean performance of different treatment groups remained constant but the underlying genetic architecture changed considerably. Methods are now becoming available for the analysis of genetic and environmental effects on human behaviour across both time [8] and variables [23].

This reason justifies another longitudinal twin study directed to a wider range of cognitive skills. The Louisville study has relied on well-tried and standard tests of ability such as the WPPSI and WISC, a sensible strategy in view of the considerable problems should a test turn out to be of dubious reliability or validity after several years' use. However, tests such as the Wechsler series were never really designed for analysis of the subtests, although this is now a common practice as several recent reviews point out [3]. Nor did they set out to provide systematic coverage of a theoretically formulated set of abilities incorporating Piagetian tests and other developments in cognition, as has been tried in the British Ability Scales [32].

In addition to attempting coverage of a wider spectrum of cognitive skills, we have sought to broaden our information on the twin situation in general. This area has never received much attention [31, 37], even though cognitive abilities do not develop in isolation from biological or social variables. It is important to be able to integrate such information into the newer biometrical analyses, rather than merely to estimate genetic and environmental components with no knowledge of what the environmental variables might be. For example, if specific environmental influences between twins are detected [23], the cause of such differences could be anything from the twin transfusion syndrome [22] to the effects of separating the twins in school. Much is known about the biological variables in the twin situation [31], and there are certain behaviours such as handedness, where biological factors much be considered if a coherent view of the genetic determinants is to emerge [14].

Apart from the work on parental attitudes in relation to perceived zygosity [21], the social factors relevant to the twin situation have largely been ignored except by the NIMH Twin and Siblings Study Section [6]. A study of the responses of 150 members of clubs belonging to the Australian Multiple Birth Association directed us to some of the areas of concern felt by parents of twins. These include: (1) the perinatal period, especially when twins were not diagnosed until late in pregnancy or when it was planned to release one twin from hospital before the other, a problem noted elsewhere [16]; (2) the practical, financial, emotional and marital stresses accompanying the birth of twins; (3) the reaction of older siblings (especially those 2–3 years older)to the arrival of twins; and (4) twins in the early school years, particularly when there exist marked differences in ability.

The questionnaire program described below indicates our attempt to assess the long-term significance of such problems for the development of the children, beyond the immediate difficulties they must bring to the families. However, one criticism that can be made of any volunteer sample, especially one with the large commitment required for a longitudinal study, is that it attracts families with problems, whereas those experiencing no difficulties are less likely to participate. Fortunately, this is currently being checked by comparing the responses of families in the La Trobe Twin Study with those enrolled in the Australian National Twin Registry, run by Dr. Martin of Canberra and Dr. Mathews of Melbourne. They have some 4,000 families with twins below the age of 12 years (over 25% of the twins in Australia in this age range) and a comparison of this sample with our smaller and more committed longitudinal sample provides an essential check on this source of bias.

MATERIALS AND METHODS

Subjects

The sample at present comprises some 950 children from 290 families. There are approximately 260 sets of twins plus their siblings, in addition to 50 cousins. The cousins are included because they provide a control group, genetically related to the twins, but from families without twins. These numbers are lower than one would wish for adequate biometrical analyses [7], but are the maximum that existing facilities permit. At first, recruitment was through parents-of-twins clubs, but now is principally through hospitals, infant welfare centres, and preschools. The twins clubs initially proposed this research collaboration and have been very helpful in distributing consent forms to these other points of contact.

The main aim is to follow children between the ages of 3 and 15 years. The lower limit was chosen because few of the tests applicable to children younger than this can be used throughout childhood, and one aim of the project was to utilise a series of tests relevant to as wide an age range as possible. Children younger than 3 are being enrolled, but there are not the resources to study these in detail at the present time. Children over 3 are being enrolled because of the importance of starting with children of different ages. A formal sequential cohort design is impractical with children [25], but the entry into the Twin Study of children at different ages is important because of (1) changing attitudes on everything from twin diagnosis and bedrest to separation in school, which would matter if a single cohort were used, and (2) the influence of repeated testing on behaviour, partly through practice effects, but more through its influence on the attitudes of the parents and children.

All testing is carried out within 2 weeks of the children's birthdays in a 5-m mobile laboratory parked at their home or school. We travel to the children because the considerable suburban sprawl of Melbourne would otherwise discourage many families from participating if they had to make several lengthy trips a year with different children in the family to a central laboratory. The mobile laboratory was specially built for this project and has two compartments so that twins can be tested simultaneously but separately.

Test Procedure

The information obtained from each child is of three types: physical and behavioural measures plus social and profile data, each of which can be considered briefly in turn.

Physical measures. These (Table 1) are quite conventional except for the photographs, the blood pressure, and the stereopsis and visual acuity measures. The photographs were taken in order to study craniofacial development, since young children may be reluctant to undergo repeated caliper measurements. The relation between photographs and the underlying bone structure remains questionable, but we are currently investigating a sample of 200 Down syndrome children where standardised photographs and radiographs of the head were obtained in the course of treatment. The blood pressure measures are justified by the considerable interest now being shown in "tracking" of blood pressure during childhood [38] but are complicated by the testing situation. The stress created by the novelty situation of the caravan or the testing procedure may influence blood pressure, so measures are taken both before and after testing. Testing for visual and auditory problems is important because of its relevance to the children's performance on the ability tests, but there may also be theoretical implications. For example, is ambylopia more likely in "mirror-image" identical twins?

Beyond any scientific merit, the physical tests have been chosen because they are neither too long nor too traumatic for the children. For the latter reason, blood typing has not so far been required for the entire sample, but has been confined to some 140 children whose parents requested it specifically, because of considerable uncertaintly over the zogosity. Other children have been assessed by means of standard questionnaire items [31].

Behavioural measures. The choice of behavioural tests is far more difficult and some of the criteria are listed in Table 2. The first two areas are self-explanatory, the practical criteria centering around the need to keep the children's enthusiasm so that they will agree to testing in subsequent years, and the theoretical points being covered briefly in the introduction.

The integrative criteria refer to the fact that a developmental twin study provides considerable information on the factors influencing performance in the normal population and that these may in turn be of help in studying more specialised groups, such as the three listed in the table that are interests of our department. For example, the Alternation Learning task has differentiated within a retarded group when conventional testing did not [15]; Knox Cubes is part of the Queensland Test and Pacific Islands Test widely used with Aborigine and Papua–New Guinea children [27]; and dyslexic children score very poorly on Speed of Information Processing and Concepts of Left and Right, whereas their Peabody or Block Design performance is slightly above average [28].

TABLE 1. Physical Measures in La Trobe Twin Study

1) Weight
2) Standing height
3) Sitting height
4) Head circumference
5) Frontal and side facial photographs
6) Skin-fold thickness on left and right arms
7) Pulse
8) Systolic and diastolic blood pressure
9) Ishihara test of colour vision
10) Visual acuity using NVRI chart or Sheridan-Gardiner cards
11) Stereopsis using Frisby and/or Titmus Fly tests
12) Audiometry
13) Dermatoglyphics

At start and at end of testing session

TABLE 2. Criteria for Choice of Behavioural Tests in La Trobe Twin Study

Practical
  1) Enjoyable for the children
  2) Moderately short
  3) Not involving elaborate equipment or instructions
  4) Suitable for as wide an age range as possible and for repeated testing
  5) Not duplicating exactly tests likely to be administered in school

Theoretical
  6) Covering a wide range of cognitive skills
  7) Relating to theoretical issues in the development of cognition
  8) Differentiating between groups when standard intelligence tests do not
  9) Reported to differ between twins and singletons

Integrative
  10) Appropriate for retarded children
  11) Useable with Aboriginal children in tribal communities
  12) Relevant to the deficits in children with specific dyslexia

Table 3 lists the final choice of tests, grouped for convenience under descriptive headings, which are not intended to refer to possible factor loadings. All are standard tests [3], except for Card Sorting [4], Concepts of Left and Right [20], and the Dominance tests, which comprise a series of at least three actions the child performs with the hand, eye, or foot. The reliabilities are published figures taken, where more than one value was given, for the group most closely resembling the

TABLE 3. Behavioural Measures Used in the La Trobe Twin Study for Children Three Years and Upwards (exact selection depends on age and ability)

Area	Test	Duration (minutes)	Reliability
Language	Reynell Language Scales (< 7 years) (comprehension)	5–7	0.96–0.45
	Peabody Picture Vocabulary Test (word recognition)	4–10	0.68–0.88
	Dailey Language Facility Test	2–4	0.90
Memory	Immediate and Delayed Visual Memory – BAS	3–6	0.63*
	Forward and Backward Digit Span – WISC	2–4	0.78
	Knox Cube – Queensland Test	2–5	0.61–0.77
Information processing	Card Sort (< 8 years) – Connolly	5–10	Unknown
	Speed of Information Processing (> 8 years) – BAS	2–5	0.81*
Spatial ability	Mazes – WPPSI or Porteus	2–5 or 5–20	0.87 or 0.95
	Block Design – WPPSI or BAS	5–7 or 5–15	0.82 or 0.85*
Learning ability	Animal House (< 7 years) – WPPSI	2–5	0.77
	Alternation Learning – Jensen	3–15	0.96
Developmental stage	Concepts of Left and Right – Laurendeau and Pinard	1–4	0.92
Lateralization	Purdue Pegboard	2–3	0.60–0.76
	Hand, Eye, and Foot Dominance	2–3	Unknown

*British Ability Scales (BAS) reliabilities are not yet available: These estimates are from other very similar tests.

Twin Study sample. The Reynell Scales become less reliable as children get older, but have turned out to be important at the start of the session, since the actions required using appealing stimulus objects put the child at ease.

Much preliminary work went into the choice of these tests and after 1 year of full-scale testing, only the BAS Visual Memory tasks proved unsatisfactory, since children are very easily distracted from these. Administration of some of the other tests has had to be modified slightly but the only change being contemplated is the introduction of a time limit to the Porteus mazes, to cope with the child who spends an inordinately long time planning a solution.

Questionnaires. These draw heavily on some of the studies reviewed by Vandenberg [31] and on the NIMH forms [6]. For example, their Pregnancy, Birth, and the First Month of Life Scale, and Recent Family Changes were the bases, respectively, for the questionnaires in Table 4, entitled gestation, birth, and the first three months of life, and family changes and stress. However, the format has been changed considerably, so that wherever possible all children in the family,

TABLE 4. Questionnaires in La Trobe Twin Study

A) Stages of childhood	
1) Gestation, birth, and first 3 months	
2) Three months to 3 years	Plus twin supplements
3) Preschool	
4) Primary school	
B) Information from parents	
5) Basic demographic information	
6) Family changes and stresses	
7) The child during the last year	Repeated annually
8) How I see having twins—father and mother separately	
C) Information from children	
9) How I see being a twin	
10) How I see having twins in the family	
D) Information from teacher	
11) Stamp Behaviour Study Technique	
12) Bristol Social Adjustment Scale	Depending on age
E) Information from tester	
13) Behaviour and attitude checklist	
F) For younger children	
14) Infant Temperament Questionnaire (4–8 months)	
15) Toddler Temperament Scale (1–3 years)	
16) Behavioural Style Questionnaire (3–7 years)	

both twins and singletons, are rated on adjacent columns of the questionnaire. This has necessitated twin supplements to each questionnaire, containing questions specifically related to twins and in these the entries for both twins are made next to each other rather than on separate forms. We believe this is important, especially when retrospective information is being obtained. The parent may not be able to give an answer in absolute terms, but may be able to rate the children relative to each other. In addition, when the parent is completing the form, the impact of twins can be viewed in relation to the impact of any single child in the family.

Together these questionnaires provide a comprehensive picture of the family from the viewpoints of biology, behaviour, and the attitudes of the family members to each other. These can be closely related because, for example, preeclampsia, vaginal bleeding, and morning sickness may be more than just biological concomitants of pregnancy but may have postnatal influences on the way the mother acts towards the child or children [6]. The questionnaires to be completed by the parents are mailed to them 10–14 days before the visit and any queries are dealt with when the children are being tested. The questionnaires for the children are answered by them at the end of the testing session, to ensure completion without the parents' seeing their answers, which could bias the children's responses. These questionnaires have sections relevant to children between 8 and 15 years. Presenting the material in structured interviews has been tried with younger children but with little success.

The remaining questionnaires include standard ones completed by the teacher in respect of each child in the family and mailed back to the Twin Study without the reply being seen by the family. The Stamp Technique is an Australian questionnaire for preschool children and the Bristol Scale has proved very successful with Australian children [1], with essentially no modification from the original British version. In contrast, the well-known and widely used Carey questionnaires in Section F have elicited unfavourable comments from parents, and the American version used at present will have to be considerably shortened and modified. The final questionnaire is completed by the tester and is a 37-item checklist designed by Sattler [29] on the child's behaviour in the test situation.

In each year of testing, these questionnaires provide some 1,500–2,000 items of information, on average, for every family. Although family members may decline to complete particular test items, refusal to complete entire questionnaires is surprisingly rare and largely confined to adolescent siblings of twins.

We feel one reason for this high response rate is that the questionnaires are based in part on comments and queries we have received in discussion with families with twins and the parents and children therefore generally appreciate the point behind specific items. This may not be so apparent with the Carey questionnaires, which are not designed with the needs of the twin family in mind and could explain their lower completion rate. A detailed description of these questionnaires will be prepared once sufficient numbers have been collected for multivariate analysis, but in the meantime copies of the questionnaires are available on request.

One other practical point must be considered. Such extensive records are of little use, unless it is possible to integrate information from the various questionnaires and tests. To take a hypothetical but plausible example, one may want to examine the behaviour in the school of siblings who have twins 2 or 3 years younger and of above average abilities, according to whether or not the siblings had a prolonged period of stress when the twins were born and who still resent the twins. This requires relating information from the family history, the behavioural tests and questionnaires to the parents, siblings, and teachers. Our approach has been to use the commercial data base management package, System 1022®, which allows this sort of programming problem to be solved easily, as well as permitting very efficient storage of all the records and rapid reorganisation of the data base as questionnaires are revised.

RESULTS AND DISCUSSION

Two questions will be studied in order to indicate the initial results and possibilities of this Twin Study: 1) To what extent do the cognitive tests differentiate between twins and singletons and between first- and second-born twins? The former is vital, if we are to study the causes of twin-singleton differences and the latter provides some justification for the questionnaire approach. Since first- and second-born twins experience very different risk factors at delivery [22], any investigation of the pre-, peri-, and postnatal history should detect some difference between at least these groups. 2) Are parents realistic in their judgment of each twin's ability, attitudes, etc, or are they over- or understating the differences between each twin in order to stress their individuality or sameness? Are the parents prepared to distinguish between the twins and are the twins prepared to distinguish between each other?

A comparison between the test results, teacher's assessment, and parents' responses to relevant questionnaire items would clarify the answers to the first part of question 2. Concerning the second point, a problem in any longitudinal study is that one is providing new information (eg, on intellectual ability) or raising questions previously not thought about. In effect, one is intervening in the family situation and perhaps altering the parents' or the twins' perceptions of each other. This altered expectation may influence actions or lead to a self-fulfilling prophesy.

Although the importance of this bias may be limited for longitudinal studies in general [25], the possibility of making such comparisons between the children is far greater in the twin situation, where children of the same age are together in very similar environments. We are approaching this problem by comparing in successive years the test results with the questionnaire items on which the parents and the children will differentiate the twins. In conversation during the visit to the home, such comparisons of the children do occur, but parents may not be prepared to make them when completing the questionnaires.

The results presented here are based on a sample of families with twins aged 6–15 years who had a singleton sibling in the same age range and where all the children had been tested and the necessary questionnaires completed. As this search was done just halfway through the first year of testing, only 95 children fitted these criteria with 29 sets of twins (16 boy-boy, 10 girl-girl, and three boy-girl).

Cognitive Tests

The twin-sibling and first-born differences are summarised in Table 5 for those comparisons significant at $P < 0.05$. The twin-sibling comparisons are overwhelming, since differences are absent only on the two tests where this might have been predicted, namely Forward Digit Span, which usually has a far lower correlation with cognitive ability than Backward Digit Span and Concepts of Left and Right, where the five possible developmental stages may not detect within-stage differences between groups. The general indications are that girls performed better than boys, with female twins being superior and male twins the most inferior.

Sex and twin-singleton differences have been reported [26, 34], although rarely are they so widespread. It is reassuring that the one test (Block Design, Level and Power) on which both male and female twins outperformed their siblings, fits with Koch's observation [18] of twin superiority on spatial tests. The one test on which male twins scored higher than the other groups was the Peabody Picture Vocabulary Test where their average centile rank was 77 ± 3, compared with 58 ± 6

TABLE 5. Summary of Cognitive Assessment

Test	Twins and siblings	First- and second-born
Porteus Mazes	FT = FS > MS > MT	
Forward Digit Span	All equal	
Backward Digit Span	FS > FT = MT = MS	
Knox Cube	FS = FT = MS > MT	
Block Design — Level	FT = MT = MS > FS	
Block Design — Power	FT > MT > MS = FS	
Concepts of Left and Right	All equal	
Speed of Information Processing	FT > FS = MT = MS	Second > First
Immediate Visual Memory	FT = FS > MS > MT	First > Second
Delayed Visual Memory	FT = FS = MS > > MT	First > > Second
Peabody Picture Vocabulary Test	MT > FS = MS > FT	First > Second
Alternation Learning — plan A	FT = FS = MS > MT	First > Second
Alternation Learning — plan B	FT = FS > MS > MT	
		N = 16 males, 10 females* (in each group)

Key: FT = Female twins (N = 2.3, 6–13 yr); FS = Female siblings (N = 19, 7–15 yr); MT = male twins (N = 35, 7–15 yr); MS = male siblings (N = 18, 6–15 yr). = no significant difference; > difference significant at P < 0.05; > > difference significant at P < 0.01.

*To avoid confounding with sex differences, only like-sex twins have been used for these comparisons.

in female twins. Although this indicates they recognize more words, they may not be able to use them as well. A smaller sample assessed on the Dailey Language Facility Test suggests this is the case, as does their very poor performance on Delayed Visual Memory. Male twins are only 10 centiles below male siblings on the immediate task but are 22 centiles below them on the delayed task, where verbal information processing becomes important.

Delayed visual memory is also the task on which second-born twins perform more poorly than first-born. The birth order effects are confined to only a few tests and include one (Speed of Information Processing) where second-born twins do better. It remains to check the birth history items on the questionnaires to find if these relate in any way to the observed differences on the tests. Birth order effects in twins are not usually found for conventional intelligence tests [26], which would explain their absence here from tests such as Block Design, an adequate measure of nonverbal intelligence.

The next priority is to compare twins and siblings with their singleton cousins. The present data indicate that twins, especially the girls, are often superior to their

TABLE 6. Summary of Questionnaire Results

Perception of twins by mothers and children

1) Almost all mothers believed strongly in treating their twins as individuals and all children saw their parents as doing so.
2) The mothers saw the twins as being closer to each other than the twins considered themselves to be.
3) Mothers were far more likely to judge the twins as being jealous of each other than were the twins to admit this.

Reactions of boys and girls to being a twin (male N = 33, female N = 20)

1) Boys were more enthusiastic about being a twin than were girls.
2) Girls would like to have twins when they were adults, whereas the boys would not.
3) Boys but not girls disliked being called "the twins."
4) More boys than girls sleep in the same bedroom but more girls would prefer to share the same bedroom.
5) More boys considered they were dressed alike and girls had a stronger preference for being dressed differently.

---

siblings, in contrast to the twin deficiencies so frequently reported [26, 34]. It may be a function of the tests, the sample, or the sex differences, but it could also be that the siblings are scoring lower than singletons without twins as a possible detrimental effect from the amount of parental attention given to the twins. Whatever the reason, there are certainly sufficient group differences to warrant closer scrutiny.

Questionnaire Comparisons of the Twins

The emphasis here will be on those sections of the questionnaires where mothers (not all fathers completed the forms) were asked to compare the first- and second-born twin or where the twins were asked to compare each other. The former are contained in "How I see having twins in the family," where the first- and second-born twins are compared on a 5-point scale with respect to 22 attributes, and in the Development in Primary School questionnaire, where parents simply have to check which twin is "easier to manage," "more distractable," etc. Again there were 22 attributes, some worded slightly differently from those on the other questionnaire. The corresponding situation for the twins comprised several practice trials, after which they had to complete 20 items of the form:

I am more confident   1 2 3 4 5   My twin is more confident

(with instructions "Circle the number closest to what you feel at the present time"). Rather than discuss in detail the other areas covered in these questionnaires, some relevant results are summarised in Table 6. It is interesting that the children without exception perceived the parents as trying to treat them in many different situations as individuals rather than as a pair. The lower part of the table dealing with the attitudes of the twins to being twins lists specific questionnaire items on which there were sex differences significant at P > 0.05.

What seems clear is that there is no general sex difference in preference for different aspects of being a twin, but rather that any differences depend on the specific question. Sex differences were also found in the responses of the siblings of the twins, in that girls were more likely to have a close relationship with one of the twins, whereas boys generally felt less important than the twins and felt the parents fussed over them too much.

The comparisons of the twins can be approached by considering on which items mothers are most or least likely to differentiate their twins. Items were ranked by the frequency with which the mothers checked the neutral category or left the item blank. Although the ranking varied to some extent, there was excellent agreement between the two questionnaires, the five items with the highest differentiation on both forms including:

easy-going   dominant   persistent   aggressive   withdrawn

and the five with the least differentiation including:

intelligent   competent   likeable   healthy   loving

In summary, mothers seem more willing to accept or to admit differences in personality rather than in physical or mental capabilities or affection.

An alternative approach is to compare the ratings of the first- and second-born twins. The two questionnaires agreed on four items with differences significant at $P < 0.05$, such that first-born twins were:

more dominant   more independent   better coordinated   less loving

To find mothers willing to accept differences in "loving" is not inconsistent with the previous analysis. Although most mothers ranked both twins equal on this, the few who did not always chose the second-born as "more loving." Data from an unpublished survey by the Australian Multiple Birth Association and from other questionnaires of our own may explain this result.

Second-born twins in Australia are more likely to spend time in humicribs and to be kept longer in hospital after the birth. Mothers can fail to bond to these children [16] and may compensate for this or for the other perceived superiorities of the first-born by considering the second-born as more "loving." Whether the cognitive performance differences associated with birth order (Table 4) reflect this maternal influence or only the original differences in medical history remains to be determined.

The data from the twins themselves reveal far fewer items at the extremes of high or low differentiation. Both boys and girls are very unlikely to distinguish themselves from their cotwins on any item concerned with being liked by other family members. The only items on which they will admit differences are the objective ones of "I read more," "I talk less," and "I am poorer at drawing," these being common to both sexes. One affective item showed a significant ($P < 0.05$) difference, girls being more likely to indicate differences on "I am less shy."

Summing over all 20 items, boys were much more likely (P < 0.001) to give a neutral response or no response at all. Whether this reflects an inability to understand the verbal concepts involved (as discussed earlier), boredom with the test situation, or less of a tendency in boys to analyse each other in this way is unclear. An examination of the tester's checklists, and also the fact that boys and girls differentiate on the same three items, indicate that it is not boredom, and it seems likely that all three factors contribute to this sex difference.

CONCLUSIONS

The combination of assessment by testing and questionnaire advocated here brings a developmental perspective to the approach used by Koch [18] except that she studied twin pairs who were the only children in families and matched them with singletons from two-child families. Such an approach can be termed "transactional," with the major aim being "to emphasize the constant interplay and mutual influence of environmental and organismic factors across developmental time" [25, p 342]. Or, to paraphrase Bronfenbrenner [2, p 513], the aim is to advance research on twin children beyond being "the science of the strange behavior of children in strange situations with strange adults for the briefest possible periods of time."

The initial results discussed here are encouraging. The behavioural tests indicate a wide variety of sex and twin-sibling differences which, while not readily interpretable at the present time, are at least consistent with each other and with published information: for example, the same ordering of the four groups on both the Level and Power measures of Block Design or on both Alternation Learning tasks, greater differences on Backward than Forward Digit Span, and Delayed than Immediate Visual Memory, and lower scores on several tests for male twins and for second-born twins.

The questionnaires are more difficult to assess. The biological items have not been discussed here but they are of obvious value in considering the effects of birthweight, prematurity, and other complications on subsequent behaviour [14, 22, 26, 31, 35]. The birth-order effects reported here are larger than one would expect in children of this age range [26, 35] and may reflect the wider range of behaviours being sampled. A problem with any questionnaire method is the temptation to include more and more questions on the basis that "they may be useful sometime in the future." Already we have had one instance of this. Recent suggestions of a connection between the fertility drug, Clomid, and polar body fertilisation [11] led us to examine in more detail records of those nonidentical twin pairs whose mothers reported using this drug. In seven of the ten pairs tested to date, the physical and/or behavioural intrapair differences are much greater than normal, which may fit with a polar-body explanation.

The other questionnaire items dealing with attitudes and behavioural reports are another matter. Vandenberg [31] summarises how such information can be used to test many of the assumptions of the twin method, and some other problems for longitudinal surveys, such as parental expectations, have been discussed earlier. Martin and Gross [24] attempted an examination of the relationship between the perceived degree of closeness between one twin and the other in 16 pairs of MZ and 16 pairs of DZ male adolescent twins, as ascertained by questionnaire, and field dependency, as measured by the Embedded Figures Test. Although no relationship was found between expressed closeness and field dependency, the relationship between these two variables and an objective measure of intelligence was significant. The design of the present Twin Study obviously allows the possibility of behavioural validation of questionnaire data, as well as exploration of the relationship between data gathered by questionnaire and those obtained by more objective methods. The results discussed here do show considerable reliability between questionnaires to the mothers and between boys and girls in the case of the twins themselves. However, reliability is not enough and Dibble and Cohen's questionnaire approach [6] has been attacked on the ground that it is an easy way to collect a massive but inadequate data base in a short space of time [19, p 402]. Since we have drawn extensively on Dibble and Cohen's material, this criticism applies equally to the questionnaire method we advocate. It is appropriate to conclude with a general justification of the questionnaire method, based on our experience with the first 600 replies in our twin study.

The Use of the Questionnaire Method

The children join this study at varying ages from shortly after birth until 15 years of age, so few are available to be followed prospectively through gestation and birth or their early years when so much of relevance to their present level of development has already occurred.

The only two methods of gaining this essential information retrospectively would appear to be by questionnaire or interview. Despite the well-known limitations of the questionnaire method — careless or random responding, misunderstood questions, dependence on memory, unduly restrictive questions, etc — it seemed to be the most practical method to employ.

A great proportion of the information required is factual or profile data (name, sex, age, marital status, etc), and questionnaires allow the respondent to refer to records the family may have. Some of the data are quite personal and the greater anonymity of this method over the interview avoids some bias effects — the respondent is free from any pressure of being observed and the completed forms show only code numbers, not names. Time considerations were also of utmost importance since the respondents are busy mothers and the formal testing procedure already involves 1–2 hours of their time. It is much more convenient for them to be able to answer in their own time, without small children under foot, and is probably also less time-consuming than an interview.

Where opinions are sought, restricted responding or closed questions are used predominantly, with a minimum of open questions. Replies are therefore more precise and scoring is easier and more exact. However, although the questionnaires are mailed out, they are collected after the testing session and the respondent has the opportunity to clarify or elaborate on questions or answers where so desired.

For purposes of analysis, the standardization of the wording means both questions and answers can be readily computer-coded and the mass of information fully utilized. Although qualitative depth is obviously decreased, this has been minimised by making the response categories as comprehensive as possible. They are based on an extensive survey of the relevant literature, as well as on discussions with interested persons, and are revised as new information comes to hand.

Overall, despite the built-in limitations of the method, a higher level of standardisation is obtainable than would be with the interview, and there exists the opportunity to check for reliability. Validity can be examined by comparison with the objective data or the replies to the same questions by other members of the family or the teacher. One must achieve a compromise between depth and breadth of questioning and the sample size. The sample sizes needed for biometrical analyses are such [7] that only the questionnaire method is feasible for obtaining the required information.

ACKNOWLEDGMENTS

We thank Dr. R.J. Mitchell and Mrs. M. Blake for bloodtyping services, Drs. B.D. Bowden and N.G. White for advice on the physical measurements, and the staff of the Australian Council of Educational Research for help with the behavioural test battery. Ms. M. Ross provided invaluable assistance in the testing of the children and the general running of the project. The cooperation of Mrs. P. Stewart and many other members of the Australian Multiple Birth Association is gratefully acknowledged.

REFERENCES

1. Bell S: "An Evaluation of the Bristol Social Adjustment Guides." Unpublished Master's thesis, La Trobe University, 1978.
2. Bronfenbrenner U: Towards an experimental ecology of human development. Am Psychol 32:513–531, 1977.
3. Buros OK: "The Seventh Mental Measurements Yearbook." Highland Park: Gryphon Press, 1972.
4. Connolly K: Response speed, temporal sequencing and information processing in children. In Connolly K (ed): "Mechanisms of Motor Skill Development." New York: Academic Press, 1970 pp 161–188.
5. De Fries JC, Vandenberg SG, McClearn GE: Genetics of specific cognitive abilities. Ann Rev Genet 10:179–207, 1976.
6. Dibble EO, Cohen DJ: The interplay of biological endowment, early experience, and psychosocial influence during the first year of life: An epidemiological twin study. In Anthony EJ, Childland C (eds): "The Child in His Family." vol 6, New York: Wiley-Interscience, 1980.
7. Eaves LJ: Computer simulation of sample size and experimental design in human psychogenetics. Psychol Bull 77:144–152, 1972.
8. Eaves LJ, Eysenck HJ: Genetic and environmental components of inconsistency and unrepeatability in twins' responses to a neuroticism questionnaire. Behav Genet 6:145–160, 1976.
9. Eysenck HJ: "The Structure and Measurement of Intelligence." Berlin: Springer-Verlag, 1979.
10. Fischbein S: Intra-pair similarity in physical growth of monozygotic and dizygotic twins during puberty. Ann Hum Biol 4:417–423, 1977.
11. Fischer KM, Polesky HF: Polar body conceptions and Clomid twins. Paper presented at American Society of Human Genetics Annual Meeting, Minneapolis, 1979.
12. Garfinkle-Claussner AS: "Genetic and Environmental Influences on the Development of Piagetian Logico-Mathematical Abilities and Other Specific Cognitive Abilities: A Twin Study." Unpublished doctoral dissertation, University of Colorado, 1979.

13. Hay DA: Genetical and maternal determinants of the activity and preening behaviour of D. melanogaster reared in different environments. Heredity 28:311–336, 1972.
14. Hay DA, Howie PM: Handedness and differences in birthweight of twins. Percept Mot Skills 51:666, 1980.
15. Jensen MB: Alternation learning and mental pathology: Test procedures and findings. J Psychol 50:211–225, 1960.
16. Klaus MH, Kennell JH: "Maternal-Infant Bonding." St. Louis: Mosby, 1976.
17. Klausmeier HJ, Allen PS: "Cognitive Development of Children and Youth: A Longitudinal Study." New York: Academic Press, 1978.
18. Koch H: "Twins and Twin Relations." Chicago: University of Chicago Press, 1966.
19. Koupernik C: The Dakar discussion: A review. In Anthony EJ, Koupernik C (eds): "The Child in His Family." vol 3, New York: Wiley, 1974, pp 395–404.
20. Laurendeau M, Pinard A: "The Development of the Concept of Space in the Child." New York: International Universities Press, 1970.
21. Lytton H: Do parents create, or respond to, differences in twins? Dev Psychol 13: 456-459, 1979.
22. MacGillivary I, Nylander PPS, Corney G (eds): "Human Multiple Reproduction." London: Saunders, 1975.
23. Martin NG, Eaves LJ: The genetical analysis of covariance structure. Heredity 38:79–95, 1977.
24. Martin TO, Gross RB: A comparison of twins for degree of closeness and field dependency. Adolescence 14:739–745, 1979.
25. McCall RB: Challenges to a science of developmental psychology. Child Dev 48:333–344, 1977.
26. Mittler P: Biological and social aspects of language development in twins. Dev Med Child Neurol 12:741–757, 1970.
27. Ord IG: "Mental Tests for Pre-Literates." Melbourne: Jacaranda Press, 1970.
28. Rosewarne RC: "A Study of the Familial Nature of Reading Disability." Unpublished Honours thesis, La Trobe University, 1979.
29. Sattler JM: "Assessment of Children's Intelligence." Philadelphia: Saunders, 1974.
30. Savic S: "The Development of Speech in Twins and Non-Twins." Unpublished doctoral dissertation, University of Belgrade, 1977.
31. Vandenberg SG: Twin studies. In Kaplan AR (ed): "Human Behavior Genetics." Springfield, Illinois: Thomas, 1976, pp 90–150.
32. Warburton FW: The British Intelligence Scale. In Dockrell WB (ed): "On Intelligence." London: Methuen, 1970, pp 71-98.
33. White BL, Watts JC: "Experience and Environment: Major Influences on the Development of the Young Child." vol 1, Englewood Cliffs, New Jersey: Prentice Hall, 1973.
34. Wilson RS: Twins: Patterns of Cognitive Development as measured on the Wechsler Preschool and Primary Scale of Intelligence. Dev Psychol 11:126–134, 1975.
35. Wilson RS: Mental development in twins. In Oliverio A (ed): "Genetics, Environment and Intelligence." Amsterdam: North Holland, 1977, pp 305–334.
36. Wilson RS: Synchronies in mental development: An epigenetic perspective. Science 202:939–948, 1978.
37. Zazzo R: Genesis and peculiarities of the personalities of twins. In Nance WE (ed): "Twin Research: Psychology and Methodology." New York: Alan R Liss, 1978, pp 1–11.
38. Zinner SH, Margolius HS, Rosner BR, Kass EH: Does hypertension begin in childhood? Studies of the familial aggregation of blood pressure in childhood. In New MI, Levine LS (eds): "Juvenile Hypertension." New York: Raven Press, 1977, pp 45–53.

Twin Research 3: Intelligence, Personality,
and Development, pages 251–253
© 1981 Alan R. Liss, Inc., 150 Fifth Avenue, New York, NY 10011

The Impact of Twin Research in Developmental Studies on Models of Human Development:

A Discussion of the Papers Presented by Drs. Wilson, Fischbein, Bouchard, and Hay, at the Symposium, "Twin Research in Developmental Studies"

Reuven Kohen-Raz
Division of Special Education, School of Education, Hebrew University, Jerusalem

We must certainly admit that the four papers that have been presented at this symposium have been well coordinated and concerted as to their content and scope. In fact, the three presentations of Wilson, Fischbein, and Bouchard encompass three important periods of the human life-span: infancy (Wilson), adolescence (Fischbein), and adulthood (Bouchard), while Hay's investigations cover another pertinent aspect of human development, on which I shall elaborate later. It seems that the interesting findings that have been reported fundamentally change our outlook on human development; actually, they are prone to shatter the existing traditional models of developmental psychology. That is to say, the current, widely accepted conceptualisation of development is based on the so-called "cumulative model," which represents a rather vague compromise of the "nature-nurture controversy" in the sense that genetic effects are considered to operate very early in development, but hereafter they are increasingly overshadowed by "cumulative" environmental factors, which lead either to "cumulative" adaptation or "cumulative" deterioration of the interaction process between the human organism and his surroundings. In striking contrast to this perspective, we have been taught by the results reported by the three first speakers that there are constant and continuous genetic effects on physical and mental development in humans throughout the life-span. However, these effects are neither linear nor straightforward; they may emerge at certain points of development, submerge and reemerge hereafter according to genetically predetermined laws which we are only beginning to conceive.

In addition to this general change of view, it becomes more and more clear that there are at least three types of genetic effects, which must be duly differentiated and which hitherto have been in part unknown or misinterpreted. The first type is manifest in the hereditary transmission of organismic structures and functions, a phenomemon which is very well known and on which we need not to elaborate here. The second type clearly demonstrated by Wilson's study on physical and mental growth rhythm in early childhood, by Fischbein's investigation on concordance in height, weight, and mental development in adolescent twins, and by Bouchard's impressive discoveries on astonishing parallelisms in quality and timing of vocational choice, incidence of disease, sexual aberrations, etc in MZ twin pairs reared apart — has been aptly described as a mechanism of a genetic timetable or a genetic clock, which consists in a genetic program determining when and how intensively a certain structure or function should crystallize, dominate, or submerge. Furthermore, there seems to be, within the same organism, more than one timetable and more than one genetic clock system. In fact, one of the intriguing objectives of future research is the way how these various "programs" and "schedules" interact between themselves. As an example, Wilson has shown to us that there appears to be no linkage between the rhythm of growth in height and mental abilities in infants, while each of these functions clearly grows according to its own specific timetable. However, some of our research has indicated that, at preadolescence, mental and physical growth spurts might occur in predetermined interdependence.

Finally, there is a third type of genetic effect, possibly the most complex one, but perhaps also the most pertinent for psychology and education, which seems to be the core objective of Hay's research. As you well know, animal instincts are geared to interact with what has been described by Lorenz as the "average expectable environment." In other words, the genetic timetable may be sufficient to guarantee the encounter of the animal's organism with relevant environmental stimuli necessary for its survival. Humans obviously cannot rely on an expectable probability that environmental objects, energy sources, and supportive agents will be available when genetically rooted (and timed) needs emerge and require satisfaction. Therefore the human organism has the capacity to change and to create his environment; as formulated by Fischbein: "There is an active, creative impact of the individual on his environment." The important discovery that has been conveyed to us, especially by Fischbein's paper, is the genetic root of this mechanism; that is to say, the way a human organism chooses his diet, patterns of verbal-social interaction, etc, appears to be determined by the genotype in a way similar to the previously described "genetic clock system."

As already mentioned, Hay's comprehensive design to investigate patterns of physical, mental, and social interaction within twin pairs and between pairs and their siblings in the context of the life space of the total family, promises to shed new light on the very complex effects of this last, third type of genetic mechanism. Possibly, by comparing the situation of twins reared apart, investigated by Bouchard, to the complementary status of twins growing up together in close contact, as studied by Hay, we shall be able to gather insight on such complicated issues as the clash between a genetic program to shape a certain way of interaction with an MZ twin who is compelled to implement the same program vis-à-vis his twin sibling. Obviously, Hay's design is ideally suited to get to grips with the relevant variables related to this intriguing problem.

It is evident how all these new perspectives that we have gained this morning are prone to change current concepts and practices in education and developmental clinical psychology, which unfortunately seem to remain fixated to already-obsolete models of human development. Let me conclude with my appreciation of Dr. Wilson's initiative to have chosen so well four speakers whose papers have admirably converged on focal issues in twin research relevant to developmental studies. If they had not come from different countries and thus from different "genetic pools," we might duly suspect that their presentations had been "genetically pre-programmed."

Twin Research 3: Intelligence, Personality,
and Development, pages 255—259
© 1981 Alan R. Liss, Inc., 150 Fifth Avenue, New York, NY 10011

The Social Development of Twins in Longitudinal Perspective: How Stable Is Genetic Determination Over Age 2 to 9?

Hugh Lytton and Denise Watts
Department of Educational Psychology, University of Calgary, Canada

Whether a genetic contribution to the variance of a given trait can be shown repeatedly at different ages is an important aspect of demonstrating convincingly that the trait in question is at least partly under genetic control. How can one claim it is, if a contribution by the genes to the phenotypic expression of the trait can be shown only at one age, since the genotype must be a life-long property of the organism? A longitudinal investigation of the social development of male twins, seen first at 2½, and again when they were 8–10 years old, presented us with a welcome opportunity to examine this question.

METHOD

First let us describe the investigation and its procedures at age 2. Its aim was to trace the origin of the social characteristics of young boys—their "temperament," if you like—in their interactions with their parents, as well as in possible genetic predisposition. The sample consisted of 46 male sets of twins (17 MZ, 29 DZ), as well as of 44 singleton boys. The main plank of the study was the naturalistic observation of the interactions of the twins with their parents in an unstructured situation in the home.

The observation method has been described in a number of articles and in a recent book [6]. We observed each family over two sessions, usually 1 week apart, round about suppertime, each time for 3 hours before the children went to bed. In addition to both twins, the mother was present for almost the entire time, and the father whenever possible, although we had some single-parent twin families. We asked that the twins and at least one parent stay in the room and suggested that they follow their normal routine and behave as naturally as possible in the presence of an observer who did her best to merge with the

Supported by the Social Sciences and Humanities Research Council of Canada, Grant 410-78-0003-R2.

furniture. We therefore did not otherwise control the comings and goings of the parents, or of other siblings or relatives who would often be present, and we took rough-and-tumble play, TV watching, supper and preparation for bed, all in our stride. The observer dictated a continuous record of the twins' actions, including verbalizations, and of the actions by others that impinged on them in a whispered code into a microphone.

We also interviewed the mother about her perceptions of the twins and about her childrearing attitudes and practices. Based on both the interview and the observations, the observer allotted ratings for the child characteristics of interest, ie, attachment, independence, compliance, internalization of standards, and maturity of speech, and for the mother's childrearing characteristics, eg, consistency in the enforcement of rules, use of reasoning, warmth, etc.

A follow-up study has just been completed, with the twins about 8–10 years old. A few twin pairs had moved out of our reach and a few refused to participate, but 37 pairs cooperated in the study—two of them in only a limited way. The twins were given standardized achievement and intelligence tests at school, and their teachers rated them on cognitive and social characteristics and filled out Rutter's Children's Behavior Questionnaire designed to measure social maladjustment [10].

Both mothers and fathers were given interviews, adapted from the earlier interviews to take account of the difference in age, and ratings were allotted parallel to the 2-year ratings, plus a score for maladjustment, based on a questionnaire for parents, parallel to the one for teachers [11]. We found that observation of completely unstructured interaction in the homes now would be much less fruitful and meaningful than at age 2, because of the twins' greater self-consciousness. To get a first-hand assessment of the children's interactions with their parents, we arranged some structured tasks in which both parents and twins took part. The tasks involved manual construction, a game, and discussion, and were videotaped. They are a compromise and a far cry from the free, unstructured behavior that we observed at age 2. However, we derived from them measures such as dominance, cooperativeness, etc.

RESULTS

The 2-year data were submitted to a biometric-genetic analysis and to a classical genetic analysis [2, 5]. The results of the two analyses were, gratifyingly, almost identical. However, only the rating for independence and the rate of child speech (number of utterances per minute) showed significant genetic components [5]. The largest portion of the variance of the other characteristics was explained by between-families environmental effects. We attributed the meagerness of the genetic harvest to the relatively small sample, but perhaps it was also due to the fact that the measures were based on behavior which, at age 2, is notoriously fluctuating and volatile—although reliabilities between two scores for ratings and experimental scores were quite satisfactory.

We now come to the genetic analysis of the 9-year measures. Significance of the "heritabilities" (h^2) was tested by the F ratio of the within-pairs DZ variance divided by the within-pairs MZ variance. Some of the heritability figures were higher than 1 and therefore these figures must not be taken too literally as "proportions of variance explained by genetic factors." What is important is whether or not the F ratio shows a significant genetic component. We used as a second criterion the difference between MZ and DZ intraclass correlations and, where this was found to be significant, too, we can more confidently accept the genetic component as "real."

Let us first discuss physical and cognitive attributes. Height and weight had important genetic components by both criteria, as you might expect—these results simply confirm the validity of the analysis. *Verbal* IQ (Crichton Vocabulary Scale) [9] would have a negative, ie, impossible, heritability, if calculated, and the DZ intraclass correlation was larger than the MZ one. These relationships, in fact, duplicated what we found for the Peabody Vocabulary Test at age 2. The ability to acquire vocabulary in our sample is heavily dependent on environmental factors and only insignificantly on genetic factors. *Nonverbal* IQ (Raven's Matrices) [9], however, had a genetic component that was just significant, and the genetic variance was confirmed by both criteria. Spelling (test measure), similarly, showed a significant genetic component by both criteria. The variance of some teacher ratings (for intellectual ability, reading, and mathematics) was explainable to a significant extent by genetic factors, but only by the F-test criterion. The greater similarity of MZ twins on these teacher ratings is not likely to be due to teachers entertaining a stereotype of MZ twins' alikeness, since being in the same or different classrooms did not significantly affect the differences in ratings. (Parents, also, do not create greater similarity for their own MZ twins, but rather react to their genetic likeness [4].) Teachers rated speech maturity on the basis of the coherence and correctness of the child's speech in relation to his age group. The speech maturity rating also showed significant genetic variance by the F-test criterion. At age 2 it was the *rate* of speech that displayed a significant genetic component; the maturity rating did not. The genetic determination of speech thus appears to remain stable from age 2 to 9, if we are willing to equate the two different measures of the ability.

We now come to the social characteristics, most of which were also assessed at 2, with modifications for age. The teacher rating of compliance had a genetic component, confirmed via both methods of assessing significance. A seeming genetic component in the teacher rating of independence must, however, be treated with great scepticism, since one correlation (for DZ) was negative. The mother's independence rating of the 2-year-olds had significant genetic variance, but her rating at age 9 had not, although the father's independence rating showed heritability—but only by the difference between the MZ and DZ correlations. In view of the inconsistent and doubtful significance of the genetic components, we cannot claim stability of genetic determination for this trait. The heritability of attachment to mother is somewhat doubtful, since the h^2 was greater than 1.

The maladjustment scores, assigned by mother, father, and teacher, showed a consistent significant genetic component across all three raters, which strengthens confidence in the finding. The Antisocial Conduct and Neurotic Indices are subsets of the Maladjustment Total and genetic factors seemed to explain some variance in the Antisocial Index (by teacher's and mother's assessments) but not in the Neurotic Index. None of the variables derived from the observed family interaction tasks, eg, dominance, showed any significant genetic variance.

Whereas 47% of the physical and cognitive variables tested showed significant heritability, only 29% of the social characteristics did so. Thus the analysis demonstrates less genetic determination in social aspects than in physical and cognitive aspects of the personality—a result in line with findings from many previous investigations [cf 3].

To sum up: How much stable genetic variance could we detect in parallel measures at age 2 and age 9? The measures, we should emphasize, were parallel, but not identical at the two ages: The ratings were modified in accordance with expectations for age; the vocabulary tests were different ones.

Speech was the one characteristic that showed consistent heritability, but only if we are willing to equate the amount of speech at 2 with the speech maturity rating at 9. Independence had a significant heritability at 2, but only a doubtful one at 9. Compliance, however, showed significant genetic variance at age 9 only, and then only in its manifestation at school, not at home. Attachment to mother acquired dubiously significant heritability at 9. Conscience and vocabulary IQ consistently failed to show any genetic variance at either age. In view of the consistent genetic component in speech competence (quantity or quality), it is surprising that the ability to acquire vocabulary and define words, etc, should be influenced only by environmental factors. It therefore seems that the two abilities are distinct.

DISCUSSION AND CONCLUSIONS

The inconsistent findings of genetic variability from age 2 to age 9 may be due to the scales, eg for independence and compliance, measuring somewhat different functions at the two ages, particularly if assessed in different locales—school or home. Or inconsistency may be due to the smallness of the sample which produced unstable twin differences. However, where we have solid grounds for expecting genetic variance, such as in height and weight, even the small sample displayed significant heritability. Various other arguments have been put forward to explain the conflicting phenomena of emerging and disappearing genetic components over age, eg a change from an expressive to a suppressive environment, or vice versa [cf 1]. However, such claims are difficult to evaluate empirically for ordinary human characters. We noted more characteristics with significant genetic variance at age 9 than 2. This is not damaging to a genetic hypothesis for these traits, since it is likely that genetic determination will emerge more clearly, when the traits can be measured more stably in middle childhood. Lack of consistency such as has been demonstrated over later ages by other researchers must, however, lead to more serious questioning of the genetic hypothesis.

Many of the traits we studied are "adaptive," ie, they increase Darwinian fitness, and such traits can be expected to be highly selected for. It has been argued that when there is directional selection for the high expression of a trait, the relevant genes will be built in species-wide, so that there is very little genetic variability left [7, 8]. This would mean low heritability for such adaptive traits. Unfortunately for this argument, speech—surely an adaptive trait that helps to ensure the survival of the species—was the one characteristic that showed consistent genetic variance in our research.

Heritability can be assessed by different methods, and results across methods, samples, and ages are often only patchily significant. Before accepting a genetic component as "real," one should therefore require a replicated demonstration of significant heritability, be it via several methods, or for several ages or, best of all, across several samples.

This investigation has demonstrated stable genetic variance over age in speech competence. It has also demonstrated genetic factors in replicated form at age 9 for the social characteristics of compliance and social deviancy, for nonverbal IQ and spelling ability, and for height and weight. This is something. However, in general, attempts to replicate genetic analyses over several samples have shown that the reliable demonstration of genetic determination for most *social* characteristics, as opposed to cognitive ones, remains an elusive goal.

ACKNOWLEDGMENTS

Our thanks are due the statistical consultant for the project, Bruce Dunn. We are indebted to Bill Yuzwak for carrying out the field work, to Deborah Twaddle for the data analysis, and to the project secretary, Linda Culshaw. We would also like to thank all of the participating school boards, principals, and teachers, the Calgary public health nurses, and their director, Miss Frances Moore, for their cooperation and assistance.

REFERENCES

1. Dworkin RH, Burke BW, Maher BA, Gottesman II: A longitudinal study of the genetics of personality. J Person Soc Psychol 34:510–518, 1976.
2. Haseman JK, Elston RC: The estimation of genetic variance from twin data. Behav Genet 1:11–19, 1970.
3. Loehlin JC, Nichols RC: "Heredity, Environment and Personality: A Study of 850 Sets of Twins." Austin: University of Texas Press, 1976.
4. Lytton H: Do parents create, or respond to differences in twins? Dev Psychol 13:456–459, 1977.
5. Lytton H: Genetic analysis of twins' naturalistically observed behavior. In Nance WE (ed): "Twin Research: Psychology and Methodology." New York: Alan R Liss, 1978, pp 43–48.
6. Lytton H: "Parent-Child Interaction: The Socialization Process Observed in Twin and Singleton Families." New York: Plenum Press, 1980.
7. McClearn GE, DeFries JC: "Introduction to Behavioral Genetics." San Francisco: Freeman & Co, 1973.
8. Plomin R, Rowe D: Genetic and environmental etiology of social behavior in infancy. Dev Psychol 15:62–72, 1979.
9. Raven JC, Court JH, Raven J: "Raven's Progressive Matrices and Vocabulary Scales." London: HK Lewis and Co Ltd, 1978.
10. Rutter M: A children's behaviour questionnaire for completion by teachers: Preliminary findings. J Child Psychol Psychiatry 8:1–11, 1967.
11. Rutter M, Tizard J, Whitmore K: "Education, Health and Behaviour." London: Longman, 1970.

Twin Research 3: Intelligence, Personality,
and Development, pages 261 – 268
©1981 Alan R. Liss, Inc., 150 Fifth Avenue, New York, NY 10011

Genetic Aspects of Temperamental Development: A Follow-Up Study of Twins From Infancy to Six Years of Age

Anne Mari Torgersen
Department of Child Psychiatry, Ullevål Hospital, Oslo, Norway

The recent interest in temperamental individuality has prompted a few studies on the influence of genetic factors on the development of temperamental characteristics in the child. Some researchers seem to hypothesize that temperament is the genetic aspect of personality and that careful research will reveal some few basic temperamental traits.

The study to be reported here has an opposite approach to this question. It starts out with a number of defined temperamental traits that are claimed by other researchers to be of clinical importance, and tries to investigate to what degree these traits are influenced by hereditary factors. One of the most outstanding efforts to define clinically relevant temperamental aspects in the child has been provided by Thomas and Chess and co-workers in their New York Longitudinal Study [4, 5]. Their nine temperamental categories have been utilized in this study and are the following: activity, regularity of body functions, approach or withdrawal to new situations, adaptability, intensity of emotions, threshold of responsivity, mood, distractibility, and attention-span/persistence.

MATERIALS AND METHODS

In a follow-up study these nine temperamental characteristics were evaluated in a group of 53 same-sexed twin pairs at three age levels: 2 months, 9 months, and 6½ years. On the basis of questionnaires and blood and serum typing, 34 pairs were classified as monozygotic (MZ) and 16 as dizygotic (DZ), and three pairs had an uncertain zygosity diagnosis. Follow-up data at 6 years were obtained on 32 MZ pairs and 16 DZ pairs.

Temperamental Assessment

Data on temperament were obtained by semistructured interviews with the mothers in their homes at the two age periods in infancy—2 and 9 months—and in the follow-up study when the twins were 6 years old. As in the protocols from the New York Longitudinal Study, detailed objective descriptions of the child's behavior in different routine situations of daily life were obtained. The object of the interview was to determine *how* the child reacted to various situations rather than *what* the child actually did. Even if the questions concerned different age-appropriate behavior criteria at succeeding age periods, the definitional identity of each temperamental category was maintained over time. The interviews were tape-recorded and transcribed.

All the information related to temperament in the interviews was evaluated. During scoring, the mother's description was evaluated on five-point scales as to how typical a child's behavior was in different situations.

In the infant study, the clustering of items to temperamental categories relied mainly on concepts proposed by Thomas et al [4]. All the scoring was performed by the author, who was at that time blind as to the twins' zygosity. Methodological details from this infant study can be found in a previous publication [7].

In the 6-year study, the same definitions of temperament were used in the item construction and scoring. The scoring was this time done by one who was not familiar with the twins or their zygosity. Interview protocols from 20 children were then rescored by the author to determined interscorer reliability. Items with interscorer consensus lower than 80% within one scale-point, and also items impossible to score in more than 70% of the children, were excluded. After principal component factor/analysis within each temperamental category, items that had factorial loadings lower than 0.30 were also excluded.

Only three of the initial 14 items in distractibility met these criteria. The relationships between these three items were also so low (Chronbachs alpha = 0.20) that the whole category was excluded from further analysis. The final numbers of items within the other temperamental categories varied from 4 to 9, and the internal consistency within each category was sufficiently high (the Cronbachs alpha were between 0.64 and 0.73), with the exception of regularity, which had comparatively low internal consistency (Chronbachs alpha = 0.46). The reason for retaining regularity for further analysis is that the items in this category have high interscorer reliability, and the category is of special interest because of its relationship to behavioral problems reported by Thomas et al [5, 6]. (Methodological details from the 6-year study can be found in another publication [8].)

Statistical Procedures

A heritability index has been calculated by means of two different statistical models: the F ratio between intrapair variances proposed by Vandenberg [9] and the modified F' ratio proposed by Christian et al [1]. This modified F' ratio takes into consideration the variation in the total variances within the two zygosity groups, and are calculated when the probability of differences between the total variances of the two zygosity groups is less than 0.20 on a two-tailed test, again according to Christian et al [1].

RESULTS

At all ages, both in infancy and at 6 years of age, the MZ cotwins were more alike than the DZ cotwins in all the temperamental categories studied. These differences between the two zygosity groups are analyzed in Tables 1–3.

Table 1 shows that at the age of 2 months, the Vandenberg F ratio is significant for three temperamental categories (regularity, threshold, and intensity). Only one temperamental category, mood, required the new calculation of Christian's F' ratio, which was higher and now statistically significant.

TABLE 1. F Values of the Twin Variances in Temperament at 2 Months

Temperamental Category[a]	Within-pair variances F	Total variances F_T	Component estimates F'
Act.	1.52	1.21	
Reg.	4.98***	1.10	
Appr.	0.83	1.26	
Ad.	0.57	1.10	
Int.	2.55*	1.42	
Thr.	2.82**	1.35	
Mood	1.54	1.90°	2.36**
Dis.	1.40	1.12	

[a]See text for definition.
°:P < 0.20, two-tailed test.
*:P < 0.05.
**:P< 0.01.
***:P < 0.001.

TABLE 2. F Values of the Twin Variances in Temperament at 9 Months

Temperamental Category[a]	Within-pair variances F	Total variances F_T	Component estimates F'
Act.	5.26***	1.30	
Reg.	12.86***	1.13	
Appr.	6.77***	1.20	
Ad.	2.28*	1.05	
Int.	5.32***	1.14	
Thr.	9.90***	1.15	
Mood	3.31**	1.35	
Dis.	3.94***	1.54°	1.15
Pers.	4.40***	2.83°	1.68

[a]See text for definition.
°:P < 0.20. Two-tailed test.
*:P < 0.05.
**:P < 0.01.
***:P < 0.001.

TABLE 3. F Values of the Twin Variances in Temperament at 6 Years

Temperamental Category[a]	Within-pair variances F	Total variances F_T	Component estimates F'
Act.	11.34***	1.07	
Reg.	4.22***	1.55°	1.06
Appr.	8.80***	1.03	
Ad.	2.23*	1.32	
Int.	9.56***	1.08	
Thr.	2.91**	1.79°	2.73**
Mood	3.32**	1.97°	1.40
Pers.	5.13***	1.07	

[a]See text for definition.
°:$P < 0.20$. Two-tailed test.
*:$P < 0.05$.
**:$P < 0.01$.
***:$P < 0.001$.

Table 2 shows the results at age 9 months. Here, Vandenberg's F ratio is statistically significant for all the temperamental categories studied. The F_T ratio of the differences in total variances between MZ and DZ pairs is significant for distractibility and persistence, and when Christian's F' ratios were calculated, nonsignificant F ratios for these two categories appeared.

Table 3 shows that at the age of 6 years all the categories had significant F ratios. Three categories needed recalculation of their F ratios according to Christian. With these calculations both mood and regularity got nonsignificant F' ratios, whereas threshold maintained its significance.

The same data are presented graphically in Figure 1. The F ratios used are those proposed by Vandenberg. Christian's F' ratios, suggested with a mark on the figure, do not alter the tendency in the figure significantly. As can be seen from Figure I, for the categories of activity, approach, intensity, and persistence, the differences in level of intrapair similarity between the two zygosity groups are higher at 6 years than in infancy. The other categories are either very similar at all ages, like adaptability and mood, or the F ratios are lower at 6 years, as for regularity and threshold.

DISCUSSION

The results from this study show that the importance of genetic factors differs from one age level to another within the same temperamental category, and also from one category to another. The level of statistical significance of these factors varies with the method used, Christian's method often giving lower F ratios.

For some temperamental categories genetic factors seem to be of great importance at 9 months but not at 6 years. For other categories the contrary is the case. When the evidence for the importance of genetic factors is high in

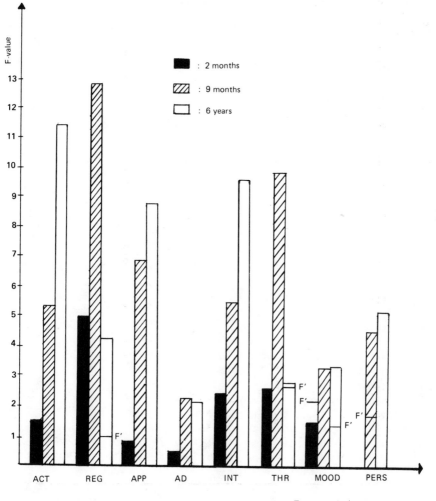

Fig. 1. The F value of the twin variances in temperament at 2 months, at 9 months, and at 6 years.

infancy and low at 6 years (regularity and threshold), it may be that these behavior styles are easily modified by environmental factors *in spite of* a strong genetic influence on early development of the trait. When, however, the evidence of the importance of genetic factors is stronger at 9 months than at 2 months, and stronger at 6 years than in infancy (activity, approach, and intensity), at least three explanations may be given: 1) Genetic influence may have

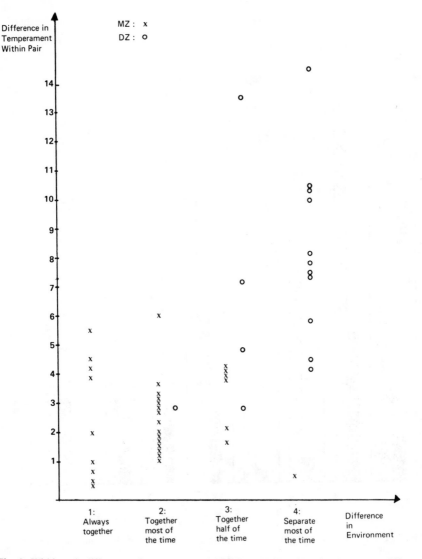

Fig. 2. Within-pair differences in temperament in DZ and MZ twin pairs that spent different degrees of time together.

been masked in the earlier age because of perinatal environmental influences; 2) an interaction between hereditary and environmental factors is at work; or 3) the measures may have a low reliability at early age.

Some evidence has been found supporting masking phenomena in the period from 2 to 9 months. The changes from infancy to 6 years are easier to explain by means of an interaction theory: The more different the twins are in temperament at infancy, the more different will be their reactions to the environment, and consequently the more different will be their individual development.

It is interesting that the same temperamental categories that were lowest in heritability, namely mood and adaptability, or were most easily modified by environment, as regularity, are among the same categories that have been reported to correlate with behavioral problems. Thomas et al [5] found that children who were referred by their parents because of behavioral problems, more often than other children in the group, had the "difficult child syndrome," which means negative mood, irregularity, low adaptability, withdrawal and high intensity.

Graham et al [2] also found that irregularity and low malleability, which is much like adaptability, were the two temperamental categories that were among the most predictable for developing emotional problems. Furthermore, they found that the only significant difference between the risk group of children of neurotic parents and the control group was higher negative mood scores in the risk group.

It thus seems that some of the temperamental traits—mood, adaptability, and regularity, which are most relevant for the development of behavioral problems in children—are the same as those found in this study to be most influenced by environmental factors.

A well-known critical comment to twin studies is that the greater similarity in MZ than in DZ twin pairs can also be caused by the more similar environment of the MZ twin pairs. This criticism has been met by studies of MZ twins with a different degree of similarity in their environment, with the finding that MZ cotwins do not vary in likeness in personality according to the variation in their environment similarity [3].

Similar results were also obtained in this study when one kind of environmental similarity was studied: namely, the degree to which the 6-year-old twins play and stay together or apart.

Figure 2 shows that the mean total within-pair differences in all temperamental categories were not significantly higher in the group of MZ twins who most often played with different friends than among the MZ pairs who were unseparable and always stayed together.

However, a closer look at the figure shows that the variations in environmental likeness are too small to give this explanation any significant value. As for temperamental differences, the environmental differences were significantly greater for almost all the DZ twins than the MZ. This gives no opportunity to compare a group of MZ twins with every similar environment with another group of MZ twins with differences in the environment to the degree it exists for DZ twins.

CONCLUSIONS

This study has confirmed that genetic factors play a role in the development of temperamental aspects of behavior. However, this conclusion should be considered in the light of the following four points: 1) The same categories that seem to be of importance in the development of behavioral problems in childhood were least influenced by hereditary factors, or easily modified by environmental factors; 2) the results can be seen from an interactionistic viewpoint; 3) the conclusions differ according to the statistical methods used; 4) the classic criticism to the twin method concerning the shared environment effect should be taken into account.

REFERENCES

1. Christian JC, Kang KW, Norton JA Jr: Choice of an estimate of genetic variance from twin data. Am J Hum Genet 26:154–161, 1974.
2. Graham P, Rutter M, George S: Temperamental characteristic as predictors of behavior disorders in children. Am J Orthopsychiatry 43:328–339, 1973.
3. Plomin R, Willerman L, Loehlin, JC: Resemblance in appearance and the equal environments assumption in twin studies of personality traits. Behav Genet 6:43–52, 1976.
4. Thomas A, Birch HG, Chess S, Hertzig ME, Korn S: "Behavioral Individuality in Early Childhood." New York: New York University Press, 1963.
5. Thomas A, Chess S, Birch HG: "Temperament and Behavior Disorder in Children." New York: Brunner/Mazel, 1968.
6. Thomas A, Chess S: "Temperament and Development." New York: Brunner/Mazel, 1977.
7. Torgersen AM, Kringlen E: Genetic aspects of temperamental differences in infants. J Am Acad Child Psychiatry 17:433–444, 1978.
8. Torgersen AM: Temperamental categories in 6-year-old children: A factor analysis. (Unpublished), 1980.
9. Vandenberg SG: Contributions of twin research to psychology. In Manosevitz M, Lindzeg C, Thiessen DD (eds): "Behavioral Genetics." New York: Appelton-Century-Crofts, 1966, pp 145–164.

Twin Research 3: Intelligence, Personality,
and Development, pages 269–278
© 1981 Alan R. Liss, Inc., 150 Fifth Avenue, New York, NY 10011

Heredity and Temperament: A Comparison of Twin Data for Self-Report Questionnaires, Parental Ratings, and Objectively Assessed Behavior

Robert Plomin
Institute for Behavioral Genetics, University of Colorado, Boulder

INTRODUCTION

At the 1980 Temperament Research Symposium in New Haven, Connecticut, a definition of temperament received considerable consensus: Temperament involves those dimensions of personality that are largely genetic or constitutional in origin, exist in most ages and in most societies, show some consistency across situations, and are relatively stable, at least within major developmental eras. The genetic criterion for temperament is the focus of this paper. It would seem that the obvious task for behavioral geneticists is to point to those dimensions of personality that have a substantial genetic component. However, this task is not so straightforward as it might appear.

I shall focus on twin data as they relate to the issue of heredity and temperament. Important conclusions concerning self-report questionnaire data have emerged recently, but these conclusions have not previously been examined in relation to parental rating data or objectively assessed behavior, sources of data more pertinent to the assessment of temperament in childhood than self-report measures. For this reason, I shall compare twin results for self-report questionnaires, parental ratings, and objectively assessed measures of personality.

SELF-REPORT QUESTIONNAIRES

Because temperament refers in part to personality dimensions with an inherited component, a discussion of temperament and heredity must begin with the general domain of personality. A most important conclusion arose from the work of Loehlin and Nichols [6], *Heredity, Environment and Personality: A*

Supported in part by grants from the National Institute of Child Health and Human Development (HD-10333) and the National Science Foundation (BNS-7826204). The report was written while the author was supported by a Research Scientist Development Award (AA-00041) from the National Institute on Alcohol Abuse and Alcoholism.

Study of 850 Pairs of Twins. They concluded that all personality traits are influenced by heredity to the same moderate extent: "Identical twins correlate about 0.20 higher than fraternal twins, give or take some sampling fluctuation, and it doesn't much matter what you measure" (p 35). For personality measures, Loehlin and Nichols found a median identical (MZ) twin correlation of 0.50 and a median fraternal (DZ) twin correlation of 0.32 for the 18 scales of the California Psychological Inventory in two half-samples of their large group of adolescent twins. Moreover, they found no evidence for differential heritability among traits. In other words, no trait showed consistently greater differences between MZ and DZ correlations than any other trait. For example, heritability differences among traits in one half-sample did not replicate in the other half-sample. The absence of significant differential heritability follows from the finding that all personality dimensions show moderate (about 0.40) heritability; when differences in heritability are slight, huge samples are needed to detect such differences. For example, over 500 pairs of each type of twin are needed to demonstrate a significant difference between a heritability of 0.40 (based on an MZ correlation of 0.50 and a DZ correlation of 0.30) and a heritability of 0.60 (based on an MZ correlation of 0.60 and a DZ correlation of 0.30). Over 2,000 pairs of each type of twin are needed to demonstrate significant differential heritability when the heritabilities differ by 0.10 or less.

Who would have thought that all personality traits are influenced by heredity to the same moderate degree? A reasonable explanation is that this conclusion might be limited to the California Psychological Inventory, which has a number of problems such as item overlap on various scales [5]. However, when Loehlin and Nichols conducted additional analyses of over 1,000 personality and related items grouped into 70 clusters, these analyses yielded similar results. Personality clusters showed MZ correlations of about 0.50 and DZ correlations of about 0.30. Although self-concepts, ideals, goals, and vocational interest clusters yielded generally lower twin resemblance and an activities cluster yielded higher twin resemblance, the difference between the MZ and DZ correlations was consistently about 0.20 for these diverse domains.

The same conclusion emerges from other studies. For example, Vandenberg [19] reviewed major twin studies of personality and reported twin correlations for 32 different personality scales in six studies. The median MZ correlation was 0.45 and the median DZ correlation was 0.21, a difference of 0.24. Most of the personality scales showed moderate heritability. Thus results from other studies are in agreement with Loehlin and Nichols's conclusion, particularly when one takes into account the large standard errors involved in the other studies, which are considerably smaller than Loehlin and Nichols's sample (an average sample size of 75 MZ pairs and 70 DZ pairs). One exception to this general rule may be extraversion, for which the MZ correlation is about 0.50 but the DZ correlation is near zero [4].

If most personality dimensions are moderately heritable, an obvious implication for temperament research is that twin studies cannot point to a subset of personality dimensions that are substantially more heritable than others. Other important implications follow. Large twin samples are needed to detect significant heritability if the expected MZ correlation is 0.50 and the expected DZ correlation is 0.30. Power analyses [2] show that a sample of 250 MZ and 250 DZ twin pairs is needed to detect a significant (P < 0.05) correlational difference of this magnitude 80% of the time. Samples of 50 pairs of each type of twin have only 32% power to detect such a difference; this means that a significant difference between MZ and DZ correlations will be detected only about a third of the time. Thus studies that report that some personality dimensions are significantly heritable and other dimensions are not heritable must be evaluated in terms of the power of their sample size to detect significant heritability.

Another even more mischievous implication is that, in order for small twin samples to show significant heritability, the pattern of twin correlations must violate the twin model. For example, with 25 pairs of each twin type, if the MZ correlation were 0.50, a *negative* DZ correlation is needed to produce a significant difference in correlations.

These problems are not obvious in the literature because the pattern of twin correlations is not always considered. Often studies report only the significance level of the difference between MZ and DZ correlations or the F ratio of intrapair differences without presenting the MZ and DZ correlations. Also, Holzinger's H is still sometimes computed even though it is clearly an inappropriate estimate of heritability. Holzinger's H always yields a plausible heritability estimate regardless of the implausibility of the pattern of twin correlations [13].

PARENTAL RATINGS

It should be noted that the previous discussion pertains to self-report questionnaire data. What about the parental ratings that are more commonly used to assess temperament in children? Loehlin and Nichols's conclusion appears to apply here as well, but with an interesting twist. Although MZ correlations are about 0.50, the DZ correlations are lower than 0.30 and often are negative. As a result, the differences between the MZ and DZ correlations are too large to explain with the usual twin model, and Falconer [3] heritabilities are often greater than 1.0.

I shall document this with my own data. Because I am interested in temperament in infants and young children, I conducted several twin studies using parental ratings instruments. The Buss-Plomin [1] EASI Temperament Survey was used in a study of 2- to 6-year-old twins (60 MZ and 51 DZ pairs). For midparent ratings the median twin correlations for 11 scales were 0.56 for MZ and −0.12 for DZ twins. The results for single-parent ratings by the mothers and fathers were similar. "Cross-correlations"—where the mother rated one twin and the father rated the twin partner—also yielded a negative DZ correlation. The median MZ cross-correlation is lower because rater agreement (in this case, the correlation between mothers' and fathers' ratings of their children which is only about 0.40 as shown by Lyon and Plomin [7]) creates a ceiling for the twin cross-correlations.

A parental rating instrument called the Colorado Childhood Temperament Inventory (CCTI) was used in a study of 1- to 7-year-old twins (36 MZ and 31

DZ pairs). The CCTI is an amalgamation of the EASI Temperament Survey and factors derived from the New York Longitudinal Study. For the six CCTI scales, the median MZ correlation was 0.60 and the DZ correlation was 0.06 [15]. The CCTI was also used in an unreported study of twins (53 MZ and 33 DZ pairs) from 5 to 11 years of age. The median MZ correlation in that study was 0.55 and the median DZ correlation was −0.10.

Loehlin and Nichols's book also contains some confirmatory data. The parents of the adolescent twins in their sample rated the temperament of their twins as infants and as preschoolers. In the appendix to their book, twin discordances are listed for these items. For the sum of the infant temperament items, the DZ discordance was more than four times greater than the MZ discordance (0.68 vs 0.16); in the preschool years, the DZ discordance was nearly three times greater than the MZ discordance (2.27 vs 0.83).

Although there are twin studies using parental interviews, it is not yet possible to determine whether parental interviews will yield twin correlations similar to those for parental ratings. One study [18] did not present twin correlations and the other [20] reported percentages of mothers who indicated that their twins were the "same" or "different" on various behavioral dimensions. The former study found significant intrapair F ratios for all variables for 9-month-old twins, although only three of nine scales showed significant MZ-DZ differences when the twins were 2 months old. The latter study found very few significant differences in MZ and DZ concordances from 1 to 7 years, although it should be noted that the method used in this study is quite different from those used in other studies.

The usual pattern of parental rating correlations—MZ correlations of about 0.50 and DZ correlations that are much lower than 0.30—violates the twin model in the sense that, for a heritable trait, DZ twins should be about half as similar as MZ twins because DZ twins have half of their segregating alleles in common on the average. Although epistasis can lead to slightly lower-than-expected DZ correlations, epistasis is not likely to explain MZ-DZ differences of this magnitude and it cannot explain negative DZ correlations. I suspect that the argument used by Fulker et al [4] to explain low DZ correlations for extraversion (that within-family contrasts affect twins' personalities) applies even more strongly to parental ratings. Speculations aside, the large MZ-DZ correlational differences result in significant heritability for nearly all dimensions. The results do not provide evidence for differential heritability among the personality dimensions. Thus twin studies using parental ratings are congruent with Loehlin and Nichols's conclusion that there is no evidence for differential heritability. For self-report data, Loehlin and Nichols concluded that heritability is generally moderate with median MZ correlations of about 0.50 and DZ correlations of about 0.30. For parental rating data, MZ correlations are also about 0.50; however, DZ correlations are lower than 0.30 and frequently negative, thus resulting in artifactually large heritability estimates.

OBJECTIVELY ASSESSED BEHAVIOR

On the basis of both self-report and parental rating data, it appears that nearly all personality dimensions are influenced by heredity. Before we accept the radical conclusion that heredity affects all personality traits to the same moderate extent, studies of objectively assessed behavior should also be examined. It is not unreasonable to suppose that an individual's perception and report of his own personality or a mother's perception and report of her children may reflect genetic and environmental factors different from objectively assessed behavior.

Very few behavioral genetic studies of personality have used measures other than self-report or parental rating questionnaires. I was able to find only six twin studies using test situations and these sampled quite limited behaviors—perseveration, decision time, and body sway susceptibility [14]. Four small studies involving objective observations, as well as two recent observational studies of 1- to 3-year-old children [8, 16], found no evidence of genetic influence on social behavior directed toward mothers, although the latter study found significant genetic influence on social behavior directed toward a stranger.

These two recent studies yield results different from self-report and parental rating data. For 24 observational measures in the study by Plomin and Rowe [16], the median MZ correlation was 0.29 and the DZ correlation was 0.20, suggesting only slight genetic influence. For six of the measures, the DZ correlation was greater than the MZ correlation, something rarely seen in self-report or parental rating data. However, a critical problem in interpreting the results of this study is that no test-retest reliability data were available. Low reliability can in part explain the differences between these results and those of self-report and parental rating studies because reliability creates a ceiling for twin correlations. In their observational study of 19 MZ and 29 DZ pairs, Lytton et al [8] studied the stability of interactive behavior between parents and their twin children, using behavioral counts, ratings, and experimental measures. Reliability was only moderate (primarily 0.40 to 0.50) and it was particularly low for measures involving counts of behavior. Nonetheless the twin correlations were generally very high, much higher than the reliabilities. However, there was little difference between MZ and DZ correlations—for 11 observational variables, the median correlations were 0.76 for MZ twins and 0.71 for DZ twins. Ratings in the home based on observation as well as interviews yielded median correlations of 0.68 and 0.59, respectively, for MZ and DZ twins; experimental measures in a playroom yielded median correlations of 0.42 and 0.27, respectively. The authors concluded that "there is little genetical variance expressed in these measures of child behavior." A similar conclusion was reached for a follow-up study at 9 years of age [9].

In a recent study of 87 pairs of 5- to 12-year-old twins [14], videotape observations in standardized situations, objective tests, and mechanical measures were used to assess such diverse behaviors as activity, fidgeting, vigilance, selective attention, and aggression. Two-month, test-retest reliability was collected for all measures. The twins were studied individually in a large playroom equipped with a one-way mirror through which time-sampled videotape observations were made. Activity was measured by a week-long assessment using pedometers; fidgeting was rated from videotapes of the children after they were told to lie still in a beanbag chair for 9 minutes; vigilance was measured by a version of the continuous performance test; selective attention was assessed by the Goldman-Fristoe-Woodcock test, in which the child listens through headphones to pick out a signal word from background noise that increases in intensity during the test; and aggression was measured by play with a large, inflated "Bobo" clown. Details of the procedure and the measures can be found in Plomin and Foch [14].

Although rater reliability was high for all videotape measures, test-retest reliability was nonsignificant for some measures (most notably, the free-play observational measures), and these measures were deleted from subsequent analyses. Age-corrected twin correlations yielded results quite different from those obtained for self-report or parental rating data. Although the twin correlations yielded the usual finding of substantial genetic influence for height and weight, the twin correlations provided little evidence of genetic influence upon objectively assessed and reliable measures of personality. Although samples of this size (54 and 33 DZ pairs) can detect only substantial genetic effects, the pattern of twin correlations was not even suggestive of genetic influence for selective attention and the aggression measures. The DZ correlations for these measures were as great as or greater than the MZ correlations. The only significant difference between MZ and DZ correlations came from a very unusual pattern of correlations for the week-long pedometer assessment of activity. The MZ correlation was 0.99 and the DZ correlation was 0.94. The high level of the correlations is responsible for detecting significant but slight genetic influence.

The most interesting aspect of these results in the present context is that the objective measures yielded a diverse pattern of results from the high correlations for activity level to MZ and DZ correlations of about 0.40 for the various selective attention and aggressiveness measures to correlations of about zero for measures such as vigilance. Thus results for objectively assessed behavior stand in sharp contrast to twin results for self-report and parental rating questionnaires.

DISCUSSION

One caveat needs to be discussed. I have defined the word "objective" somewhat arbitrarily to include observational ratings of specific behaviors and scores from test situations. The fact that the objective measures are molecular (narrow, specific), whereas the self-report and rating assessments are molar (broad and global), introduces a confound in the comparison between self-report and parental rating data on the one hand and objectively assessed behavior on the other. Molar measurements represent generalizations over numerous specific behaviors, across time, and over various situations. Thus the differences in twin results that I have presented may be a result of differences in the dimension of molar-molecular assessment rather than differences between self-report/rating versus objective assessment.

I investigated this possibility by examining the few studies that permitted a comparison of twin results for molar and molecular measures within each of the three methods of assessment. Because the vast majority of self-report personality questionnaires involves molar items such as "I enjoy social gatherings just to be with people," data are not available to determine adequately whether molecular measurements yield similar results. However, Loehlin and Nichols [6] used the 324-item Objective Behavior Inventory which includes questions about such specific behaviors as participation in sports, religious, and musical activities. Fifteen clusters of these items yielded results similar to the molar personality ratings, although the level of twin correlations was generally higher. The median MZ correlation was 0.64 and the median DZ correlation was 0.49. There was no evidence for differential heritability among the activity clusters.

As another comparison of molecular and molar items, I chose four CPI items (52, 70, 319, 321) that are somewhat specific and behavioral in nature and had reasonable endorsement frequencies, and I compared these items to cognates that are more molar (CPI items 251, 418, 320, and 361, respectively). For example, CPI item 319—"In a group, I usually take the responsibility for getting people introduced"—is more specific than the related CPI item 320—"I would be willing to describe myself as a pretty strong personality." These two groups of items yielded very similar twin correlations. For the "molecular" items, the median MZ correlation was 0.28 and the DZ correlation was 0.13. For the "molar" items, the median MZ and DZ correlations were 0.27 and 0.16, respectively. The individual item correlations were close to these median correlations, providing no evidence for differential heritability for either group of items and suggesting again that the molar-molecular distinction does not substantially change the picture of twin correlations for self-report questionnaires.

Turning to parental ratings, it should be noted that the data presented earlier involved molar ratings such as "Child is always on the go." Studies of more molecular ratings yield higher twin correlations, but the same basic pattern as more molar ratings. For example, Conners's Parent Symptom Rating questionnaire was completed by parents of 5- to 11-year-old twins [12]. This questionnaire asks about the occurrence of such specific behavioral problems as bullying, shyness, and stealing. The median MZ correlation was 0.79 (53 pairs) and the median DZ correlation was 0.29 (33 pairs). Nearly all the behaviors showed significant heritability with no suggestion that any behavior was more heritable than any other.

In order to provide another molecular-molar comparison for parental rating data, I selected five "molecular" items and five "molar" items from Loehlin and Nichols's [6] parental ratings of their twins as adolescents. An example of the molecular items (242, 260, 264, 266, 273) is "Usually decides what the two of them will do together." An example of the molar items (241, 256, 273, 279, 282) is "Is more interested in helping others." Once again, the molecular items showed greater twin resemblance than the molar items, but the pattern of twin discordances for both groups of items was similar to the basic pattern usually observed for parental ratings. For the molecular items, the median discordance for MZ twins was 0.23; for DZ twins, it was 0.55. For the molar items, the median discordances were 0.42 and 0.66, respectively. Neither group of items suggested any differential heritability—the DZ-MZ differences in discordances were all about 0.20.

These few results suggest as a working hypothesis that the molecular-molar distinction does not explain the more differentiated twin results obtained for objectively assessed behavior.

Data to compare more or less molecular measures within studies of obejc-tively assessed behavior are rare, but their results are heuristically important. There are objective studies that I did not discuss earlier because they involved molar ratings by observers other than parents. An important example of this approach is the Bayley Infant Behavior Record (IBR), which is used to rate an infant's personality after administering the Bayley Scales of Infant Develop-ment. The IBR primarily includes global ratings such as "Responsiveness." In a twin study using the IBR, Matheny et al [11] found that MZ twins were gen-erally more similar than DZ twins, with little suggestion of differential her-itability. The median MZ correlations were 0.63 for 1-year-olds and 0.46 for 2-year-olds; the median DZ correlations were 0.36 and 0.35, respectively. Ex-ceptions included two molecular behavioral items, banging and mouthing, for which both the MZ and DZ correlations were about 0.60. This again suggests generally higher twin correlations for molecular ratings as well as differential heritability for objective and molecular assessments of behaviors, but not for molar assessments. These results are similar to those in a more recent publica-tion [10] in which it was concluded that "the general feature of the correlations was that almost all factors had higher correlations for the identical pairs than for the fraternal pairs." Similarly, a study involving observers' molar ratings of behavior in children [17] found that MZ correlations were generally and sub-stantially higher than DZ correlations for molar ratings such as "Friendliness."

My tentative conclusion is that molar personality ratings by objective ob-servers do not yield the differentiated twin results typical of objective assess-ments, which usually involve more molecular measures. In summary, molecular behavioral ratings tend to yield generally higher twin correlations than do molar ratings for self-reports, parental ratings, and objective assessments. The pattern of twin correlations remains characteristic of self-report questionnaires and parental ratings for both molecular and molar measures. However, for objective assessments, molar measures appear to yield less differentiated twin results than molecular measures. These conclusions are summarized in Table 1.

One additional implication of these conclusions should be mentioned. I have emphasized genetic information available from twin studies because of its im-portance to the study of temperament. However, these same comparisons bear on Loehlin and Nichols's [6] second major conclusion: For personality, envi-ronmental influences operate almost exclusively within families, making family members different from one another. Most investigators of personality and temperament have assumed that environmental influences, such as childrearing practices, affect children in a family similarly and therefore lead to between-family environmental variance. Because differences within pairs of identical twins are environmental, twin studies estimate within-family environmental variance as that portion of variance not shared by identical twins. For self-report questionnaires, for which the identical twin correlation is 0.50, it is esti-mated that 50% of the variance is accounted for by within-family environmental

TABLE 1. Typical Results of Twin Studies of Personality as a Function of the Type of Measurement[a]

	Molar measures			Molecular measures		
	rMZ	rDZ	Differential heritability?	rMZ	rDZ	Differential heritability?
Self-report questionnaires	0.50	0.30	No	0.70	0.50	No
Parental ratings	0.50	0.00	No	0.80	0.30	No
Objective assessments	0.50	0.30	No	Varied	Varied	Yes

[a]See text for explanation. The twin correlations are illustrative only. The confidence to be placed in them is a function of the amount of data available, which is in the following approximate order from most to least: molar self-report, molar parental ratings, molecular objective assessments, molecular self-report, molecular parental ratings, and molar objective assessments.

influences and that genetic differences account for the rest of the reliable variance. For parental rating data, the identical twin correlation tends to be about the same, 0.50, and the estimate of within-family environmental variance is also about 0.50. However, as we have seen, parental rating data do not fit the assumptions of the twin model because fraternal twin correlations are often negative and result in heritability estimates greater than 1.0. Molecular measures of objectively assessed personality yield diverse results, and thus do not permit a general conclusion about the locus of environmental influence when personality is assessed objectively rather than by means of self-report questionnaires or parental ratings. Finally, because molecular ratings tend to yield higher twin correlations, they will result in higher estimates of between-family environmental influences for self-report and parental rating data.

In closing, I would emphasize that my conclusion is *not* that objective assessments of molecular behaviors are a panacea for the measurement of personality and temperament. It is simply noteworthy that objective assessments of behavior appear to yield twin results less perplexing than those based on self-report or parental rating data, where significant heritability is found for all dimensions and where within-family environmental effects are the rule rather than the exception. As usual, more data are clearly needed, but these results may motivate researchers to collect such data despite the tremendously greater costs in time and energy required for most objective assessments as compared to paper-and-pencil measures.

REFERENCES

1. Buss AH, Plomin R: "A Temperament Theory of Personality Development." New York: Wiley Interscience, 1975.
2. Cohen J: "Statistical Power Analysis for the Behavioral Sciences." New York: Academic Press, 1977.
3. Falconer DS: "Introduction to Quantitative Genetics." New York: Ronald Press, 1960.

4. Fulker D, Parisi P, Eysenck HJ, Gedda L: "A Comparative Study of Individual Differences in Personality: An Italian Twin Study." Paper presented at the Third International Congress on Twin Studies, Jerusalem, June 1980.
5. Horn JM, Plomin R, Rosenman R: Heritability of personality traits in adult male twins. Behav Genet 6:17–30, 1976.
6. Loehlin JC, Nichols RC: "Heredity, Environment, and Personality: A Study of 850 Twins." Austin: University of Texas Press, 1976.
7. Lyon M, Plomin R: The measurement of temperament using parental ratings. J Child Psychol Psychiatry, 21:1–7, 1980.
8. Lytton H, Martin NG, Eaves L: Environmental and genetical causes of variation in ethological aspects of behavior in two-year-old boys. Soc Biol 24:200–211, 1977.
9. Lytton H, Watts D: "The Social Development of Twins in Longitudinal Perspective: How Stable is Genetic Determination from Age 2 to 9?" Paper presented at the Third International Congress on Twin Studies, Jerusalem, June 1980.
10. Matheny AP: Bayley's Infant Behavior Record: Behavioral components and twin analyses. Child Dev (in press), 1980.
11. Matheny AP, Dolan AB, Wilson RS: Twins: Within-pair similarity on Bayley's Infant Behavior Record. J Genet Psychol 128:263–270, 1976.
12. O'Connor M, Foch TT, Sherry T, Plomin R: A twin study of specific behavioral problems of socialization as viewed by parents. J Abnorm Child Psychol 8:189–199, 1980.
13. Plomin R, DeFries JC, McClearn GE: "Behavioral Genetics: A Primer." San Francisco: Freeman, 1980.
14. Plomin R, Foch TT: A twin study of objectively assessed personality in childhood. J Pers Soc Psychol 39:680–688, 1980.
15. Plomin R, Rowe DC: A twin study of temperament in young children. J Psychol 97:107–113, 1977.
16. Plomin R, Rowe DC: Genetic and environmental etiology of social behavior in infancy. Dev Psychol 15:62–72, 1979.
17. Scarr S: Genetic factors in activity motivation. Child Dev 37:663–673, 1966.
18. Torgerson AM, Kringlen E: Genetic aspects of temperamental differences in infants: A study of same-sexed twins. J Am Acad Child Psychiatry 17:433–444, 1978.
19. Vandenberg SG: Hereditary factors in normal personality traits. In Wortis J (ed): "Recent Advances in Biological Psychiatry," vol. IX. New York: Plenum Press, 1967, pp 65–104.
20. Wilson RS, Brown AM, Matheny AP: Emergence and persistence of behavioral differences in twins. Child Dev 42:1381–1398, 1971.

Twin Research 3: Intelligence, Personality,
and Development, pages 279—282
© 1981 Alan R. Liss, Inc., 150 Fifth Avenue, New York, NY 10011

Assessment of Temperament in Twin Children: A Reconciliation Between Structured and Naturalistic Observations

Adam P. Matheny, Jr.
University of Louisville, School of Medicine, Kentucky

Twins offer a unique resource for studying the origins and development of temperament in that they allow for the appraisal of differences and similarities for patterns of reactions taking place within contexts highly matched for biological and social variables. In the Louisville Twin Study, the development of several methods for the longitudinal assessment of temperament of twin infants and preschoolers has taken advantage of the strengths of structured and naturalistic observations. These methods have included the following: 1) neonatal evaluations, 2) semistructured interviews with parents, 3) temperament questionnaires developed by Carey and associates [1, 2] from the work of the New York Longitudinal Study, 4) ratings on the Bayley Infant Behavior Record (IBR) made during mental testing, and 5) ratings from direct observations. Each of these sources of information has been considered as yielding comparatively unique views of the twins under different circumstances, and as Lytton [3] has suggested, each has its own relative utility.

In regard to parental reports, obtained either from interviews or from questionnaires, the cumulative observations of parents have been central fixtures of the study. Parents witness behaviors inaccessible to laboratory observations and perform like "computers of average transients" in that they distill large naturalistic samples of children's behavior by isolating or tracing invariant features among those samples. The comparative yield of this type of data source has been established; however, it remains to be demonstrated what relations exist between parental observations and those observations gained more formally.

On-site direct observations of twins were originally gained during unstructured ("free play") conditions occurring during a 3- to 4-hour visit to the study. After considerable pilot work, it became obvious that the course of the entire visit and especially the format of periods for direct observations should be structured to provide standardized episodes for twins together, with and without parents, and each twin alone. When each twin was observed alone, comparable sets of activities were necessary in order to provide a common experiential reference for comparisons within pairs as well as with other children. In addition, the direct observations required the creation of more structured age-specific reference tasks. These tasks, called "vignettes," were expected to challenge the children, very much like natural challenges in the home, and, as a consequence, developmental expectations set the limits for the tasks. For convenience and because of our extensive experience with the IBR, the categories of behaviors assessed during the visit paralleled those rated by the IBR for the highly structured Bayley mental testing.

Throughout a visit, videotapes were made within episodes when twins and parents were first seen together ("orientation"), twins were together without parents, each twin was alone, and twins and parents were reunited. Ratings from the videotapes were supplemented with similar ratings from other periods not videotaped: photographs of the family, physical measurements of the twins. In combination, ratings of temperament were available from the parents and from direct observations; the former were naturalistic according to source, the latter both structured and naturalistic.

Given the large number of observations, there remain the problem of reducing the data to a smaller set of quantifiable characteristics of temperament and the corollary problem of establishing interrelations among structured and naturalistic observations. Both of these problems were explored by preliminary analyses essentially examining the multimethod—multitrait matrices yielded for the twins.

In a pilot study involving about 50 pairs of twins, temperament data were available for 3, 6, 9, 12, 18, and 24 months. Data analyses were performed at every age, but for illustrative purposes, analyses for three aspects of temperament (emotionality, activity, and attention span) and two ages (6 and 18 months) are presented. To reduce the number of dimensions of temperament and to show the contributions from the different kinds of observations, principal components analyses were performed. The measures consisted of the ratings from videotapes of four periods during a visit, parental ratings from the temperament questionnaires, IBR ratings made during Bayley mental testing, and ratings made while the twins were being measured for weight, length, and head circumference. The principal components according to dimensions of temperament, measures, and age are presented in Table 1.

One should note that the component labeled "emotionality" has loadings of equivalent magnitude from parental ratings and from direct observations. Regarding the parental ratings, it is of interest that the categories of temperament contributing to the component were those comprising the easy-difficult continuum formulated by Thomas and Chess [4]. Moreover, rational combinations of the measures provided correlations of the same order as those anticipated from the principal components analyses.

TABLE 1. Multimethod Measures of Temperament: Principal Components at
6 and 18 Months

Principal component and measure		Loadings	
		6 Months	18 Months
EMOTIONALITY			
Emotional	Orientation	0.17	0.72
tone/Rated	Twins together	0.07	0.51
during videotaped	Twin alone	0.75	0.60
periods	Reunions	0.62	0.52
Temperament	Adaptability	0.75	0.55
questionnaire—	Intensity	0.48	0.48
Categories	Mood	0.60	0.41
IBR rating—Emotional tone		0.13	0.65
Physical measure rating—Emotional tone		0.75	0.52
ACTIVITY			
Activity—	Orientation	0.58	0.46
Rated during	Twins together	0.61	0.13
videotaped	Twin alone	0.43	0.43
periods	Reunions	0.62	—
Temperament questionnaire—Activity		0.66	0.55
IBR rating—Activity		0.73	0.66
Physical measure rating—Activity		—	0.64
ATTENTION SPAN			
Attention span—	Orientation	0.51	0.34
Rated during	Twins together	0.30	0.39
videotaped	Twin alone	0.60	0.68
periods	Reunions	0.18	0.56
Temperament questionnaire—Persistance/Attention		0.73	0.48
IBR rating—Task orientation composite score		—	0.82

The components labeled "activity" and "attention span" also provided a multivariate perspective of the twins' behaviors as viewed jointly by parents and trained observers. The magnitudes of the loadings, particularly at 18 months, point to the fact that there were shared common features within each behavioral domain. To the extent that the diverse sources of observations contributed to those domains, there were obvious connections between structured and naturalistic observations.

Apparently, there can be a reconciliation between seemingly disparate measures of temperament, especially if analytical techniques are applied to the complementary aspects of the measures and isolate dimensions that underly those measures. As a consequence, coordination of measures from the different sources might make it possible to create standardized scores for each dimension and represent each twin's profile of temperament in the form of standard scores. It remains to be seen if this approach provides empirical evidence, from twin studies, for genetic influences upon temperament.

REFERENCES

1. Carey WB, McDevitt SC: Revision of the Infant Temperament Questionnaire. Pediatrics 61:735, 1978.
2. Fullard W, McDevitt SC, Carey WB: "Toddler Temperament Scale." Unpublished test. Philadelphia: Temple University, 1979.
3. Lytton, H: Comparative yield of three data sources in the study of parent-child interaction. Merrill-Palmer Quart. 20:53–64, 1974.
4. Thomas A, Chess S: "Temperament and development." New York: Brunner Mazel, 1977.

Twin Research 3: Intelligence, Personality,
and Development, pages 283—286
© 1981 Alan R. Liss, Inc., 150 Fifth Avenue, New York, NY 10011

Twinship as Handicap: Fact or Fiction?

Denise Watts and Hugh Lytton
Department of Educational Psychology, University of Calgary, Canada

METHOD

The sample for the original study [2] consisted of 136 2-year-old boys, 46 sets of identical (MZ) and fraternal (DZ) twins, and 44 singletons. At the time of the follow-up, 43 of the original twin pairs were relocated and 37 of these (15 MZ, 22 DZ) were available for participation in the investigation. A new control group of 37 male singletons was included. The singletons were chosen randomly from the same schools as the twin pairs for whom they served as controls. The mean age of both groups was 9 years, 6 months. All subjects were white and English speaking. There were no significant differences between the social class of the twins and the singletons as measured by fathers' occupations or mothers' education.

Twins and singletons were compared in two broad areas: pre- and perinatal, or "biological," factors, and academic and social competence in the school setting. During the earlier investigation, pre- and perinatal information had been collected from hospital records for the twin sample. Variables such as the presence of various complications of pregnancy and delivery, gestational age, birthweight, and age at time of discharge from hospital were included. Similar information was obtained for the singleton boys at this time through telephone interviews with their mothers. Unfortunately, these data were susceptible to the unreliability that invariably accompanies retrospective recall of events.

To obtain the academic and social competency data, each child was assessed individually at school. The test battery included measures of verbal and nonverbal intellectual ability (the Crichton Vocabulary Scale and the Raven's Progressive Matrices [3]), school achievement (the Peabody Individual Achievement Test [1]), and moral development. The classroom teacher rated the children on a variety of characteristics such as reading achievement, independence, and relationships with peers. Height and weight measurements were taken by the school nurse.

Supported by the Social Sciences and Humanities Research Council of Canada, grant 410-78-0003-R2.
This paper presents a report on the first results of the follow-up investigation of a longitudinal study of twins, begun in 1971.

In order to compare the twins and the singletons on the various measures, the mean scores of the twin pairs and the scores of their singleton controls were submitted to correlated t-test analyses. For nominal variables such as presence or absence of toxemia during pregnancy, chi-square analyses were performed between the singletons and a randomly selected twin from each pair.

RESULTS

Examination of the biological data indicated greater stress on the twins than on the singletons during pregnancy, delivery, and the early perinatal period. More twin mothers experienced toxemia during pregnancy and more twins than singletons had breech deliveries. Twins had a lower mean birthweight than singletons and spent a longer period of time in hospital prior to discharge, indicating some necessity for prolonged observation and medical care. This biological weakness was borne out by the twins' higher scores on the variable Total Stress Index, which is the number of stresses out of a possible six which a child displayed.

In the original investigation it had been shown that social class, as indexed by mother's education, was associated with many of the child characteristics, and that certain differences that appeared to be due to twinship were actually more strongly related to differences in mother's education between the two groups [2]. Therefore, in spite of the fact that twins and singletons in the follow-up did not differ significantly on the mother education variable, a separate covariance analysis was carried out for each of the criterion variables, with twinship as the independent variable and mother's education as the covariate. All of the twin-singleton differences in the biological data remained significant when the influence of mother's education had been removed.

Out of 30 school-related variables, six showed a significant difference between twins and controls. Verbal IQ was lower for the twin group, although nonverbal IQ showed no appreciable difference. As expected, twins' lower ability was accompanied by significantly lower achievement test scores—specifically in the areas of reading comprehension and mathematics—as well as in the overall achievement score. More twins than singletons had failed a grade and the number of twins involved in speech therapy at school was also significantly greater. It was interesting and somewhat surprising to us that although standardized tests of ability and achievement indicated considerable twin-singleton differences, teachers' ratings of the same abilities, as well as other social characteristics, revealed no noticeable differences.

A separate covariance analysis was also performed on the school data. When the effect of mother's education had been controlled for, only verbal IQ and the mathematics achievement score continued to show significant differences between the two groups.

DISCUSSION AND CONCLUSIONS

What do these findings suggest in regard to the question posed by this paper? Are twins indeed a "handicapped" group?

The biological differences appear to indicate that twins' earliest days are marked by potentially more hazardous conditions than singletons experience. However, the initial physical weakness seems to have been overcome by age 9. Twins and controls were very similar in height and weight and there were no significant differences in the numbers of twins and singletons with identified vision or hearing defects.

Although the physical condition of the twins appears to have improved over time, the fact remains that they appear to display a verbal deficit in comparison to single-born children. At 2 years of age, twins were inferior to singletons on several indices of language development. During a standard 6-hour observation period, twins spoke less than singletons and their speech was rated as less mature by the observers. Vocabulary IQ scores were also lower for the twins.

This verbal immaturity, evident at 2, has persisted, showing itself in a considerably lower verbal IQ, even when the mother's education has been controlled for. The higher incidence of sample twins in the school speech therapy program also indicates a continuing lag in the development of adequate speech skills. It is not difficult to imagine some direct connection between twins' lack of facility with verbal processes and their lower achievement test scores, especially in the area of reading, which in turn would be related to an increased probability of having to repeat a grade.

So once again the question is posed as to whether we can consider twinship as a handicapping condition. There can be no doubt that, within this relatively small sample, the scores of singletons on tests of ability and achievement were consistently superior to those of the twins. It should be noted, however, that both groups scored above average for their age according to the norms provided for the tests, suggesting that the "deficiency" of the twins is relative rather than absolute in nature. Nevertheless, in light of the apparent persistence of the weakness and the fact that verbal skills are crucial for overall academic achievement, this potentially limiting factor cannot be overlooked.

One of the major aims of this research has been to examine the relationships between parent practices and attitudes and child characteristics. Based on evidence from the initial investigation, the conclusion was drawn that parents' lesser speech to individual twins at 2 years was an important factor in the poorer verbal competence they displayed, although pre- and perinatal complications may also play a part. We will now have the opportunity to link the earlier parent and child measures with measures from the 9-year follow-up, and it is hoped that this analysis will provide further clues to interrelationships that may be significant in twin development.

ACKNOWLEDGMENTS

We are indebted to Bill Yuzwak for carrying out the field work, to Deborah Twaddle for the data analysis, and to the project secretary, Linda Culshaw. Statistical consultant for the project was Bruce Dunn. We would like to thank all of the participating school boards, principals, and teachers, the Calgary public health nurses, and their director, Miss Frances Moore, for their cooperation and assistance.

REFERENCES

1. Dunn LM, Markwardt Jr. FC: "Peabody Individual Achievement Test," vol I and vol II. Circle Pines, Minnesota: American Guidance Service Inc, 1970.
2. Lytton H, Conway D, Sauve R: The impact of twinship on parent-child interaction. Personality Soc Psychol 35:97–107, 1977.
3. Raven JC, Court JH, Raven J: "Raven's Progressive Matrices and Vocabulary Scales." London: H.K. Lewis and Co Ltd, 1978.

Subject Index

Adolescence
  growth and development in, 211–25
  personality in, 99–118
Adoption, 17–19, 21–23, 102–8
Analytic ability, 44
Artistic interests, 23, 129–30

Behavioral development, 238–40, 248
Biological families, 102–18
Birth order, 246, 247
Blood groups, 123, 124
Brain lateralization, 45, 48

Causal model, 62–64, 68–70
Cognitive abilities, 220–25
  and adoption, 21–23
  and environment, 9–16, 55–58
  and family attitudes, 243–45
  logicomathematical concepts, 51–58
  resemblance of, in MZ twins, 35–40
  and twin mating, 65–71
  and twin study, 21–23
  see also intelligence
Cryptophasia, 6

Darwin, Charles, 61–62
Development
  adolescent, 211–25
  human, 251–53
  mental, 201–8
  synchronized infant, 199–208
  temperamental, 261–68
  twin, 25–32, 227–33, 236–39, 251–53
Dizygotic twins, 121–25

Ego phenomenology, 149–53
Environment
  and adolescent growth and development, 211–25
  and cognitive ability, 9–16, 55–58
  and development, 252
  and genetics, 27–32
  and intelligence, 21–23
  and obsessionality, 163–68
  and perception, 135–36
  and personality, 87–91, 97, 99–100, 102, 118, 146, 155–61
  rearing, 189–98
  and sex differences, 45

Family
  attitudes, 236–49
  biological vs adoptive, 102–18
  and personality, 102, 106–8, 114–18
Fears, 169–73, 187
Fecundity, 62

Genetics
  and adolescent growth and development, 211–25
  correlation between spouses of twins, 80–84
  and development, 252–53
  and environment, 27–32
  and intelligence, 9, 17–19
  and intelligence in opposite-sex twins, 45, 49
  and mating selection, 77–80
  multivariate behavioral, 25–32
  and obsessionality, 163–68
  and personality, 87–89, 91, 92, 96–97, 99–118, 147, 225–59

PROGRESS IN CLINICAL AND BIOLOGICAL RESEARCH

Series Editors
Nathan Back
George J. Brewer

Vincent P. Eijsvoogel
Robert Grover
Kurt Hirschhorn

Seymour S. Kety
Sidney Udenfriend
Jonathan W. Uhr

Part B: **Biology and Epidemiology**
Part C: **Clinical Studies**

DATE DUE

Demco, Inc 38-293